Each volume of this series of companions to major philosophers contains specially commissioned essays by an international team of scholars, together with a substantial bibliography, and will serve as a reference work for students and nonspecialists. One aim of the series is to dispel the intimidation such readers often feel when faced with the work of a difficult and challenging thinker.

The significance of Friedrich Nietzsche for twentieth-century culture is now no longer a matter of dispute. He was quite simply one of the most influential of modern thinkers. His attempts to unmask the root motives underlying traditional Western philosophy, morality, and religion have deeply affected subsequent generations of philosophers, theologians, ̇   ̇ lists, and playwrights. Nietzsche thou̇   ̇e ̇ences of the triumph of Enlightenmė̇   ̇ and i̇ so doing laid the foundations for the phi̇ ̇ȯ̇̇cal agenda of the twentieth century, the "post-Nietzschean age."

The opening essay of this Companion provides a chronologically organized introduction to and summary of Nietzsche's published works, while also providing an overview of their basic themes and concerns. It is followed by three essays on the appropriation and misappropriation of his writings, and a group of essays exploring the nature of Nietzsche's philosophy and its relation to the modern and postmodern world. The final contributions consider Nietzsche's influence on the twentieth century in Europe, the U.S.A., and Asia.

THE CAMBRIDGE COMPANION TO

NIETZSCHE

The Cambridge Companion to

NIETZSCHE

Edited by

Bernd Magnus
University of California, Riverside

and

Kathleen M. Higgins
University of Texas at Austin

CAMBRIDGE
UNIVERSITY PRESS

For David and Julie
&
For Bob

CAMBRIDGE UNIVERSITY PRESS
Cambridge, New York, Melbourne, Madrid, Cape Town,
Singapore, São Paulo, Delhi, Tokyo, Mexico City

Cambridge University Press
The Edinburgh Building, Cambridge CB2 8RU, UK

Published in the United States of America by Cambridge University Press, New York

www.cambridge.org
Information on this title: www.cambridge.org/9780521367677

First published 1996
Reprinted 1996, 1997, 1999

A catalogue record for this publication is available from the British Library

ISBN 978-0-521-36586-4 Hardback
ISBN 978-0-521-36767-7 Paperback

CONTENTS

v

CONTRIBUTORS

ERNST BEHLER, Professor and Chair of the Department of Comparative Literature at the University of Washington, is the author of *Confrontations: Derrida, Heidegger, Nietzsche* (1991) and coauthor (with Aldo Venturelli) of *Friedrich Nietzsche* (1994). His recent publications include *Frühromantik* (1992) and *German Romantic Literary Theory* (1994). He is the editor of the in-progress *The Complete Works of Friedrich Nietzsche*.

KATHLEEN MARIE HIGGINS is Professor of Philosophy at the University of Texas at Austin. She is the author of *Nietzsche's "Zarathustra," The Music of Our Lives*, and coeditor (with Robert C. Solomon) of *Reading Nietzsche, The Philosophy of (Erotic) Love*, and *From Africa to Zen*, among other books and articles.

R. J. HOLLINGDALE has translated most of Nietzsche's published works, and books by many other German authors, classic and contemporary; and he has published a substantial study, *Nietzsche*, as well as his biography, *Nietzsche: The Man and His Philosophy*. He is honorary president of the British Nietzsche Society.

BERND MAGNUS, Professor of Philosophy and Humanities at the University of California, Riverside, was the founding Executive Director (with Walter Kaufmann) of the North American Nietzsche Society. Among his books are *Nietzsche's Existential Imperative*, and (with Stanley Stewart and Jean-Pierre Mileur) *Nietzsche's Case: Philosophy as/and Literature*, as well as books on Heidegger, Derrida, and Marx.

ALEXANDER NEHAMAS is Carpenter Professor of Philosophy and Humanities at Princeton University, where he teaches philosophy

vii

and comparative literature and chairs the Council on the Humanities. He is the author of *Nietzsche: Life as Literature*, cotranslator of Plato's *Symposium* and *Phaedrus*, and the author of a forthcoming book on Socrates and philosophy as "the art of living."

GRAHAM PARKES studied philosophy and psychology at Oxford and the University of California, Berkeley, and now teaches at the University of Hawaii. He is the editor of and contributor to *Heidegger and Asian Thought, Nietzsche and Asian Thought*, and the author of *Composing the Soul: Reaches of Nietzsche's Psychology*.

ROBERT B. PIPPIN is Professor of Social Thought and Philosophy, and Chair of the Committee on Social Thought, at the University of Chicago. His books include *Kant's Theory of Form, Hegel's Idealism: The Satisfactions of Self-Consciousness*, and *Modernism as a Philosophical Problem: On the Dissatisfactions of European High Culture.* He is currently at work on a book about Hegel's ethical theory.

JÖRG SALAQUARDA is Professor of Philosophy in the school of Protestant Theology of the University of Vienna, having previously taught in Berlin and Mainz. His areas of specialization include philosophy of religion and continental philosophy, especially the work of Schopenhauer and Nietzsche. His extensive publications include original work in his fields of specialization as well as translations from English to German. He is managing coeditor of *Nietzsche-Studien* and *Monographien und Texte zur Nietzsche-Forschung*.

RICHARD SCHACHT, Jubilee Professor of Liberal Arts and Sciences at the University of Illinois, Urbana-Champaign, is the author of *Nietzsche*, and the editor of *Nietzsche, Genealogy, Morality*. His interests center on issues relating to human nature, value theory, and social theory. His recent books include *The Future of Alienation* and *Making Sense of Nietzsche*. He is the current Executive Director of the North American Nietzsche Society.

ALAN D. SCHRIFT is Associate Professor of Philosophy at Grinnell College. His books include *Nietzsche's French Legacy: A Genealogy of Poststructuralism, Nietzsche and the Question of Interpretation: Between Hermeneutics and Deconstruction*, and he is the editor, with Gayle L. Ormiston, of *The Hermeneutic Tradition: From Ast to*

Ricoeur and *Transforming the Hermeneutic Context: From Nietzsche to Nancy.*

ROBERT C. SOLOMON is Quincy Lee Centennial Professor of Philosophy at the University of Texas at Austin. His books include *About Love, Continental Philosophy Since 1750, From Rationalism to Existentialism, In the Spirit of Hegel, A Passion for Justice,* and *The Passions.* He has edited *Nietzsche: A Collection of Critical Essays* and (with Kathleen Higgins) *Reading Nietzsche, The Philosophy of (Erotic) Love,* and *From Africa to Zen.*

TRACY B. STRONG is Professor of Political Science at the University of California, San Diego, and editor of the journal *Political Theory.* His books include *Friedrich Nietzsche and the Politics of Transfiguration, The Idea of Political Theory, Right in Her Soul: The Life of Anna Louise Strong,* and, most recently, *Jean Jacques Rousseau and the Politics of the Ordinary.* He is presently working on the relationship between aesthetics and political thought in the early twentieth century.

Introduction to The Cambridge Companion to Nietzsche

The importance to the humanities and to our culture of the nineteenth-century German philosopher and writer Friedrich Nietzsche may require little motivation or discussion. He was quite simply one of the most influential modern European thinkers. His attempts to unmask the root motives which underlie traditional Western philosophy, morality, and religion have deeply affected subsequent generations of philosophers, theologians, psychologists, poets, novelists and playwrights. Indeed, one contemporary English-speaking philosopher, Richard Rorty, has characterized the entire present age as "post-Nietzschean." That is because Nietzsche was able to think through the consequences of the triumph of the Enlightenment's secularism – captured in his observation that "God is dead" – in a way that determined the agenda for many of Europe's most celebrated intellectuals after his death in 1900. An ardent foe of nationalism, anti-Semitism, and power politics, his name was later invoked by Fascists and Nazis to advance the very things he loathed.

It might also be useful to recall that, according to Martin Heidegger, Nietzsche is the consummation of the Western philosophical tradition, the thinker who brings metaphysics to its end; that Michel Foucault frequently regarded Nietzsche as the progenitor of his own genealogical method and its stress on discursive practices; that Jacques Derrida considers Nietzsche the deconstructive thinker *par excellence*. All this serves as eloquent testimony to Nietzsche's claim, voiced in *The Antichrist* and elsewhere, that some persons are born posthumously; for that observation certainly applies to his own case. It is no accident, therefore, that the last published edition of the *International Nietzsche Bibliography*, edited by Herbert Reichert and Karl Schlechta in 1968 – long before the recent explosion of inter-est in Nietzsche – lists more than 4,500 titles in 27 languages de-voted to Nietzsche. And it must not be forgotten that Nietzsche's importance has not been confined to philosophy or even to humanis-tic study. One much discussed recent critic, Allan Bloom, argued the controversial thesis that America's very cultural life – the mis-education of its citizens as well as its misguided public philosophy – is to be traced to a superficial version of (what the author considered) Nietzsche's virulently infectious nihilism.[1] Indeed, without endors-ing Allan Bloom's diagnosis or thesis about Nietzsche's etiological role in the "closing" of the American mind, it is no exaggeration to say that Nietzsche's influence has become unavoidable in our cul-ture. Whether one reads G. Gordon Liddy's misappropriations, goes to a movie, or merely turns on the television, Nietzsche seems al-ways to be already there. For example, Eddie Murphy quotes from Nietzsche at length in a climactic moment in the movie "Coming to America"; a rock music group names itself "The Will to Power"; and even the teen-age "Dr. Howser" of the wretched (and now mercifully canceled) "Doogie Howser, M.D." television show can be heard say-ing, "As Nietzsche said: 'Whatever doesn't destroy me makes me stronger.'" Could one cite illustrations of Nietzsche's "appropria-tion" more banal, more crude and pervasive, than these? Nietzsche's name and epigrams are invoked everywhere nowadays, indiscrimi-nately selling ideas as well as products.

From the mid-1890s until today, a century later, Nietzsche's name has been invoked and enlisted repeatedly in the service of every conceivable political and cultural movement and agenda – from early-twentieth-century emancipatory feminism to later fascism and Nazism, from a Faustian modernism to recent versions of post-modernism. Nor is it the case any longer that Nietzsche's pervasive influence is confined primarily to continental European philoso-phers and politics, intellectuals, and American popular culture. Rather, his critique of traditional morality has become a force in the reflections of some leading Anglophone philosophers, such as Ber-nard Williams,[2] Richard Rorty,[3] Martha Nussbaum,[4] Alasdair MacIn-tyre,[5] and Philippa Foot.[6]

Given this ubiquity, it is not surprising that Nietzsche commenta-tors disagree about most aspects of his thinking, especially about what an *Übermensch* [superhuman being] is supposed to be, what eternal recurrence asserts, whether he had developed or had intended to formulate a full-blown theory of the will to power, as well as what his perspectivism may be said to assert. These are disagreements concerning the substance, goal, and success of Nietzsche's attempted transvaluation of all values. On the other hand, there is considerably less disagreement about identifying the deconstructive aspect of his work, the sense in which he sought to disentangle Western metaphysics, Christianity, and morality in order to display what he took to be their reactive decadence. Put crudely and misleadingly, there is considerably less disagreement concerning the negative, deconstructive side of Nietzsche's thinking than there is about the positive, reconstructive side.

These, then, appear to be the two faces of Nietzsche that are recognized by virtually all critics. One face looks at our past and vivisects our common cultural heritage at its roots; the other seems to be turned toward the future, suggesting visions of possible new forms of Western life. The negative, deconstructive, backward-glancing Nietzsche is the face which seems to be more easily recognized by his commentators and his critics. But when one tries to examine in detail Nietzsche's positive, reconstructive face, one is beset by an immediate difficulty. For this other, future-directed face turns out to be not one profile but at least two possible ones. One sketch of Nietzsche's positive profile portrays his remarks about truth, knowledge, superhumanity, eternal recurrence, and will to power as his answers to perennial, textbook philosophical problems: his theory of knowledge, his moral philosophy, and his ontology. On this reading of his reconstructive side, Nietzsche seems to be shattering the foundations of past theories as one demolishes false idols, in order to erect his own, better phoenix from their ashes. In admittedly quite different ways, this seems to be an orientation common to the work of Danto,[7] Wilcox,[8] Clark,[9] and Schacht;[10] or perhaps it is a framework toward which their work points.

The alternative profile of this reconstructive side of Nietzsche rejects the positive/negative dichotomy itself and depicts him instead as attempting to liberate us precisely from the felt need to provide theories of knowledge, or moral theories, or ontologies. Despite admitted differences, enormous ones, this seems to be a useful way of capturing an orientation suggested by the work of Alderman,[11] Derrida,[12] Nehamas,[13] Deleuze,[14] Strong,[15] Shapiro,[16] and Rorty,[17] for example. The first version of his reconstructive portrait assimilates Nietzsche's project to the great tradition of "the metaphysics of presence" – to the tradition epitomized by Plato, Descartes, and Kant. The alternative portrait sees the negative, deconstructive side of Nietzsche as already *constructive*, in the therapeutic manner of the later Wittgenstein, late Heidegger, Derrida, Rorty, and Foucault.[18]

What is at the bottom of these conflicting portraits, perhaps, is an unarticulated difference scarcely recognized among Nietzsche scholars, not to say philosophers generally. It is the difference between those who believe that one is paying him a compliment by reading Nietzsche as "a philosopher" who gives Kantian style answers to textbook questions, and those who view that characterization as depreciating his more broadly "therapeutic" achievement.

A nice illustration of this bifurcated state of affairs is what seems to be occurring in discussions of Nietzsche's perspectivism. What seems to be occurring among Nietzsche scholars is not only a difference of detail – a difference about how to construe Nietzsche's remarks about "knowledge," "truth," "correspondence," and "perspective" – but a metaphilosophical split about the *point* of Nietzsche's perspectivism. For many commentators, Nietzsche's perspectivism is, roughly, his theory of knowledge. It wants to assert four distinguishable claims: (1) no accurate representation of the world as it is in itself is possible; (2) there is nothing to which our theories stand in the required correspondence relation to enable us to say that they are true or false; (3) no method of understanding our world – the sciences, logic, or moral theory – enjoys a privileged epistemic status; (4) human needs always help to "constitute" the world for us. Nietzsche tends to run (1)–(4) together; often he confuses them. But the most serious difficulty for Nietzsche's perspectivism lies elsewhere: the self-reference problem. Are we to understand his many naturalistic and historical theses as accurate representations of the world as it is in itself, as corresponding to any facts of the matter, as privileged perspectives, ones which are conditioned by no need whatsoever? If we are, then Nietzsche's perspectivism is self-contradictory in all four versions mentioned. But that is just to say either that the theories Nietzsche offered are not to be taken perspectivally – in which case his perspectivism must be abandoned – or that they are only perspectives, in which case they may not be true and may be superseded.

To say that they may not be true, however, is just to say that what he maintains may be "false." But how can he then maintain that there is nothing to which our theories stand in the required correspondence relation to enable us to determine whether they are true or false? Further, in saying that there is no truth did Nietzsche mean to say something true? If he told the truth, then what he said was false, for there had to be a truth to be told for him to say, truly, that there is no truth. If what he said is false, on the other hand, then it is false to assert that there is no truth. But then at least something is true in an unmitigated sense. Similarly, if every great philosophy is really only "the personal confession of its author and a kind of involuntary and unconscious memoir" (BGE 6), then what is Nietzsche himself confessing? What is his involuntary and unconscious memoir *really* about? Perhaps the best way to understand his perspectivism, then, is to construe it in a neo-Kantian way, as providing a transcendental standpoint in which putative "facts" about human needs and human neurophysiology play a role not unlike that of Kant's categories and forms of intuition.

However, there is another, second, and quite different way to construe Nietzsche's perspectivism remarks: Nietzsche's "perspectivism" is not a *theory* of anything, and it is most certainly not a *theory* of knowledge. To say that there are only interpretations (or perspectives) is to rename all the old facts "interpretation." The point of the renaming is to help us set aside the vocabulary of accurate representation which still holds us in its Platonic thrall. Similarly, to say that "truth" is "error" is not to offer a theory of truth so much as it is to rename it. So Nietzsche's tropes concerning "truth" and "error," "fact" and "interpretation" are best understood as rhetorical devices to help the reader to understand and confront the widely shared intuition that there must be something like a final truth about reality as such which it is the goal of philosophy to disclose. The reader's own penchant for the God's-eye view is surfaced and called into question. Indeed, a theory of knowledge is not something Nietzsche has; the yearning for its possession is what his tropes parody. Knowledge is the sort of thing about which one ought to have a theory primarily when the Platonically inspired God's-eye view has seduced us, primarily when we construe knowledge on the analogy of vision – the mind's eye seeing the way things really are – primarily when we see philosophy as culture's referee, allowing or barring moves made elsewhere in culture which claim to be items of knowledge. Yet this is precisely the picture of philosophy and inquiry Nietzsche urges ought to be set aside. Put oversimply, "knowledge" and "truth" are compliments paid to successful discourse, as Rorty and others have suggested. To give an account of such success is always to say why this specific item is "true" or "known" – for example, the superiority of the heliocentric over the geocentric account of planetary motion. There can be explanations and illustrations of successful discourse on a case by case basis, illustrations and explanations of the relative attractions of various competing concrete proposals; but there is no way to slide an unwobbling pivot between "theory" and "reality" which will register an unmediated fit between word and world. There can only be a misconceived "theory of" successful discourse, on this view.

But how are we to choose between such conflicting interpretations of Nietzsche's remarks about perspectivism, not to mention the large array of alternative interpretations not easily captured by this oversimplification?

The case of the "will to power" is equally messy, but for different reasons. These are primarily textual and conceptual. Even if there exists a doctrine, one that can be unpacked "analytically" as a psychological principle, is it to be grasped ontologically, as discarded notes from the *Nachlass* [his literary estate] seem to suggest? How is the will to power to be understood as an assertion of the way things are, rather than as a figure for the self in quest of self, a self in transformation? In the end, the will to power may well reduce to the view that if one must do metaphysics – and perhaps Nietzsche's final recommendation is that this comfort is better given up – then one buys the picture of language as accurate representation, of theory as correspondence to facts; one buys the ultimate and decidable purchase of mapping metaphors along with the correspondence theory of truth. To mitigate the force of that picture, think of Nietzsche's remarks concerning will to power as recommending that we think instead of "things" as events and as families of events. On such a view, the paradox is that a world of only wills, only events, is necessarily formless and formed at the same time. Formless, because wills conceived as events are form-giving while possessed of no fixed or inherent structure of their own, apart from their contextual articulation, apart from what Nietzsche called their "interpretation."

Formed, because wills conceived as families of events are always acting upon one another, are always imposing form upon one another. The paradox is intractable. If we are no longer to think of "wills" as "things," we can form no clear mental image of them. They elude representational thinking. Insofar as we do form a clear mental image, a representation, the formless antecedent eludes us. We invariably picture an entity which has already been formed, structured. We grasp only an "interpretation." Consequently, will to power is the general characterization of this action of will upon will, in which form is imposed by will upon will, that is, by event upon event, in which there is visible only the articulation which we call "the world."

Grasping things as events *simpliciter* is counterintuitive, to be sure, for it requires that we abandon the notion that events consist of items, that they are constituted *by* the interaction *of* things. Indeed, prepositional language fails us here, for we are asked to grasp the world as a family of events constituted by and consisting of no-thing in particular, a "world" of relations without relata. This difficulty in stating Nietzsche's position is not restricted to his discussion of the will to power. It is a recurring problem in making Nietzsche's argument plain, that in order to state his position or argument one must frequently resort to a vocabulary whose use often depends upon the very contrasts he sought to displace or set aside.

This specific feature of Nietzsche's central themes has been characterized elsewhere as the "self-consuming" character of his concepts, categories, and tropes.[19] A self-consuming concept is one which requires as a condition of its intelligibility (or even its possibility) the very contrast it wishes to set aside or would have us set aside. The notion of will to power as relation(s) without relata appears to be self-consuming in the sense specified, as may be the notion of invoking the analogy between seeing and knowing, which Nietzsche's perspectivism explicitly does, in order to set aside the dominating visual metaphorics of traditional epistemology. The notions of eternal recurrence and the ideal life may also be usefully viewed – as a preliminary approximation – as self-consuming concepts. The usefulness of viewing some of Nietzsche's most discussed themes as self-consuming is that, so regarded, they resist reification, resist reduction to substantive, traditional philosophical doctrines. Moreover, so regarded, their fluidity is not merely an accidental feature but a typical feature. Like the literary figure catachresis, Nietzsche's major themes seem necessarily both to solicit and to reject literal interpretation at the same time. The noun phrase "table leg," for example, is a literal expression. There is no other literal expression for which "table leg" is a metaphorical substitute, place-holder, or stand-in. Yet, at the same time, "table leg" is itself a metaphor, since tables can be said to have "legs" only in a metaphorical sense, the sense in which a good glass of cabernet sauvignon may be said to have "legs." The catachresis "table legs" is *both* literal and metaphorical or is *neither* literal nor metaphorical at the same time. And Nietzsche's central themes seem to exemplify a similar paradoxical quality.

Nietzsche's presentation of eternal recurrence is central to his philosophic project. It is the generating thought of his *Zarathustra*, the thought which most divides commentators.[20] It is unarguably the subject of two of Zarathustra's speeches – "On the Vision and the Riddle" and "The Convalescent" – and is fully rehearsed in *The Gay Science* under the heading *"Das Grösste Schwergewicht"* [The Greatest Stress]. That entry (#341) concludes by asking its interlocutors two questions framed as one:

If this thought [of eternal recurrence] were to gain possession of you, it would transform you, as you are, or perhaps crush you. The question in each and every thing, "Do you want this once more and innumerable times more?" would weigh upon your actions as the greatest stress. Or how well disposed would you have to become to life and to yourself to *crave nothing more fervently* [*um nach nichts mehr zu verlangen*] than this ultimate eternal confirmation and seal?

In Nietzsche's various published writings in which we are invited to think through the notion of eternal recurrence, we are asked the question "How well disposed would one have to become to oneself and to life to crave nothing more fervently than the infinite repetition, without alteration, of each and every moment?" Nietzsche invites his reader to imagine a finite number of possible states of the universe, each destined to recur eternally, and asks his reader's reaction to this imagined state of affairs. Presumably most persons should find such a thought shattering because they would always find it possible to prefer the eternal repetition of their lives in an edited version rather than to crave nothing more fervently than the recurrence of each of its horrors. Only a superhuman being (an *Übermensch*) could accept recurrence without emendation, evasion, or self-deception, a being whose distance from conventional humanity is greater than the distance between man and beast, Zarathustra tells us in the Prologue to *Thus Spoke Zarathustra*.

But what sort of creature would desire the unaltered repetition of its exact life, would prefer each and every moment of its life just as it is, and would prefer this to any alternative possibility it could imagine? What sort of attitude is suggested by a person, a quester, who could regard his or her life as Leibniz's God regarded the world: the best of all possible worlds?

If the notion of a self-consuming concept is to be of use in understanding Nietzsche's remarks concerning the will to power, eternal recurrence, the ascetic ideal, and the *Übermensch*, then it should also be of use in motivating the sense in which these central themes in Nietzsche generate one version of an old question: Is Nietzsche playing the same philosophical game with different rules or is it now a different game? Is Nietzsche offering new critiques of the tradition, followed by substantive epistemic, moral, and ontological theories on which the critiques depend, or is he suggesting that we cease to speak in this way? Perhaps Nietzsche's critiques just *are* the new game, as they are for Foucault. As in psychotherapy, the negative act of being deprived of something – say, a cherished neurosis – just *is* the gift-giving virtue.

Because of the conflict of interpretations still with us today, this anthology is designed for the use of those reading Nietzsche for the first time as well as those already more familiar with his work. Our opening essay, "Nietzsche's Works and Their Themes," provides an introduction to each of Nietzsche's philosophical writings and an overview of the basic concerns and concepts they are thought to involve. Chronologically organized, this lead essay should be of particular value to those with limited previous experience reading Nietzsche. Those who have done more substantial and sustained reading of Nietzsche might elect to skip this essay – although we do not recommend this – and move directly to the essays which are more concerned with interpretation and analysis.

The first trio of essays which follows our overview concerns Nietzsche's life as well as the appropriation and misappropriation of his writings.

R. J. Hollingdale's "The Hero as Outsider" considers the discrepancy between the facts of Nietzsche's life and the popular, constructed image of Nietzsche as the solitary, suffering, lunatic-genius. Hollingdale argues that Nietzsche has become the object, perhaps the victim, of a legend that has developed a life of its own. Ironically or perhaps deliberately, Nietzsche himself helped create the tradition of legendary freelance philosophers, for he endorsed a view of Schopenhauer as a legendary figure in his Schopenhauer as Educator. While Nietzsche was not overly concerned with realism in his portraits of his heroes, it is likely that he would be deeply disturbed by what Hollingdale regards as one of the consequences of his own legend – the fact that many enamored of the Nietzsche legend seldom pay much attention to his books.

Jörg Salaquarda, in "Nietzsche and the Judaeo-Christian Tradition," offers a religious biography of Nietzsche. Nietzsche was steeped in the Christian tradition, was influenced by it, and was profoundly knowledgeable about it. Indeed, his initial rejection of Christianity grew out of the theological studies that he pursued during his early university years. Educated in the historical mode of Biblical criticism that was popular at the time, Nietzsche became convinced that Christianity's claims to authority and absolute truth were no longer credible. Although Nietzsche did not develop a systematic and fully coherent case against Christianity in any traditional sense, and despite shifts in the extremity of his opposition, Salaquarda contends that Nietzsche's discussions of Christianity reveal more continuities than discontinuities. Even the genealogical method, which Nietzsche employs in Toward the Genealogy of Morals[21] to undercut belief in Christianity and the philosophical, moral, and intellectual habits that he considers linked to it, stem fundamentally from the same historical orientation that originally initiated his loss of faith. Nietzsche's tendency to become more strident in his polemics against Christianity in his later writings stems not from a change of conviction but from his growing disturbance over the inertia of his contemporaries, who seemed unwilling to draw the conclusions that their own intellectual and religious convictions entailed.

In "Nietzsche's Political Misappropriation," Tracy B. Strong sets out to explain the peculiar fact that Nietzsche has been declared an ally by political advocates across the political spectrum: progressive democratic leftists, feminists, socialists, romantics, anarchists, American neoconservatives, social Darwinists, and Nazis. Strong sheds light on this question by reading *The Birth of Tragedy* as a political work that shows how the ancient Greeks constructed a political identity for themselves. The Apollonian and Dionysian principles that Nietzsche viewed as constitutive of Greek tragedy – principles that respectively urge one to take appearances at face value and to recognize that the world has no ultimate foundation – required the Greek to assume an aesthetic stance toward phenomena. By providing a dual perspective toward the self, these principles undercut the possibility of a Greek's finding identity in terms of a single "meaning."

Encouraging his contemporaries to pursue identity as the Greeks did, by interpreting the world mythically and open-endedly, without closure, Nietzsche's own writing resists all attempts to establish a single correct "meaning" of his texts. Political appropriations that profess to have discovered such a meaning in Nietzsche are essentially projections of the readers' own political concerns, Strong argues. Ironically, however, Nietzsche's writings lend themselves to such projections, precisely because he deliberately wrote in a fashion that sought to preclude any definitive, canonical reading.

The second ensemble of essays, a quartet, consider Nietzsche primarily as a philosopher.

Richard Schacht considers some of Nietzsche's specific strategies in "Nietzsche's Kind of Philosophy." Schacht takes issue with certain contemporary deconstructivist readings that regard Nietzsche as rejecting the philosophical enterprise altogether. Nietzsche was committed to philosophy, Schacht argues, albeit philosophy of a nonstandard sort. Primarily concerned with the nature and quality of human life, the problems he thought about concerned morality, religion, psychology, and aesthetics more than the metaphysical and epistemological concerns that are often considered the philosophical "mainstream." Indeed, Nietzsche saw certain mainstream concerns and positions as rooted in dubious presuppositions, and much of his work involves efforts to remove them from the agenda by exposing their questionable foundation.

Denying that any single perspective on reality is "objective," in the sense of being canonically binding for all persons, times, and places, Nietzsche urges a recognition of the perspectival nature of all knowledge. Nietzsche's perspectivism led him to examine particular "cases" in human experience, the case of the Greeks, for example, and the case of Richard Wagner. Nietzsche's philosophy is also consistently antidogmatic, Schacht points out. He insists on the provisional nature of all of our suppositions, and, accordingly, the kind of philosophy that Nietzsche advocates is open-ended in character, experimentally employing models and metaphors from various domains and eager to draw upon the diversity of human experience.

In "Nietzsche's *Ad Hominem:* Perspectivism, Personality, and *Ressentiment* Revisited," Robert C. Solomon focuses on one of Nietzsche's more striking and peculiar philosophical devices, his employment of the *ad hominem*. Defined as the fallacy of attacking the person instead of the position, the *ad hominem* argument is usually considered inadmissible in philosophical argumentation. Solomon contends, however, that the *ad hominem* is an appropriate expression of Nietzsche's conviction, linked to his perspectivism, that the person and the philosopher are inextricably connected. Insofar as any philosophical outlook is a particular person's interpretation, it makes good philosophical sense to ask what kind of person formulated it, Solomon argues. Nietzsche therefore defends a radically contextualized understanding of what it means to assert a philosophical claim. Nietzsche views philosophy as emerging from one's living engagements. So understood, philosophy should admit *ad hominem* arguments and dispense with the pretension that anyone's arguments are purely "objective" in a sense that divorces theory from theorist.

In "Nietzsche, Modernity, Aestheticism," Alexander Nehamas considers Nietzsche's perspective on modernity. Nehamas rejects the readings of Jürgen Habermas, Richard Rorty, Martin Heidegger, and Alasdair MacIntyre, who characterize Nietzsche as, respectively, a nostalgic romantic, an ironist convinced of reality's blind contingency, the last metaphysician, and a radical relativist. Nehamas regards each of these descriptions as overly simplistic. Nietzsche, he contends, did not believe that we were beyond the need to demand truth or beyond the need to make choices and evaluate some possibilities as superior to others. What Nietzsche has abandoned is the quest for absolute truth, universal values, and complete liberation. For this reason, Nehamas characterizes Nietzsche as a postmodernist. Never-

theless, Nietzsche urges us to attend to goals and truth in local contexts, and to make choices on aesthetic grounds, taking artistic decisions as a model for all choice.

Robert B. Pippin also considers Habermas's interpretation of
Nietzsche in "Nietzsche's Alleged Farewell: The Premodern, Modern, and Postmodern Nietzsche." Unlike Nehamas, however, Pippin does not consider Nietzsche a postmodern thinker. Pippin
challenges Habermas's characterization of Nietzsche as a counter-
Enlightenment thinker. Pippin contends instead that Nietzsche
did not place much emphasis on the Enlightenment or modernity
as such. What does concern him is the nihilism that he believes
has arrived in our era. Indeed, Nietzsche is dissatisfied with the
current situation, but he does not prefer the premodern or some
postmodern alternative to the modern era. Instead, Nietzsche's
self-irony in the presentation of his ideas reflects his recognition
that he himself is implicated in modernity, a feature especially
evident in his commitment to attending to the tensions inherent
in the modern situation.

The final three papers in this anthology consider Nietzsche's influence on the twentieth century. Ernst Behler's "Nietzsche in the
Twentieth Century" traces the stages of the European and American
reception of Nietzsche over the past hundred years. Among the high
points of this chronology are: the early biographies written by Nietzsche's sister and Lou Salomé, the object of his unrequited love;
Georg Brandes's presentation of the first public lectures on Nietzsche's philosophy, lectures that presented him as radically aristocratic; the interest in Nietzsche exhibited by George Bernard Shaw
and other British socialists; Nietzsche's influence on such literary
figures as André Gide, Thomas Mann, Gottfried Benn, and Robert
Musil; the influential academic interpretations of Georg Simmel,
Karl Jaspers, and Martin Heidegger; Walter Kaufmann's rescue of
Nietzsche from National Socialism; and some of the recent German
and French interpretations of the "new Nietzsche" that became
available after the unreliable editing of Nietzsche's posthumous
notes by his fascist sister was exposed and a scholarly edition of his
complete works and letters made available.

Alan D. Schrift continues the saga of Nietzsche's influence in
France in "Nietzsche's French Legacy." Schrift locates this influence within the context of developments in recent French thought,

and he focuses primarily on the "poststructural" interpretations that were formulated after the waning of the structuralist movement. One tendency among the poststructuralist thinkers is to emphasize "the will to power" in their readings of Nietzsche. They also tend to place considerable emphasis on Nietzsche's style, contending that the style is an essential part of the content of a philosophical work. Schrift considers the interpretations of Gilles Deleuze, Jean Granier, Bernard Pautrat, and Sarah Kofman as poststructuralist thinkers who place emphasis on Nietzsche's style and thereby bring under-appreciated thematics to light. Schrift goes on to analyze the work of Jacques Derrida, Michel Foucault, Gilles Deleuze, and Jean-François Lyotard as moving beyond Nietzsche's work but nonetheless "Nietzschean" in its adherence to a number of Nietzschean themes.

Nietzsche's influence is not limited to Europe and America. Graham Parkes examines Nietzsche's Asian reception in "Nietzsche and East Asian Thought: Influences, Impacts, and Resonances." Parkes begins by indicating the slender extent of Nietzsche's own knowledge of Asian thought. Similarly, Nietzsche's initial impact on Japan and China was more enthusiasm based on rumor than detailed scholarly knowledge. However, Nietzsche came to be a significant concern of twentieth-century Japanese thinkers. Besides being a central influence on such literary figures as Mishima Yukio and Akutagawa Ryūnosuke, Nietzsche has had an important impact on the thinking of Watsuji Tetsurō and the philosophers of the Kyoto School (especially Nishitani Keiji).

One omission which will strike some readers is the lack of any discussion of recent feminist readings of Nietzsche. When the contents of this book were originally conceived many years ago, however, feminist discussions of Nietzsche were much more common in the French-speaking world than in the English-speaking world. Moreover, many of the leading French feminist interpretations of Nietzsche are only now being translated and published. Nevertheless, if this anthology were being assembled today for the first time, the topic of feminism would certainly justify more discussion than it, unfortunately, receives here, despite the fact that no single treatment of Nietzsche and feminism, in English, has as yet managed to define the parameters of that debate – as has arguably been done by most of the contributors on the topics covered in this anthology.

NOTES

1 This is spelled out in Allan Bloom's popular book (admittedly designed for the general audience), *The Closing of the American Mind: How Higher Education Has Failed Democracy and Impoverished the Souls of Today's Students*, Foreword by Saul Bellow (New York: Simon and Schuster, 1987), Part 2, esp. pp. 217–26.

2 In addition to his celebrated *Ethics and the Limits of Philosophy*, see especially his "Nietzsche's Minimalist Moral Psychology," in *European Journal of Philosophy*, volume 1, number 1 (1993), pp. 1–14.

3 See especially his *Contingency, Irony, and Solidarity* (Cambridge University Press, 1989).

4 See especially her essay "Pity and Mercy: Nietzsche's Stoicism," in *Nietzsche, Genealogy, Morality*, edited by R. Schacht (University of California Press, 1994); but also her discussions of Nietzsche in *The Fragility of Goodness* (Cambridge University Press, 1986) and *Love's Knowledge* (Oxford University Press, 1990).

5 See his "Genealogies and Subversions" in his *Three Rival Versions of Moral Enquiry* (University of Notre Dame Press, 1990); also see his earlier discussion of Nietzsche in *After Virtue* (University of Notre Dame Press, 1984, second edition) in which the choice in morality reduces to Aristotle or Nietzsche, as in Chapter 18, "After Virtue: Nietzsche or Aristotle, Trotsky and St. Benedict."

6 See her "Nietzsche's Immoralism" in *The New York Review of Books*, 13 June 1991, pp. 18–22, reprinted in Schacht's op cit.

7 Arthur C. Danto, *Nietzsche as Philosopher* (New York: The Macmillan Company, 1965).

8 John T. Wilcox, *Truth and Value in Nietzsche* (University of Michigan Press, 1974).

9 Maudemarie Clark, *Nietzsche on Truth and Philosophy* (Cambridge University Press, 1990).

10 Richard Schacht, *Nietzsche* (London: Routledge and Kegan Paul, 1983).

11 Harold Alderman, *Nietzsche's Gift* (Ohio University Press, 1977).

12 Jacques Derrida, *Spurs* (University of Chicago Press, 1979) and *Otobiography* (New York: Schocken Books, 1985).

13 Alexander Nehamas, *Nietzsche: Life as Literature* (Harvard University Press, 1985).

14 Gilles Deleuze, *Nietzsche et la philosophie* (Presses Universitaires de France, 1962); translated by Hugh Tomlinson as *Nietzsche and Philosophy* (Columbia University Press, 1983).

15 Tracy B. Strong, *Friedrich Nietzsche and the Politics of Transfiguration* (University of California Press, 1975).

16 Gary Shapiro, *Nietzschean Narratives* (Indiana University Press, 1989)
    and *Alcyone: Nietzsche on Gifts, Noise, and Women* (State University
    of New York Press, 1991).

17 Richard Rorty, *Contingency, Irony, Solidarity* (Cambridge University
    Press, 1989).

18 Compare this contrast with Steven Taubeneck's "Translator's After-
    word" titled "Nietzsche in North America: Walter Kaufmann and Af-
    ter," in *Confrontations: Derrida, Heidegger, Nietzsche*, by Ernst Behler
    (Stanford University Press, 1991): "Danto, Magnus, and Schacht, each
    with his own suggestions, offer principles different from Kaufmann's as
    alternative bases for understanding Nietzsche. Nehamas and Krell high-
    light to differing extents the roles of Nietzsche's many styles. Bloom,
    among those who use Nietzsche for other arguments, retains the
    humanistic-anthropological emphasis and adds a critique of the politics;
    Rorty downplays the politics and drops the belief in a foundational hu-
    man nature" (p. 176).

19 See especially Chapter 1 of *Nietzsche's Case: Philosophy as/and Litera-
    ture* by Bernd Magnus, Stanley Stewart, and Jean-Pierre Mileur (New
    York and London: Routledge, 1993).

20 For discussion, see ibid., and "Deconstruction Site: 'The Problem of
    Style' in Nietzsche's Philosophy," by Bernd Magnus, in *Philosophical
    Topics* 19, 2 (Fall 1991):215–43.

21 In the editors's contributions to this volume, the titles *On the Geneal-
    ogy of Morals* or *The Genealogy of Morals*, and *Untimely Meditations*
    will not be used. Instead, the titles now appearing (and/or soon to ap-
    pear) in the twenty-volume set, *The Complete Works of Friedrich Nietz-
    sche*, edited by Ernst Behler, will be used instead. However, this standard-
    ization has *not* been imposed on other contributors to this anthology
    who have not already adopted such changes themselves (as Behler and
    Parkes have, for example, in this volume).

    The title of Nietzsche's *Zur Genealogie der Moral* has previously
    been consistently translated in English either as *The Genealogy of Mor-
    als* or *On the Genealogy of Morals*. Both translations are misleading, yet
    their usage continues to this day. Had he wanted to convey *the* geneal-
    ogy of morals, the book's title would have been *Die Genealogie der
    Moral*. At best, therefore, the title of Nietzsche's text might be either
    Toward the Genealogy of Morals or *On the Genealogy of Morals*, but
    not *The Genealogy of Morals*.

    The title is better translated as *Toward* [not *The* or *On*] *the Genealogy
    of Morals*, in our view, since the contraction "zur" is quite different than
    the German definite article or the prepositions "von" (on; about) or even
    "über." And as is very clear from the works of the period (Z and BGE)

whenever Nietzsche wanted to write "on" a topic (in the sense of "about" rather than "toward") he used the preposition "von," not the contraction "zur." In *every* case in which Nietzsche wrote "on" a subject in *Zarathustra* – for example, from "On the Three Metamorphoses" in Part One to "On Science" in the concluding Part Four – he consistently used the preposition "von." Most compellingly, however, in *Beyond Good and Evil*, the book immediately preceding GM, the fifth numbered part (entries 186–203) bears the title "zur Naturgeschichte der Moral" ["toward the natural history of morals"]. Nietzsche would most assuredly have written "von der . . . " or "über der . . . " if he had intended to write "on the natural history of morals." Parenthetically, Walter Kaufmann's translation of this interesting chapter simply begs the question by refusing to translate the German "zur" altogether. Instead, the header for this fifth part of BGE is translated by Kaufmann as "the natural history of morals." "Zur" silently disappears, leaving in its wake the mistaken impression that Nietzsche is writing "the" natural history of morals rather than feeling his way "toward" it.

This difference betweeen the prepositions "toward" and "on" in Nietzsche's GM title is not a niggling difference. It is philosophically significant, because "*on* the genealogy of morals" suggests an antecedent topic upon which one is remarking; whereas "*toward* the genealogy of morals" does not imply the prior existence of the subject or method upon which Nietzsche is remarking. The one preposition ("toward") suggests that Nietzsche is working *in the direction of* the genealogy of morals in a way that the preposition "on" does not suggest.

A similar case concerning a lack of nuance in previously existing translations is corrected by Richard Gray's nuanced and novel retranslation of the title *Unzeitgemäße Betrachtungen* as *Unfashionable Observations* [in press] in the complete English language edition of Nietzsche's published and unpublished writings now in progress, mentioned above, rather than translating it as *Untimely Meditations* or *Unmodern Observations* as had been done hitherto. (Capital letters used above such as Z, BGE, and GM are abbreviations of Nietzsche's titles, for example, *Thus Spoke Zarathustra, Beyond Good and Evil, Toward the Genealogy of Morals*. This practice occurs throughout this volume. The reader should be able to infer without difficulty the intended title from the abbreviation.)

Part I   Introduction to Nietzsche's Works

1 Nietzsche's works and their themes

Interpretation of Nietzsche's thought is a complex enterprise. Because of his avoidance of any conventional philosophical system and his many experiments with styles and genres, Nietzsche's writings seem to demand a sense of active reading. The "Nietzsche" that emerges from scholarly discussion typically depends on the interests of the interpreter and especially often those of the interpreter's discipline. Themes which are taken to be most central to Nietzsche's philosophy often depend on which works are regarded as most important or most accessible; but the relative importance which attaches to each of Nietzsche's works is by no means obvious. Indeed, Nietzsche scholarship has experienced fads with regard to given points of interest. As we will consider below, *Thus Spoke Zarathustra*'s celebrity outside of Germany declined after the Nazis invoked it for propagandistic purposes, while Nietzsche's early essay "On Truth and Lies in a Nonmoral Sense" has assumed new importance in recent literary-critical discussion, in part because it suggests that all language is metaphoric.

In what follows, we shall trace the chronology of Nietzsche's writings, mentioning themes that are prominent in each work. We shall also indicate central interpretive issues provoked by particular works and themes. While the Nietzsche that emerges here will, of necessity, be "our" Nietzsche, we hope that this synopsis will offer a basic map of the terrain of Nietzsche's works.

THE BIRTH OF TRAGEDY FROM THE SPIRIT OF MUSIC

Nietzsche was appointed Associate Professor of philology at Basel University before he had written a dissertation, on the basis of the enthusiastic support of his supervising professor, Albrecht Ritschl. His first book was, therefore, awaited with great expectations by his fellow classicists. Unfortunately, *The Birth of Tragedy from the Spirit of Music* (1872) was far from what Nietzsche's philological colleagues had had in mind. The book, which defended a theory of the origins and functions of Greek tragedy, was largely speculative and utterly devoid of footnotes. It began by appealing to its readers' experiences with drunkenness and dreams, and it ended with an appeal to popular culture in the form of a paean to Richard Wagner.

In this work, Nietzsche theorizes that Greek tragedy was built upon a wedding of two principles, which he associated with the deities Apollo and Dionysus. The Apollonian principle, in keeping with the characteristics of the sun god Apollo, is the principle of order, static beauty, and clear boundaries. The Dionysian principle, in contrast, is the principle of frenzy, excess, and the collapse of boundaries.

These principles offered perspectives on the position of the individual human being, but perspectives that were radically opposed to one another. The Apollonian principle conceived the individual as sufficiently separate from the rest of reality to be able to contemplate it dispassionately. The Dionysian principle, however, presents reality as a tumultuous flux in which individuality is overwhelmed by the dynamics of a living whole. Nietzsche believed that a balance of these principles is essential if one is both to recognize the challenge to one's sense of meaning posed by individual vulnerability and to recognize the solution, which depends on one's sense of oneness with a larger reality. Greek tragedy, as he saw it, confronted the issue of life's meaning by merging the perspectives of the two principles.

The themes of Greek tragedy concerned the worst case scenario from an Apollonian point of view – the devastation of vulnerable individuals. Scholarship had concluded that the chanting of the chorus was the first form of Athenian tragedy. Nietzsche interpreted the effect of the chorus as the initiation of a Dionysian experience on the part of the audience. Captivated by music, audience members abandoned their usual sense of themselves as isolated individuals and felt themselves instead to be part of a larger, frenzied whole.

This sense of self as part of a dynamic whole gave a different ground for experiencing life as meaningful than one would recognize in the more typical Apollonian condition, which entails a certain psychic distance. Feeling oneself to be part of the joyous vitality of the whole, one could take participation in life to be intrinsically wonderful, despite the obvious vulnerabilities one experiences as an individual. The aesthetic transformation of the audience member's sense of the significance of individual life aroused a quasi-religious affirmation of life's value. "It is only as an *aesthetic phenomenon* that existence and the world are eternally *justified*," Nietzsche concluded.[1]

The function of characters and drama later added to tragedy depended on the fundamental, enthralled experience of oneness with the chorus, according to Nietzsche. Already incited to a Dionysian state before the tragic hero appeared on stage, the audience would see the character before them as a manifestation of the god Dionysus. Unfortunately, Euripides restructured tragedy in such a way that the chorus's role was diminished. Euripides wrote plays that would encourage an Apollonian stance of objective interest in the drama. Nietzsche contended that in his attempt to write "intelligent" plays, Euripides had killed tragedy. He had done so, moreover, because he had fallen under the influence of Socrates.

The Birth of Tragedy is the first of many works in which Nietzsche re-evaluates the traditional view that Socrates was the quintessential philosopher. Although granting that Socrates was a turning point in world history, Nietzsche contends that Socrates was responsible for directing Western culture toward an imbalanced, exaggerated reliance on the Apollonian point of view. A defender of reason to an irrational degree, Socrates had taught that reason could penetrate reality to the point that it could correct reality's flaws. This had become the fundamental dream of Western culture, a dream that was later manifested in the modern approach to scholarship. Unfortunately, the optimism of the Socratic rational project was doomed to failure. Reason itself, through Kant, had pointed to its own limits. Whatever reason might accomplish, it could not "correct" the most basic flaws in human reality – the facts of human vulnerability and mortality.

The Birth of Tragedy also involves an indictment of contemporary culture as well as an account of the significance of tragedy. Contemporary culture's reliance on reason and its commitment to scientific optimism had rendered the modern individual largely oblivious to the Dionysian character of reality – a character which engulfed all individuals in the flow of life but which also rendered everyone subject to death and devastation. The repression of vulnerability was psychologically disastrous, in Nietzsche's view. The only hope for modern culture was that it might turn to myth, which could compensate for the culture's excesses, before a crisis.

Nietzsche's defense of Wagner as a cultural hero emerged in connection with this endorsement of myth as the necessary antidote to reason. Nietzsche believed that Wagner's operatic embodiments of Germanic myths had the potential to effect a new merger of the Apollonian and Dionysian principles, with redemptive effects on German culture. Nietzsche's great expectations of Wagner were not only central to his first book – they were also fundamentally important to him personally. Nietzsche and Wagner shared an enthusiasm for Schopenhauer, and for a number of years Nietzsche was a personal friend of Wagner's, visiting him regularly at his home in Tribschen – and sufficiently close to have been sent on one occasion to do some of the Wagners' Christmas shopping.

Nietzsche's endorsement of Wagner in the context of a philological work struck many of his professional colleagues as jarring. One, Ulrich von Wilamowitz-Möllendorf, responded to *The Birth of Tragedy*'s publication with a hostile pamphlet called *"Zukunftsphilologie"* ["Philology of the Future"], playing on Wagner's grandiose aspirations to create a *Kunstwerk der Zukunft* [artwork of the future]. The pamphlet presented *The Birth of Tragedy* as thoroughly unscholarly, filled with omissions and inaccuracies. With Nietzsche's encouragement, his friend Erwin Rohde wrote a pamphlet (October 1872) replying to Wilamowitz-Möllendorf, entitled *Afterphilologie* [Ass's Philology], which emphasized Wilamowitz-Möllendorf's own inaccuracies in citing from *The Birth of Tragedy*.

The Birth of Tragedy failed initially to secure esteem for Nietzsche among his philological colleagues. Nevertheless, the work has had enduring influence. In particular, the analysis of Apollo and Dionysus has had an impact on figures in diverse fields, among them Thomas Mann and C. G. Jung.[2]

THE *UNFASHIONABLE OBSERVATIONS*

Nietzsche wrote "David Strauss, the Confessor and the Writer" (1873), the first of his *Unfashionable Observations*, at the behest of

Richard Wagner. David Strauss was an eminent theologian, whose *The Life of Jesus Critically Examined* (1864) had had a tremendous impact due to its demystification of Jesus' life.³ Strauss had contended that the supernatural claims made about the historical Jesus could be explained in terms of the particular needs of his community. Although Strauss defends Christianity for its moral ideals, his demythologizing of Jesus appealed to Nietzsche.

Nevertheless, Wagner had been publicly denounced by Strauss in 1865 for having persuaded Ludwig II to fire a musician-rival. Not one to forget an assault, Wagner encouraged Nietzsche to read Strauss's recent *The Old and the New Faith* (1872), which advocated the rejection of the Christian faith in favor of a Darwinian, materialistic, and patriotic worldview. Wagner described the book to Nietzsche as extremely superficial, and Nietzsche agreed with Wagner's opinion, despite the similarity of his own views to Strauss's perspective on religion.

This *Unfashionable Observation*, accordingly, was Nietzsche's attempt to avenge Wagner by attacking Strauss's recent book. In fact, the essay is at least as much a polemical attack on Strauss as on his book, for Nietzsche identifies Strauss as a cultural "Philistine" and exemplar of pseudoculture. The resulting essay appears extremely intemperate, although erudite, filled with references to many of Nietzsche's scholarly contemporaries. The climax is a literary tour de force, in which Nietzsche cites a litany of malapropisms from Strauss, interspersed with his own barbed comments.

Not surprisingly, the elderly Strauss was stunned and stung by Nietzsche's essay. He wrote to a friend, "The only thing I find interesting about the fellow is the psychological point – how one can get into such a rage with a person whose path one has never crossed, in brief, the real motive of this passionate hatred."⁴ Nietzsche, apparently, had some qualms after his essay was published. When he heard that Strauss died six months after its publication, he wrote to his friend Gerdsdorff, "I very much hope that I did not sadden his last months, and that he died without knowing anything about me. It's rather on my mind."⁵

Nietzsche's second *Unfashionable Observation*, "On the Advantages and Disadvantages of History for Life" (1874)," is "unfashionable" because it questions the apparent assumption of nineteenth-century German educators that historical knowledge is intrinsically valuable. Nietzsche argues, in contrast, that historical knowledge is valuable only when it has a positive effect on human beings' sense of life. Although he acknowledges that history does provide a number of benefits in this respect, Nietzsche also contends that there are a number of ways in which historical knowledge could prove damaging to those who pursued it and that many of his contemporaries were suffering these ill effects.

Nietzsche contends that history can play three positive roles, which he terms "monumental," "antiquarian," and "critical." *Monumental history* brings the great achievements of humanity into focus. This genre of history has value for contemporary individuals because it makes them aware of what is possible for human beings to achieve. *Antiquarian history*, history motivated primarily out of a spirit of reverence for the past, can be valuable to contemporary individuals by helping them to appreciate their lives and culture. *Critical history*, history approached in an effort to pass judgment, provides a counterbalancing effect to that inspired by antiquarian history. By judging the past, those engaged in critical history remain attentive to flaws and failures in the experience of their culture, thereby avoiding slavish blindness in their appreciation of it.

The problem with historical scholarship in his own time, according to Nietzsche, was that historical knowledge was pursued for its own sake. He cited five dangers resulting from such an approach to history: (1) Modern historical knowledge undercuts joy in the present, since it makes the present appear as just another episode. (2) Modern historical knowledge inhibits creative activity by convincing those made aware of the vast sweep of historical currents that their present actions are too feeble to change the past they have inherited. (3) Modern historical knowledge encourages the sense that the inner person is disconnected from the outer world by assaulting the psyche with more information than it can absorb and assimilate. (4) Modern historical knowledge encourages a jaded relativism toward reality and present experience, motivated by a sense that because things keep changing present states of affairs do not matter. (5) Modern historical knowledge inspires irony and cynicism about the contemporary individual's role in the world; the historically knowledgeable person comes to feel increasingly like an afterthought in the scheme of things, imbued by a sense of belatedness.

Although Nietzsche was convinced that the current approach to history was psychologically and ethically devastating to his contemporaries, particularly the young, he contends that antidotes could reverse these trends. One antidote is the *unhistorical*, the ability to forget how overwhelming the deluge of historical information is, and to "enclose oneself within a bounded *horizon*."[6] A second antidote is the *suprahistorical*, a shift of focus from the ongoing flux of history to "that which bestows upon existence the character of the eternal and stable, towards *art* and *religion*."[7]

Nietzsche's third *Unfashionable Observation*, "Schopenhauer as Educator" (1874), probably provides more information about Nietzsche himself than it does about Schopenhauer or his philosophy. As R. J. Hollingdale remarks, this is almost wholly about Schopenhauer as "an exemplary type of man."[8]

Schopenhauer, in Nietzsche's idealizing perspective, is exemplary because he was so thoroughly an individual genius. Schopenhauer was one of those rare individuals whose emergence is nature's true goal in producing humanity, Nietzsche suggests. He praises Schopenhauer's indifference to the mediocre academicians of his era, as well as his heroism as a philosophical "loner."

Strangely, given Schopenhauer's legendary pessimism, Nietzsche praises his "cheerfulness that really cheers" along with his honesty and steadfastness.[9] But Nietzsche argues that in addition to specific traits that a student might imitate, Schopenhauer offers a more important kind of example. Being himself attuned to the laws of his own character, Schopenhauer directed those students who were capable of insight to recognize the laws of their own character. By reading and learning from Schopenhauer, one could develop one's own individuality.

Nietzsche intended to write a fourth *Unfashionable Observation* devoted to the profession of classical philology. He began dictating "We Philologists" in 1875, but this meditation was never finished.[10] Nevertheless, the notes that remain are extensive, and they offer insight into Nietzsche's aspirations as a classicist and his disillusionment with the profession as practiced. In its critique of contemporary education, the notes share an elective affinity with the *Observation* on history. Unfortunately, Nietzsche argued, classical philology was pursued as a relentless labor for its own sake, without concern for its relevance to contemporary life.

Classical scholarship as knowledge of the ancient world cannot, of course, last forever; its material is exhaustible. What cannot be exhausted is the perpetually new adjustment of our own age to the classical world, of measuring ourselves against it. If we assign the classicist the task of understanding *his own* age better by means of the classical world, then his task is a permanent one. – This is the antinomy of classical scholarship. Men have always, in fact, understood *the ancient world* exclusively in terms of *the present* – and shall *the present* now be understood in terms of *the ancient world?* More precisely: men have explained the classical world to themselves in terms of their own experience; and from this they have acquired of the classical world in this way, they have *assessed,* evaluated their own experience. Hence experience is clearly an absolute prerequisite for a *classicist.* Which means: the classicist must first be a man in order to become creative as a classicist.[11]

"Richard Wagner in Bayreuth" (1876), the fourth and final of Nietzsche's published *Unfashionable Observations,* was intended as a paean to Wagner, somewhat akin to "Schopenhauer as Educator." Nietzsche's relationship to Wagner had been strained by the time he wrote this essay, however, and the tension is evident in the text, which emphasizes Wagner's psychology (a theme that would preoccupy Nietzsche in many of his future writings). Nietzsche himself may have been concerned about the extent to which the essay might be perceived as unflattering, for he considered not publishing it. Ultimately, Nietzsche published a version of the essay that was considerably less critical of Wagner than were earlier drafts, and Wagner was pleased enough to send a copy of the essay to King Ludwig.[12]

A break with Wagner was probably inevitable for Nietzsche. Wagner showed considerable arrogance toward the younger Nietzsche, whom he frequently treated on the order of a servant. The personal styles and sensibilities of the two men clashed. Wagner was brash and vain; Nietzsche, in contrast, was extremely polite. Thus, Nietzsche was annoyed by Wagner's rude denunciations; Wagner, in contrast, suggested to Nietzsche's physician that his headaches were the consequences of excessive masturbation. Nietzsche's disgust at the philistinism of Wagner's followers provoked him to leave a Bayreuth festival in 1876, and the final break was precipitated by Wagner's opera *Parsifal,* which struck Nietzsche as hypocritically religious.

The break with Wagner was extremely significant to Nietzsche. The importance of the relationship is evident from the extent to which Nietzsche's works analyze Wagner and "artists" more generally. Among the works of Nietzsche's final lucid year were two on Wagner, *The Case of Wagner: A Musician's Problem* (1888) and *Nietzsche contra Wagner: Documents of a Psychologist* (1895), an edition of passages on Wagner assembled from Nietzsche's various books.

EARLY ESSAYS

Besides the four *Unfashionable Observations*, Nietzsche drafted a number of additional essays in the early 1870s which he never elected to publish. These include "The Philosopher: Reflections on the Struggle between Art and Knowledge," "On the Pathos of Truth," "The Philosopher as Cultural Physician," "Philosophy in Hard Times," "The Struggle between Science and Wisdom," "On Truth and Lies in a Nonmoral Sense," and "Philosophy in the Tragic Age of the Greeks."[13] These manuscripts reveal considerable thematic overlap. Nietzsche apparently intended to integrate the various drafts into a single book, a companion to *The Birth of Tragedy*, but this integration never occurred.[14] Nevertheless, "On Truth and Lies in a Nonmoral Sense" and "Philosophy in the Tragic Age of the Greeks" have received sufficient scholarly attention and commentary to warrant discussion here.

Nietzsche's early essay "On Truth and Lies in a Nonmoral Sense" (1873) makes some claims designed to startle those who see philosophy as essentially a quest for truth in the correspondence sense, a search for accurate representation. He contends instead that "truth" is a mode of illusion and that the schemes our intellects impose upon things by means of language, while practically useful, are fundamentally deceptive. Moreover, while language is always metaphoric, one usually forgets that this is so, imagining that the conceptual schemes of one's own construction are permanent fixtures. In fact, Nietzsche argues somewhat paradoxically, reality is a flux that language cannot capture. Most famously, Nietzsche contends,

What then is truth? A movable host of metaphors, metonymies, and anthropomorphisms: in short, a sum of human relations which have been poetically and rhetorically intensified, transferred, and embellished, and which, after long usage, seem to a people to be fixed, canonical, and binding. Truths are illusions which we have forgotten are illusions; they are metaphors that have become worn out and have been drained of sensuous force, coins which have lost their embossing and are now considered as metal and no longer as coins.[15]

The stock of "On Truth and Lies in a Nonmoral Sense" has risen in the eyes of many scholars over the past few decades, primarily because it analyzes truth in terms of metaphor. Many literary theorists and philosophers influenced by literary criticism, in particular, interpret Nietzsche as defending a view of "truth" that treats it as an illusion foisted upon us by language. Truth, on this view, amounts ultimately to a mode of rhetoric.[16] The essay's striking images have also inspired reflection and commentary from contemporary literary critics.[17] For example, Nietzsche describes the human being's lack of self-knowledge as follows:

Does nature not conceal most things from him – even concerning his own body, in order to confine and lock him within a proud, deceptive consciousness, aloof from the coils of the bowels, the rapid flow of the blood stream, and the intricate quivering of the fibers! She threw away the key. And woe to that fatal curiosity which might one day have the power to peer out and down through a crack in the chamber of consciousness and then suspect that man is sustained in the indifference of his ignorance by that which is pitiless, greedy, insatiable, and murderous – as if hanging in dreams on the back of a tiger.[18]

Among philosophers less influenced by recent literary theory, however, the essay has more typically been seen as an early statement of Nietzsche's thoughts on truth that he was later to revise and supplant with more philosophically sophisticated views. Maudemarie Clark, for instance, contends that, "Far from a precocious statement of Nietzsche's lifelong views, ... ["On Truth and Lies"] belongs, according to my interpretation, to Nietzsche's juvenilia."[19]

Nietzsche also wrote a manuscript primarily about the early Greek philosophers, drawing on a series of lectures that he gave during the summer of 1872 on the pre-Platonic philosophers. He worked on this project until his visit to the Wagners at Easter of 1873. Nietzsche set this manuscript aside after this visit, when Wagner incited him to write the essay on David Strauss, which led Nietzsche to the idea of a whole series of *Unfashionable Observations*.

The unpublished manuscript that exists, "Philosophy in the Tragic Age of the Greeks" (1873), however, gives insight into Nietzsche's approach to both classics and philosophy. Nietzsche treats the pre-Platonic philosophies as archetypes for all basic philosophical moves and postures, which he does not separate from the types of individuals expressing them. Most striking to Nietzsche was the fact that these early thinkers took the ordinary as cause for wonder. He also emphasizes two other problems of importance to these thinkers: the purposes in nature and the value of knowledge.[20]

HUMAN, ALL TOO HUMAN

Nietzsche is often said to have entered a new period with the publication of *Human, All Too Human, a Book for Free Spirits* (1878). The book is considerably more "positivistic" than his earlier writings.[21] It aims at debunking unwarranted assumptions more than at defending a grand interpretation of its own, and it marks the high point of Nietzsche's interest in and applause for natural science. The book is deliberately anti-metaphysical.

Nietzsche describes what he means by *"free spirits"* in the preface to the second edition of *Human, All Too Human*. Free spirits contrast with the typical human being of his era, who was, as the title suggests, all too human. Free spirits, in contrast, are ideal companions that do not yet exist but may appear in the future. They are those who have freed themselves from the fetters of acculturation, even the bonds of reverence for those things they once found most praiseworthy. The dangerous period of the free spirit is introduced by the desire to flee whatever has been one's previous spiritual world, a desire that leads to a reconsideration of matters that previously had been taken for granted. The ultimate aim of this liberation is independent self-mastery and supreme health in a life of continual experimentation and adventure. This ideal is akin to images Nietzsche develops later, particularly in "On the Three Metamorphoses" in *Thus Spoke Zarathustra* and in the description of the philosophers of the future in *Beyond Good and Evil*.

Although Nietzsche suggests a perspectival view in the unpublished "On Truth and Lies" essay, *Human, All Too Human* is the first published work in which he defends his famed *perspectivism*, the view that "truths" are one and all interpretations formulated from particular perspectives.[22] Scholars take various positions on the matter of how radical this position is. On one extreme are those who see this as a brand of neo-Kantianism that simply spells out the implication of Kant's theory that the world as it appears to us is constructed by our particular human faculties. On the other extreme are those who read Nietzsche's perspectivism as a radical form of relativism, one which denies any basis for preferring one perspective to another.

Philosophers in the Anglo-American tradition are also especially fond of examining Nietzsche's perspectivism from the standpoint of the famed "liar's paradox." The liar's paradox afflicts the liar who claims, "Everything I say is false." If that sentence is taken as true, it is actually false, since it would itself be a true claim made by the liar. Nietzsche has been accused of adopting a similarly paradoxical position. If all knowledge claims are interpretations, that should hold also for the claim that all knowledge claims are merely interpretations. But if this is so, according to some, Nietzsche has undermined the status and force of his own claim. Others, however, see no reason why Nietzsche would not acknowledge that his own claims are interpretations, pointing to textual passages where he seems to do just that.[23]

Nietzsche's perspectivism figures importantly in his debunking critique of morality, which is first presented in *Human, All Too Human*. Nietzsche denies that morality is anything but perspectival. Contrary to the claims of moralists, morality is not inherent in or determined by reality. It does not limn human nature. Instead, it is the invention of human beings. Moreover, morality has not been the same in every culture and at every time. Nietzsche explicitly contrasts Christian and Greek moral thought, typically claiming that Greek thought had been vastly superior.

Personally, Nietzsche considered the book a breakthrough because it openly articulated his unconventional conclusions for the first time. It also sealed the break with Richard Wagner, who received the book with stony silence. Nietzsche also considered himself to have moved beyond the sway of Schopenhauerian metaphysics by this point.

Human, All Too Human also represents a stylistic departure from Nietzsche's earlier writing. While his previous works had typically been in the forms of essays or similarly structured longer works,

Human, All Too Human is the first of Nietzsche's "aphoristic" works. That is, it is written as an assembly of short discussions (sometimes literally aphorisms) which are strung together like beads, often without obvious connections between adjacent fragments. This appearance is often deceptive, however. Nietzsche orders his fragments to achieve a given effect, suggesting but not dogmatically asserting comparisons and contrasts, while challenging his readers to draw their own conclusions.

From *Human, All Too Human* onward, the fragmentary "aphoristic" style predominated in Nietzsche's writings. The biographical motivation for composing in this style may have been largely one of necessity – Nietzsche's migraines were so oppressive and visually impairing that he had to resort to intermittent bursts of writing and dictation as a method.[24] Nevertheless, Erich Heller rightly notes that this format suits this thinker, who was avowedly antisystematic.[25] This is particularly evident in Nietzsche's many gems of psychological insight, which are offered as verbal snapshots of disparate vignettes, usually without over-arching commentary. Moreover, this style is a suitable vehicle to reflect the movements and discontinuities of thought on given topics, an issue with which Nietzsche was profoundly concerned.[26]

In 1886, Nietzsche published a second edition of *Human, All Too Human*, in which the previously published work was made Volume I of a two-volume work. Volume II consisted of two aphoristic works that Nietzsche had written and published separately, *Appendix: Assorted Opinions and Sayings* (1879) and *The Wanderer and His Shadow* (1880). These books were more conventionally aphoristic than the earlier volume, largely consisting of extremely terse, condensed formulations. Schopenhauer and Wagner receive more direct attacks than previously, and Nietzsche is more strident in his rejection of metaphysics on the grounds that (like historical scholarship) it is not approached with sufficient attention to its value (or lack of value) for actual living.

DAYBREAK

Daybreak: Thoughts on Moral Prejudices (1881) goes further than *Human, All Too Human* in elaborating Nietzsche's critique of Christian morality. It is perhaps also more masterful than the earlier work in its artful use of "aphoristic" juxtaposition to engage the reader in his or her own reflections. Indeed, Nietzsche seems bent on conveying a particular type of experience in thinking to his readers, much more than he is concerned to persuade his readers to adopt any particular point of view.[27]

Nietzsche criticized the Christian moral worldview on a number of grounds that he was to develop further in his later works. His basic case rests on psychological analyses of the motivations and effects that stem from the adoption of the Christian moral perspective. In this respect, *Daybreak* typifies Nietzsche's *ad hominem* approach to morality. Nietzsche asks primarily, "What kind of person would be inclined to adopt this perspective?" and "What impact does this perspective have on the way in which its adherent develops and lives?"[28]

Nietzsche argues that the concepts that Christianity uses to analyze moral experience – especially sin and the afterlife – are entirely imaginary and psychologically pernicious. These categories deprecate human experience, making its significance appear much more vile than it actually is. Painting reality in a morbid light, Christian moral concepts motivate Christians to adopt somewhat paranoid and hostile attitudes toward their own behavior and that of others. Convinced of their own sinfulness and worthiness of eternal damnation, Christians are driven to seek spiritual reassurance at tremendous costs in terms of their own mental health and their relationships to others.

For instance, Christians feel that they need to escape their embodied selves because they are convinced of their own sinfulness. They are convinced of their own failure insofar as they believe themselves sinners and believe themselves to be bound by an unfulfillable law of perfect love. In order to ameliorate their sense of guilt and failure, Nietzsche contends, they look to others in the hope of finding them more sinful than themselves. Because the Christian moral worldview has convinced its advocates that their own position is perilous, Christians are driven to judge others to be sinners in order to gain a sense of power over them. The Christian moral worldview thus encourages uncharitable judgments of others, paradoxically despite its praise of neighbor love.

The fundamental misrepresentation of reality offered by the Christian moral worldview provokes dishonesty in its adherents, particularly in appraisals of themselves and others. It also encourages them to despise earthly life in favor of another reality (one that Nietzsche claims does not exist). Still further psychological damage to the believer results from the Christian moral worldview's insistence on absolute conformity to a single standard of human behavior. Nietzsche contends that one size does not fit all where morality is concerned, and that most of the best and strongest individuals are least capable of living according to the mold. Nevertheless, Christians are urged to abolish their individual characters, and to the extent that they fail to do so they reinforce their own feelings of inadequacy.

Nietzsche's picture of Christian morality seems dismal. He regards it as the motivation for attitudes that are self-denigrating, vindictive toward others, escapist, and antilife. Nietzsche never alters this basic assessment of the moral framework of his own tradition; instead, he continues to develop these themes in all his later discussions of morality and ethics.

THE GAY SCIENCE

Nietzsche's *The Gay Science* (1882)[29] [*Die Fröhliche Wissenschaft*] proposes an antidote to the condition of contemporary scholarship [*Wissenschaft*]. As opposed to what he saw as contemporary scholars' antlike drudgery in amassing facts, he recommends "the *gay science*" – a kind of scholarship that would be light-hearted and deliberately "superficial – out of profundity," as he claims that the Greeks were. Aware of the murkier aspects of human experience, the ancient Athenians responded by taking aesthetic delight in life and becoming "adorers of forms, of tones, of words."[30] In his own era, in which many felt belated in history and incapable of transforming reality, Nietzsche proposed that this would be the appropriate convalescence for scholars, as it had been for him in his personal life.

The most famous statement in *The Gay Science* is the claim, "God is dead."[31] It appears twice, first in Section 108, which opens Book Three:

New struggles. – After Buddha was dead, his shadow was still shown for centuries in a cave – a tremendous, gruesome shadow. God is dead; but given the way of men, there may still be caves for thousands of years in which his shadow will be shown. – And we – we still have to vanquish his shadow, too.[32]

Somewhat surprisingly, the section that follows this statement seems to drop this theme and attacks the contemporary attitude toward science instead. An extended theme in the work, however, is the danger that science will be treated as the new religion, serving as a basis for retaining that same damaging psychological habit that the Christian religion developed.

The more famous appearance of the statement "God is dead," however, arrives in Section 125, entitled *The Madman.* " The madman in the section appears in the marketplace and makes this announcement, rather frantically, to the scientific atheists who are gathered there. They merely laugh. The madman tells them, *"We have killed him* – you and I. All of us are his murderers." He explains as best he can to his listeners, who respond only with silence. Finally, he breaks the lantern he is carrying on the ground and says, "I have come too early . . . ; my time is not yet. . . . This deed is still more distant from them than the most distant stars – *and yet they have done it themselves."* The section continues with the report that the madman visited several churches later that day and sang the *requiem aeternam deo* of the funeral mass. "Let out and called to account, he is said always to have replied nothing but: 'What after all are these churches now if they are not the tombs and sepulchers of God?' "[33]

This parable suggests the inappropriateness of the popular characterization of Nietzsche as the hardened atheist who delights in nothing more than debunking other people's beliefs. Nevertheless, the perspective that Nietzsche proposes throughout *The Gay Science* is naturalistic and aesthetic, in opposition to traditional religious views.[34] Indeed, many of the work's sections might be considered practical advice for the spiritually sensitive atheist who is concerned lest he or she return to old religious habits out of desperation. Nietzsche proposes as an alternative to religious views that seek life's meaning in an afterlife, an immanent appreciation of this life in aesthetic terms. Ideal, he suggests, is the experience of *amor fati* [love of fate], in which one loves one's life, with all its flaws, just for what it is.[35]

Nietzsche's most complex and controversial image for the satisfaction that one would ideally take in one's earthly life is his "doctrine" [*Lehre*] of eternal recurrence. The concept of eternal recurrence seems to suggest that time is cyclical, with the entire sequence of all events recurring over and over again. In Nietzsche's published works, this concept is first suggested in the penultimate section of Book Four of *The Gay Science*, entitled "The Greatest Stress." The section presents a thought experiment, akin to Descartes's thought experiment of the evil genius:

What, if some day or night a demon were to steal after you into your loneliest loneliness and say to you: "This life as you now live it and have lived it, you will have to live once more and innumerable times more; and there will be nothing new in it, but every pain and every joy and every thought and sigh and everything unutterably small or great in your life will have to return to you, all in the same succession and sequence. . . ."[36]

The section goes on to ask how the reader would respond to this suggestion. Would it cause the reader to gnash his or her teeth, or would the reader imagine this prospect as divine?

The conception of eternal recurrence, often labeled a "doctrine," recurs in *Thus Spoke Zarathustra* in various forms and images.[37] In these, as in the passage from *The Gay Science*, the vision of time as cyclical is presented as something that should have existential import for an individual. The image of eternal recurrence appears to serve as a test that will determine whether an individual genuinely considers his or her life meaningful. So construed, as an *existential* theory, eternal recurrence is important primarily because it indicates a desirable attitude toward life. If one can genuinely affirm eternal recurrence, one considers one's life intrinsically valuable, worth living over and over again.[38]

Some scholars have accepted the existential construal of the theory, but elaborated it in ethical or aesthetic terms. On one reading, the theory is offered as a kind of ethical admonition to live one's life as one would if one genuinely believed that one's life would eternally recur.[39] Eternal recurrence has also been interpreted in terms borrowed from aesthetics. On this view, the doctrine provides instruction as to how to construct one's life (and one's interpretation of it) as an artistic whole, with sufficient aesthetic merit to make its recurrence desirable.[40]

Although the published passages that deal with eternal recurrence lend support to the "existential" reading, some of Nietzsche's unpublished notes suggest another reading of eternal recurrence. In his notes Nietzsche sketches various "scientific" proofs of eternal recurrence, based on the assumptions that time is infinite while configurations of energy are finite. Some scholars emphasize these formulations over the published formulations, which do not offer "scientific" demonstrations of the doctrine. These interpreters regard eternal recurrence as a *cosmological* theory that offers an account of the nature of time in the context of the universe. So understood, the doctrine is not primarily about human beings, but instead deals with the entire structure and content of the universe.[41]

The first edition of *The Gay Science* ends with the vignette that opens Nietzsche's next book, *Thus Spoke Zarathustra*. Entitled *"Incipit tragoedia"* ["The tragedy begins"], it describes the prophet Zarathustra's emergence from his mountain cave, addressing the sun, and beginning the descent that will commence his teaching mission. The passage plays with the imagery of Plato's famous "Myth of the Cave" from Book 7 of the *Republic*. Zarathustra, although a fictional character in Nietzsche's works, is modeled on the Persian prophet of the same name, founder of the Zoroastrian religion. In his discussion of his choice of this figure in *Ecce Homo*, Nietzsche's description suggests that he sees the Persian prophet as an appropriate alternative to the Christian worldview (which he frequently describes in terms of "good and evil"):

Zarathustra was the first to consider the fight of good and evil the very wheel in the machinery of things: the transposition of morality into the metaphysical realm, as a force, cause, and end in itself, is *his* work. But this question is at bottom its own answer. Zarathustra created this most calamitous error, morality; consequently, he must also be the first to recognize it. Not only has he more experience in the matter, for a longer time, than any other thinker – after all, the whole of history is the refutation by experiment of the principle of the so-called "moral world order" – what is more important is that Zarathustra is more truthful than any other thinker. His doctrine and his alone, posits truthfulness as the highest virtue.... To speak the truth and to *shoot well with arrows*, that is Persian virtue.... The self-overcoming of morality, out of truthfulness; the self-overcoming of the moralist, into his opposite – into me – that is what the name of Zarathustra means in my mouth.[42]

THUS SPOKE ZARATHUSTRA

Nietzsche's *Thus Spoke Zarathustra: A Book for All and None* is probably his most famous work – and also the work least popular among philosophers, at least in the Anglo-American tradition.[43] This is probably partially because it is written in fictional form. Many philosophers who want to treat issues discussed by Zarathustra prefer to find what they regard as similar discussions elsewhere in Nietzsche's works and to avoid the need to factor the fictionality of the work into their reading.[44] *Zarathustra* is also well designed to frustrate twentieth-century philosophy of the analytic tradition, which seeks conceptual clarity at the expense of rhetorical form, indeed often insists on the separation between a concept and the vehicle of its expression. The subtitle itself reveals the book's propensity for paradox; and Zarathustra's stance as a pontificating sage chimes poorly with the analytic effort to subject insinuated authority to critical conceptual analysis. Moreover, the employment of *Zarathustra* by the Nazi war effort to inspire German soldiers did little to improve the book's reception in the Anglo-American world.[45]

Nevertheless, the book is philosophically interesting, in part because it does employ literary tropes and genres to philosophical effect. *Zarathustra* makes frequent use of parody, particularly of the Platonic dialogues and the New Testament. This strategy immediately presents Zarathustra on a par with Socrates and Christ – and as a clear alternative to them. The erudite allusions to works spanning the Western philosophical and literary traditions also play a philosophical role, for they both reveal Nietzsche's construal of the tradition he inherited and flag points at which he views it as problematic.

Much of the book consists of Zarathustra's speeches on philosophical themes, and these often obscure the plotline of the book. The book does involve a plot, however, which includes sections in which Zarathustra is "off-stage," in private reflection, and some in which he seems extremely distressed about the way his teaching and his life are going. Heidegger sees the plot as essential to the kind of teaching that Zarathustra effects. Zarathustra attempts to instruct the crowds and occasional higher man that he encounters in the book; but his most important teaching, in Heidegger's view, is his education of the reader, accomplished through demonstrative means. Zarathustra teaches "by showing."

Indeed, Zarathustra stands in the tradition of the German Bildungsroman, in which a character's development toward spiritual maturity is chronicled. Zarathustra can be seen as a paradigm for the modern, spiritually sensitive individual, one who grapples with nihilism, the contemporary crisis in values in the wake of the collapse of the Christian worldview that assigned humanity a clear place in the world.[46]

In the popular imagination, Nietzsche's idea of "the Superman" [Übermensch] is one of his most memorable and significant ideals. In fact, however, the concept of the Übermensch [superhuman being] is actually discussed rather little in the book.[47] The topic is the theme of the first speech in "Zarathustra's Prologue,"[48] which he presents to a crowd gathered for a circus. The audience interprets Zarathustra as a circus barker and the speech as an introduction to a performance by a tightrope walker. The concept is mentioned recurrently in Part I as something of a refrain to Zarathustra's speeches. But the word "Übermensch" rarely occurs after that.

In addition, the notion of the Übermensch is presented in more imagistic than explanatory terms. The Übermensch, according to Zarathustra, is continually experimental, willing to risk all for the sake of the enhancement of humanity. The Übermensch aspires to greatness, but Zarathustra does not formulate any more specific characterization of what constitutes the enhancement of humanity or greatness. He does, however, contrast the Übermensch to the last man, the human type whose sole desire is personal comfort, happiness. Such a person is "the last man" quite literally, incapable of the desire that is required to create beyond oneself in any form, including that of having children.

The status of the Übermensch concept has been much debated among Nietzsche scholars.[49] Among the issues are the following: Is the notion presented to establish a set of character traits as most desirable, or does it represent instead an ideal attitude?[50] Is the Übermensch an attainable goal? Is it a solipsistic goal? Is it an evolutionary goal in a Darwinian sense? Does the doctrine stand in any particular relationship to Nietzsche's other doctrines? In particular, does it describe the type of person who would be able to affirm eternal recurrence?[51] What is to be made of the fact that the notion of the

Übermensch is virtually abandoned after Part I of *Zarathustra*? Does Nietzsche give up on the idea?[52] Does he mean it to be implicit in Zarathustra's later speeches? Does the theme of eternal recurrence supplant that of the *Übermensch* as the fundamental theme of the book?

Zarathustra's opening speech, besides proposing the *Übermensch* as the ideal for humanity also places emphasis on this world as opposed to any future world. "Let your will say: the *Übermensch* shall be the meaning of the earth! I beseech you, my brothers, remain faithful to the earth, and do not believe those who speak to you of otherworldly hopes!"[53] In particular, Zarathustra urges that human beings reassess the value of their own bodies, indeed their embodiment. For too long, dreaming of the afterlife, Western humanity has treated the body as a source of sin and error. Zarathustra, in contrast, insists that the body is the ground of all meaning and knowledge, and that health and strength should be recognized and sought as virtues.[54]

Another prominent theme in *Zarathustra* is its emphasis on the relative importance of will. In part, this emphasis follows Schopenhauer in claiming that will is more fundamental to human beings than knowledge. However, Nietzsche stresses the will's attempt to enhance its power, whereas he views Schopenhauer as placing greater stress on the will's efforts at self-preservation. Nietzsche's famous conception of will to power makes one of its few published appearances in *Zarathustra*.

"Indeed, the truth was not hit by him who shot at it with the word of the 'will to existence': that will does not exist. For, what does not exist cannot will; but what is in existence, how could that still want existence? Only where there is life is there also will: not will to life but – thus I teach you – will to power."[55]

The formulation "will to power" has received considerable attention by Nietzsche scholars and by a larger spectrum of society as well. Easily exploited by the Nazi war effort and utilized by murderers Leopold and Loeb as justification for their crime, this theme has had an unsavory history beyond the world of scholarship. Scholars have endeavored to set the record straight, but they have disagreed as to the significance and importance of "will to power" in Nietzsche's thought.

Some scholars have argued that its appearance reveals the extent to which Nietzsche remains Schopenhauerian in his thinking, despite the changed formulation he proposes.[56] Some have contended that the idea is a cornerstone of Nietzsche's thought, observing that some of Nietzsche's notes reveal his definite plans to write a book about it.[57] Others have pointed to the paucity of published mentions of "will to power" and suggested that this idea was not particularly central to Nietzsche.[58] Scholars disagree on whether the will to power should be viewed as a psychological observation or a metaphysical doctrine, and they have also disagreed on whether Nietzsche intended this primarily as an explanation of human behavior or a more general cosmological account.[59]

Those discussions of will that appear in *Zarathustra* particularly occur in connection with the doctrine of eternal recurrence.

"To redeem those who lived in the past and to recreate all 'it was' into a 'thus I willed it' – that alone should I call redemption. . . . All 'it was' is a fragment, a riddle, a dreadful accident – until the creative will says to it, 'But thus I will it; thus shall I will it.' "[60]

Much of the plot of *Zarathustra* concerns his efforts to formulate his idea of eternal recurrence. At times, the idea possesses him in the form of visions and dreams. At others, he seems reluctant to state it categorically or to accept its implications. During a particularly despairing moment, he shudders at the implication of his doctrine that "the rabble," the petty people who comprise most of the human race, will also recur. The eagle and snake who have been his companions urge him to stop speaking and to sing instead. They suggest their own formulation of eternal recurrence, which is perhaps one of the clearest suggestions of how eternal recurrence might give one a sense of meaning in life. And yet, it is not Zarathustra's words one reads.

"And if you wanted to die now, O Zarathustra, behold, we also know how you would then speak to yourself . . .

" 'Now I die and vanish,' you would say, 'and all at once I am nothing. The soul is as mortal as the body. But the knot of causes in which I am entangled recurs and will create me again. I myself belong to the causes of the eternal recurrence. I come again, with this sun, with this earth, with this eagle, with this serpent – not to a new life or a better life or a similar life: I come back eternally to this same, selfsame life, in what is greatest as in what is smallest, to teach again the eternal recurrence of all things, to speak again the word of the great noon of earth and man, to proclaim the *Übermensch* again to men. I spoke my word, I break of my word: thus my eternal lot wants it; as a proclaimer I perish. The hour has now come when he who goes under should bless himself. Thus *ends* Zarathustra's going under.' "[61]

The fact that Zarathustra objects to the recurrence of the rabble is indicative of Nietzsche's elitism.[62] Consistently, Nietzsche and Zarathustra contend that human beings are not equal. Nietzsche objects to the democratic movements of his era in favor of more aristocratic forms of social organization that would place control in the hands of the talented, of necessity not the majority.

Nietzsche is also often reputed to be a sexist, in large part because of a famous line that appears in *Zarathustra*: "You are going to women? Do not forget the whip!" What is rarely remembered is the fact that this line is not spoken by Zarathustra, but instead by an old woman in partial objection to Zarathustra's romanticized image of male and female roles. The line certainly requires interpretation; but it should not be construed as a straightforward statement of Nietzsche's views.[63]

Nietzsche's alleged sexism is a complex topic. In some of his writings he mouths the inflammatory misogynistic imagery of Schopenhauer's "On Women," arguably the most notorious denunciation of women in German.[64] At other times, he presents psychological vignettes depicting interactions among women and men; frequently in these, he seems to be sympathetic to women.[65] He frequently personifies abstract ideas in female form, and he appeals to stereotypical images of women, although in the latter cases he often plays with the images or refers explicitly to male perceptions of women.[66] The passages in *Beyond Good and Evil* dealing with women are often read as stridently antifeminist; but Nietzsche significantly prefaces these immoderately modulated passages with a confessional remark akin to what one would expect in a male consciousness-raising group:

Whenever a cardinal problem is at stake, there speaks an unchangeable "this is I"; about man and woman, for example, a thinker cannot relearn but only finish learning – only discover ultimately how this is "settled in him." At times we find certain solutions of problems that inspire strong faith in us; some call them henceforth *their* "convictions." Later – we see them only as steps to self-knowledge, signposts to the problem we *are* – rather, to the great stupidity we are, to our spiritual *fatum*, to what is *unteachable* very "deep down."

After this abundant civility that I have just evidenced in relation to myself I shall perhaps be permitted more readily to state a few truths about "woman as such" – assuming that it is now known from the outset how very much these are after all only – *my* truths.[67]

Nietzsche's biography might also be brought to bear on his views on women. He was raised in a family of women of rigidly moralistic views. His marriage proposals were all rebuffed; and the women whom he seemed most to admire, Lou Salomé and Cosima Wagner, were strong-willed individuals who did not especially subscribe to conventional roles for women. No doubt, Nietzsche had many motivations for complicated reactions to "woman as such." At any rate, his published references to women present more a suggestive interpretive puzzle than a coherent statement.

Nietzsche claims that he wrote the first three parts of the four-part *Zarathustra* in ten-day outbursts, although it is evident from his notes that he had plans in mind for a considerably longer period. The work was published in various segments and sizes. Parts I and II were published together in 1883, and Part III was published in 1884. Part IV was published in a limited edition in 1885. Nietzsche distributed Part IV to a few friends, but he wanted them to keep the book quiet. Only in 1892 was Part IV published in a public edition.

Part IV certainly contrasts with the other three parts. The narrator's voice is more critical of Zarathustra and of claims it reports. The plot is more prominent. It is, moreover, funny. Besides involving an irreverent parody of the Last Supper and Plato's Symposium, it involves a number of characters, called the "higher men," who ludicrously personify Zarathustra's teachings. The higher men have each taken one of Zarathustra's doctrines as fundamental – so much so that each exaggerates one feature of Zarathustra's perspective. They represent a kind of "worst case scenario" for Zarathustra as teacher.

Zarathustra, moreover, appears more ludicrous himself in Part IV than in the earlier three parts. He makes foolish mistakes in identifying the higher men; and when the higher men slip in their atheism, he reacts, contrary to his own insight, like a defender of the faith. Nevertheless, he sees through his own folly and responds with *laughter*. He resolves at the end of the book that his pity for the higher men, expressed in inviting them to dine in his cave, will have been his "final sin." Throwing off his error as those burdened by original sin could not, he begins his teaching mission once again, descending from his mountain cave as he did at the beginning of the book.

Part IV has been a source of controversy among Nietzsche scholars. Some are convinced that the book is stronger without Part IV,[68] and others apparently seem comfortable relegating Part IV to the status of a postscript.[69] Recently, however, a number of commentators have reassessed the importance of Part IV, offering accounts of why Nietzsche would have felt the need for a comic finale to an otherwise tragic work.[70] These readings suggest that Nietzsche had a more ironic perspective on Zarathustra's prophetic stance than traditional readings have appreciated.

BEYOND GOOD AND EVIL

Beyond Good and Evil: Prelude to a Philosophy of the Future (1886) represented a shift in Nietzsche's basic goals as an author. "After the Yes-saying part of my task had been solved, the turn had come for the No-saying, No-*doing* part: the revaluation of our values so far, the great war. . . ."[71]

Nietzsche goes on to describe *Beyond Good and Evil* as "a *critique of modernity*."[72] The modernity attacked includes culture broadly construed; but Nietzsche appears to be especially concerned with the direction of philosophy and its role in future history. Indeed, the subtitle is "*Prelude to a Philosophy of the Future*." The book opens with a Preface and first section that are often witty in criticizing traditional philosophy and its presuppositions. After the famous opening line about truth being a woman, Nietzsche asks, "Are there not grounds for the suspicion that all philosophers, insofar as they were dogmatists, have been very inexpert about women?"[73]

Nietzsche attacks particularly the dogmatism of philosophers. Philosophers have typically regarded themselves as seekers of truth – but from the book's beginning, Nietzsche casts suspicion on their motives. Philosophers, he argues, have simply assumed that truth is valuable, without inquiring as to whether this is so. They have posed their conclusions as objective, while in fact "every great philosophy so far has been . . . the personal confession of its author and a kind of involuntary and unconscious memoir."[74] Unwittingly, philosophers have sought to impose their own moral outlook on nature itself, and read into it what they have wanted to find.

Nietzsche proposes a reassessment of the way philosophy has been practiced in physiological and psychological terms, recognizing how much against the grain his approach will seem.

A proper physio-psychology has to contend with unconscious resistance in the heart of the investigator, it has "the heart" against it: even a doctrine of the reciprocal dependence of the "good" and the "wicked" drives, causes (as refined immorality) distress and aversion in a still hale and hearty conscience – still more so, a doctrine of the derivation of all good impulses from wicked ones. If, however, a person should regard even the affects of hatred, envy, covetousness, and the lust to rule as conditions of life, as factors which, fundamentally and essentially, must be present in the general economy of life (and must, therefore, be further enhanced if life is to be further enhanced) – he will suffer from such a view of things as from seasickness.[75]

Nietzsche proposes a new direction for philosophy, and a different kind of person as philosopher. Philosophers, on this view, should be free spirits and great experimentalists, as opposed to the mere "philosophical laborers" that are often thought to be philosophers.[76] The philosopher has "the most comprehensive responsibility" and "the conscience for the over-all development of man," and should utilize religion, education, and political and economic conditions in accordance with this responsibility.[77] *Beyond Good and Evil* makes explicitly political suggestions, although it is more concerned to propose a type of political arrangement (akin to that of Plato advocating philosopher-kings) than to argue for specific policies.

Central to the agenda of Nietzsche's future philosophers is a reconsideration of the value of conventional morality from a physio-psychological perspective. For the first time, in *Beyond Good and Evil* Nietzsche proposes to develop "a natural history of morals." He implies with this formulation that morality has changed over time. He also suggests that morality can be naturalistically described, that it is not a revelation from another, divine level of reality.

Nietzsche goes so far in employing naturalistic terms in his analysis that he describes the morality of his tradition as a "herd morality." In other words, people follow the same direction as others for the same reason that cows and sheep follow other cows and sheep. Nietzsche surely recognizes that many readers will find comparison between their moral beliefs and animal behavior offensive. (Presumably, however, he has Scripture on his side, in that the New Testament frequently refers to the faithful as "a flock.")

Nietzsche also suggests that multiple moralities have existed at the same time, and that they reveal their adherents' psychological perspective, which can be either healthy or sick. In particular, he suggests that master morality and slave morality are radically different in outlook. Master morality, typified by those in positions of power, involves a primary judgment of oneself as good, and a judgment of others in reference to one's own traits. Slave morality, by contrast, as the moral outlook of those who are oppressed, is primarily concerned with the reactions those in power might have to any contemplated act. Although slaves hate the master and everything the master represents, they still refer their behavior primarily to the master. Even self-esteem is achieved by reference to the master. Judging the master with hostility, they come to see him (or her?) as "evil," and only then come to judge themselves, relatively, as "good." Nietzsche develops this account of master and slave morality much more thoroughly in *Toward the Genealogy of Morals*, as we shall see.

The concept of will to power appears prominently in *Beyond Good and Evil*. Again, Nietzsche takes issue with Schopenhauer's emphasis on will to life: "A living thing seeks above all to *discharge* its strength – life itself is *will to power*; self-preservation is only one of the indirect and most frequent *results*."[78] Although emphatic in stressing will, Nietzsche is equally emphatic in denying freedom of the will. In fact, he considers the defense of freedom of will to be simply a manifestation of the asserter's desire for power.

'Freedom of the will' – that is the expression for the complex state of delight of the person exercising volition, who commands and at the same time identifies himself with the executor of the order – who as such, enjoys also the triumph over obstacles, but thinks within himself that it was really his will itself that overcame them.[79]

Will to power is also enlisted as a potential basis for explaining physiology and physiologically grounded behavior. Significantly, however, as in many other instances Nietzsche poses this "reduction" as a thought experiment.

Suppose, finally, we succeeded in explaining our entire instinctive life as the development and ramification of one basic form of the will – namely, of the will to power, as my proposition has it; suppose all organic functions could be traced back to this will to power and one could also find in it the solution of the problem of procreation and nourishment – it is one problem – then one would have gained the right to determine all efficient force univocally as – will to power. The world viewed from inside, the world defined and determined according to its "intelligible character" – it would be "will to power" and nothing else.[80]

This picture of the will to power is sometimes interpreted as a basic cosmological theory, and understood as the ontological ground of Nietzsche's perspectivism. If will to power is seen as the fundamental stuff of which reality is composed, one can read the quest of each thing for its own power, or enhancement, as inherently situated, ontologically located in a position that is distinct from that of every other entity.

Nietzsche's perspectivism, however, is discussed in more psychological terms elsewhere in *Beyond Good and Evil*. Nietzsche suggests that the perspective different individuals have of human reality depends on their relative stature as human beings. Nietzsche frequently adopts the image of height, describing those who see others from a higher vantage as having a more comprehensive view that is incommensurable with the perspective of those below them. Nietzsche emphasizes the importance of this order of rank, and he often claims that the human species consists of a proliferation of types, some of which are more valuable (or higher) than others. Of greatest importance for Nietzsche is the individual genius, on whom culture most depends. Nietzsche's view on this matter is unrepentently elitist: "For every high world one must be born; or to speak more clearly, one must be *cultivated* for it: a right to philosophy – taking that word in its great sense – one has only by virtue of one's origins; one's ancestors, one's 'blood' decide here, too."[81]

TOWARD THE GENEALOGY OF MORALS

Toward the Genealogy of Morals: A Polemic (1887) is as popular among philosophers as *Zarathustra* is unpopular.[82] The book's structure is more evidently argumentative than many of his other works. It is written in the form of three sustained essays on interrelated topics. The clarity of *Genealogy* is, however, deceptive. While the book does appear to have the structure of an argument (despite its subtitle "A Polemic"), what it presents is more a reading of a number of moral phenomena, a reading whose literal meaning and practical import are far from straightforward.

The book's three essays offer accounts of the origins of our conceptions of the "good," the experience of bad conscience, and practices of asceticism. The book's first essay begins with a critique of utilitarianism. Nietzsche contends that "the good" did not originally refer to that which maximized pleasure and minimized pain. Instead, it referred primarily to the self-description of the person who employed it. However, the individual's specific understanding of the term depended on whether he or she represented the perspective of a master or that of a slave. Those with the outlook of masters, as we have seen above, understood "good" as referring precisely to their own selves and their qualities. They concluded that those who differed from themselves are to that extent "bad." Those with the less healthy perspective of slaves, in contrast, understood themselves to be "good" only derivatively. Judging their masters "evil," they concluded that they were "good," in the negative sense of lacking the masters' evil traits.

Nietzsche suggests, on the basis of this analysis, that Christian morality is inherently structured as a form of slave morality. Slave morality depends on a fundamental disposition of *ressentiment* [resentment, understood as a basic character trait, more nearly the sense in which the poet John Milton characterized it as a sense of "injured merit"] toward the masters, and it accomplishes revenge imaginatively, by means of passing judgment. The strong, active traits of the masters are vilified by the slavish, who come to regard their own passivity and weakness as virtues. Nietzsche suggests this pattern pervades the moral ideals of Christianity. Many modes of self-assertion and self-expression are analyzed as sins on the Christian scheme, while passive suffering is deemed characteristic of the blessed.

The second essay of *Genealogy* traces the origin of *bad conscience* in the human disposition to cruelty. Nietzsche recounts the "festive" history of punishment,[83] contending that punishment is gratifying because it involves the imposition of one's will upon that of another. Bad conscience is a manifestation of the same joy in cruelty, but in this case the cruelty is directed inward. Nietzsche suggests that this introjection of cruelty resulted from humanity's acquisition of consciousness and the subsequent suppression of external manifestations of instinct: "All instincts that do not discharge themselves outwardly *turn inward* – this is what I call the *internalization* of man: thus it was that man first developed what was later called his 'soul.' "[84]

Nietzsche analyzes bad conscience, the soul's taking sides against itself, as a disease, but a disease that is "pregnant with a future."[85] Bad conscience, according to Nietzsche, motivated many of humanity's greatest accomplishments. It also motivates apparently "selfless" behavior. Nietzsche analyzes this apparent selflessness as the subjugation of one part of the soul by another, and "the delight that the selfless man, the self-denier, the self-scarificer feels from the first: *this* delight is tied to cruelty."[86]

Bad conscience, combined with humanity's joy in cruelty, according to Nietzsche, is also the basis for monotheism, particularly that of Christianity. Bad conscience motivates a feeling of guilt and indebtedness. At earlier moments in history, feelings of indebtedness were directed toward one's ancestors, whose imagined power became greater as the power of one's tribe increased. This escalation of power reached its climax in the idea of a supreme, all-powerful God.

The notion of an omnipotent deity raises feelings of guilt to extreme heights. In Christianity, guilt was viewed as so extreme that only God himself could redeem humanity from it, as the orthodox view of the Crucifixion contends. Guilt in relation to God is expiated, according to this perspective, as guilt to anyone is expiated – by means of a drama of punishment that gratifies the spectator's lust for cruelty. Nietzsche sees this conception of God as poisonous: "Indeed, the prospect cannot be dismissed that the complete and definitive victory of atheism might free mankind of this whole feeling of guilty indebtedness toward its origin, its *causa prima*. Atheism and a kind of *second innocence* belong together."[87]

Nietzsche's third essay suggests a genealogical account of yet another feature of the Christian moral worldview, its advocacy of *ascetic ideals*. The person who is self-denying, on this worldview, is seen as a kind of exemplar. Ascetic ideals appear paradoxical, for they appear to involve a lively passion for what is contrary to life. Nietzsche concludes that these strange passions must themselves be in the interest of life, despite appearances to the contrary. Again, he sees *ressentiment* and lust for power at work. "An ascetic life is a self-contradiction: here rules a *ressentiment* without equal, that of an insatiable instinct and power-will that wants to become master not over something in life, but over life itself."[88]

Asceticism is an expression of lust for power as it is manifest in those who are declining, or decadent. Those who feel themselves declining seek self-protection, primarily. "This, I surmise, constitutes the actual physiological cause of *ressentiment*, vengefulness, and the like: a desire to deaden pain by means of affects."[89]

This desire, Nietzsche argues, is fulfilled by the ascetic priest. To those in pain, the Christian moral worldview (and those of other ascetic doctrines) tells them that they are to blame. This produces an orgy of feeling,[90] constructed around the sufferer's sense of guilt. Feelings of guilt reverse the feeling that one's life is declining: "life again became *very* interesting . . . "[91] Thus, the paradox of the ascetic perspective is only apparent. The interpretation upon which this perspective depends is actually enlivening, even though it is achieved at the apparent expense of self-esteem.

Nevertheless, Nietzsche views the long-term impact of ascetic ideals as psychologically and physiologically damaging. The practices of asceticism weaken the body and the will. Like other moral phenomena Nietzsche analyzes in *Genealogy*, asceticism accomplishes a gradual poisoning of those who embrace it. Ironically, ascetic ideals offer palliatives to those who are already sick, but these palliatives themselves make the sick sicker in the long term.

Nietzsche concludes the third essay by suggesting that the modern scientific worldview, which might be seen as an alternative to the Christian moral worldview, is no improvement but is instead an extension of it. The scientific worldview itself is based on faith, in this case faith in truth. Moreover, this faith itself motivates asceticism, for it encourages one to quash one's desires in the pursuit of truth, however painful the latter might be.

Genealogy ends inconclusively, with the modern antidote to the Christian worldview exposed as yet another manifestation of the same basic disposition. Nietzsche hints that other alternatives may be possible. "In the most spiritual sphere, too, the ascetic ideal has at present only one kind of real enemy capable of *harming* it: the comedians of this ideal – for they arouse mistrust of it.[92] Again, as in

Zarathustra and *The Gay Science*, Nietzsche proposes the comedic or parodic overcoming of the ascetic ideal as positive remedies to the nihilism of his era, presumably once it is understood that our suffering is as much a product of our basic beliefs and self-descriptions as it is a consequence of any "facts" of the matter. Yet Nietzsche does not develop this suggestion. Instead he concludes with a psychological observation suggested by the ascetic ideal and its associated moral phenomena, an observation that reaffirms that will is psychologically fundamental:

We can no longer conceal from ourselves *what* is expressed by all that willing which has taken its direction from the ascetic ideal: this hatred of the human, and even more of the animal, and more still of the material, this horror of the senses, of reason itself, this fear of happiness and beauty, this longing to get away from all appearance, change, becoming, death, wishing, from longing itself – all this means – let us dare to grasp it – *a will to nothingness*, an aversion to life, a rebellion against the most fundamental presuppositions of life; but it is and remains a *will!* . . . And, to repeat in conclusion what I said at the beginning: man would rather will *nothingness* than *not* will.[93]

Nietzsche's genealogical method of analysis does not lead him to many specific, literal proposals. He typically leaves the direction of responding to his analyses up to the reader. Nietzsche's method of offering genealogical accounts of given human concepts and practices has been extremely influential, most notably in the work of Michel Foucault. Like Nietzsche, Foucault utilizes genealogy to undermine the notion that humanly constructed concepts are "given" and unchangeable.[94]

THE WORKS OF 1888

The final year of Nietzsche's productivity was 1888; it was spectacularly prolific. Nietzsche wrote five books in 1888, beginning with *The Case of Wagner: A Musician's Problem* (1888).

As Nietzsche acknowledges, the case of Wagner was a personal problem for him; and he cannot resist the occasion as an opportunity to register volleys of witty barbs against Wagner and his music. Nevertheless, Nietzsche now sees the problem posed by Wagner as symptomatic of his entire culture. Wagner and modernity are both thoroughly decadent. Here, Nietzsche treats his aesthetic descriptions of Wagner's style as characterizations of the tendencies of the entire modern era. Both, he contends, lack integrity, manifesting instead an "anarchy of the atoms" in which "life no longer dwells in the whole."[95]

Nietzsche concludes the body of the book – in self-conscious imitation of Wagner's own bombastic pronouncements – with his own bombastic and moralistic triumvirate of anti-Wagnerian demands for art:

That the theater should not lord it over the arts.
That the actor should not seduce those who are authentic.
That music should not become an art of lying.[96]

Although more comprehensive and synoptic in scope, *Twilight of the Idols, or How to Philosophize with a Hammer* (written 1888; published 1889) similarly suggests the importance of Wagner to Nietzsche, if only as a negative and appropriately unmentioned model. The title, *Götzendämmerung*, puns on the title of one of Wagner's operas, *Götterdämerung* [*Twilight of the Gods*]. At the same time, it casts Nietzsche as one who, like Francis Bacon, exposes as "Idols" certain deceptive tendencies of the human mind that stand in need of correction.

The subtitle, "How to Philosophize with a Hammer," reinforces this impression of Nietzsche's intentions. Presumably, it alludes to Martin Luther's image of God sculpting the soul with a hammer, although Nietzsche's image is both more crude and more comic: "Another mode of convalescence . . . is *sounding out* idols. . . . For once to pose questions here with a *hammer*, and, perhaps, to hear as a reply that famous hollow sound which speaks of bloated entrails – what a delight for one who has ears even behind his ears."[97] Presumably, the hollow idols that the hammer detects are not long for the world, and the hammer itself might well be an implement of destruction. Nietzsche's use of the hammer metaphor, however, is ambiguous like Luther's, in which the hammer both smashes the sinner's pride and provokes the beginning of a positive process of transformation. And Nietzsche identifies his hammer with a "tuning fork," not with a sledgehammer, one must also be reminded.

Nietzsche announces in the book's Preface that the transformation he has in mind is the "revaluation of all values." He describes this as a "question mark, so black, so tremendous that it casts shadows upon the man who puts it down."[98] The notion of re-valuating all values is perplexing; evaluation occurs in terms of some value, while Nietzsche allegedly wants to call *all* values into question. But what value speaks here? How can a perspectivist assume a view from nowhere?

Some of the specific values that Nietzsche questions in *Twilight of the Idols*, however, are familiar from and refer to his other works. His primary targets are the "Idols" of philosophers and moralists, with the aspirations of Germans serving as a lesser target. The body of the book opens with a series of aphorisms, followed by an *ad hominem* attack against Socrates, the demigod of philosophy.[99] The next two sections continue the assault on traditional philosophers' worship of reason and their variously articulated faith in a "true world" beyond the apparent one.[100] The next several sections succinctly state Nietzsche's case against Christian morality and moralism in general. Nietzsche proceeds to vivisect the values of Germany and then launches into a series of attacks on a variety of contemporary ideas, people, and phenomena, which he titles "Skirmishes of an Untimely Man."[101]

The book draws to a close with a recapitulation of some of Nietzsche's views of antiquity. He applauds the Romans at the expense of the Greeks, and he gives Plato peremptory dismissal. What he values primarily in the Greeks, he claims, is the conception of *Dionysus*, which he associates with a naturalistic version of eternal recurrence.

What was it that the Hellene guaranteed himself by means of these mysteries? *Eternal* life, the eternal return of life; the future promised and hallowed in the past; the triumphant Yes to life beyond all death and change; *true* life as the over-all continuation of life through procreation, through the mysteries of sexuality. For the Greeks the *sexual* symbol was therefore the venerable symbol par excellence, the real profundity in the whole of ancient piety. Every single element in the act of procreation, of pregnancy, and of birth aroused the highest and most solemn feelings. In the doctrine of the mysteries, *pain* is pronounced holy: the pangs of the woman giving birth hallows all pain; all becoming and growing – all that guarantees a future – involves pain. That there may be the eternal joy of creating, that the will to life may eternally affirm itself, the agony of the woman giving birth *must* also be there eternally.

All this is meant by the word Dionysus . . .[102]

Nietzsche contrasts this significance of Dionysus directly with that of the suffering Christ. "It was Christianity, with its *ressentiment* against life at the bottom of its heart, which first made something unclean of sexuality: it threw *filth* on the origin, on the presupposition of our life."[103] Siding with Dionysus against Christianity, Nietzsche closes with his own salute to embodiment, to sexuality in particular: "This new tablet, O my brothers, I place over you: become hard!"[104]

Revaluation remains on Nietzsche's mind when he writes his next work, *The Antichrist* (written 1888, published 1895). "Revaluation of all values!" is, in fact, the closing statement of the book. Nietzsche's notoriety for hostility against Christianity stems largely from this work, his most vitriolic attack on that collection of religions. Although his complaints against Christianity, and particularly against its moral worldview, had been developed in a number of earlier works, his sarcastic tone and extreme hyperbole in *The Antichrist* is more continuous and deftly wielded than in any other work, possibly accepting the *Unfashionable Observations* essay on David Strauss.

The Antichrist offers a historical and psychological account of the development of Christianity from Judaism. Significantly, Nietzsche sharply distinguishes between the teachings of Jesus and the institution of Christianity that developed, largely under the influence of Paul, the principal villain of the book. "In Paul was embodied the opposite type to that of the 'bringer of glad tidings': the genius in hatred, in the vision of hatred, in the inexorable logic of hatred."[105] Jesus is presented, in contrast, as "blissed out," in Gary Shapiro's apt phrase.[106]

Using the expression somewhat tolerantly, one could call Jesus a "free spirit" – he does not care for anything solid: the word kills, all that is solid kills. The concept, the experience of "life" in the only way he knows it, resists any kind of word, formula, law, faith, dogma. He speaks only of the innermost: "life" or "truth" or "light" is his word for the innermost – all the rest, the whole of reality, the whole of nature, language itself, has for him only the value of a sign, a simile.[107]

Although Nietzsche considers this perspective both childlike and a decadent avoidance of pain, this portrait of Jesus is not devoid of respect. Something akin to admiration is evident in further passages.

The "kingdom of God" is nothing that one expects; it has no yesterday and no day after tomorrow, it will not come in "a thousand years" – it is an experience of the heart; it is everywhere, it is nowhere."[108]

This 'bringer of glad tidings' died as he had lived, as he had taught – *not to* 'redeem men' but to show how one must live.[109]

In contrast, Nietzsche has little good to say about the institution, the scaffolding that developed around Jesus. Those who constructed the Church, beginning with Paul, fomented lies about Jesus and his aims. They attached their own interpretation to his death, one steeped in *ressentiment*; and they interpreted the "kingdom" not as an inner state but as a promised future life. Recapitulating and further explicating his previous complaints against Christianity, Nietzsche concludes that it is thoroughly harmful. "I call Christianity the one great curse, the one great innermost corruption, the one great instinct of revenge, for which no means is poisonous, stealthy, subterranean, *small* enough – I call it the one immortal blemish of mankind."[110]

On his forty-fourth birthday, October 15, 1888, Nietzsche began to write his intellectual autobiography, *Ecce Homo: How One Becomes What One Is* (written 1888; published 1908). The dedication suits the spirit of affirming eternal recurrence:

On this perfect day, when everything is ripening and not only the grape turns brown, the eye of the sun just fell upon my life: I looked back, I looked forward, and never saw so many and such good things at once. It was not for nothing that I buried my forty-fourth year today: I had the *right* to bury it; whatever was life in it has been saved, is immortal. The first book of the *Revaluation of All Values*, the *Songs of Zarathustra*, the *Twilight of the Idols*, my attempt to philosophize with a hammer – all presents of this year, indeed of its last quarter! *How could I fail to be grateful to my whole life?* – and so I tell my life to myself.[111]

As an autobiography, *Ecce Homo* is certainly nonstandard. It is extremely stylized, indeed it defies any traditional genre, and it emphasizes matters such as food, climate, and daily routines. The tone is also immodest at times to the point of megalomania. At one point, for instance, Nietzsche exclaims, "I am no man, I am dynamite."[112] The combination of this tone with the self-adulatory chapter titles – "Why I Am So Wise," "Why I Am So Clever," "Why I Write Such Good Books," and "Why I Am a Destiny" – has led some to conclude that Nietzsche was already mad when he wrote the book.

What such readers are missing is the humor involved in chapter titles that reverse Socrates's pose of modesty when he insisted that he was wise because he knew he was not wise.[113] Lost also to that perspective is Nietzsche's philosophical purpose in emphasizing matters usually unannounced in autobiographies, a purpose that he explains in the book itself.

> One will ask me why on earth I've been relating all these small things which are generally considered matters of complete indifference: I only harm myself, the more so if I am destined to represent great tasks. Answer: these small things – nutrition, place, climate, recreation, the whole casuistry of selfishness – are inconceivably more important than everything one has taken to be important so far. Precisely here one must begin to *relearn*. . . . All the problems of politics, of social organization, and of education have been falsified through and through because one mistook the most harmful men for great men – because one learned to despise "little things," which means the basic concerns of life itself.[114]

Nietzsche's final work of 1888, *Nietzsche contra Wagner: Documents of a Psychologist* (published 1895), is a short anthology of edited passages from other works, all having to do with Wagner. According to the Preface, written on Christmas 1888, the book is offered to psychologists. The upshot, Nietzsche contends, is that he and Wagner are antipodes.[115]

NACHLASS

Besides his published works, Nietzsche left a vast number of notes, sketches, and literary fragments, known as the *Nachgelassene Fragmente*, or the *Nachlass*. These have been passed on to posterity in a scrambled form, thanks to the mangled editing job by Nietzsche's sister, Elisabeth Förster-Nietzsche, and her fascistic and racist compatriots. The edition that resulted enlisted a hodge-podge of notes taken from a variety of contexts and arranged in a fashion that emphasized themes that appeared friendly to the ideals of National Socialism. This edition was published as *The Will to Power*, a title that Nietzsche had envisioned for a work that remained unwritten when he collapsed.[116]

Elisabeth promoted this "work" as Nietzsche's masterpiece, a perspective that was adopted by Martin Heidegger in his influential works on Nietzsche.[117] Heidegger went so far as to claim that Nietzsche's most important book was one that he had never completed and that his central thought was never fully developed: "What Nietzsche himself published during his creative life was always foreground. His philosophy proper was left behind as posthumous, unpublished work."[118] Those critical of Heidegger's analysis of Nietzsche, on the grounds that it is more concerned with reinforcing Heidegger's philosophical perspective than it is with fidelity to Nietzsche, have typically been especially appalled by this methodology, which facilitated Heidegger's reading his own concerns into Nietzsche's works.

Few Nietzsche scholars since Heidegger have gone as far as he in enlisting the *Nachlass* in their readings of Nietzsche. Nevertheless, the status of the *Nachlass* has been a central debate in recent Nietzsche scholarship. The opposing views are those of the "lumpers," who treat the *Nachlass* as on a par with Nietzsche's published works, and the "splitters," who draw a sharp distinction between the published and unpublished work.[119] While some scholars defend one position theoretically and practice another, the positions scholars take on the status of the unpublished material often has repercussions for how significant they consider certain themes in Nietzsche's work as a whole. In particular, lumpers and splitters often divide over the importance of the concept of the will to power (which is mentioned rarely in published works) and the cosmological version of the doctrine of eternal recurrence (which appears only in unpublished works).

The purpose of this overview of Nietzsche's works has been merely to provide a first approximation of what each of his texts is "about." This task, we are keenly aware, is dangerous. Alternative summaries could have been written; and surely greater subtlety and nuance are required than we have been able to provide in this introductory survey. That, however, is precisely the purpose and justification of the essays which follow.

NOTES

1 Friedrich Nietzsche, *The Birth of Tragedy* [together with *The Case of Wagner*], trans. Walter Kaufmann (New York: Random House, 1967), hereafter noted as "BT," p. 52; *Kritische Gesamtausgabe: Werke*, ed. G. Colli and M. Montinari, 30 vols. in 8 parts (Berlin: Walter de Gruyter, 1967ff), hereafter indicated as "KGW," III/1, p. 43. See also BT, p. 22.

2 Nietzsche's analysis of Apollo and Dionysus is also sufficiently flexible to suggest perspectives on a variety of phenomena. Tracy B. Strong's "Nietzsche's Political Misappropriation" (in this volume), for instance, discusses *The Birth of Tragedy* and its duality of deities in terms of a theory of politics. Alexander Nehamas's "Nietzsche, Modernity, Aestheticism" (also in this volume) discusses *The Birth of Tragedy* in connection with Nietzsche's critique of modernity.

3 Jörg Salaquarda's "Nietzsche and the Judaeo-Christian Tradition" (in this volume) suggests that *The Life of Jesus* was at least somewhat influential for Nietzsche's own views of Christianity.

4 David Strauss to Rapp, December 19, 1873; cited in J. P. Stern, "Introduction," in *Untimely Meditations*, trans. R. J. Hollingdale (Cambridge: Cambridge University Press, 1983), p. xiv. See the entire introduction for further information about the context and analysis of Nietzsche's *Untimely Meditations* (pp. vii–xxxii).

5 Nietzsche to Gersdorff, February 11, 1874, in J. P. Stern, "Introduction," p. xiv. Although the David Strauss essay was arguably Nietzsche's most hostile, Nietzsche made systematic use of *ad hominem* arguments in many of his works. See Robert C. Solomon, "Nietzsche's *Ad Hominem*: Perspectivism, Personality, and *Ressentiment* Revisited" (in this volume).

6 Friedrich Nietzsche, "On the Uses and Disadvantages of History for Life," in *Untimely Meditations*, trans. R. J. Hollingdale (Cambridge: Cambridge University Press, 1983), p. 120.

7 Ibid., p. 120. Jörg Salaquarda (in "Nietzsche and the Judaeo-Christian Tradition") considers the importance of Nietzsche's analysis of history for his historically based critique of Christianity. Alexander Nehamas (in "Nietzsche, Modernity, Aestheticism") also discusses this analysis, focusing on its significance in Nietzsche's more general critique of modernity.

8 See R. J. Hollingdale, "The Hero as Outsider" (in this volume). Hollingdale describes the legend that grew up around Schopenhauer as a prototype and precursor for the legend that came to surround Nietzsche, as well as the basis for Schopenhauer becoming so significant to both Wagner and Nietzsche.

9 Friedrich Nietzsche, "Schopenhauer as Educator," in *Untimely Meditations*, trans. R. J. Hollingdale (Cambridge: Cambridge University Press, 1983), p. 135.

10 Despite the fact that Nietzsche never completed "We Philologists," William Arrowsmith included the unfinished text ("We Classicists") in his edition of the *Untimely Meditations*, [*Unfashionable Observations*] whose title he translates *Unmodern Observations*. See Friedrich Nietzsche, *Unmodern Observations*, ed. William Arrowsmith, trans. Herbert

Golder, Gary Brown, and William Arrowsmith (New Haven: Yale University Press, 1990). In his introductions to the various finished meditations, Arrowsmith, a classicist himself, also stresses the extent to which each of the *Unfashionable Observations* reveal Nietzsche's relative preference for antiquity over modernity and address contemporary philological issues.

11 Friedrich Nietzsche, "*Wir Philologen*," Sec. 7, included in part in "Nietzsche on Classics and Classicists," selected and translated by William Arrowsmith, *Arion*, II, No. 1 (Spring, 1963): 10–11; KGW, VI/1, no. 3 (62), p. 107.

12 See Ronald Hayman, *Nietzsche: A Critical Life* (New York: Oxford University Press, 1980), p. 184ff.

13 All but the last of these essays, along with additional plans and outlines from the early 1870s, appear in *Philosophy and Truth: Selections from Nietzsche's Notebooks of the Early 1870's*, trans. and ed. Daniel Breazeale (Atlantic Highlands, New Jersey: Humanities Press; Sussex: Harvester Press, 1979). The last is published separately: Friedrich Nietzsche, *Philosophy in the Tragic Age of the Greeks*, trans. Marianne Cowan (Chicago: Henry Regnery Company, 1962).

14 See Daniel Breazeale, "Introduction," in *Philosophy and Truth*, trans. and ed. Breazeale, p. xxvi and xlv.

15 Nietzsche, "On Truth and Lies in a Nonmoral Sense," in *Philosophy and Truth*, trans. and ed. Breazeale, p. 84. See also Richard Schacht's "Nietzsche's Kind of Philosophy" (in this volume).

16 See, for example, Paul de Man. *Allegories of Reading* (New Haven, Connecticut: Yale University Press, 1979). For a philosophical discussion of Nietzsche's essay and poststructuralist readings of Nietzsche, see Alan D. Schrift, *Nietzsche and the Question of Interpretation: Between Hermeneutics and Deconstruction* (New York: Routledge, 1990), especially pp. 124ff.

17 See, for example, J. Hillis Miller, "Dismembering and Disremembering in Nietzsche's 'On Truth and Lies in a Nonmoral Sense,' " in *Why Nietzsche Now?*, ed. Daniel O'Hara (Bloomington: Indiana University Press, 1985), pp. 41–54.

18 Friedrich Nietzsche, "On Truth and Lies in a Nonmoral Sense," in *Philosophy and Truth*, trans. and ed. Breazeale, p. 80.

19 Maudemarie Clark, *Nietzsche on Truth and Philosophy* (Cambridge: Cambridge University Press, 1990), p. 65.

20 Graham Parkes's "Nietzsche and East Asian Thought: Influences, Impacts, and Resonances" (in this volume) discusses Nietzsche's praise for Heraclitus's intuitive powers, which may have had an impact on the Japanese thinker Watsuji Tetsurō's reading of Nietzsche.

21 For example, see R. J. Hollingdale's "The Hero as Outsider" (in this volume). Indeed, Nietzsche himself used the expression "positivism" in a description of his aspirations with respect to the book in one of the prefaces he drafted but did not use. See Erich Heller, "Introduction," in Friedrich Nietzsche, *Human, All Too Human*, trans. R. J. Hollingdale (Cambridge: Cambridge University Press, 1986), p. xiii.

22 The centrality of perspectivism in Nietzsche's thought is suggested by the number of essays in this volume alone that emphasize it: See Nehamas, "Nietzsche, Modernity, Aestheticism"; Robert B. Pippin, "Nietzsche's Alleged Farewell: The Premodern, Modern, and Postmodern Nietzsche"; Jörg Salaquarda, "Nietzsche and the Judeao-Christian Tradition"; Richard Schacht, "Nietzsche's Kind of Philosophy"; Solomon, "Nietzsche's *Ad Hominem*: Perspectivism, Personality, and *Ressentiment* Revisited"; and Tracy B. Strong, "Nietzsche's Political Misappropriation."

23 See, for example, *Beyond Good and Evil: Prelude to a Philosophy of the Future*, trans. Walter Kaufmann (New York: Random House, 1966), hereafter indicated as "BGE," Section #22, pp. 30–1: "Supposing that this also is only interpretation – and you will be eager enough to make this objection? – well, so much the better."

24 See Hayman, *Nietzsche: A Critical Life*, p. 198 and p. 215.

25 Erich Heller, "Introduction," in Nietzsche, *Human, All Too Human*, p. xvii.

26 The preface to the second edition of *The Gay Science* discusses the art of the philosopher as the spiritual transposition of various states of health. See Friedrich Nietzsche, "Preface for the Second Edition," *The Gay Science: With a Prelude in Rhymes and an Appendix of Songs*, trans. Walter Kaufmann (New York: Random House, 1974), hereafter indicated as "GS," p. 35.

27 See Michael Tanner, "Introduction," in Friedrich Nietzsche, *Daybreak: Thoughts on the Prejudices of Morality*, trans. R. J. Hollingdale (Cambridge: Cambridge University Press, 1982), pp. ix–xi. See also Kathleen Marie Higgins, *Nietzsche's Zarathustra* (Philadelphia: Temple University Press, 1987), pp. 43–6.

28 See Robert C. Solomon, "Nietzsche's *Ad Hominem*: Perspectivism, Personality, and *Ressentiment* Revisited" (this volume) for further discussion of this approach. See also Jörg Salaquarda, "Nietzsche and the Judeao-Christian Tradition" (this volume) for further discussion of Nietzsche's conceptions of Christian morality and Christian psychology.

29 The first edition of *The Gay Science*, published in 1882, consisted of four books. Nietzsche added a fifth book to his second edition, which appeared in 1887.

30 GS, "Preface for the Second Edition," p. 38.
31 As Robert Pippin notes in "Nietzsche's Alleged Farewell: The Premodern, Modern, and Postmodern Nietzsche" (this volume), this statement was first made by Hegel in the *Phenomenology of Spirit*. There, however, it appears as a description of a particular condition of consciousness rather than a blanket characterization of the modern condition.
32 GS, #108, p. 167.
33 GS, #125, pp. 181–2. See Ernst Behler's "Nietzsche in the Twentieth Century," Alexander Nehamas's "Nietzsche, Modernity, Aestheticism," Jörg Salaquarda's "Nietzsche and the Judaeo-Christian Tradition," and Alan D. Schrift's "Nietzsche's French Legacy" (all in this volume) for discussions of this parable.
34 Alexander Nehamas has made much of Nietzsche's aestheticism in *Nietzsche: Life as Literature* (Cambridge, Massachusetts: Harvard University Press, 1985). In this volume, Nietzsche's (alleged) aestheticism, and particularly Nehamas's construal of it, is discussed in Alexander Nehamas's "Nietzsche, Modernity, Aestheticism," Graham Parkes' "Nietzsche and East Asian Thought: Influences, Impacts, and Resonances," Robert Pippin, "Nietzsche's Alleged Farewell: The Premodern, Modern, and Postmodern Nietzsche," Richard Schacht's "Nietzsche's Kind of Philosophy," and Robert C. Solomon's "Nietzsche's *Ad Hominem*: Perspectivism, Personality, and *Ressentiment* Revisited."
35 Graham Parkes considers the Japanese reception of this concept in "Nietzsche and East Asian Thought: Influences, Impacts, and Resonances" (in this volume).
36 GS, #341, p. 273.
37 Robert Gooding-Williams has suggested a reading of Zarathustra in which the plot's unfolding is analyzed in terms of changes in the way the doctrine of eternal recurrence is formulated. See Robert Gooding-Williams, "Recurrence, Parody, and Politics in the Philosophy of Friedrich Nietzsche," dissertation, Yale University, 1982.
38 For further discussion of the existential reading of the doctrine of eternal recurrence, as well as alternative readings, see Bernd Magnus, *Nietzsche's Existential Imperative* (Bloomington: Indiana University Press, 1978).
39 See Tracy B. Strong, *Friedrich Nietzsche and the Politics of Transfiguration* (Berkeley: University of California Press, 1975), pp. 270–1. See also Robert C. Solomon, *From Rationalism to Existentialism: The Existentialists and Their Nineteenth-Century Backgrounds* (New York: Harper and Row, 1972), p. 137.
40 For such an aestheticist reading, see Alexander Nehamas, *Nietzsche: Life as Literature* (Cambridge, Massachusetts: Harvard University Press, 1985), pp. 141–65.

41 For a discussion of eternal recurrence viewed as a cosmological doctrine, see, for example, Arthur C. Danto, *Nietzsche as Philosopher: An Original Study* (New York: Columbia University Press, 1965), pp. 203–9.

42 Friedrich Nietzsche, *Ecce Homo: How One Becomes What One Is* [together with *Toward the Genealogy of Morals*], trans. Walter Kaufmann (New York: Random House, 1967), hereafter indicated as "EH," pp. 327–8.

43 See Ernst Behler's "Nietzsche in the Twentieth Century" (in this volume) for a discussion of Thomas Mann's critical reaction.

44 See, for example, Richard Schacht, *Nietzsche* (New York: Routledge, 1983), pp. xiii–xiv.

45 About 150,000 copies were distributed to the troops, and *Zarathustra* was among the three most popular works among German soldiers. For further discussion of the Nazi employment of Nietzsche, see Steven E. Aschheim, *The Nietzsche Legacy in Germany, 1890–1990* (Berkeley: University of California Press, 1992), pp. 128–63.

46 The theme of Nietzsche's perspective on nihilism is discussed in this volume in Ernst Behler's "Nietzsche in the Twentieth Century," Alexander Nehamas's "Nietzsche, Modernity, Aestheticism," Graham Parkes's "Nietzsche and East Asian Thought: Influences, Impacts, and Resonances," Robert Pippin's "Nietzsche's Alleged Farewell: The Premodern, Modern, and Postmodern Nietzsche," and Alan D. Schrift's "Nietzsche's French Legacy." The essays by Nehamas and Pippin address, in particular, Jürgen Habermas's contention that Nietzsche addressed nihilism by abandoning Enlightenment rationalism in favor of a "postmodern" irrationalism.

47 See Ernst Behler's "Nietzsche in the Twentieth Century" for a discussion of George Bernard Shaw's interest in and use of this concept.

48 Graham Parkes's "Nietzsche and East Asian Thought: Influences, Impacts, and Resonances" discusses Zarathustra's encounter with a hermit saint during his descent from his mountain cave.

49 Besides Behler's discussion, the concept is also discussed in this volume in Graham Parkes's "Nietzsche and East Asian Thought: Influences, Impacts, and Resonances," Robert Pippin's "Nietzsche's Alleged Farewell: The Premodern, Modern, and Postmodern Nietzsche," and Alan D. Schrift's "Nietzsche's French Legacy."

50 See, for example, "Nietzsche's Philosophy in 1888: *The Will to Power* and the *Übermensch*," *Journal of the History of Philosophy* 24, 1 (January 1986): 79–98. See also Bernd Magnus, "The Use and Abuse of *The Will to Power*," in *Reading Nietzsche*, Robert C. Solomon and Kathleen M. Higgins, eds. (New York: Oxford University Press, 1988): 218–325.

51 See Bernd Magnus, "Perfectibility and Attitude in Nietzsche's *Übermensch*," *Review of Metaphysics* 36 (March 1983): 633–60.

52 For reflections on this possibility, see Bernd Magnus, "The Deification of the Commonplace: *Twilight of the Idols*," in *Reading Nietzsche*, Robert C. Solomon and Kathleen M. Higgins, eds. (New York: Oxford University Press, 1988): 152–81.

53 Friedrich Nietzsche, *Thus Spoke Zarathustra*, in *The Portable Nietzsche*, ed. and trans. Walter Kaufmann (New York: Viking, 1968), hereafter indicated as "TSZ," p. 125.

54 See Graham Parkes's "Nietzsche and East Asian Thought: Influences, Impacts, and Resonances" for further discussion of the theme of the body in Nietzsche.

55 TSZ, p. 227.

56 See, for example, Ivan Soll, "Reconsiderations of Nietzsche's *Birth of Tragedy*," in *Reading Nietzsche*, eds. Robert C. Solomon and Kathleen M. Higgins (New York: Oxford University Press, 1988), pp. 104–31. Soll argues that Nietzsche exaggerated his differences with Schopenhauer in his later works, and that Nietzsche largely developed his philosophy with Schopenhauerian premises.

57 The most notorious defense of this position is offered by Martin Heidegger, *Nietzsche*, 2 vols. (Pfullingen: Verlag Günther Neske, 1961). See also the following translations: Martin Heidegger, *Nietzsche, Volume One: The Will to Power as Art*, ed. and trans. David F. Krell (San Francisco: Harper and Row, 1979); Martin Heidegger, *Nietzsche, Volume Two: The Eternal Recurrence of the Same*, ed. and trans. David F. Krell (San Francisco: Harper and Row, 1984); Martin Heidegger, *Nietzsche, Volume Three: The Will to Power as Knowledge and Metaphysics*, ed. David F. Krell, trans. Joan Stambaugh, David F. Krell, and Frank A. Capuzzi (San Francisco: Harper and Row, 1987); and Martin Heidegger, *Nietzsche, Volume Four: Nihilism*, ed. David F. Krell, trans. Frank A. Capuzzi (San Francisco: Harper and Row, 1982).

58 See, for example, Bernd Magnus, "Nietzsche's Philosophy in 1888: *The Will to Power* and the '*Übermensch*,' " *Journal of the History of Philosophy* 24 (January 1986): 79-99. See also Julian Young, *Nietzsche's Philosophy of Art* (Cambridge: Cambridge University Press, 1992), pp. 1–2.

59 See the following articles in this volume for a further sense of the range of positions taken by scholars on the idea of the will to power: Ernst Behler's "Nietzsche in the Twentieth Century," Graham Parkes's "Nietzsche and East Asian Thought: Influences, Impacts, and Resonances," and Alan D. Schrift's "Nietzsche's French Legacy."

60 TSZ, pp. 251–3.

61 TSZ, p. 333.

62 For further discussion of Nietzsche's elitism, see Graham Parkes's "Nietzsche and East Asian Thought: Influences, Impacts, and Resonances" (in this volume).

63 Nietzsche might also be seen as sexist because he personifies Life and Wisdom as women in *Zarathustra*, posing Zarathustra as the lover of both and a bit confused as to who is who.

64 Schopenhauer's "On Women," occurs in *Parerga and Parilipomena: Short Philosophical Essays*, trans. E. F. J. Payne, in 2 vols., Vol. II (Oxford: Clarendon Press, 1974), pp. 614–26. For Nietzsche's repetition of Schopenhauerian images, see, for example, BGE, #232–39, pp. 162–70.

65 This is particularly evident in *The Gay Science*. See, for example, GS, #71, pp. 127–8, which concludes, "In sum, one cannot be too kind about women."

66 Presumably, his opening remark in *Beyond Good and Evil*, "Supposing truth is a woman – what then?" (BGE, p. 2) has been interpreted as sexist because it utilizes stereotypical images of women. See Richard Schacht's "Nietzsche's Kind of Philosophy" (in this volume) for such an interpretation. Ofelia Schutte also objects to Nietzsche's preference for female personifications of abstractions over actual women. See Ofelia Schutte, "Nietzsche's Psychology of Gender Difference," in *Critical Feminist Essays in the History of Western Philosophy*, ed. Bat-Ami Bar On, in 2 vols. (Albany: State University of New York Press, 1993–94). An example of Nietzsche's explicit discussion of male fantasy occurs in GS, #59, pp. 122–3.

67 BGE, #231, p. 162.

68 See, for example, R. J. Hollingdale, *Nietzsche: The Man and His Philosophy* (Baton Rouge: Louisiana State University Press, 1965), p. 190.

69 See, for example, Laurence Lampert, *Nietzsche's Teaching: An Interpretation of "Thus Spoke Zarathustra."* (New Haven: Yale University Press, 1987).

70 Among these are Anke Bennholdt-Thomsen, who sees Part IV as a satyr play that follows a tragedy (as in the traditional Athenian formula); Gary Shapiro, who analyzes the section in terms of carnival and sees the turn to humor as a renunciation of the text's claim to narrative authority; and Kathleen Marie Higgins, who contends that Part IV is modeled on Menippean satire in order to reveal the limitations of doctrinal formulations and to suggest the importance of transfiguring failure through laughter. See Anke Bennholdt-Thomsen, *Nietzsches "Also Sprach Zarathustra" als literarisches Phaenomen. Eine Revision* (Frankfurt: Athenaeum, 1974), pp. 196, 205, 210–11; Gary Shapiro, "Festival, Carnival and Parody in *Zarathustra IV*," in *The Great Year of Zarathustra (1881–1981)*, ed. David Goicoechea (New York: Lanham, 1983), pp. 60–1; Kathleen Marie Higgins, *Nietzsche's "Zarathustra"* (Philadelphia: Temple University Press, 1987), pp. 203–32.

71 EH, p. 310.

72 Emphasis ours. Ibid., p. 310.

73 BGE, p. 2. See Alan D. Schrift's "Nietzsche's French Legacy" (in this volume) for a discussion of Derrida's reading of this image of truth as a woman. For Derrida's discussion see Jacques Derrida, *Spurs: Nietzsche's Styles* trans. B. Harlow (Chicago: The University of Chicago Press, 1979).

74 BGE, #6, p. 13.

75 BGE, #23, p. 31.

76 BGE, #211, pp. 135–6.

77 BGE, #61, p. 72.

78 BGE, #13, p. 21.

79 BGE, #19, p. 26.

80 GS, #36, p. 48.

81 BGE, #213, p. 140.

82 Just among the essays in this volume, for example, five devote attention to this work; and particularly Nehamas's construal of it is discussed in Robert Pippin, "Nietzsche's Alleged Farewell: The Premodern, Modern, and Postmodern Nietzsche"; Jörg Salaquarda, "Nietzsche and the Judaeo-Christian Tradition"; Alan D. Schrift, "Nietzsche's French Legacy"; Robert C. Solomon, "Nietzsche's *Ad Hominem*: Perspectivism, Personality, and *Ressentiment* Revisited"; and Tracy B. Strong, "Nietzsche's Political Misappropriation."

83 See Friedrich Nietzsche, *On the Genealogy of Morals*, trans. Walter Kaufmann and R. J. Hollingdale (together with *Ecce Homo*, trans. Walter Kaufmann) (New York: Random House, 1967), hereafter indicated as "GM," II, 7, p. 69.

84 GM, II, 16, p. 84.

85 GM, II, 16, p. 85.

86 GM, II, 18, p. 88.

87 GM, II, 20, p. 91.

88 GM, III, 11, p. 117.

89 GM, III, 15, p. 127.

90 See GM, III, 20, p. 139.

91 GM, III, 20, p. 141.

92 GM, III, 27, p. 160.

93 GM, III, 28, p. 163.

94 For further discussion of Foucault's use of Nietzsche's methodology, see Alan D. Schrift, "Nietzsche's French Legacy" (in this volume).

95 Friedrich Nietzsche, *The Case of Wagner* (together with *The Birth of Tragedy*), trans. Walter Kaufmann (New York: Random House, 1967), hereafter indicated as "CW," 7, p. 170.

96 CW, 12, p. 180.

97 Friedrich Nietzsche, *Twilight of the Idols*, in *The Portable Nietzsche*, trans. and ed. Walter Kaufmann (New York: Viking Penguin, 1968), hereafter indicated as "TI," Preface, p. 465.

98 TI, Preface, p. 465.

99 For a discussion of this and the role of other *ad hominem* attacks by Nietzsche, see Robert C. Solomon, "Nietzsche's *Ad Hominem:* Perspectivism, Personality, and *Ressentiment* Revisited" (in this volume).

100 For a discussion of the section "How the 'True World' Finally Became a Fable," see Richard Schacht, "Nietzsche's Kind of Philosophy" (in this volume).

101 See Graham Parkes's "Nietzsche and East Asian Thought: Influences, Impacts, and Resonances" (in this volume) for a discussion of the conception of the individual that emerges from Nietzsche's "Skirmishes."

102 TI, "What I Owe to the Ancients," 4, pp. 561–2.

103 TI, "What I Owe to the Ancients," 4, pp. 561.

104 TI, "The Hammer Speaks," p. 563.

105 A, 42, p. 617.

106 See Gary Shapiro, "The Writing on the Wall: *The Antichrist* and the Semiotics of History," in *Reading Nietzsche*, ed. Robert C. Solomon and Kathleen M. Higgins (New York: Oxford University Press, 1988), p. 200.

107 Friedrich Nietzsche, *The Antichrist*, in *The Portable Nietzsche*, trans. and ed. Walter Kaufmann (New York: Viking Penguin, 1968), hereafter indicated as "A," 32, p. 605.

108 A, 34, p. 608.

109 A, 35, pp. 608–9.

110 A, 62, p. 656. For further discussion of *The Antichrist*, see Richard Schacht, "Nietzsche's Kind of Philosophy," and Jörg Salaquarda, "Nietzsche and the Judaeo-Christian Tradition" (both in this volume).

111 EH, p. 221. *The Songs of Zarathustra* are a series of poems, published under the title *Dionysus Dithyrambs* in 1891.

112 EH, p. 326.

113 For a discussion of Nietzsche's systematic use of the trope hyperbole, and the question of his styles, see Magnus et al., *Nietzsche's Case: Philosophy as/and Literature* (New York and London: Routledge, Chapman and Hall, Inc., 1993).

114 EH, p. 256; KGW, VI/3, pp. 293–4.

115 Friedrich Nietzsche, *Nietzsche contra Wagner*, in *The Portable Nietzsche*, trans. and ed. Walter Kaufmann (New York: Viking Penguin, 1968), p. 662.

116 Ernst Behler's "Nietzsche in the Twentieth Century" (in this volume) discusses Elisabeth's impact on Nietzsche's life as well as her role in editing the *Nachlass*. Behler also describes the more recent efforts made by scholars to reconstruct the *Nachlass* in its original chronology. Graham Parkes's "Nietzsche and East Asian Thought: Influences, Impacts, and Resonances" (also in this volume) discusses the influence of *The Will to Power* on the Japanese reception of Nietzsche.

117 See Ernst Behler's "Nietzsche in the Twentieth Century" for further discussion of Heidegger's interpretation of Nietzsche.

118 Martin Heidegger, *Nietzsche*, vol. 1, trans. David Krell (New York: Harper and Row, 1979), pp. 8–9.

119 This distinction was formulated in Bernd Magnus, "Nietzsche's Philosophy in 1888: *The Will to Power* and the *Übermensch*," *Journal of the History of Philosophy* 24, 1 (January 1986): 79–98. See also Bernd Magnus, "The Use and Abuse of *The Will to Power*," in *Reading Nietzsche*, eds. Robert C. Solomon and Kathleen M. Higgins (New York: Oxford University Press, 1988), pp. 218–325.

Part II The Use and Abuse of Nietzsche's Life and Works

2 The hero as outsider

I. THE NIETZSCHE LEGEND

For many years Nietzsche lived in a room in a house in Sils-Maria, in the Upper Engadine in Switzerland. The room is kept as he lived in it and it has often been photographed. It contains a bed, a writing-table with a lamp on it and a wash-table, and a small sofa. The walls are of wood, and the floorboards are partly covered with a carpet. There is a single window and through it you can see part of the village of Sils and the slopes of the mountains that lie beyond it. It is a typical small room in an Alpine village house.

He lived in this room in the summer months and would have lived in it all the year round if the winters had not been too cold for him. The winters in the Upper Engadine can be very cold.

From this room he wrote on 20 July 1888 that he had succeeded in securing a publisher for a book on the aesthetics of French drama by the Swiss author Carl Spitteler. This "little piece of humanity on my part," he said, was "my kind of revenge for an extremely tactless and impudent article by Spitteler on my entire literature" which had appeared the previous winter. He added: "I have far too high an opinion of the talent of this Swiss to let myself be disconcerted by a piece of *loutishness*."[1]

Though Spitteler's article, which appeared in the Bern *Bund* on 1 January 1888, clearly failed to win Nietzsche's approval, it must have given him some satisfaction nonetheless, for it was the first general account of his "whole literature" to appear anywhere. The modesty of the accommodation he occupied in Sils-Maria corresponded to the modesty of the reputation he enjoyed while he lived there. At the beginning of 1888 he was known to almost no one.

A quarter of a century later another journal, the British *Educational Review*, published an article called "Did Nietzsche Cause the War?" The war it meant was the world war that had started in 1914. Nietzsche's reputation was by now not at all modest.

Here is Clarence Darrow, writing in 1916: "Since his death, no philosopher on earth has been so talked of as Nietzsche . . . The universities of the world have been turned upside down by Nietzsche . . . Nietzsche has helped men to be strong – to look the world in the face."[2]

Here is Giovanni Papini, writing in 1922: "I declare to you I do not know of any modern life nobler, purer, sadder, lonelier, more hopeless than that of Friedrich Nietzsche." Nietzsche was "pure, saintly, martyred"; it was "of love, shut in and unappeased, that Nietzsche died. We slew him – all of us – by our common human behavior."[3]

And here is Alfred Bäumler, writing in 1937: "When today we see German youth marching under the sign of the swastika, our minds go back to Nietzsche's *Untimely Meditations*, in which this youth was invoked for the first time . . . And when we call out to this youth 'Heil Hitler!' we greet at the same time, with the same cry, Friedrich Nietzsche!"[4]

What these, and other comparable denunciations which I shall refer to later, have in common is that they are implausible. "Did Nietzsche Cause the War?" invites the answer "No." The connection between the *Untimely Meditations* of 1873–6 and National Socialism is invisible to the sober reader. And Darrow and Papini would excite even in someone who knew nothing of Nietzsche the suspicion they are being carried away from reality by an excess of emotion.

Anyone at all interested in Nietzsche and his philosophy will have encountered claims as to his status and character which, though they may conflict or even be incompatible with one another, share this element of implausibility. They belong to a cloudier, less palpable, and less believable world than that occupied by the room in Sils-Maria.

The world they belong to is not the real world but the world of legend. They refer to – or rather are – Nietzsche as legend.

2. THE NATURE OF LEGEND

Legend is fiction presented as truth. The word is often used as if it were synonymous with myth, but legends differ from myths in that, while myths, being fictions about gods, are necessarily set in what is imagined as the very remote past, legends, being fictions about heroes, can attach themselves to the people or events of any period, including the most recent.

A half-conscious awareness of this is probably manifested in the misuse of the word "legendary" as a term of high approval, as in "the legendary gathering at Woodstock." The person using the word does not intend to assert that the event never took place but that it was so singular it has become the subject of legend. "Legendized" is the correct word.

If I speak, then, of Nietzsche as legend I am not using the word in a metaphorical sense but saying that Nietzsche's life became legendized, became the subject of a legend. Though the facts of his life are of consequence to anyone who wants to understand why he thought as he did, they are of small cultural significance compared with that of the legend.

Very many people to whom Nietzsche's philosophy is and must remain wholly unfamiliar are entirely familiar with the legend. His idealized head – the stiff black hair, the deep-sunk eyes staring at a point about fifteen feet in front of them, the overarching eyebrows, and, fronting all like the scoop of a bulldozer, the "Nietzsche mustache" – has for nearly a century been a familiar icon: that is to say, a sacred symbol bearing some of the features of the thing symbolized.

The imprecision, some of it willful, with which such freighted words as "legend" are employed today – how many legends in their own lifetime can you think of from, say Valentino to Jim Morrison? – makes it necessary for us to become clear in our minds what a genuinely legended figure is and, beyond that, how it could come about that as unpromising a candidate as a German philosopher could become a figure whose portrait is as immediately recognizable as that of any statesman or film actor.

3. THE *NACHMÄRZ* REPRESSION

The conditions which made it possible for a German philosopher to become a legend and culture star have their origin in the period of reaction and repression that followed the failure of the German revolution of March 1848. The agitated period that preceded the revolt in Berlin is known as the *Vormärz* [Before March], the reactionary pe-

riod that followed it as the *Nachmärz* [After March].⁵ Restrictions
on what would now be called civil liberties and freedom of expression became general and were applied not only to political and social
life but to almost every region of public activity; and among the
most affected regions was philosophy.

Convinced that revolutionary acts could only be a direct consequence of revolutionary ideas, and that revolutionary ideas could in
turn only be a direct consequence of philosophical theories, the representatives of a reinvigorated state and church purged the philosophy departments of the universities of everything that struck them
as being subversive of the existing order. The purge was mild enough
compared with comparable exercises in our own century, but it was
based on the same belief that ideas can be ordered out of existence
and that if philosophers are instructed to abandon them they will do
so. This belief is false, however, and when it is acted on it necessarily produces effects different from those foreseen.

As every philosophical topic of interest to anyone but a professional logician or epistemologist was banished from the German
universities of the 1850s – and that was the practical outcome of the
political and ecclesiastical censorship – philosophy was not brought
to heel or reduced to an obedient servant of state and church, as was
of course the intention. What happened was that German philosophy split into two: into an academic philosophy to which no one any
longer paid attention and whose reputation sank to an unprecedented low for Germany, and a freelance philosophy existing outside
and independently of the university whose practitioners were able to
discuss those questions, alone of interest to the nonacademic public,
which the academic philosopher was inhibited from approaching.

4. THE SCHOPENHAUER LEGEND

The first large beneficiary of this creation of a freelance market in
philosophy was Schopenhauer. For thirty years Schopenhauer had
been willfully hostile to the academic establishment of his time and
apparently determined to fail to become part of it; as a consequence
his influence had been severely limited. Now the *Nachmärz* repression handed him a public: a German audience eager to listen to
"philosophy," to which academic philosophy, however, no longer
dared to say anything. Aided by a finer literary style than any Ger-

man philosopher had hitherto had at his command, he then became not only the most widely read philosopher in Germany but also the pioneer of a species of literary figure previously unknown to German letters: the freelance philosopher sustained only by the popularity his performance procured him.

It was quite possibly Schopenhauer's exceptional success, combined with his isolation as a hostile exile from the academic world, that now assisted to produce what has been called a "transference of interest from the problems of philosophy to the men who produce this philosophy."[6] Interest in the private lives of Kant or Hegel had been largely limited to the enjoyment of anecdote. Kant's punctuality, by which you could set your watch each day as he walked past the window, represented the normal level of engagement with the life and personality of Kant. Generally speaking, Kant, Hegel, Fichte were "philosophy professors," and that summed up their characters.

This relative indifference to what these men themselves were like was, moreover, not confined to the nonacademic world, in which they had never been popular in the ordinary sense of the word. Academic discussion of their philosophies, even vigorous partisanship for or against, was conducted almost as though these philosophies had produced themselves. The degree of abstractionism attained to – the atmosphere produced of self-enclosed mind-problems lacking a "real" or "human" dimension – was among the reasons university philosophy ceased to have contact with the larger German public. This certainly contributed to the decline of the word "academic" to a pejorative word meaning "having no relevance to the affairs of the real world."

But the type of freelance philosopher who was an outcome of the *Nachmärz* bifurcation of German philosophy was, in strong contrast to this, all but compelled to exhibit publicly at least some aspects of his personality if only because they were his only credentials, or at any rate the only ones he could decently present in his posture as a thinker existing outside and above the system and its "qualifications." And that "transference of interest from the problems of philosophy to the men who produce this philosophy" would naturally have been promoted by such higher visibility.

Interest in Schopenhauer thus swiftly took a personal turn – but it was a personal turn of a specific and fateful kind. It is aptly symbolized by the fact that his earliest influential advocate was quite happy for Schopenhauer to refer to him as his disciple: a word recalling, if not the relationship of Jesus's disciples to Jesus, at least that of Plato to Socrates. Objectively, Schopenhauer's life had hardly more to recommend it as an object of public interest than the lives of Kant or Hegel had. Nor was his personality calculated to excite general affection or sympathy. Yet when in this case the interest of the public was transferred from the philosophy to the man, it was transferred not to the real man but to the man as he represented himself to be and as, under his guidance and inspiration, his "disciple" Julius Frauenstädt depicted him.[7]

In Frauenstädt's presentation the neurotic genius – misanthropic, misogynist, and irascible to the point of caricature – is inverted into a patient and passive sufferer of misfortunes he had in reality mostly brought upon himself. Although there exists no evidence that anyone was ever exceptionally hostile toward Schopenhauer, Frauenstädt's 1849 essay, "Stimmen über Arthur Schopenhauer" ["Prejudices about Arthur Schopenhauer"] has for its theme the academic stupidity, blindness and malevolence responsible for burying the greatest contemporary philosopher in silence and obscurity for a quarter of a century. If you ask why he should have been singled out for such treatment, the answer is that he was a genius and all the rest were mediocrities defending their territory against him: which sounds plausible until you reflect that Kant and Hegel were, presumably, also "geniuses" yet were spared comparable persecution.

It is plain that Frauenstädt's interest in the facts of Schopenhauer's life was confined to those which he could put to use, and he was not interested at all in discovering the true motivations behind his subject's actions. What he was writing was not biography or even, in the last resort, polemic on behalf of Schopenhauer's Weltanschauung (worldview); what he was writing was legend.

5. THE PRECONDITIONS OF THE SCHOPENHAUER LEGEND

The Schopenhauer legend is the medieval legend of the knight errant translated from the physical to the mental sphere. Alone, more likely to be opposed and hindered than aided and succored by those about him, he ranges through the world in search of adventures of the mind. He slays falsehoods and rescues truths; he enters into dialectical combat and always wins; grown old, he leaves as his legacy a model mode of being and way of life: fearless independence.

For such a legend to come into existence two things had to occur together: Schopenhauer had actually to possess an exceptional mind and the German academic world had to have no place for him. During the greater part of his life his estrangement from the university had been largely of his own doing, but with the advent of the *Nachmärz* purge it became enforced: no one would have been permitted during that period to teach what Schopenhauer taught ("atheism," for example).

Thus it was not until about 1850 that the necessary concrete reality existed upon which the legend could be erected. There were other reasons for Schopenhauer's sudden rise to fame and influence after so lengthy a period of obscurity, but these conditions contributed most to the fact that the real Schopenhauer so quickly vanished behind the legend of the solitary knight errant of truth.

6. NIETZSCHE'S ENCOUNTER WITH THE SCHOPENHAUER LEGEND

Such a legend may seem to be only a harmless piece of storytelling. It might even seem to benefit its subject inasmuch as it may attract to him the attention of those to whom a "philosophy professor," however gifted, would make no appeal. But the advantages it may have are outweighed by the disadvantage that the legend is capable of existing in the absence of the philosophy of which it was initially created to be the vehicle. The knight errant can go his merry way inspiring thousands to a life of fearless independence while the "truths" he rescues disappear into the background mist. And this is what happened in the case of Schopenhauer.

To Richard Wagner, who first read Schopenhauer's masterpiece, *The World as Will and Idea*, in 1854, the philosopher was the great resolver of the riddle of life, and it was in this sense that he sought to propagate his philosophy. Schopenhauer the man, whether the real man or the legend, hardly enters into Wagner's writings about him. A generation later, however, we find that Nietzsche is capable of revering Schopenhauer almost as greatly as Wagner had done, while first doubting, then denying, and finally ignoring his philosophy.

It is a commonplace of commentary on Nietzsche's early essay

"Schopenhauer as Educator" that it contains next to nothing about Schopenhauer's philosophy. It is almost wholly concerned with Schopenhauer as an exemplary type of man, or at least of philosopher. Academic philosophers, Nietzsche says, are harmless and pusillanimous, "and of all their art and aims there could be said what Diogenes said when someone praised a philosopher in his presence: 'How can he be considered great, since he has been a philosopher for so long and has never yet *disturbed* anybody?' But if this is how things stand in our time," he goes on,

then the dignity of philosophy is trampled into the dust; it has even become something ludicrous, it would seem, or a matter of complete indifference to anyone: so that it is the duty of all its true friends to bear witness against this confusion, and at the least to show that it is only its false and unworthy servants who are ludicrous or a matter of indifference. It would be better still if they demonstrated by their deeds that love of truth is something fearsome and mighty. Schopenhauer demonstrated both these things – and will demonstrate them more and more as day succeeds day.[8]

In "Schopenhauer as Educator" it is not Schopenhauer's philosophy but Schopenhauer's legend which "educates"; and what it educates to is an admiration for and determination to live a life of fearless independence in the service of truth. That what this "truth" amounts to is in the last resort a matter of indifference, a position almost but not quite arrived at in the essay, is declared unambiguously in a quatrain Nietzsche subsequently wrote on Schopenhauer:

> Was er lehrte, ist abgetan;
> Was er lebte, wird bleiben stahn;
> Seht ihn nur an –
> Niemandem war er untertan!
>
> [What he taught has been done away with;
> How he lived will remain;
> You have only to look at him –
> He was subject to no one!]

To Nietzsche at least the philosophy of which the legend was once the vehicle is dead, but the legend lives vigorously on.

7. POETIC JUSTICE?

Perhaps the hackneyed term "poetic justice" is applicable to what happened to Nietzsche when he too became a famous freelance German philosopher. Like Schopenhauer he philosophized outside and in hostile independence of the academic world (technically he was even more "independent" than Schopenhauer, inasmuch as, unlike Schopenhauer, he possessed no philosophical degree); like Schopenhauer he had command of a literary style out of the reach of the academic philosophers of his time; like Schopenhauer he was in his personal life a "solitary"; and like Schopenhauer he acquired "disciples" who, heirs of those who had transferred their interest from the problems of philosophy to the men who produced this philosophy, embraced his legend and ignored his books.

8. NIETZSCHE'S ILLNESS

Let us return to the room in Sils-Maria. It is the mid-1880s and the Nietzsche legend does not yet exist. The "proud and lonely truth-finder" – Nietzsche's description of Heraclitus[9] but before long to be applied to him – is a chronic invalid wondering whether Sils is still warm enough or whether, with winter coming on, he must remove to somewhere warmer. He feels more truly at home in the high Alps than he does anywhere else and likes to celebrate their coldness and remoteness in rhapsodic prose: but his nervous system can endure only so much of them.

Here is how he came to be living in this way. It is a medical story with a strong bearing on the character of the legend and especially on its more megalomaniac features. A few years ago it was a story that could no longer be told of anyone, but things have of course changed in the medical sphere since a few years ago.

Nietzsche attended the university at Bonn for a short time. His friend and fellow student Paul Deussen tells us that in February 1865 Nietzsche told him he had gone on a trip to Cologne, and that the cab-driver who had driven him around had, without his wishing it, taken him to a brothel. "I suddenly saw myself surrounded by half-a-dozen apparitions in tinsel and gauze who looked at me expectantly," Deussen says Nietzsche told him. "I stood for a moment speechless. Then I made instinctively for a piano in the room as to the only living thing in that company and struck several chords. They broke the spell and I hurried away."[10]

Deussen, who became one of the West's great Sanskrit scholars, was celebrated among his friends and acquaintances for the quality of his memory. The brief anecdote he relates is thus of importance because it connects us in what are almost certainly Nietzsche's own words with the probable origin of his illness. It also exposes as legend the story of Nietzsche the great mind "driven insane" by solitude, lack of understanding, and the vulgarity of the world around him – by Papini's "love shut in and unappeased" – as the aspect of it that conflicts most crassly with reality.

In 1867 Nietzsche, now a student at Leipzig, was treated by two Leipzig doctors for a syphilitic infection; but there existed no cure for syphilis and the disease took its course. In 1869 he was appointed to the chair of classical philology at the university of Basel, in Switzerland; in 1871 he began to suffer from recurring migrainelike headaches, stomach disorder and general exhaustion, and in the February of that year he was granted leave of absence from Basel "for the purpose of restoring his health." No such restoration was possible, however, and the symptoms persisted. As the consequence of a general breakdown at Christmas 1875, he was again allowed time off from teaching, and in October 1876 the university let him go for a full year. In April 1879 he sustained so violent and protracted an attack of migraine and vomiting that he decided he must ask the university to release him for good, and he was retired on a pension.

Hereafter he conducted what he called a "daily battle against headache" and against a "laughable diversity" of ailments which continued until, in the autumn of 1888, everything suddenly cleared up, he experienced a feeling of boundless euphoria, and in the first days of 1889 collapsed into insanity. He was taken to a psychiatric clinic, where he was diagnosed as suffering from "paralysis progressiva." During the course of the next eleven years he slowly but inexorably declined into the condition commonly called general paralysis of the insane, and during his final years he was plainly aware of nothing.

Except for the extended length of time that elapsed between mental breakdown and death, which is atypical, this progress exhibits most of the typical symptoms of destruction by syphilis, and Nietzsche's story of being taken to a brothel is a plausible account of where he contracted it. His medical history is exceptionally well documented but in no way mysterious or uncommon.

Nietzsche's mental breakdown initially ignited two opposite reactions in the relatively few people who already knew something of what he had written. On the one hand there were those who, already disturbed by his works, recalled or were informed that his father had died of "encephalomalacia" and thus felt entitled to conclude that Nietzsche had perhaps "inherited" insanity from him and had been mad all along. That this is an unscientific conclusion hardly needs pointing out. The word, obtained by translating the vernacular words for "brain" and "soft" into Greek and putting them together, describes a condition of the brain. The supposition that this condition produces "insanity," which can then be transmitted genetically, however, is really a piece of folklore, on a level with Wagner's discovery, communicated by letter to Nietzsche's physician, that the cause of Nietzsche's headaches and general malaise was "excessive masturbation." The thinking here, again, is prescientific.

The other reaction to Nietzsche's breakdown was to idealize it into an "ascent" above and beyond the concerns of the mundane world. Here is Gabriele Reuter, writing in the 1890s: "I stood trembling beneath the power of his glance. . . . It seemed to me that his spirit dwelt in boundless solitude, endlessly distant from all human affairs";[11] Ernst Bertram, writing in 1918, refers to an "ascent into the mystic";[12] Rudolf Steiner refers to the "unfathomable exultation" of Nietzsche's facial expression.[13] Here, true to the nature of legend, fiction replaces fact: a spirit dwelling in boundless solitude usurps in the legend the place occupied in the real world by the author of Nietzsche's philosophy.

9. NIETZSCHE'S EARLY LIFE

Nietzsche's life can be divided into four unequal parts: 1844–69, child, youth, student; 1869–79, university professor; 1879–89, freelance philosopher; 1889–1900, invalid. Of the books he published or intended to publish, three, *The Birth of Tragedy*, the four-part *Untimely Meditations*, and the first part of *Human, All Too Human*, belong to the second division. The remainder – the second and third parts of *Human, All Too Human*, *Daybreak*, *The Gay Science*, the four parts of *Thus Spoke Zarathustra*, *Beyond Good and Evil*, *On the Genealogy of Morals*, *The Wagner Case*, *Twilight of the Idols*, *The Anti-Christ*, *Ecce Homo*, *Nietzsche contra Wagner* and the *Dithyrambs of Dionysus* – belong to the third. The multitude of notebook entries some of which were published after his death under the title *The Will to Power* also belong to this third period. It was only in this period, 1879–89, that Nietzsche's life assumed the form that supplied the necessary real foundation upon which the legend could subsequently be erected.

Nietzsche was born on 15 October 1844 in the village of Röcken, near the town of Lützen, which is near the city of Leipzig. At the time he was born, Röcken was in Prussian Saxony, and Nietzsche was thus a citizen of Prussia. All the above-mentioned places are now in what was called eastern Germany until 1989.

Nietzsche's father was the village Lutheran pastor, and his father's father had been a superintendent, the Lutheran equivalent of a bishop. Nietzsche's mother was the sixth of the eleven children of the pastor of a neighboring village. He was his parent's first child, and he was named after the reigning king of Prussia, of whom Pastor Nietzsche was an admirer. The king's birthday was also 15 October, which meant that when he was a boy, Nietzsche's birthday was a public holiday. He could hardly have been born more comfortably embedded in the church and state that were to reassert their authority in the *Nachmärz* 1850s.

Nietzsche's origin in a country parsonage is worth dwelling on because it supplies a corrective to the "proud and lonely truth-finder" element of the legend which conflicts with and obscures the fact that he was in reality a product of that *Pfarrhaustradition* [parsonage tradition] to which so many of Germany's intellectual elite have belonged. The facts of his biography second the conclusion to which an unprejudiced reading of his works, and especially a reading in the chronological order of their production, must surely lead – that his origins lay not in the clouds but in Protestant Christianity, of which he is manifestly an outcome. From the point of view of the Catholic church, the sin of Protestantism is its refusal to accept faith on authority – a refusal which must in the end lead to a loss of faith. Protestantism is a halfway stage between belief in God and atheism. From this point of view Nietzsche's origin in Protestantism must seem unquestionable: he must, indeed, if one takes him seriously, appear as the inevitable end of the course inaugurated by Luther. This way of viewing Nietzsche possesses over the legend of the solitary seer the advantage that it is sustained by biography: Nietzsche was in fact the heir of generations of Protestant clergymen and, in his own person, a son of the parsonage.

The earliest stage of Nietzsche's existence came to an end when his father died of "encephalomalacia," and the family – he, his mother, his younger sister, Elisabeth, and two maiden aunts – had to vacate the manse to the pastor's successor. Nietzsche was then four-and-a-half years old. The family moved to Naumburg, a small town in Thuringia in eastern Germany. Nietzsche lived there from 1850 until he left for the Pforta boarding school in 1858. His mother remained there for the rest of her life, and he was returned there after his mental collapse of 1889.

In 1850 Naumburg was still surrounded by a wall; the gates were shut at night. The Kaisersaschern of Thomas Mann's novel *Doctor Faustus* is modeled on Naumburg, and the word it irresistibly brings into mind is "medieval." The town could, of course, not have been truly medieval in 1850; but the exaggeration contained in the image assists toward an understanding of Nietzsche's subsequent attitude toward "the Germans" and his answers to the question "What is German?"

Here again biography acts as a corrective to legend. Before the era of German predominance in Europe that followed the foundation of the Reich in 1871, conservatism, inertia, and a sinister kind of quaintness were the characteristics universally ascribed to German society and the German nature. Germany was the European backwater where all things that are outmoded could be expected to have their home; and we must remember that this Germany, which anyone now living can experience only in imagination, was Nietzsche's real world during his formative years.

The first effect on a new reader of Nietzsche's writings of the 1880s, on which his reputation rests, is the feeling how "modern" he is, and this modernity obscures his origins and thus to some degree the sources of his judgments. It is a little as though a writer residing in Connecticut had been born and raised in Mississippi: his answer to the question "What is American?" might easily startle his neighbors who had spent their whole lives in New England.

From 1858 to 1864 Nietzsche attended Schulpforta. It was already clear to him that he was not going to follow his father and grandfathers into the church. He had no specific idea of what he was going to do; but Pforta placed a strong emphasis on the Greek and Roman classics. He discovered these presented him with no difficulty, and he thus became a classicist. There seems to have been no other reason for this choice of discipline.

"Classical philology," as the study of the life, language, and letters of antique Greece and Rome was called in Germany, was a field in which Nietzsche later distinguished himself, and it is probably not too much to say that he revolutionized the way in which we perceive the Greeks. Of even greater consequence than the influence he had on Greek studies, however, was the influence his Greek studies had on him. Their most general effect was to demonstrate to him that a high civilization – the highest, indeed, as he quickly came to think – could be raised on a moral foundation wholly at variance with the Christian; and that Christian morality was not the only one. It would be right to call Nietzsche one of the great Hellenophiles: only he had first to redefine Hellas before he could admire it.

Nietzsche's universities were, as indicated, Bonn and Leipzig. At Bonn he studied theology and philology, but soon dropped theology. At Leipzig he discovered Schopenhauer and Wagner and became the star philological student. In 1869 he was appointed to the chair of classical philology at Basel at the almost unprecedentedly youthful age of twenty-four and awarded his doctorate by Leipzig without examination, on the basis of work he had already published. Basel wanted him to change his nationality from Prussian to Swiss. The first part of this request he was able to comply with, but he never achieved the residential qualification necessary for the granting of Swiss citizenship. He was thus for the remainder of his life stateless.

Nietzsche taught at Basel, very successfully it seems, for a little under ten years. He gained a modest notoriety with his first book, *The Birth of Tragedy*, which now enjoys a reputation as a counter-blow to the "sweetness and light" school of Hellenism. On its publication in 1872, however, it was considered seriously unscholarly for the work of a professor of classical philology; and its vehement advocacy of Wagner placed his academic career increasingly in jeopardy. In an overview of his life, however, Nietzsche's Basel years seem transitional. It was not until his incapacitation through illness had compelled him to relinquish an academic life that he became, in every really important respect, himself.

10. NIETZSCHE AS SOLITARY WRITER

Nietzsche now entered upon the decade of independence which constitutes the essential material of the legend, but which the legend falsifies in essential respects. The life he led was an unusual one, certainly, but there are many witnesses to the groundlessness of the legend which depicts him as a remote, self-enclosed ascetic wholly devoted to a solitary pursuit of the higher truth. On the contrary, almost every report we have speaks of him as being to an uncommon degree urbane and civilized.[14] Everyone who remarks on the matter, for instance, notes the attention he paid to dress: he never appeared in public without being well turned out.

Because he was often ill, Nietzsche was often in bed throughout the day; and because he was a writer, he was often equally out of the public eye because he was sitting behind a desk. The latter point needs to be stressed. If we take into account the mass of unpublished material he wrote as well as the published books, we come to realize that between his thirty-fifth and forty-fifth years Nietzsche wrote a very great deal. Whatever else he might have done or suffered during these years, he was for much of the time sitting alone writing. This is something you have to forget if you want to see him, as the legend would have you see him, as being to an abnormal degree solitary and a loner.

The "solitude" that characterized Nietzsche's existence was, indeed, soberly considered only the solitude of the unmarried man without family: it was in no sense a life lived in desert isolation. Where he lived was dictated by his medical condition, inasmuch as he needed warmth in winter and coolness in summer. He spent summers in Switzerland – from the summer of 1881 in Sils-Maria – in winter on the French and Italian Riviera, chiefly in Nice or Genoa. Sometimes he was back in Germany (Naumburg, Marienbad, Leipzig), sometimes in Venice. When he collapsed he was staying in Turin. Except for his returns to the room in Sils, he never established himself anywhere but was repeatedly on the move, and this may perhaps be considered the sign of a restlessness abnormal in a man as sick as he was; notice, however, that his choice of resting-places does not suggest precisely asceticism.

The hook by which the legend attaches itself to the real man is in fact not any self-sought solitude but Nietzsche's intellectual independence as a philosopher during this decade, of which his footloose wanderings through Germany–Switzerland–France–Italy can be seen as an objective correlative. That he was perforce "free" of the university and never afterward attached himself to any other place or institution offers a biographical parallel to the freedom which characterized his thinking. It also provides a hold for the legend of the unencumbered solitary to cling to. This consideration does not, however, apply to the paralytically immobile icon of the self-absorbed "thinker," which people who have never read a line of what he wrote have no difficulty in recognizing as "Nietzsche." It is the idealized head, not of Nietzsche as a thinker, but of Nietzsche as he appeared during the only time the graphic artists who created the icon ever saw him, which was when he had ceased to think at all.

II. THE ROLE OF ELISABETH FÖRSTER-NIETZSCHE

After Nietzsche's mental breakdown the most important figure in his life was his sister, Elisabeth, who was the chief instrument in the creation of the legend. Though many others made their contribution, it is she who is in the last resort responsible for the fact that Nietzsche is so much better known than his books are.

Two years younger than her brother, Elisabeth survived him by thirty-five years, or by forty-six if we add the eleven years of his incapacitation. While he was still quite unknown to the world at large she founded the "Nietzsche Archive" in the family home at Naumburg and then transferred it to a villa in Weimar, the cultural capital of Germany. Her role model seems to have been Wagner's widow, Cosima Wagner, who after Wagner's death preserved his "heritage" at Bayreuth something in the style of the priestess of a mystery cult. Elisabeth aimed to do the same for Nietzsche. The difference between them was that Cosima understood Wagner very well and acted in what was almost certainly the way in which he would have acted had he been alive, whereas Elisabeth seems to have had no notion of what Nietzsche stood for, or of what philosophy is, or of what is meant by intellectual integrity.

Elisabeth Förster-Nietzsche's inadequacies are copiously documented and are not, at this time, in need of further substantiation. Until his suicide in 1889, Elisabeth had been married to Bernhard Förster, an anti-Semitic politician and proto-Nazi, and they had together founded a colony, New Germania, in Paraguay. After her husband's death and the colony's apparent failure – it has in fact survived to the present day in a rudimentary form – she returned to Germany and adopted Nietzsche as a substitute "life-task." So far as she could she imposed Förster's values on the "Nietzsche Archive" and adapted Nietzsche in accordance with them. Ignorant of philosophy, she visualized a "philosopher" as a hybrid of solitary seer and elevated saint, and this is how Nietzsche appears in her biographies of him. Ultimately, he is to her a commodity, which she marketed in exchange not so much for money as for prestige, for a place of prominence in the new Germany.

Assisted by an acute commercial sense and the new copyright laws, Elisabeth gained control of everything Nietzsche had written – to prevent anyone else from acquiring it was one of the functions of the Archive – and as "Nietzsche's sister" laid claim to a unique ability to understand and interpret him. The legend we have been discussing was an outcome of her efforts.[15] Others more talented (to put it mildly) than Elisabeth contributed to the propagation of this legend, and in select cases (e.g. Stefan George) to its greater refinement and intellectualization; but the heart of it remained unaffected and it has come down to us intact.

12. THE DAMAGE CAUSED BY THE NIETZSCHE LEGEND

The Nietzsche legend is the modern legend of the isolate and embattled individual: the hero as outsider. He thinks more, knows more, and suffers more than other men do, and is as a consequence elevated above them. Whatever he has of value he has created out of himself, for apart from himself there is only "the compact majority," which is always wrong. When he speaks he is usually misunderstood, but he can in any case be understood only by isolated and embattled individuals such as himself. In the end he removes himself to a distance at which he and the compact majority become mutually invisible, but his image is preserved in his icon: the man who goes alone.

As in the case of Schopenhauer, the legend possesses an obvious attractiveness. It has certainly enthralled very many who would not have found enthralling, or even comprehensible, the philosophy of which it is supposed to be the vehicle, but from which it has broken free to enjoy an independent existence. It is certainly not going too far to say that thousands who claim to have been enlightened by Nietzsche, and believe what they claim, have in reality been seduced by the legend of the man who went alone, the high plains drifter of philosophy.

There have also been many, however, who have encountered the legend and found it repellent; and they have concluded that the philosophy must also be repellent. Here the legend proves to be very harmful indeed. "Most people," I was told recently, "regard Nietzsche as a very intelligent nutter." I don't doubt that this is true. I also don't doubt that "most people" have never read a line he wrote. How, then, can they have an opinion of him, unfavorable or otherwise? They have encountered the legend, which is part of the cultural air we breathe, and have formed an opinion of that, in the illusion they were forming an opinion of the man and his philosophy.

NOTES

1 Letter to Franz Overbeck, 20 July 1888. Carl Spitteler (pseudonym of Felix Tandem, 1845–1924), a leading Swiss poet and writer, received the Nobel prize for literature in 1919.
2 Clarence Darrow, "Nietzsche," in *Athena* (1916), reprinted by Enigma Press, Mount Pleasant, Michigan, 1983.
3 Giovanni Papini, "Nietzsche," in *Four and Twenty Minds* (1922), reprinted by the Enigma Press, 1983.
4 Alfred Bäumler, "*Nietzsche und der Nationalsozialismus*" (1937), quoted in Ernest Newman, *The Life of Richard Wagner*, vol. IV (1947), p. 511.
5 The general aspect of the *Nachmärz* is familiar enough to students of German history, but the effect of the *Nachmärz* reaction specifically within the field of philosophy is treated in detail in Klaus Christian Köhnke's *Entstehung und Aufstieg der Neukantianismus* (Frankfurt am Main, 1986), to which I owe much of the present and following paragraphs.
6 Julius Ebbinghaus, *Schulphilosophie and Menschenbildung im 19. Jahrhundert* (1943), quoted in Köhnke, p.116.
7 For Frauenstädt's voluminous contribution to the Schopenhauer literature see Arthur Hübscher, *Schopenhauer-Bibliographie* (Stuttgart–Bad Cannstatt, 1981). His earliest eulogy of Schopenhauer dates from 1840; the essay "*Stimmen über Arthur Schopenhauer*," in which the legend appears small but perfectly formed, appeared in 1849; and his first full-sized book on Schopenhauer (376 pages), *Briefe über die Schopenhauer'sche Philosophie*, was published in 1854. Schopenhauer's *Parerga*

und Paralipomena, which first ignited general interest in him, appeared in Berlin in 1851.

8 "Schopenhauer as Educator," in *Untimely Meditations* (CUP, 1983), p. 194.

9 In lecture 10 of *The Pre-Platonic Philosophers.*

10 Paul Deussen, *Erinnerungen an Friedrich Nietzsche* (Leipzig, 1901), p. 24.

11 Quoted in Erich Podach, *Der kranke Nietzsche* (Vienna, 1937), p.251f.

12 Ernst Bertram: *Nietzsche: Versuch einer Mythologie* (1918), p.361.

13 Quoted in C. A. Bernoulli, *Franz Overbeck und Friedrich Nietzsche: eine Freundschaft* (Jena, 1908), vol. 2, p. 370.

14 For example, *Conversations with Nietzsche,* ed. Sander L. Gilman (OUP, 1987), contains recollections of Nietzsche by over fifty people who knew him, and he produced upon them all the impression of an almost excessively courteous and self-possessed companion. Some, it seems clear, subsequently had difficulty in identifying the Dionysian God-destroyer of the 1890s and afterward with the gentleman they had met and talked with. But all the documents relating to Nietzsche's life before his mental breakdown witness to the same thing.

15 Descriptions and, sometimes, documentation of Elisabeth's leading role in the creation of the legend and in the elevation of Nietzsche to a cult figure and culture hero can be found in most contemporary accounts of Nietzsche's life, even brief ones (e.g. the article on him in *The New Encyclopaedia Britannica,* 1982). No recommendable account of her own life exists, and probably no account is needed outside the context of her involvement with her brother.

3 Nietzsche and the Judaeo-Christian tradition

OVERVIEW

Nietzsche has been one of the most influential critics of Christianity. Like Feuerbach and other philosophers of the Hegelian Left, he was not content with merely rejecting Christianity. Instead, he developed a kind of "genetic criticism." In other words, he claimed that his critique of religion demonstrated the reasons why human beings become religious and the mechanisms by which they comprehend the religious realm.

For some time Nietzsche, the son of a Lutheran minister, was an active Christian himself. He was familiar with Christian practice, with the Bible, and with Christian doctrine. In his critique of religion, he made more use of this familiarity and knowledge than did other critics. His criticism has been effective not only through the arguments he articulated but also through the vitality of his language and the richness and splendor of his rhetoric. Emulating Luther's German translation of the Bible and Goethe's poetry and prose, Nietzsche utilized keen images and impressive similes to persuade his readers.[1]

For several years after he had lost his faith, Nietzsche relied on the historical refutation of Christianity available at the time. In this period his own critique of religion mainly recapitulated that of Schopenhauer. To a certain extent, he accepted religion as a fictitious "suprahistorical power," at the same time expecting that religion in general, and Christianity in particular, would automatically vanish with the passage of time.

Nietzsche's specific psychological, or "genealogical," critique of Christianity, with its fierce attacks, is to be found mainly in the

90

publications of the second half of the 1880s.[2] But its roots go far back. The dramatic shift in argument and tone was due to Nietzsche's "discovery," as he put it, that religion was but a superficial and popular form of an underlying morality. Thus, Nietzsche's late attacks on Christianity may be understood as his desperate struggle against the most successful form of the morality of *ressentiment*,[3] which he regarded as hostile to human life. His attacks became more severe the more he was convinced that most "modern ideas" (for example, liberalism, socialism, the politics of emancipation, etc.) were by no means anti-Christian, as their supporters intended; instead, they were themselves expressions of the Christian ideal. Nietzsche also seemed to believe that his genealogical criticism was totally new and utterly decisive, making him "a destiny."[4] In fact, Nietzsche initiated a kind of criticism that is now associated with depth psychology and sociology. And for this we are indebted to him.

Until the end, Nietzsche remained suspicious that his own analyses themselves might be based on Christian impulses, that his own critiques might instantiate rather than set aside the object of his analysis.[5] While he attacked and even cursed Christianity,[6] he never forgot to mention and stress the importance of the whole Judaeo-Christian tradition for the development of culture, indeed, of humankind.[7]

Nietzsche's criticism has uncovered temptations to which Christianity has now and again succumbed. But it has neither actually done away with Christianity nor worked out a logically irresistible refutation of it. To be sure, a Christian doctrine and practice that does not integrate Nietzsche's criticisms cannot survive under the conditions of modernity. But not all kinds of Christian doctrine and practice are rendered impossible by his critique.

BACKGROUND: NIETZSCHE'S RELIGIOUS BIOGRAPHY[8]

Nietzsche was the only son of a Lutheran minister.[9] His only other sibling was his sister Elisabeth. Both of his grandfathers had been ministers just as his father had been. In his paternal line, this clerical tradition reached back several generations. The German Protestant parsonage is famous for the surprising number of famous individuals it created. Many German artists and scholars and, above all, "people of the word" (writers, poets, philosophers, philologists, and historians) were born and raised as a minister's children. Nor should we forget "people of the tone," that is, composers and musicians. Nietzsche, who exemplified most of these talents as well, was aware and proud of this origin. From his first autobiographical sketches[10] to the highly stylized late autobiography, *Ecce Homo*, he praised the parsonage as the source of his "cleverness." He also used to condense its meaning symbolically in the person of his father: "I regard it a special privilege that I had such a father."[11]

Nietzsche was familiar, above all, with two types of religious faith: on the one hand, the practical faith of his mother, which lacked theological reflection and sophistication entirely; and, on the other, the more rationalistic tradition of his aunt Rosalie, who was the dominating theological figure in the family after the death of his father. From his early boyhood, Nietzsche was expected to follow the family tradition and become a minister himself. As late as 1864, when he studied classics *and* theology at Bonn University, he seems to have adhered to his family's expectations (if no longer wholeheartedly). When one year later he finally dropped theology, he provoked a family crisis.

Disagreement persists among Nietzsche scholars as to when, and for what reasons exactly, Nietzsche broke with Christianity.[12] In the corpus of his early notes, we find testimonies of a living faith as late as 1861. But these notes conflict with other texts in which Nietzsche submitted Christian teachings to a sober analysis or penned rather blasphemous remarks.[13] At any rate, from 1862 or so, Nietzsche was clearly already estranged from Christianity, and in 1865, when he confined his studies exclusively to classics, he overtly broke with it irrevocably.

As reason for his renunciation of Christianity, in his notes young Nietzsche offered historical criticism.[14] He had become acquainted with and had come to know and defend historical criticism himself in Schulpforta, Germany's leading Protestant boarding school to which he had been awarded a scholarship and at which he spent so much of his childhood and youth. Students there learned and were trained to handle such criticism in the course of interpreting Greek and Latin texts, but historical criticism was also applied to the Christian tradition. Nietzsche seems to have adopted this method. His first outspoken criticism of some Christian doctrines was inspired by the tension between their alleged absolutism, on the one hand, and the obvious historical relativity of their origins and traditions, on the other.[15] In his writings of the early 1870s Nietzsche made use of two additional arguments. Together with Overbeck he mocked the poverty of contemporary Christian trends. He also tried to unmask the inconsistency or "mendacity," not only of individual Christians, but of Christian doctrine as such. In the 1880s Nietzsche's criticism became more aggressive and psychological in orientation.[16]

Looking back at the whole of this life, from the perspective of the end of the 1880s, Nietzsche would assert of his early relation to Christianity that he had fundamentally been at odds with it from the beginning, and that his atheism had not been evoked by arguments, but arose "from instinct." He also would deny any personal animosity against Christians. On the contrary, he had experienced nothing but good will toward sincere Christians.[17] Moreover, he called Christianity "the best piece of ideal life" he had ever come to know,[18] Christ the Crucified "the most sublime symbol still,"[19] etc.

From childhood on, perhaps until the end of the 1870s, Nietzsche clearly favored Lutheran Protestantism, from which he himself had originated.[20] However, he was not attracted by specifically Lutheran doctrines, at least not after his apostasy. He was attracted instead by Luther's and the Lutheran tradition's (alleged or real) kinship with ideas of the Enlightenment.[21] Later, when Nietzsche's criticism of modern Christianity's uncertainty grew more radical, however, he tended especially to reject Protestantism as a kind of "hemiplegia of Christianity – and reason."[22] There is some evidence that he began, relatively, to prefer Roman Catholicism.[23]

Through the influences of Schopenhauer and Wagner, the young Nietzsche tended toward anti-Judaism and even toward anti-Semitism. When Nietzsche broke with Wagner in the second half of the 1870s, he also outgrew his earlier bias which he had acquired under their influence. And although he rejected all of the Judaeo-Christian tradition, he now strongly preferred the Old to the New Testament, especially because of the examples of human greatness evident in the earlier tradition.[24]

NIETZSCHE'S KNOWLEDGE OF THE JUDAEO-CHRISTIAN TRADITION[25]

Although Nietzsche's break with Christianity cannot be dated with precision, most scholars agree that for a number of years, perhaps through 1861, when he was confirmed, he himself had been a practicing Christian. He had taken part in prayers at home, had regularly attended formal services, had enjoyed Christian holidays amidst his family, etc. From his early childhood, furthermore, he had been regarded as a future minister and had internalized this expectation. Nietzsche, therefore, knew from his own experience what cult, prayer, sermon, reading the Holy Scripture, blessing, Christian community, etc., meant to believers, for good or ill. This personal background is strongly evident in his later psychological analyses of Christian life.[26]

Nietzsche was exceptionally familiar with Scripture. He learned spelling and biblical language from the Bible, so to speak, and the "book of books" was among the very first that the little boy tried to read himself, unaided. The lessons of the preparatory class he attended at Naumburg in 1851 consisted to a considerable extent of Bible teachings.[27] And although in Schulpforta biblical studies were considered less important than classical ones, Nietzsche knew most books of the Bible quite well when he left school. He never ceased to look up biblical quotations and phrases, and at least once he seems to have reread large parts of Scripture to prepare his attacks on Christianity in his late works.[28]

Not only *Thus Spoke Zarathustra*, in which this is most obvious, but all of Nietzsche's books contain biblical motifs, phrases, quotations, and allusions galore. The philosopher, in general, made a critical if not polemical use of this material. However, he nearly always retained the language of Luther's German translation of the Bible.[29]

During his school days and in his early studies, Nietzsche also gained his first theological insights and knowledge.[30] Already in Schulpforta he was introduced to a critical reading of Scripture and to philosophical discussion of Christian doctrines, especially of the classical proofs for God's existence (as well as Kant's arguments against their validity). At Bonn University Nietzsche, among other things, attended lectures surveying the three main theological trends of nineteenth century Protestantism. These included: the traditionalist apologetic perspective, based on a supernatural reading of the Bible; the critical school of F. Chr. Baur, who was suspicious, if not hostile, to the contemporary Church; and the "*Vermittlungstheologie*" [theology of mediation] of the church historian K. A. V. Hase.

Nietzsche carefully read the two outstanding critical works produced by the so-called Hegelian Left, works which were widely known, even beyond the more narrow borders of academic discussion. These were David Strauss's *The Life of Jesus* and Ludwig Feuerbach's *The Essence of Christianity*. But it was in the person of one of his most intimate friends from 1870 on, Franz Overbeck, with whom he shared the same lodgings for some time, (a person who was also his colleague at Basel University) that Nietzsche came to know one of the most radical members of the critical current personally. It was Overbeck who recommended to Nietzsche books that were to become influential in shaping his view of religion in general, and of Christianity and specific Christian doctrines in particular.[31]

Despite his extreme near-sightedness, Nietzsche was a diligent reader, interested in a wide variety of scientific and scholarly areas. More often than not, he developed his own ideas in the form of a critical discussion and engagement with contemporary literature. This is true also of his ideas on religion and Christianity.[32]

THE INFLUENCE OF SCHOPENHAUER[33]

Of deep and lasting influence for Nietzsche's understanding of the Judaeo-Christian tradition was Arthur Schopenhauer. Nietzsche read Schopenhauer's main work, *The World as Will and Representation*, in 1864.

Schopenhauer observed that there have been religions at all times and that they were, and are, of great importance for human beings. From this, he derived a fundamental anthropological drive,[34] which he called "*metaphysisches Bedürfnis*" [metaphysical need]. Religion and philosophy endeavor to fulfill this drive or need, but they do so in quite different ways. While philosophy argues and focuses on reasons, religion relies on authority. Therefore, Schopenhauer's attitude to "*Volksmetaphysik*" [the metaphysics of (ordinary) people],[35] as he called religion, was ambivalent. He accepted and even praised religion because it preserved the awareness that the world of everyday life experience, and also that of scientific experience, was not the true world. In Schopenhauer's opinion, the vast majority of people were and would always be incapable of proper philosophizing, and, therefore, religion could not be dispensed with. But, of course, he would have preferred that more – in fact all – people could have abandoned religious thinking and turned to philosophy. For religion was not immune to self-misunderstandings. Adherents of religions tended to exhibit three shared dispositions. They tended (i) to claim literal truth for their doctrines, which at best might be true in an allegorical sense. They tended (ii) to regard the doctrines of their respective faith-systems as true in an absolute sense, at the expense of all other doctrines, including those of philosophy. And they tended (iii) to adopt wrong ideas of the world, because religions rely on authority rather than on reasoning.

Schopenhauer argued that if religion is essentially the symbolic awareness of the same metaphysical reality which philosophy grasps in its proper sense, a religion must be better the more its fundamental doctrines resemble those of true (i.e., Schopenhauerian) philosophy. Not surprisingly, therefore, a religion would be better if it shared at least four pertinent features of Schopenhauer's philosophy. These include (i) retaining the distinction between an empirical world and a metaphysical one (in this Schopenhauer merely followed the dominant Western tradition, from Plato to Kant); (ii) acknowledging and retaining the metaphysical reality of "will," its ontological status, which is neither intelligent, nor good. In this, Schopenhauer's philosophy contradicted the very same major Western traditions which before him had embraced the distinction between an empirical and a metaphysical reality. To Schopenhauer, not only was the empirical world essentially suffering, but its suffering was based on the essence of metaphysical will as blind striving, expressed both in beings' coming into and sustaining their existence. The suffering we experience is self-imposed, from this point of view; therefore, it is guilt and punishment in one. A "better" religion, that is, one more consistent with Schopenhauerian principles, would also embrace (iii) the morality of compassion. Seeing through the empirical world's merely apparent character of multiplicity, and recognizing the metaphysical oneness of all representations (including oneself), the compassionate human being turns against the egoism of seeking his or her own advantage at the expense of all others. Finally, a religion symbolically attuned to Schopenhauerian principles would embrace a form of (iv) metaphysical pessimism. Since the striving of will essentially cannot be satisfied, there is no hope for a better life in this or in another world. This Schopenhauerian pessimism cannot be overcome by compassionate activities, but only by giving up all striving. This involves passing to a state of "holiness," which Schopenhauer described as quietist asceticism.

Apart from the fundamental weakness of all religions, then, Schopenhauer evaluated a religion more favorably the more it was dualistic and pessimistic; the more it recognized suffering and understood it as guilt and punishment in one; and the more it fostered compassion and tended to an ascetic renunciation of reality as such (understood as the apparent world).

Because Indian religions, in Schopenhauer's opinion, best exemplify all these features, he held them in the highest regard. At the other end of the spectrum, he placed national religions, like the ancient religions of Greece and Rome, religions that served political purposes and promised a better life. He considered Judaism and Islam nearly as bad, especially because of their ideas of creation ex nihilo as good and their promise of a better life. Christianity, however, Schopenhauer ranked much higher than its Near Eastern sister religions. While rejecting what he took to be the "optimistic" tendencies it shares with them, he praised some of its fundamental doctrines that better suited his own philosophy. These include the doctrine of hereditary (i.e., original) sin, the general need for redemption, suffering and death of the just (God) man, the morality of *caritas* (Christian love, which Schopenhauer understood as a kind of compassion), and Christianity's ascetic tendencies.[36]

One additional important reason for Schopenhauer's high regard for Hinduism and Buddhism was their mystical character. Schopenhauer was convinced that his philosophy, unprecedented in the dominant Western philosophical tradition, had given an adequate interpretation of mystical experience. He took pride in preserving mystical experience from fake objectifications. The crucial point, according to Schopenhauer, was that the mystical One was different from the unity of the empirical world. Instead, its essence was identical with the oneness of the metaphysical will. In contrast to the objects of the empirical world, the "object" of mystical experience was, rather, nothingness. But if we could take another point of view, this nothingness might turn out to be the true reality, compared to which "this world with all its suns and galaxies would be – nothingness."[37] However, since even our language is restricted to rendering the world as representation (the phenomenal world), we cannot adequately speak of this metaphysical "nothingness." Every attempt would falsify the core of mystical experience. Evident here is a second and decisive motive for Schopenhauer's sometimes harsh criticism of religion, besides his sympathy for Enlightenment objections to its dogmatic partisanship. In his view, the true but incommunicable reality of mystical experience should be defended against inadequate religious formulations.[38]

When Nietzsche read Schopenhauer for the first time, he had already abandoned Christianity, but he had not yet started to attack it. *The World as Will and Representation* helped him to clarify his attitude toward the religion of his youth. In his early writings he recapitulated much of Schopenhauer's philosophy of religion. Although he later rejected some parts of it, to a certain extent he never ceased to interpret Christianity along Schopenhauerian lines. To these constant Schopenhauerian presuppositions in Nietzsche's understanding of religion the following features belong above all: Because it is a religion, Christianity is essentially mythic. Therefore, its doctrines cannot be true in a strict sense, but, at best, require philosophical interpretation. Moreover, Nietzsche argued that Christianity most resembles Platonism, with which it shares a dualism which entails a devaluation of this world. Christianity – as he put it in *Twilight of the Idols* – is "Platonism for 'the People'." Further, Nietzsche regarded Christianity as a *pessimistic* religion, one which tends toward asceticism and, consequently, toward nihilism. Although agreeing with Schopenhauer that *caritas*, Christian love, is a form of compassion, Nietzsche reinterpreted it as a form of pity, which Nietzsche considered harmful to both the pitier and the pitied.

On other points Nietzsche turned against positions held by Schopenhauer. In his *Untimely Meditations*, for example, Nietzsche, too, traced philosophy and religion to a "metaphysical need" as its undeniable motivation, but he changed his view later on.[39] In addition, along with his later attacks on Christian anti-Semitism, whose adherents dreamed of an "Aryan Christianity," Nietzsche – unlike Schopenhauer – stressed the close connection between Christianity and Judaism. In this way he implicitly contradicted Schopenhauer's attempt to sever Christianity from Judaism as far as possible, both historically and logically.

Nor did the late Nietzsche share Schopenhauer's high regard for mysticism. For him, mystical experiences were by no means "deeper" than other ones, and he strongly denied that any insights whatsoever could be derived from them.[40]

Nietzsche's first argument against religions in general, and against Christianity in particular, relied on history. He argued that historical method and historical criticism of texts had rendered invalid the mythical presuppositions without which religions cannot survive. This argument appeared first in the notes, letters, and papers while he was still a Schulpforta pupil; and the mature philosopher defended this form of criticism through his very last writings and notes. The salient point of the argument is already stated clearly in the adolescent's essay *Fate and History* of 1862.[42] There he argued that historical research, especially in comparison with research in other areas, had turned central Christian doctrines into mere opinions. Traditional appeals to "the authority of the Holy Scripture," or to its "inspiration" and the like, had lost their credibility. When Nietzsche finally abandoned his theological studies, he referred again to arguments of this kind:

Every true faith is also infallible – it does accomplish what the respective faithful person hopes to gain from it. But it does not prepare a reference point whatsoever which could guarantee its objective truth. Here the paths of human beings part. If you prefer peace of mind and happiness, then better believe! But if you would like to be a disciple of truth, turn to research![43]

Historical criticism remained Nietzsche's most important argument against religion up to the beginning of the 1880s. Compared to the harsh attacks of his later writings, his early formulations were rather unpolemical in tone. Nietzsche confined himself to a skeptical attitude and did not claim that the falsity of the religious ideas and doctrines he rejected could be proven.[44] Nevertheless, he was quite outspoken in the conviction that nobody familiar with scholarly methods could any longer base his weal and woe on so a weak a foundation as that offered by religion. Starting with *Human, All Too Human*, Nietzsche pleaded for a new "historical philosophy" which was to replace "metaphysical philosophy." Metaphysics he now regarded as a mere substitute for religion; and he now came to regard Schopenhauer as the last metaphysical philosopher.

It may be objected that in his publications of the early 1870s, Nietzsche obviously did *not* favor historical criticism, but, on the contrary, rejected it as a "disease" of his time. Against the all-relativizing power of history, he seemed at this time to affirm "suprahistorical powers," among them religion, and even Christianity. "Set a couple of these modern biographers to consider the origin of Christianity or the Lutheran reformation: their sober, practical investigations would be quite sufficient to make all spiritual 'action at a distance' impossible."[45]

In this decade of the early 1870s, Nietzsche generally appealed to "culture," which he defined as "the unity of artistic style in all expressions of the life of a people."[46] Culture, he continued, needs an "unhistorical horizon," which hitherto had been provided by religions, philosophies, or art. Nothing great and no values could grow or endure in the absence of such a horizon; and unrestrained (historical) criticism would lead to barbarism, and ultimately human extinction, he thought at this time. Nietzsche's paradigm was the culture of fifth century B.C. Greece, a culture centered around tragedy. In contrast, Nietzsche's idea of barbarism was shaped by the Socratic enlightenment, which, in his view, had destroyed the Greeks' tragic attitude toward life. Richard Wagner's program of a "*Gesamtkunstwerk*" [complete artwork] would overcome the "Alexandrian" civilization that ever since had dominated the Western tradition, and it would become the foundation of a new culture. Much of this sort of argument is to be found in his first official book publication, *The Birth of Tragedy*.

During the first of the "*Bayreuther Festspiele*" [Bayreuth Festivals] in 1876, Nietzsche finally lost this hope. Looking back, he even denounced it and deplored the dishonesty of his earlier statements on religion and metaphysics.[47] According to this Nietzschean self-interpretation, he had never given up historical criticism, but had only put it aside for a time in order to help bring about a new (German) culture based on Wagnerian art and Schopenhauerian metaphysics.

Since this self-interpretation fits quite well with what we find in Nietzsche's books and notes from that decade, we need not speak of "dishonesty" on Nietzsche's part.[48] For he never *totally* rejected historical criticism, nor did he ever defend the unrestricted validity of "suprahistorical" projects. Even in his second *Untimely Meditation*, he did not maintain his original scheme of "historical illness" in opposition to "unhistorical health." The logic of the problem forced him to differentiate between *un*historical phenomena and *supra*historical ones, and to admit that being human necessarily comprises a certain amount of "historicity."[49] It is also true that Nietzsche no longer adhered to Schopenhauer's metaphysics when he praised the importance of "suprahistorical powers." For metaphysical beliefs, too, had fallen prey to his historical analysis. The evidence argues strongly, however, that he had begun to adopt and to deploy a form of F. A. Lange's "standpoint of the ideal," a neo-Kantian version of Kant's doctrine of ideas. This philosophical construct enabled him to utilize Schopenhauerian notions as fictitious but nevertheless useful unifying concepts. Nietzsche's appeals, for example, to the doctrines of "great human beings" or of religion as "metaphysics for the people" are obviously such "ideas."[50] This maneuver allowed him to advocate the growth of a new culture based on suprahistorical powers without denouncing the all-relativizing power of historical criticism.[51]

For some years Nietzsche adhered to this "standpoint of the ideal," but he seems to have felt more and more uneasy about it. Nevertheless, in his published works from *The Birth of Tragedy* onward, he defended the validity of the products of suprahistorical powers. But in his notes he left room for his doubts, at least regarding religion. In a note of the summer or fall of 1873 (we do not know the precise time frame) he put it this way: "Christianity as a whole is to be surrendered to critical history."[52]

Nietzsche made it quite clear that to adhere to a religion or to a philosophy of the metaphysical type were no longer options for him. Both – religion and conventional metaphysics – could, in his view, regain power only by a revival of myth, which he neither wished nor even regarded as possible. Historical method could not be rescinded – the less so since Christianity itself had adopted it, thus promoting its own self-dissolution. Like many a great movement, Christianity would, therefore, end in suicide.[53] "Historical refutation" remained for Nietzsche "the final refutation."

What is truth? – Who would not put up with an inference that believers like to draw: "Science cannot be true for it denies God; consequently it is not true, – for God is truth." The error is not contained within the inference but within the premise: what if God just were not truth, and if it were exactly that which was proven? if he were man's vanity, lust for power, impatience, and terror? If he were man's delighted and terrible delusion?[54]

GENEALOGICAL CRITICISM [55]

During the course of the 1880s, Nietzsche increasingly was *not* content with just "passing by" silently, as he once had urged.[56] Instead he wrote increasingly harsh and scathing attacks on Christianity, finally presenting himself as the "Antichrist" who pronounces the decisive "curse on Christianity," intent on rooting out this religion once and for all.

Why did he change his mind in this way, so dramatically and so drastically? A main reason seems to have been Christianity's inertia. Although historically outdated, it did not give way to new ideas. This problem had occurred to Nietzsche quite early, but he had put it aside for nearly a decade: "It is commendable now *to do away with the reminders of religious life* because they are faint and barren, and are likely to weaken devotion to a proper goal. Death to the weak!"[57]

Nietzsche began to suspect that even where new, secular ideas spread, they were not *really* new.[58] As Nietzsche later put it, he had made a "discovery," which he first published in *Daybreak*. According to this insight, morality remained at the foundation of the current expressions of "suprahistorical powers." Traditional Western religions and philosophies had so far been nothing but systematizations of a moral attitude. While they changed on the surface, this basic attitude remained the same and expressed itself in ever new forms.[59]

Nietzsche's famous fable of the "Madman" who announces that "God is dead" [*The Gay Science*, #125] primarily attacks the adherents of secularized versions of the old Christian moral ideal. The madman's listeners are surprised at and even mock his pronouncement of God's death. They themselves, convinced by historical criticism, are Christians no longer. They do not believe in any God whatsoever. However, in Nietzsche's opinion, they still retain the underlying morality of which Christianity is but one historical expression. Thus, they cannot understand the urgency of the madman's words, "this deed is still more distant from them than the most distant stars – and yet they have done it themselves."[60]

Nietzsche's increasingly polemical attacks on Christianity were intended to make people aware of the real meaning and consequences of "the death of God." Nietzsche insisted that his contemporaries must take up the task of a "revaluation of all values," a task which had become imminent as well as urgent. As in other areas of his philosophy, Nietzsche tried to accomplish his goal in several different ways. Some of the more important elements of his own attempted transvaluation of values included the following: First, he drew psychological profiles of the founders of religions to make obvious the gap between their doctrines and their real motives. Second, he uncovered the social developments that rendered possible or favored the growth of Christianity. Third, he rendered intelligible the psychological and physiological states likely to dispose individuals to accept Christian morality. Finally, fourth, he sketched states of mind that motivated interest in keeping this type of morality alive and stable, in whatever disguise. It does not follow from this that Nietzsche developed a conventionally systematic or coherent system of criticism. Indeed, it has sometimes been argued that Nietzsche's style of philosophizing made such a task impossible. He did not always draw the same conclusion in his various analyses. In *The Antichrist*, for example, he blamed Paul for being "the (true) founder of Christianity," while he cast others, among them Jesus, in that role in earlier texts.[61] When he spoke of a morality of the weak, he characterized the weak variously as "slaves," average human beings, weak people in general, etc.

Although Nietzsche consciously avoided systems, it was not his aim to speak in paradoxes or to contradict himself. Some basic themes occur now and again in his later works and establish, in effect, the framework of his genealogical criticism (his attack on Christianity's origins). Among these themes one finds that, first, historical criticism is a presupposition. Christianity must be analyzed genealogically, it is argued, because, although it has been outdated by historical criticism, it is still alive and flourishing in the form of a particular morality and absolutist moralistic impulse. Second, Nietzsche argued that resentment[62] is fundamental to Christian morality. As an antidote and in contrast, genealogical analysis tries to show that Christianity is only one form of the morality of "resentment," if it is historically the most important and virulent one. By the term "resentment" [*ressentiment*], Nietzsche designated a psychological disposition (although, according to his later analyses, this disposition is physiologically conditioned). It is motivated by weakness and the often self-deceptive lust for revenge. Resentment is essentially *reactive*, and it is this reactive character of any morality based on resentment (particularly of Christianity) that Nietzsche rejected.[63] Third, Nietzsche tended to argue in his mature years that the "strong" should despise Christianity. Since Christianity is based on "slave morality," it must be a point of honor for the "strong" to overcome it. For them it is "indecent" to still be Christians.[64] Fourth, the mature Nietzsche seemed to assert with regularity that religion is necessary primarily or solely for the weak. In order to fight the influence of Christianity, therefore, Nietzsche would have it be replaced by another religion – one which also appealed to the weak but was free of resentment. "A European Buddhism perhaps could not be dispensed with,"[65] Nietzsche asserts. A fifth recurring theme in the framework of his genealogical criticism is the insistence that the genealogical method should be applied to Christianity. At first glance it is not obvious to everyone that Christian and post-Christian morality and values are based on resentment. Nietzsche therefore developed a genealogical method, combining psychological and historical research as instruments for detecting this underlying and sustaining motivation. Perhaps a most controversial element in the framework of Nietzsche's genealogical critique is, sixth, the thesis that human beings are essentially will to power. In his genealogical analyses Nietzsche did not simply restate the methods of history and psychology that were prevalent in his era. Instead, he developed his own methods based on an epistemology and ontology of "the will to power."[66] He construed cognition (or knowledge) as interpretation by a "power-center" (the individual human being), and he held that the individual employs knowledge to manage its relations to other power-centers. Perhaps equally controversially, the mature Nietzsche seems to have argued consistently that the value and importance of cognitions depend not only, not even primarily, on an individual's intellectual capacity and degree of knowledge. Instead, they depend primarily on the force and courage of the "will to power" involved. Finally, eighth, Nietzsche's genealogical framework argued that because there is no "thing in itself," it makes no sense to ask whether his ontology corresponds to the way things really are. Crucial to Nietzsche's ontology is the (conscious or unconscious) attempt by a power-center to increase its power. One method for accomplishing an increase of power is to construct a convincing account of its origin, along with the origins of others. Such an account, if accepted, can serve to weaken the power of an enemy by presenting the enemy's origin as "human, all-too-human."[67]

THE GENESIS OF CHRISTIANITY OUT OF RESENTMENT[68]

In keeping with the tradition of modern political philosophy, Nietzsche started his analysis in On the Genealogy of Morals with a hypothetical reconstruction of the emergence of human society. He pictured two different groups of "Vormenschen" [proto-humans], the one a small but well organized "pack of blond beasts of prey, a conqueror and master race," the other "a populace perhaps tremendously superior in numbers but still formless and nomadic." Both of them still lived in the state of "semi-animal" consciousness, which means that they could and did act according to their impulses and drives.

Nietzsche was interested in the outcome of the conflict that would occur between these groups or, more aptly put, in the development that such a conflict would initiate.[69] In contrast to the other tales of primordial warriors, in Nietzsche's account the hitherto unorganized nomads did not either win or die, but instead they were subdued. They became slaves and could no longer act according to their own impulses, but had to act in accordance with their masters' will.

This slavery initiated a thoroughgoing transformation of the slaves' minds. In order to survive, they had to repress any immediate expression of their drives. Since these drives did not vanish, the slaves had to learn to change them, or rather to alter their direction. Nietzsche speaks of a process of "internalization" that took place. In terms of depth psychology, this painful process included "Triebverzicht" [drive denial], "Triebaufschub" [drive deferral], and, above all, "Triebverschiebung" [drive displacement]. By these means, the "interior sphere" of the human psyche grew, and by means of it the "Vormenschen" developed into human beings – our forefathers.

Thus, the slaves' original drives and impulses were not extirpated, but only redirected. When aggression, cruelty, lust for power, et cetera, could no longer be expressed directly, on penalty of death, these drives turned inward: "Almost everything we call 'higher culture' is based on the spiritualization and intensification of *cruelty* – this is my proposition; the 'wild beast' has not been laid to rest at all, it lives, it flourishes, it has merely become – deified."[70] The result of this transformation and internalization was *conscience*, which, under these circumstances, primarily made itself felt as *bad* conscience. Since this annoying inner tension[71] called for relief, the suffering slaves projected someone – or something – they could make responsible for their misery, specifically, a hostile demon. This identification of the responsible one called for a further step, the projection of someone else who is able and willing to fight and subdue the Fiend – namely, the supreme God.

In *On the Genealogy of Morals* Nietzsche ascribed only part of this religious project to the slaves themselves, who settled for a God of consolation and belief in future happiness in an afterlife.[72] From the "strong" among the slaves, however, there arose another, important type of human being. Those who had lost influence among their peers discovered the possibility of regaining power as leaders of the slaves.[73] These "ascetic priests" offered to the slaves a new scapegoat on which to blame their sufferings: their own sinfulness. Combined with the promise of redemption for those who believed in God, and in God alone, this interpretation became irresistible. Historically appearing first in Judaism and reformulated in the Christian tradition, it brought about the first "revaluation of values."[74] The new interpretation of the ascetic priests succeeded by inspiring the slaves with a strong "sense of power" ["*Gefühl der Macht*"] that finally enabled them to overcome even the "masters."[75]

One may ask, what was wrong with this interpretation in Nietzsche's view? Did it not, eventually, free the slaves? According to Nietzsche, exactly the contrary took place: This interpretation also enslaved the masters! The solution of the ascetic priests did not heal the disease of weakness. It worked and still works only as long as the weak are disposed to stay weak, and it only helps them to deal with their inner conflict.[76] Nietzsche understood himself as an "*Arzt der Kultur*" [physician of culture] who would break through this vicious circle. His new "revaluation of all values" aimed at replacing all moralities of the resentment type with a new, more sophisticated, master morality, a morality of self-expression.

DISCUSSION AND EVALUATION OF NIETZSCHE'S CRITIQUE OF RELIGION

Until the 1960s, most Christian authors dealing with Nietzsche's criticisms claimed that he had only a superficial knowledge of his subject.[77] This view is untenable, and has since been abandoned.[78] Of course, it is possible that Nietzsche's understanding of Christianity is problematic, if not false, or at least in need of correction in some respects. For example, there are good reasons to question whether Christianity was fundamentally an ascetic religion as Nietzsche, together with Schopenhauer and Overbeck, had maintained. Also, the general identification of Christian love with *"Mitleid"* [compassion or empathy construed as pity] remains problematic. At least, one should differentiate between a weak sense of *"Mitleid"* (understood as "pity"), which Nietzsche seems to have had in mind in his discussions, and an active *"Mitleid"* (understood as "compassion") that grows out of awareness of the evils of the world and motivates one to fight against them.[79]

There are other areas, however, in which Nietzsche grasped and criticized essential trends in Christianity precisely and perspicuously. Surely the development of Protestantism in our century exhibits many of the tendencies Nietzsche describes. Its liberal wing has to a large extent accepted the standards and findings of scholars and scientists, but this wing runs the risk of losing the specifically religious character of Christianity. By contrast, the adherents of fundamentalism tend toward falsity in their escapism into a kind of "double bind" consciousness, accepting the modern world's technology and premises, but at the same time maintaining ideas irreconcilable with this world view. These, along with comparable groups in other religions, fall prey to Nietzsche's criticism. If there are legitimate defenses of the Judaeo-Christian tradition against Nietzsche's attacks, the religions in question should confront and overcome his arguments.

Christian theology, at least in principle, has in the meantime attempted to integrate and overcome Nietzsche's type of critique. Christian churches have long defended themselves against historical criticism of Scripture.[80] But even in Nietzsche's lifetime, theologians and churches had learned to accept historical criticism. At least in the major Christian churches and denominations, including Roman Catholicism, nobody may enter the clergy without being familiar, at least, with the elements of historical criticism.

Nietzsche was aware of the beginning of this trend. He thought it would accelerate the decline of Christianity. However, theology and philosophy of religion have instead offered distinctions and models that allow them to claim the absolute truth of their faith in spite of the relativism of their respective expressions. Examples include Bultmann's construal of faith as one form of "being-in-the-world" (following Heidegger), and Hare's description of it as a "blik" (a significant kind of experience, but one which cannot be analyzed in cognitive terms).

The kernel of these and other theories is the distinction between faith as a fundamental perspective and the specific facts that are the subject of historical research. If faith pretends to report facts which are shown to be inaccuracies, it is rightly criticized by historical scholarship.[81] But from his own ontological presupposition of perspectivism, Nietzsche cannot simply reject the claim that faith may throw new light on given facts. Moreover, if there are no facts at all, as Nietzsche taught, but only interpretations,[82] what is wrong with a Christian scholar construing the *meaning* of historical events in terms of a specific Christian perspective? At least, Nietzsche should consent as long as Christian scholars identify the *historical actuality* of persons and events in accordance with the standards and methods of secular history.

Nietzsche was well aware of this, but it did not prevent him from rejecting Christianity. It was precisely the perspective of Christian faith – or, at least, what he took to be the distinctive perspective of the Judaeo-Christian tradition – that he rejected. Nevertheless, the concepts and models offered by modern theology have called into question Nietzsche's claim that raising historical consciousness has destroyed the foundation of any religion, including Christianity. Nietzsche may legitimately fight against Christian interpretations because they are *Christian*. But if he attacks them because they are *interpretations*, himself referring to the standards of historical scholarship, he contradicts his own philosophical insights.

Nietzsche's genealogical criticism of the Judaeo-Christian tradition presupposes that religion is dependent on morality, indeed that it is in some sense an expression of morality born of resentment. In this respect, it is a *reductionist* theory of religion.

Reductionist theories were common in the epoch of the Enlightenment. Young Schleiermacher, Hegel's older contemporary, was the first influential German philosopher-theologian who argued, in opposition to Kant's moral interpretation of religion, that such theories missed the core of religion. Ever since, a certain phenomenological approach has stressed the autonomy of religion. Such approaches tend to admit that religion permeates all areas of a culture and, in turn, is influenced by them. But they rightly add that religion is more than just a popular morality or science or the like. Religion is *experienced* by human beings in a specific way.[83] Those who adopt this "phenomenological" approach have not adopted one uniform hypothesis on the nature of religion or religious experience. But they have offered some arguments in favor of religion's autonomy and independence that are worth consideration.

Nietzsche's genealogies do more than claim that religion was dependent on morality, however. They argue critically that Christianity was the religious expression of a morality of resentment, a reactive morality that is hostile to life as such. To assess this charge it is advisable to distinguish between Nietzsche's description of resentment as a psychological attitude, on the one hand, and his suggestion that Judaeo-Christian religions are merely expressions of resentment. While the discovery of resentment in general has been an important psychological insight of lasting value, the association of Christianity with resentment remains problematic, as the German phenomenologist Max Scheler has rightly indicated.

A second distinction may also be helpful. Nietzsche is certainly right when he stresses that reactive responses such as envy, hatred, and resentment threaten to poison *all* areas of human relations, including religious interactions. We might even add that the religious area is especially prone to the impact of resentment. But it does not follow from this putative fact that the Judaeo-Christian tradition has from its very beginning been nothing but the outcome and expression of resentment.

NOTES

1 Therefore, in interpreting Nietzsche we must take his rhetoric into consideration. E. Biser has proposed a specific Nietzsche-hermeneutics especially for understanding the way he dealt with Christianity. See Biser, 1980, and Biser, 1982.

2 BGE, GM, AC, and others.

3 For a discussion of the meaning and role of *ressentiment* in Nietzsche's philosophy see Robert C. Solomon's essay in this volume.

4 Cf. EH, "Why I Am a Destiny."

5 Cf., for example, "How we, too, are still pious," GS, 5th book [1887!], #344. Nietzsche concludes his considerations as follows: "[. . .] you will have gathered [. . .] that even we [. . .] godless anti-metaphysicians still take our fire, too, from the flame lit by a faith that is thousands of years old, that Christian faith [. . .] that God is the truth, that truth is divine." [Translation by Walter Kaufmann.]

6 "Curse on Christianity" is the subtitle of AC. Cf. Salaquarda, 1973, 128ff.

7 Cf. especially Grau, 1958.

8 Cf. Bohley 1987, 1989; Pernet.

9 Cf. Janz, I, pp. 23–64.

10 Cf. especially BAW, I, p. 38: "Peace and quiet hovering over a parsonage, impressed their indelible traces in my mind, as may be recognized generally that the first impressions received by our psyche are the most imperishable ones." [My translation.]

11 EH, "Why I Am So Clever," 2 [my translation, for in the new Critical Edition by Colli and Montinari, the hitherto known #2 was replaced by another text, not yet known to Walter Kaufmann when he translated EH]. The same symbolic condensation and elevation of his father is to be found already in the boy's first notes. Of course, they pertain to his father–*image*, rather than his real father.

12 Cf. Deussen; H.-J. Schmidt, 1991, vol. I.

13 H.-J. Schmidt argues that Nietzsche already lost his faith in his childhood as a result of his beloved father's terrible suffering and premature death. Although Schmidt's painstaking reading of the poems and notes Nietzsche wrote at the age of ten to fourteen suggests that Nietzsche was already concerned with religious questions and problems as a boy, the material gives little support to his central hypothesis.

14 Cf. especially his reflections on *Fate and History* (BAW, II, pp. 54ff.).

15 Cf. #2 below.

16 Cf. #3 below.

17 EH, "Why I Am So Clever," #1 and #7. [Translation by Kaufmann.]

18 Letter to Overbeck, June 23, 1881. [My translation.]

19 PW, Fall 1886-Fall 1887: VIII, 2[96]. [My translation.]
20 Cf. Grau, 1958, 1972.
21 Cf. Nietzsche's letter to Rohde, February 28, 1875, in which he complained about the intentions of their common friend Romundt to convert to Roman Catholicism.
22 AC, 10. [My translation.]
23 Cf. MO, 226, where Nietzsche starts with contrasting Catholic "generosity" to Lutheran stubbornness, but ends by rejecting both traditions for dealing only with illusions.
24 D, 38; BGE, 52; etc. Cf. Kaufmann, pp. 298–300, and Lonsbach.
25 Cf. Figl, 1984, pp. 47–120.
26 This is evident, for example, in his awareness of the Christian roots of his anti-Christian criticism; or in his unmasking of secular forms of Christian morality; or in his sympathetic description of the emotions connected with prayer; and the like.
27 Cf. Nietzsche's first autobiography, BAW, I, pp. 8ff.
28 Cf. Kaempfert's voluminous evidence of the impact of biblical language on Nietzsche's work.
29 Cf. Hirsch, Bluhm.
30 Cf. Benz, Ernst, Figl, 1984, pp. 71ff.
31 See, for example, a study on Paul by the New Testament scholar H. Luedemann. (Cf. Salaquarda, 1974, English version, pp. 103ff.) See also the history of the Reformation by the Roman Catholic church historian J. Janssen.
32 The Antichrist, for example, shows not only the influence of Renan and Jacolliot, authors whom Nietzsche explicitly quoted, but also of Tolstoy, Dostoyevsky, Wellhausen, and others.
33 Cf. Goedert, 1978, Salaquarda, 1988, A. Schmidt.
34 Cf. especially The World as Will and Representation (hereafter noted as "WWR"), II, Chapter 17. [Quotations from that chapter are my translation.]
35 Nietzsche's "Platonism for 'the people' " (BGE, Preface [translated by R. J. Hollingdale]) might be a free adaptation of this phrase.
36 Schopenhauer stressed the spiritual similarities of Hinduism and Buddhism, on the one hand, and Christianity, on the other. He also hoped that scholars someday would find evidence for a historical connection between the traditions. Cf. Salaquarda, 1992.
37 WWR, I, end of 4th book.
38 When Wittgenstein, who had carefully read WWR in his youth, expressed the famous "Schweigegebot" [precept of silence] at the end of his Tractatus, he may have been recalling this Schopenhauerian conclusion. Cf. Clegg.
39 Cf. SE, 5, with GS, 151, where he derives "metaphysical need" from

religion that had become habitual. (Metaphysical) philosophy he now regarded as a compensation that flourished in the relatively short period between the end of religious belief and the end of expectations earlier premised on that belief.

40 Cf., for example, HAH, 8.
41 Cf. Grau, 1958, Figl, 1982 (2), pp. 54–73.
42 BAW, II, pp. 54–9.
43 Letter to Elisabeth Nietzsche, June 11, 1865. [My translation.]
44 Cf., for example, HAH, 9.
45 UAH, 7. [Translated by A. Collins.]
46 DS, 1. [My translation.]
47 Cf., especially, PW, Fall 1883: VII, 16[23].
48 At least not as a conscious dishonesty, although it may have been what Sartre called "*mauvaise foi*" [bad faith].
49 A phenomenon that Heidegger later called "*Geschichtlichkeit.*"
50 Cf. Stack, Salaquarda, 1978.
51 In UAH, 9, Nietzsche confessed that he regarded the relativity of all things and opinions as "true," but also as "fatal." This statement best shows his inner conflict.
52 III, 29[203] . [My translation.]
53 Cf., for example, BT, 11.
54 D, 93. [My translation.]
55 Cf. Goedert, 1978; Grau, 1958: Figl, 1982 (1), 1982 (2), pp. 73-83; Valadier.
56 Za, III, "On Passing By." In PW, Summer-Fall 1973: III, 29[203], Nietzsche wrote: "what is called for seems to be only a thoughtful and due abstinence; by it I honor religion though it is dying." [My translation.]
57 PW, 1871: III, 9[94]. [My translation.]
58 Cf. Mueller-Lauter, pp. 81–94 ("*Nihilismus und Christentum*").
59 For example, in the nineteenth century's Christianity, which Nietzsche despised no less than Tolstoy and Kierkegaard had done; or in liberalism, socialism, the cult of the State, etc.
60 GS, 125. [Translation by W. Kaufmann.] Cf. GS, 108.
61 Cf. Salaquarda, 1973, English version, pp. 103–10.
62 Nietzsche developed this conception in GM, First Essay. Cf. Scheler.
63 In his "Law against Christianity," which was originally to be the end of *The Antichrist*, Nietzsche announced along the way: "Fight until death to corruption [*Laster*]. Christianity is corruption." (KGW, VI/3, p. 252.) [My translation.]
64 AC, 55. [My translation.] See also sections that follow.
65 PW, May-July, 1885: VII, 35[9]. [My translation.] See also sections that follow.
66 Cf. the pioneering study by Mueller-Lauter.

67 Cf. the three types of "history so far as it serves (human) life," which Nietzsche had described in his second *Untimely Meditation*. The genealogies of his later writings involve what he there terms "critical history." He had claimed of critical history that although "it is not justice that sits in judgment here [. . .] it would generally turn out the same if Justice herself delivered it [. . .]": UAH, 3. [Translation by A. Collins.]

68 Cf. GM, Second Essay, Sections 16–25. [Translation by W. Kaufmann.]

69 There are striking parallels to Hegel and Marx's famous "master-slave dialectics." Cf. Wandel, pp. 65–85.

70 BGE, 229. [Translation by R. J. Hollingdale.]

71 Closely related to what Freud later called "the uneasiness in culture."

72 This reminds one of Marx's dictum concerning religion as an "opium of/ for the people."

73 As a crucial historical example, Nietzsche presents the religious leaders of the exiled Jews in the fifth century, B.C.

74 BGE, 46. See also the sections that follow.

75 Cf., for example, the image of the "cage of concepts" by which the Teutonic nobility was weakened (TI, "The 'Improvers' of Mankind").

76 Stated in terms of depth psychology again: The adherent of a religion of resentment is a neurotic who has become comfortable with his neurosis and resists therapy. Cf. Freud's interpretation of religion as "collective neurosis" in *The Future of an Illusion*.

77 Cf. Köster; Willers, pp. 22–32.

78 Cf. Barth, as an early example. The works of Biser, Figl, Köster, Willers, Valadier, and others present examples of Christian interpretations that take Nietzsche's criticisms seriously.

79 Schopenhauer himself had already pointed out this difference. (Cf. Goedert, 1977.) That it might be helpful in the case of Nietzsche, too, was first suggested by J. Stambaugh.

80 Islam maintains this defense to the present day. Some fundamentalist tendencies in Judaism and Christianity follow the same line.

81 In AC, 51, Nietzsche ironically alludes to Cor. I, 13, 2: While faith is not able to move mountains, it is well able to set down mountains where none are.

82 PW, End of 1886–Spring 1887: VIII, 7[60].

83 Cf. the relevant studies from R. Otto to M. Eliade.

BIBLIOGRAPHY

Abbreviations

BT   Birth of Tragedy
DS   David Strauss, the Confessor and the Writer

UAH   On the Use and Abuse of History
SE   Schopenhauer as Educator
HAH   Human, All too Human
MO   Mixed Opinions . . .
D   Dawn
GS   Gay Science
Za   Thus Spoke Zarathustra
BGE   Beyond Good and Evil
GM   On the Genealogy of Morals
TI   Twilight of the Idols
AC   The Antichrist
EH   Ecce Homo
PW   Posthumous Writings
      (Quotations are established by time of origin, and by part and ms. –
      numbers from the KGW; e.g. PW Fall 1883: VII 25[204])
BAW   Beck-Ausgabe, Werke (5 vols. of Nietzsche's early notes)
KGW   Kritische Gesamtausgabe, Werke, ed. Colli and Montinari

Quotations from *letters* are established by naming the receiver and the date.

Ausmus, H. J. "Nietzsche and Eschatology," in: JR 58/1978, 347–64.
Baeumer, M. L. "Nietzsche and Luther: A Testimony to Germanophilia," in *Nietzsche and the Judaeo-Christian Tradition*, 143–60.
Balkenohl, M. *Der Antitheismus Nietzsches: Fragen und Suchen nach Gott*. Paderborn, 1976.
Barth, Karl. *Kirchliche Dogmatik* III/2, Zürich, 1979, 276–93. Trans. by G. W. Bromiley and T. F. Torrence as "Humanity without the Fellow-Man: Nietzsche's Superman and Christian Morality," in *Nietzsche and the Judaeo-Christian Tradition*, 353–74.
Benz, E. *Nietzsches Ideen zur Geschichte des Christentums und der Kirche*, Leiden, 1956.
Biser, E. "Gott ist tot." *Nietzsches Destruktion des christlichen Bewusstseins*, München, 1962.
    Gottsucher oder Antichrist? Nietzsches provokante Kritik des Christentums, Salzburg, 1982.
    "Das Desiderat einer Nietzsche-Hermeneutik," in *Nietzsche-Studien* 9/1980, 1–37.
    "Nietzsche: Critic in the Grand Style," trans. by T. F. Sellner, in *Nietzsche and the Judaeo-Christian Tradition*, 16–28.
    "The Critical Imitator of Jesus: A Contribution to the Interpretation of Nietzsche on the Basis of a Comparison," trans. by T. F. Sellner, in *Nietzsche and the Judaeo-Christian Tradition*, 86–99.

(Hg.): *Besieger Gottes und des Nichts. Nietzsches fortdauernde Provokation*, Düsseldorf, 1982.

Blondel, E. "Der christliche Antichrist. Zu Nietzsches Religionskritik," in *Dem Nichts entkommen*, 42–67.

Bluhm, H. "Das Lutherbild des jungen Nietzsche," in PMLA 58, 1943, 264–88.

"Nietzche's Idea of Luther in *Menschliches, Allzu-menschliches*," in PMLA 65, 1950, 1053–68.

"Nietzsche's View of Luther and the Reformation in *Morgenröte und Fröhliche Wissenschaft*," in PMLA 68, 1953, 111–27.

"Nietzsche's Final View of Nietzsche and the Reformation," PMLA 71, 1956, 75–83.

Bohley, R. "Über die Landesschule zur Pforte. Materialien aus der Schulzeit Nietzsches," in *Nietzsche-Studien* 5/1976, 298-320.

"Nietzsches Taufe," in *Nietzsche-Studien* 9/1980, 383–405.

"Nietzsches christliche Erziehung I," in *Nietzsche-Studien* 16/1987, 164–96.

"Nietzsches christliche Erziehung II," in *Nietzsche-Studien* 18/1989, 377–95 (= Bohley 4).

Bucher, R. *Nietzsches Mensch und Nietzsches Gott. Das Spätwerk als philosophisch-theologisches Programm*, Frankfurt am Main, 1986.

Clegg, J. S. "Logical Mysticism and the Cultural Setting of Wittgenstein's *Tractatus*," in 59. *Schop.-Jb.*, 1987, 29–47.

Copleston, F. C. "St. Thomas and Nietzsche" (The Aquinas Papers 2), London, 1944, 1955.

Deussen, P. *Erinnerungen an Fr. Nietzsche*, Leipzig, 1901.

Dibelius, M. "Der 'psychologische typus des Erlösers' bei Fr. Nietzsche," in DVLG 22/1974, 61–91.

Düringer, A. *Nietzsches Philosophie und das heutige Christentum*, Leipzig, 1907.

Ernst, J. "Quellen zu Nietzsches Christentumspolemik," in ZRG 4/1952.

Figl, J. "Interpretation als philosophisches Prinzip. Fr. Nietzsches universale Theorie der Auslegung im späten Nachlass (MTNF 7)," Berlin, 1982 (1).

"Die Religion als Kulturphänomen – Gegenstand der Kritik Nietzsches," in Biser (ed.), *Besieger Gottes und des Nichts*, 1982 (2), 52–83.

Dialektick der Gewalt. Nietzsches hermeneutishe Religionsphilosophie, Düsseldorf, 1984.

Goedert, G. *Nietzsche. Critique des valeurs chrétiennes. Souffrance et compassion*, Paris, 1977.

"Nietzsche und Schopenhauer," in *Nietzsche-Studien* 7/1978, 1–26.

Grau, G.-G. *Christlicher Glaube und intellektuelle Redlichkeit. Eine religionsphilosophie Studie über Nietzsche*, Frankfurt, 1958.

"Nietzsche und Kierkegaard. Wiederholung einer Unzeitgemässen Betrachtung," in *Nietzsche-Studien* 1/1972, 297–333. Trans. by W. Rader as "Nietzsche and Kierkegaard," in *Nietzsche and the Judaeo-Christian Tradition*, 226–51.

Hirsch, E. "Nietzsche und Luther," in *Jahrbuch der Luther-Gesellschaft* 2/3, 1921/22, 61–106.

Hohmann, W. L. *Zu Nietzsches Fluch auf das Christentum oder warum wurde Nietzsche nicht fertig mit dem Christentum* (Kl. Arbeiten z.Phil. 2), Essen, 1984.

Janz, C. P. *Nietzsche-Biographie*, 3 Bände, München, 1978/79.

Jaspers, Karl *Nietzsche und das Christentum*, Hameln, 1938.

Kaempfert, M. *Säkularisation und neue Heiligkeit. Religiöse und religionsbezogene Sprache bei Fr. Nietzsche* (Phil. Studien und Quellen 61), Berlin 1971.

Kaftan, J. *Das Christentum und Nietzsches Herrenmoral*, Berlin, 1897, 1902.

Kaufmann, W. *Nietzsche: Philosopher – Psychologist – Antichrist*, Princeton University Press, 1974.

Köster, P. *Der sterbliche Gott. Nietzsches Entwurf übermenschlicher Grösse* (MzphF 103), Meisenheim am Glan, 1972.

"Nietzsche-Kritik und Nietzsche-Rezeption in der Theologie des 20. Jahrhunderts," in *Nietzsche-Studien* 10–11/1981–2, 615–85.

Lauret, B. *Schulderfahrung und Gottesfrage bei Nietzsche*, München, 1977.

Ledure, Y. *Nietzsche et la religion de l'incroyance*, Paris, 1973.

Lectures "chrétiennes" de Nietzsche. Maurras, Papini, Scheler, de Lubac, Marcel, Mounier, Paris, 1984.

Lonsbach, R. M. *Nietzsche und die Juden. Ein Versuch*, Bonn, 1985.

Löwith, K. "Nietzsches antichristliche Bergpredigt," in *Club Voltaire* 1, München, 1963, 81–95.

"Die Auslegung des Ungesagten in Nietzsches Wort 'Gott ist tot,' " in: ders. *Heidegger – Denker in dürftiger Zeit*, Göttingen, 1965, 72–105.

Von Hegel zu Nietzsche. Der revolutionäre Bruch im Denken des 19. Jahrhunderts, Hamburg, 1978. Trans. by D. E. Green as *From Hegel to Nietzsche: The Revolution in Nineteenth Century Thought*, New York, 1964, London, 1965.

Magnus, Bernd. "Jesus, Christianity, and Superhumanity," in *Nietzsche and the Judaeo-Christian Tradition*, 295–318.

Margreiter, R. *Ontologies und Gottesbegriffe bei Nietzsche* (MzphF 160), Meisenheim am Glan, 1978.

Mueller-Lauter, W. *Nietzsche. Seine Philosophie der Gegensätze und die Gegensätze seiner Philosophie*, Berlin – New York, 1971.

Nelson, D. F. "Nietzsche, Zarathustra, and Jesus redivivus: The Unholy Trinity," in *GermR* 48/1973, 175–88. *Nietzsche and the Judaeo-Christian*

Tradition, ed. by J. C. O'Flaherty, T. F. Sellner, and R. M. Helm, Chapel Hill and London, 1985.

Pfeil, H. *Von Christus zu Dionysos. Nietzsche religiöse Entwicklung*, 1948, Meisenheim am Glan, 1975.

Rittelmeyer, F. Fr. *Nietzsche und die Religion*, München, 1907, 1920.

Salaquarda, J. "Der Antichrist" in *Nietzsche-Studien* 2/1973, 91–136.

"Dionysos gegen den Gekreuzigten. Nietzsches Verständis des Apotels Paulus," in: ZRG 26/1974, 97–124. Trans. by T. F. Sellner as "Dionysus versus the Crucified One: Nietzsche's Understanding of the Apostle Paul," in *Nietzsche and the Judaeo-Christian Tradition*, 100–29.

"Schopenhauer und die Religion," in: 69, *Schopenhauer-Jahrbuch* 1988, 321–32.

"Nietzsches Metaphysikkritik und ihre Vorbereitung durch Schopenhauer," in *Krisis der Metaphysik*, hg. von G. Abel and J. Salaquarda, Berlin and New York, 1989.

"Studien zur Zweiten Unzeitgemässen Betrachtung," in *Nietzsche-Studien* 13, 1984, 1–45.

"Lange und Nietzsche", in *Nietzsche-Studien* 7, 1978, 235ff.

"Beiträge Schopenhauers zur Religionswissenschaft," in Luethi/Kreuzer (eds.), *Zur Aktualität des Alten Testaments*, Frankfurt am Main et al., 1992, 249–58.

Scheler, M. "Das *Ressentiment* im Aufbau der Moralen," in Derselbe, *Vom Umsturz der Werte. Abhandlungen und Aufätze*, Bern, 1955, 33–147.

Schmidt A. *Die Wahrheit im Gewande der Lüge. Schopenhauers Religionsphilosophie*, Frankfurt, 1986.

Schmidt, H. J. "Fr. Nietzsche: Philosophie als Tragödie," in *Grundprobleme der grossen Philosophen*, hg. von J. Speck: Neuzeit III, Göttingen, 1983, 198–241.

Nietzsche Absconditus oder Spurenlesen bei Nietzsche, 2 vols., Berlin, 1991.

Shapiro, G. "Nietzsche contra Renan," in *Historical Theology* 21, 1982, 193–222.

Splett, J. "Dionysos gegen den Gekreuzigten. Philosophische Vorüberlegungen zur christlichen Antwort auf die Herausforderung Fr. Nietzsches," in ThPh 50, 1975, 161–82.

Stack, G. J. *Lange and Nietzsche* (MTNF 10), Berlin and New York, 1983.

Stambaugh, J. "Thoughts on Pity and Revenge," in *Nietzsche-Studien* 1/1972, 27–35.

Taureck, B. "Nihilismus und Christentum. Ein Beitrag zur philosophischen Klärung von Nietzsches Verhältnis zum Christentum," in WissWeltb 26, 1973, 115–33.

Valadier, P. *Nietzsche et la critique du christianisme*, Paris, 1974.

"Dionysus Versus the Crucified," trans. by K. Wallace, in *The New Nietzsche*, ed. by D. B. Allison, Cambridge and London, 1985, 247–61 (= Valadier 2).

Willers, U. *Fr. Nietzsches antichristliche Christologie. Eine theologische Rekonstruktion*, Innsbruck/Wien, 1988.

4 Nietzsche's political misappropriation

Il faut être absolument moderne. [It is necessary to be absolutely modern.] (Arthur Rimbaud)

There is nothing for it: one *must go forward*, that is *step by step further into decadence*. (F. Nietzsche, "For the Ear of Conservatives," *Twilight of the Idols*)

Other world! There is no other world! Here or nowhere is the whole fact. (R. W. Emerson)

I want to write here about the political uses made of Nietzsche, about what Nietzsche says about politics (broadly understood), and about the politics of reading and writing about Nietzsche. Twenty-five years ago few people would have cared. Nietzsche was a minor figure, stimulating to adolescents, without rigor, a bit silly. Now he is a minor industry in the intellectual professions. Everyone is writing about Nietzsche, some their third or fourth book. Articles appear everywhere: The bastions and inner walls of the most analytic redoubts have fallen; journals of literature both learned and popular vie for text. Nietzsche seems inexhaustible – he is available, it seems, to everyone. Everything in Nietzsche seems living. Yet if everything is living, everything about Nietzsche also seems fragile.

I want also to say something here about the various claims that have been made on Nietzsche. I do not want so much to argue that Nietzsche is or is not the ally of a particular political persuasion as much as to investigate why he lends himself to such a wide range of positions, and what it means about a writer that he can be subject to so many varying claims of political allegiance. Most importantly, I wish to raise the question of what it means for a writer, such as Nietzsche, to resist the currently available political identities.

NIETZSCHE ON POLITICS

With this in mind let us look first to what Nietzsche actually says about politics and the political. Three broad themes appear.[1] Nietzsche makes statements about contemporary political situations; he denies that morality can serve as the basis for building a society; and he attempts to analyze the nature of political identity.

First are the specific things that Nietzsche says about obviously political matters. Here his opinions, while more complex than often thought, are not of particular philosophical importance. Most contemporary politics is characterized for Nietzsche, as it would be for Weber, by the absence of rule or political leadership. "All herd and no shepherd." Nietzsche in turn links this situation to the increasingly generalized democratization of social relationships, a phenomenon that like J. S. Mill and de Tocqueville he saw as the central social phenomenon of his time. This is itself then related to the rise of socialism, a phenomenon that Nietzsche sees as a necessary further step in the evolution of slave morality.[2]

Western political and social development is of a basic piece for Nietzsche, at least since the revolutions in the politics of epistemology and interpretive authority effectuated by Socrates and Christ. Against the idea that social and political positions should be morally justified, Nietzsche reasserts one of his central claims: Social positions are not the result of desert, that is they cannot rest on a moral claim of justification. "No one deserves his happiness, no one his unhappiness."[3]

Here it is important to note that Nietzsche's wishes are not just for a leader, as if any leader would do and that people simply needed to be commanded.[4] In fact one of the greatest dangers that Nietzsche sees in the contemporary world is the existence of "leaders" who stand aloof from their political world and instrumentally manipulate it for their own ends. As the modern state becomes transformed from the arena of power (such as it had been in pre-Socratic Greece) into an instrument of power, Nietzsche asserts, a new kind of rationally choosing human being arises to make use of this tool. Armed with Socratic abstractions and self-consciousness, such individuals stand essentially outside the horizon of any community. Those who possess this instrumental self-consciousness can begin to manipulate the state for their own ends and will find themselves part of it only insofar as it is coincident with their own instincts. They use politics. In his early essay "The Greek State" Nietzsche writes:

In considering the political world of the Hellenes, *I will not hide those developments of the present in which I fear dangerous atrophies of the political sphere.* If there should exist men who through birth, as it were, should be placed outside the cultural (*Volks*) and state instinct . . . then such men will find their ultimate political aim to be the most peaceful coexistence possible of large communities, in which they will be permitted their own purpose without resistance.[5]

Such individuals tend to destroy politics and it is clear that Nietzsche finds fault in and with them. In the world in which he grew up, for instance, Nietzsche soon gives up his youthful admiration of Bismarck and comes to see the Iron Chancellor as a traitorous new Alcibiades.[6] On July 19, 1870, he writes to his closest friend Erwin Rohde that the Franco-Prussian war is disastrous, a judgment that will be finalized in his last letter, written to Jakob Burckhardt with one foot already into insanity, proclaiming that he is having Wilhelm, Bismarck, and all the anti-Semites shot."[7] Later, in the asylum, he will see one of the doctors as Bismarck.

Bismarck is emblematic for Nietzsche of the instrumentalization of the political instinct. In the *Birth of Tragedy*, Nietzsche had accused Euripides of producing an art that was "essentially an echo of his own conscious knowledge," in which the *agon* (contest or competition) itself served to reinforce the imposed order.[8] Bismarck, I might say, works in the same manner in the politics of Nietzsche's time. The resolution of the Schleswig-Holstein crisis (a dispute over who was to govern the disputed duchies of Schleswig and Holstein, a dispute which was resolved in Bismarck's favor) depended on Bismarck's convincing the Austrians to accept his particular narrative of events (which held that failure by the Austrians to yield to Bismarck's demands would enhance the cause of Socialism in a manner ultimately destructive of the Austrian empire). Like Euripides' resolution of tragic plots by means of the *deus ex machina* and "divine truthfulness," Bismarck had "guaranteed the plot" in a prologue to the action – his warnings to the Austrians of the consequences of refusing him.[9]

Nietzsche's second theme is that moral or ethical claims cannot provide the grounding for a society. Whatever a society might rest on, it cannot be a philosophical (specifically ethical) argument. Nietzsche does not, however, here join the position of a number of modern "communitarians" to the effect that society rests on a "thick" historically accreted understanding of persons-in-context.[10] Rather, he argues that moral systems are based on and derive from power relations, from politics.

This is made quite explicit in the *On the Genealogy of Morals*. In the first essay, Nietzsche sketches two moral systems reflecting structures of domination.[11] Master morality rests on a nonreflective assertion of self. The master says: "I am good, you are not like me and you are bad." "Character is destiny" in this morality. It was perfectly possible for very different persons, even enemies, to think of themselves and each other as good, even in combat.[12] The weak (not yet psychologically slaves) suffer from their domination by the unreflective masters. Not liking their suffering, they attempt to alleviate it by introducing reflection into their world – and the master's world as well. Henceforth the oppressing master will feel the need to respond to the question of "why" he oppressed. And with this a new moral configuration is introduced into the world. This one is premised upon the ability to give reasons to legitimate one's actions: one should deserve what one gets.

Slave morality – which is what now is established – is thus not simply the power inverse of master morality. It has a completely different logic. It rests on the following argument: "You oppress me and are thus evil; I am the opposite from you and am thus good." What is central here is that the identity of the slavely moral person rests on two matters. First, it is the dialectical negation of the oppression of the (once) master. Second, for it to be possible, for it to have a result, oppression has to continue to be present in the life of the slavely moral person. A threat is necessary. Nietzsche proceeds in the rest of *Genealogy* to show how the slave guarantees that s/he will be sufficiently oppressed to retain a sense of identity, of who he or she "is."

With this said, the question then becomes what is "atrophied" about modern politics. Relations of power, it appears, are at the foundation of any claim to "identity." From his first work, *The Birth of Tragedy*, Nietzsche had as one of his concerns and purposes the exploration of what one might call a politics of identity. (I shall postpone investigation of the *Birth* until a little later.) By "identity" I mean here something like what Nietzsche means when he is concerned with what it means to be, say, German. Or, as he asks at one point, "How is it possible to be Greek?" Identity is what Nietzsche refers to as the "internal connection and necessity of any true civilization" or the "dominant unity, let us call it the Hellenic will [of the Greeks]."[13] In a formal sense, I might say that I have a political identity when I can use the first person plural and first person singular pronouns to refer to the same state, when the question who are we and the question who am I are answered in the same way.[14]

If, as is the case with slave morality, one's political identity is premised upon negation, upon being the opposite of what it is not, then the nothingness at the core of that identity will eventually hollow itself out and produce the condition that Nietzsche calls "nihilism."[15] Nihilism is the state in which a being has the need to call itself continually into question, to raise continually the question of the grounds of its existence, without anything being able to count as such grounds. The last sentence of *Genealogy* claims that modern slavely moral man would rather "will the void than be void of will." That is, he will continue to exist with an identity that is premised on no-thing, rather than not exist at all.

The will is the faculty that humans have to shape the world in their own image (as memory is the way we shape the past). It is thus a particularly serious problem in modernity, since the modern will is fundamentally nihilistic. And if, as Nietzsche contends, the modern will is nihilistic, then modern politics (by which any world is established and maintained), is itself all the more nihilistic.[16] If any book is to characterize modern politics aptly, it will have to address this condition of nihilism, in the manner that *Genealogy* is premised on the fact that there is something to say about morality. If for Nietzsche the problem is to effectuate a transfiguration on the scale of that wrought by humans coming together to live in cities,[17] then what is there that can be said about the contemporary world that contains sense?

It is to the efforts to resolve this question, to figure out what sense Nietzsche meant, that we owe the multitude of readings of Nietzsche and politics. Is the diversity of claims to Nietzsche so vast that not everyone can be correct in their reading? And indeed meta-interpretations, classifications of interpretations, have arisen.[18] Does anything go? (Does heaven know who owns Nietzsche's text?) Indeed, in an age when for some the proclamation that "there is nothing outside the text" might pass as a rallying banner, to speak of "misappropriation" of a text might seem old-fashioned. For if there is nothing outside the text, then all appropriations might seem equally legitimate.

The denial of an *hors-texte* is generally taken to be the denial of independent criteria by which to judge the accuracy or validity of a reading. It seems to license any reading. Without here deciding whether or not this particular critique is valid,[19] I must note that in any case this view does not get us very far. Maybe, nothing goes. For, if all readings are valid, then all are also equally invalid.

Thus, if we wish to approach the problem of the political misappropriation of Nietzsche, or at least to investigate what that would mean, we will need to understand first what it means to appropriate or misappropriate a text. So the first question here has to be what is (mis)appropriation?

The second question is similar: What is a political misappropriation? Whatever a misappropriation is, are all misappropriations political? Is all interpretation politics, that is the imposition of power and control? We also need to know what would make a reading a political reading, that is, what are the criteria by which one might judge that a particular (mis)appropriation is political?

All of these questions are made more complex by the warnings with which Nietzsche surrounds his texts. Nietzsche warns his readers that trying to understand his texts will lead to a self-referring (perhaps frustrating, but more likely self-enhancing) exercise. He writes: "Whoever thought he had understood something of me, had made up something out of me after his own image . . . and whoever had understood nothing of me denied that I needed to be considered at all."[20] The indication here is that the texts work in such a way as to confirm the readings that readers want to make of them. As long as one seeks to treat Nietzsche's texts, in other words, as containers of meaning to be opened and shown around, the only sense one makes of them will be precisely that, one's own sense.[21]

These questions can be considered quickly here, as we will be coming back to them. The Latin root, *proprius*, carries with it connotations not only of property, but also of proper, stable, assured, and indeed of common or ordinary. I have appropriated something when I have made it mine, in a manner that I feel comfortable with, that is in a manner to which the challenges of others will carry little or no significance. A text, we might then say, is appropriated when its reader does not find him or herself called into question by it, but does find him or herself associated with it. A successfully appropriated text no longer troubles the appropriator that it has become part of his or her understanding, and it is recognized by others as "owned," not openly available for interpretation.

One might go on to say that a text is *politically* appropriated when its reader can shamelessly use it to do something, to further an argument or a position; when, in other words, the text can be called on as an authority in an argument or a struggle. The claim that a text has been politically misappropriated is a claim that the aims to which it is being put are illegitimate, or untrue to the meaning or sense of text. The claim of misappropriation, as well as that of appropriation, thus always rests on a claim that the question of the sense of the text can be resolved. A text could be successfully appropriated, but then politically misappropriated, that is, applied in an unwarranted manner.

The question of appropriation makes reference to the ownership of the meaning of a text. But a text must also be looked at in terms of its activity, not "just" its meaning. The activity of a text is not the same as its meaning. "Activity" refers rather to what kinds of responses the text requires of its readers. Some compositions, for instance some by John Cage, require from their listeners the question "Is this music?" The Holocaust, similarly, demands that we ask "why" (and at the same time denies us an answer that satisfies).[22] So our question with Nietzsche's texts must, at least eventually, be "What do they do to their readers?" And the subsequent question will then be what the politics – if any – of such activity might be.

THE POLITICS OF READING NIETZSCHE

With this in mind we turn to Nietzsche's texts. Two additional questions appear. First, many "political" readings of Nietzsche do exist: what is their legitimacy? Second, of all, or perhaps like all, great thinkers, Nietzsche has been claimed as company by a very wide range of would-be disciples. Despite the fact that he again and again tried to distance himself from would-be disciples, there is apparently no limit as to who can claim him as a forerunner. Thus we must also ask: What it is about Nietzsche's writings that permits such use? As will be clear in the rest of this essay, I am not ultimately interested in the questions "Who owns Nietzsche?" or "Who are Nietzsche's legitimate and bastard children?" Instead, I am interested in asking what it means to ask such questions. Indeed, I want to argue that Nietzsche's writing serves to break the hold that such claimed genealogies might have on us.

To speak of the "problem" of the political misappropriation of Nietzsche is to run the risk of implying that there is a "correct" appropriation. It appears to imply that Nietzsche might be thought as "on the side" of one or another political group, in the way that one would think of Edmund Burke as a man of the right and Marx as a man of the left.

Let me begin by being crude. Our (Western) political categories today derive their dimensions from the French Revolution (left–center–right) and these correspond loosely to a different understandings of the mixture of state power and educated will required to effectuate a given policy. Different combinations have given rise to different "ism's": liberalism, republicanism, conservatism, libertarianism, anarchism, and so forth. By and large when we speak of a political position or identity, these are the categories that we use. The problem of the political (mis)appropriation of Nietzsche thus must proceed first in terms of these categories.

In the contemporary English speaking world, Nietzsche is often claimed by those who see themselves on the progressive democratic (left) side of the political spectrum. Some of the reasons for these claims are historical. Many of those – I include myself to some degree among them – who first took Nietzsche seriously in the 1960s and early 1970s found in him a voice for liberation, indeed for the transfiguration of the drab world which we then felt ourselves inheriting. We were a generation who had not experienced directly the horrors of the Second World War. We were a generation for whom the civil rights movement and the new youth and student movements promised the possibility of dramatic change in society. We were a generation for whom the battles of communism and anticommunism were no longer particularly important.[23] That we were against fascism[24] went without saying or, indeed, thought. Being against communism, at least in the United States, was not an issue in a time when over 50 percent of the members of the American Communist Party were paid FBI informers. There were structures of power in place, but the reality of the political categories to which they corresponded was severely attenuated. (The "Red Scare" campaigns of the 1950s in America thus appeared as an attempt to relegitimate power structures.)

The point here is that most of the significant initial approaches to Nietzsche in the English-speaking world[25] took place, by and large, in a context in which the saliency of the political forms and categories that had governed the previous forty years had begun to relax. New, exciting political forms seemed needed. And Nietzsche was exciting. It is clear that he attracted many in the postwar generation by his claim that moral and social structures were disguised structures of domination. This also seemed true of the world around us. Nietzsche proved attractive to those who could not fit their feet comfortably in the categories of the earlier part of the century, and for whom "liberation" from the everyday inherited structures of the bourgeois world was important. However, the generation of young intellectuals that would be the new American Left were also democrats. Nietzsche thus necessarily also raised the question of whether or not the politics of structural transformation of a society (might we call it a "cultural revolution"?) and democracy were compatible.

I do not here want to argue that they – we – were right or wrong, merely that these were the politics of many of those to whom Nietzsche appealed. This was not, it should be noted, the first time that Nietzsche had inspired those on the political left. Indeed, such was a considerable portion of his appeal from the turn of the century. Let me rehearse this history briefly, as it has been recently well laid out elsewhere.[26]

Nietzsche began to be widely known and read in Europe from shortly after the onset of his insanity in 1889. From the beginning he appealed to a wide gamut of people of diverse political positions. Social democrats, such as Kurt Eisner, who was to be murdered after World War I while the head of the Bavarian Republic, found in Nietzsche "a diagnostician of genius."[27] In Germany also, anarchists, progressives hostile to laws oppressing socialists, feminists, youthful romantics of the *Wandervogel* movement,[28] all found common ground in Nietzsche's criticism of the contemporaneous bourgeois world. In France, as Geneviève Bianquais has amply demonstrated, the situation was similar.[29]

What appealed to these progressives, both in the earlier parts of the century as well as later in our contemporary world, was the unmasking trope, the ironic stance.[30] Irony is the modern progressive mode. It conveys that things are not what they seem and, most especially, that anything that claims to be some thing is clearly not entitled to that claim. The intellectual and political task of modern progressives is first one of unmasking. That which drew people with serious social concerns to Nietzsche were much the same dynamics that drew them to other cultural critics. Just as Marx had unmasked the fetishism of commodities and Freud had exposed the totems of faith, so also Nietzsche sounded out the hollowness of modern idols.

All of this is perhaps understandable, but to what politics might Nietzsche's thought then be attached and support? It is hard, on the face of it, to find in Nietzsche support for liberal egalitarian democracy in any of its modern incarnations. Thus, in many modern readings, those on the democratic left who have been attracted to Nietzsche and have wanted to enlist his thought in their projects have done so by arguing that, while Nietzsche's thought is not (really) political, his thought provides material for developing a new progressive politics. Such interpretations thus conclude that it is necessary to set aside Nietzsche's particular political judgments. William Connolly finds himself in a state of "antagonistic indebtedness" to a Nietzsche whose thought he wants to develop (and not unsuccessfully so) into a "reconstituted radicalized liberalism." Mark Warren suggests that if we free "Nietzsche's philosophy from its political straitjacket," we will find support there for the "progressive values of modern rationalism."[31] Leslie Thiele ingeniously attempts to assimilate Nietzsche to a mixture of romanticism and pragmatism that finds its most complex roots in Emerson. He argues that Nietzsche's interesting politics are confined to a "politics of the soul," which, unfortunately results in a fatal kind of isolated solipsism.[32] Most recently, Keith Ansell-Pearson has quite brilliantly established a profitable dialogue between Nietzsche and Rousseau to conclude that in Nietzsche there is a "deep incompatibility between the historical insights of his inquiry into the problem of civilization, and the political vision he develops in response to the particular historical problematic of nihilism."33

These efforts, always interesting, are politically characteristic of much of the contemporary interest in Nietzsche. But it is also true, of course, that from the beginning Nietzsche has also been claimed by many on the political right. In the early part of the century, social Darwinists, as well as out and out racists such as Frederick Lange, found inspiration in Nietzsche's writings. In France, Nietzsche influenced thinkers such as Charles Péguy, Charles Maurras and Maurice Barrès (himself a major influence on Charles DeGaulle), all of them important figures in French conservatism.

Nietzsche has also been at the center of contemporary American conservatism. Without in any way implying that a contemporary thinker of the right such as Allan Bloom is linked with such distasteful individuals as the Europeans cited above, it is, I think, no accident that Nietzsche has more index entries than any other subject in Bloom's recent best-seller *The Closing of the American Mind*. Indeed, it is one of that book's central claims that a sign of what is wrong with American society is manifest in its domestication of Nietzsche to a facile leftism.34 For writers such as Bloom and Werner Dannhauser and many of their students,35 Nietzsche is a man of the right, the greatest of the moderns in that he takes up the challenge of the ancients, the thinker who dares to raise again the old political questions of rank, domination, character, and nobility against the leveling dynamics and easy egalitarianism of liberalism.

Thus the contemporary world is characterized by apparently mutual incompatible claims as to whose Nietzsche is the "true" Nietzsche. As with Nietzsche's body with the onset of his insanity, it is a bit as if his thought has become a kind of paralyzed and paralyzing text which could only be taken care of. Nietzsche in the asylum, Nietzsche in the care of his sister, Nietzsche in the hands of his readers: Nietzsche under control. This has often been his fate in the hands of his would-be appropriators.36 There has been a political dispute for the right to claim his inheritance. The presumption is that the thought was, at the bottom, of *use* to the left, or to the right, and that the problem was to establish the superiority of one's claim. The implication of this quarrel is that Nietzsche's thought, if correctly interpreted, would align itself more with one side or with another. The presumption was then that the texts lend themselves to a "correct" (or at least more correct) interpretation.

The entire dispute over the body of Nietzsche's texts is made much more complex by the fact that it takes place against the background of the appropriations of the time between Nietzsche's death and the post-World War II era. It is well known that National Socialism claimed to find its roots in the doctrines of the *Übermensch*, the will to power, in Nietzsche's apparent validation of cruelty, in his pronouncements on greatness and destiny. Clearly and openly, the Nazis appropriated Nietzsche's remarks on racial superiority, the need for strength and ruthlessness, and war, seeking to cast Nietzsche as an intellectual ancestor of National Socialism.

Two general issues were raised by the Nazi appropriation. The first stems from the fact that of all important political movements since the French Revolution, National Socialism appears to be the least philosophically legitimated. There is, it would appear, little or no political theory of any value associated with the movement. Indeed, some have argued[37] that rational legitimation was incompatible with the very nature of the National Socialist project. From this it would follow that no thinker whose thought was legitimately of service to National Socialism could possibly be thought to be of any serious intellectual importance.

It is has become increasingly difficult to maintain this position in recent years. The (renewed) revelations about the involvement of Martin Heidegger in the practice and ideological arguments of National Socialism make it clear that a thinker of indisputable stature nevertheless perceived an "inner truth and greatness to this movement (namely the encounter between global technology and modern man)."[38] Likewise, the significance of the critique of liberalism in a thinker like the Nazi Carl Schmitt continues to have resonance.[39] One cannot argue that either of these men's association with National Socialism was a "mistake."[40] The point is that being an important thinker does not by itself exclude one from affiliations with evil.

Nor can Nietzsche's obvious importance in and of itself exclude him or differentiate him from evil. We cannot simply say that Nietzsche is a serious thinker, that there was no serious thought in Nazism, and that therefore links between the two are excluded. I need to be clear here: I am not trying here to argue that "Nietzsche was (would have been) a Nazi," but I am also not trying to exclude that possibility on the grounds that his texts "show" us that he wasn't (or would not have been). Such "refutations" depend on showing that the Nazis misread Nietzsche's texts. For a text to be misread, one has to assume that it contains a meaning, or at least does not contain certain meanings, in this case the ones that the Nazis claimed to find. Refutation here requires only that one bring to light a "correct" reading; from this it would follow that the Nazis were wrong or desperate in their reading of Nietzsche, and the question of the relationship would be closed.

Such a "meaning of the text" approach has met with much success. Indeed, perhaps no opinion in Nietzsche scholarship is now more widely accepted than that the Nazis were wrong and/or ignorant in their appropriation of Nietzsche. Credit in the English-speaking world for having demonstrated this, and thus for having again made possible the serious study of Nietzsche, is generally accorded to the late Walter Kaufmann. Kaufmann's pivotal book, *Nietzsche: Philosopher, Psychologist, Antichrist*,[41] appeared to refute once and for all the claims made by Nazi Nietzsche exponents. Kaufmann gave us a Nietzsche who participated in the philosophia perennis. His company was that of Shakespeare, Hegel, Goethe – the summits of thought. For Kaufmann, all of these thinkers stood in critical or at least problematic relation to Christianity. His Nietzsche was thus a Nietzsche fundamentally of the Enlightenment, of the company of those who freed us from authority, from tradition, from constraints on thought. What passages there were that seemed unacceptable to such *Freischwebendergeisterei* [free-floating spiritedness] were most often put down to Nietzsche's inability to free himself from the rhetoric of his times, or simply to mistakes.

Kaufmann argued, for instance, that Nietzsche was not an anti-Semite and adduced many passages in which Nietzsche clearly spoke out against anti-Semitism. Those remaining sections where Nietzsche appears to say something nasty about the Jews were often attributed to youthful desire to pander to Wagner. (Indeed, there is nothing new here. During Nietzsche's lifetime already, the anti-Semite Theodor Fritsch had complained that Nietzsche's negative judgments on anti-Semites were due to his friendship with Jews such as Paul Rée and to his fear of displeasing them.) Yet while it is relatively clear that

Nietzsche found anti-Semitism to partake of *ressentiment* (see his letter of March 23, 1887), it is also clear that he blamed Judaism for the development and furthering of slave morality. Here excuses won't do, and pulling out countertexts seems strange. Picture what one would say today in most circles about someone who announced, as did Nietzsche in 1888, that "the priestly instinct of the Jew (had) committed the . . . great crime against history."[42] Likewise, although Kaufmann suggests that Nietzsche's praise of war derives from a nineteenth-century sense of limited, instrumental warfare, it is also the case that Nietzsche speaks, apparently without distress, of "wars the like of which no one has ever known."

Clearly, there is a lot of difficulty in seeking a reasoned and reasonable interpretation of the political message or implications of Nietzsche's thought. In the face of these quandaries, some readers have suggested that there is in fact no correct political interpretation because Nietzsche does not in fact have a "real" political doctrine. Here the argument is that while Nietzsche may have commented (generally in an unfortunate manner) on political matters, such comments are a kind of category mistake on his part. His thought, it is held, is fundamentally aesthetic and only grief (epistemological, moral, and, it is held, therefore political) will come from reading him politically. One reason sometimes given as to why Nietzsche is susceptible to misuse in the political realm is that his aesthetic stance is inappropriately translated into politics. Commentators vary as to whether or not Nietzsche himself tried to do this, but they are generally clear that the attempt to do so leads to a dangerously nonmoral, or at best naive, attitude towards the political. Politics, in this understanding, requires an intersubjectively valid standard by which policy can be judged, which an aesthetic stance does not entail.

Nietzsche's position is then generally associated by these critics with the "postmodernist" view, which holds that it is always wrong to look for foundational statements (or "meta-narratives") which might provide rationally objective grounds with which different interpretations would have to come to terms.[43] A postmodern approach holds that a text or a person does not reveal it or him/herself as what or who s/he is, even *in extremis*, as there is no "thing" (in the sense of a stable entity) to recognize.

A recent major formulation of this critique of Nietzsche has been made by Jürgen Habermas. He accuses Nietzsche of romantic aesthetic nostalgia.[44] For Habermas, Nietzsche "takes leave of modernity" in favor of a stance (associated by Habermas with postmodernism as well as with archaism) that abandons the possibility of building a reasoned intersubjective consensus.[45] Insofar as the association of Nietzsche with postmodernism holds (– and to some degree it must, since Nietzsche, like the postmodernists, questions the stability of the subject –), he appears to make political action impossible, or pointless, or without standards. This is the gist of the Habermasian critique.

What is the truth of this kind of critique? Habermas has not, I think, put the pieces together correctly. It is true that Nietzsche disparages modern politics and that from the beginning of his scholarly life, Nietzsche expresses concerns about the saliency of politics in human life. When he comments about modern politics, however, it is most often to disparage not politics, but aspects of modernity. When Nietzsche says negative things about politics, he is not attacking politics per se but the modern state – the "coldest of cold monsters," as he calls it in *Thus Spoke Zarathustra*. In a text written around the time of the *Birth* he writes that there is a "Terrible danger: that the American style political agitation and this inconsistent civilization of knowledge join together."[46] However, Nietzsche looks to the Greeks, not to return to them (he is explicit that this cannot be done[47]) but to learn from them how one puts a form of life together. (It is for this reason that in the 1886 "Attempt at a Self-Critique" with which he re-prefaces the *Birth of Tragedy*, Nietzsche identifies the problem of *Wissenschaft* [scholarly inquiry] – i.e. of how one knows – as the central problem of the *Birth*.) If Nietzsche and Habermas have a quarrel, it is about the nature of modernity, but not about the desire to return to some romanticized past.

It is also true that Nietzsche praises the aesthetic; but he does not do so in favor of some formalist aesthetics, as Habermas asserts. Despite Habermas's claims that Nietzsche is a proponent of *l'art pour l'art*, Nietzsche explicitly rejects such a stance.[48] Nietzsche is in fact worried about what Habermas would call the over-instrumentalization of knowledge.[49]

From this it might seem still that the most judicious path is to say that there is nothing to say about Nietzsche and politics. This is, I think, both wrong and right. Nietzsche does seem at least occasionally to be concerned with precisely how one might achieve a politi-

cal and social identity. The most obviously political of his books –
The Birth of Tragedy – has, after all, as its central concern the examination of how it was possible to be Greek. *The Birth of Tragedy*
provides a kind of historicized transcendental deduction, not with
the intent of recreating Greece, but with that of instructing Nietzsche's contemporaries as to what would have to take place for them
to become what they were. Nietzsche's intent is not to appropriate
the Greeks, but to make what they did available again. And what is
made available is the "victory" they won. The *Birth* is, so to speak, a
lesson in how to fight, that is, a lesson in power, a lesson in politics.

Let us look then at how this first book proceeds. In the *Birth*
Nietzsche argues that the Greeks achieved a way of being in the
world, set between the chaos of Asia Minor and the rigidity of Rome,
and different from either. The problem was "to press upon its experiences the stamp of the eternal" or, as he later tried to phrase it, to
"stamp being on the nature of becoming,"[50] that is to retain one's
quality of being Greek, being in Greece, while responding to the
changes that were taking place in the Eastern Mediterranean. In the
middle of paragraphs often intended to make the reader dizzy, Nietzsche specifically notes such factors as the introduction of money, the
establishment of cities based on nontribal relations, the development of commerce, and so forth.[51]

The process of becoming Greek, Nietzsche indicates, took time.
Two principles governed this development, the Apollonian and the
Dionysian – Nietzsche is most interested in their interaction. Each
of these principles is a way of grasping the world. The Apollonian
consists in taking the world the way it presents itself to you, without looking "underneath" or behind appearance. This is the world
that Homer gives us (Nietzsche is constantly struck by how few
questions we have for Homer), and its reality is that of a continuing
dream. The Dionysian involves the acknowledgment that the world
as we experience it has no foundation in nature or necessity. The
prototype of the Dionysian man is Hamlet.

The process of becoming Greek involves working out what Nietzsche calls a "fraternal relation" between these two deities. This did
not happen all at once. Already in this first book Nietzsche insists
on the slow and evolved quality of any form of life. In Hellas, the
first "Titanic" stage established only the capacity of humans to
shape themselves in the midst of a sea of "barbarians," that is, in the

face of that which could not give itself a name. This resulted in a second stage, that of Homer, characterized by an almost pure dominance of the Apollonian. The pressure of the unformed chaotic outside, however, led to a third stage, the Doric, which Nietzsche sees as a kind of "permanent military encampment of the Apollonian" in defense against the outside. Lastly, with early Attic tragedy, a double relation was established. Placed between India and Rome, the Greeks succeed in inventing a new aesthetic/political form.[52]

The *Birth* thus reflects Nietzsche's concerns about the Greek state. The *Birth* considers how it is or was possible to be Greek. Nietzsche recognizes that tragedy not only had as its central concern the viability of the Greek identity, but more importantly that it was the embodiment of that identity. It was not just a means, a kind of pedagogical instrument, but the very form of that identity.

An implicit target of *The Birth of Tragedy* is the account of tragedy that is given by Aristotle. In the *Poetics*, Aristotle identified the high point of tragedy as the moment of *anagnorisis*, the moment at which the protagonist grasps the story which s/he has been living. Aristotle has in mind, of course, moments like the one towards the end of the *Oedipus Tyrannos* when Oedipus's own story finally becomes clear to him and when he for the first time recognizes himself, knows who he is.

At this point in the play, Oedipus cries out that all that he has done (except for his self-blinding) was set up long before by Apollo. Aristotle's account privileges, one might say, this teleological narrative. Recognition means coming to accept oneself for one's own in the terms the narrative has provided. We might describe this as a kind of self-appropriation. Aristotle's solution to the problem of Oedipus[53] places the emphasis on Oedipus's self-discovery, on his acknowledging his own tale. Self-recognition is the point and the aim.

Nietzsche is of course not refusing tragedy, but he is refusing an "Aristotelean" understanding of it[54] and such a reading is precisely what Nietzsche thinks problematic. If we read tragedy as does Aristotle, then we must understand what happens to Oedipus in terms of a tale whose telos is *anagnorisis* [recognition]. Such a reading is, I might say, almost Hegelian: Understanding only arrives at the end. The danger for a society or an individual, Nietzsche indicates, comes when it seeks to "understand itself historically," that is, in terms of a narrative that it takes to be naturally grounded.[55]

What is wrong with the narrative approach? Nietzsche associates it with the psychology of redemption, which in *On Genealogy of Morals* he later describes as the natural development of the dynamic of slave morality. The coming of the redeemer completes the story of our suffering, while maintaining the necessity of the suffering. In the *Antichrist*, Nietzsche suggests that the psychology of the redeemer rests on two physiological realities, first an "instinctive hatred of reality," and secondly, an "instinctive exclusion of all aversion, all enmity, all feeling for limitation and distancing."[56] To "hate reality" presumably means to want that there be something other than our actual situation, that there be a world not presently accessible to us. To wish to "exclude limitation and distance" means to wish that we would experience the world as our world only, with the other existing only to be converted or eliminated.[57] The identity involved in slave morality is one that involves the desire to be without limits, or which experiences all limits negatively, not as a basis for taking joy in who and what one is.[58] The accusation against Euripides and Socrates in *The Birth of Tragedy* is that they are spectators who want a whole complete story, a master and mastering narrative.[59]

The central value of tragedy, however, as Nietzsche understands it, is the denial of a single master narrative whose telos is self-recognition. The dramatic "proto-phenomenon" from which tragedy emerged was the procession of the chorus. The chorus is not, for Nietzsche, the representation of the spectator on stage, but instead a double process: "To see oneself transformed before one's eyes and to begin to act as if one had entered into another body, another character." One is not an object of contemplation for oneself here; instead, one is transformed. Nietzsche goes on to indicate that one encounters oneself "epidemically," that is, on a scale that is not only individual.[60] Moreover, the spectator is not only spectator and actor, s/he is also, in a sense, the author. In Aeschylus and Sophocles (as opposed to Euripides) the "most ingenious devices [are used] to place in the spectator's hand, as if by chance, all the threads necessary for a complete understanding."[61]

The kind of knowledge which we have from tragedy is not that of a single narrative. "All our knowledge of art is basically quite illusory, because as knowing beings we are not one and identical with that being which prepares a perpetual entertainment for itself."[62] The dramatic achievements recorded in the *Birth* rest upon the audience member's capacity to be at once spectator, author, and actor. This multiplicity enables the spectator to enter the world that Nietzsche calls "the mythical." His hope is that the example of the Greeks can help contemporary Germans to enter the mythical realm once again.

How could such a thing be accomplished? The *Birth* rests on two unspoken political hopes for its text. First, Nietzsche is very clear that he hopes that the *Birth* will succeed in combining the standard scholarly approach with his new vision of the spectator. It begins with the claim that we will have established much "for the science of aesthetics when we perceive that not just logically but with the direct certainty of vision" the Greek tragedy is bound up in the fraternal duality of the two deities.[63] Nietzsche had hoped at this point in his life at least that there would be no incompatibility between his "scholarly" and his (shall I call them) philosophical endeavors. This explains in part the depth of his depression at the uncomprehending reception his teacher Ritschl and other philologists gave to his first book.

The second hope is that there can still be in the contemporary world the kind of reader, the kind of audience, that Nietzsche had thought made the achievements of the Greeks possible. *The* Birth *is a call for those who can respond to the world mythically, that is, to respond deeply to the world as it is, in itself, with no reference to any other world, positive or negative.* Nietzsche writes:

Whoever wishes to test rigorously to what extent he is related to the true aesthetic listener or belongs to the community of the Socratic-critical persons needs only to examine sincerely the feeling with which he accepts miracles represented on stage: whether he feels his historical sense, which insists on strict psychological causality, insulted by them, whether he makes a benevolent concession and admits the miracles as a phenomenon intelligible to childhood but alien to him, or whether he experiences anything else.

"Anything else" is not a very strong call, an expression perhaps of anxiety as to whether such a spectator can still exist. But Nietzsche continues: "For in this way he will be able to determine to what extent he is capable of understanding myth as a concentrated image of the world that, as a condensation of phenomena, cannot dispense with miracles."

I think by "myth" and "condensation of phenomena" Nietzsche means something like that to which Thoreau refers when he speaks of the ability to "see eternity in a grain of sand," that is, the acknowledgment of the quality that the world has of being one, only one, and only this one. Such a world would be experienced both as an illusion and as itself, at the same time. Most people, Nietzsche makes it clear, cannot do this of themselves: "It is probable, however, that almost everyone, upon close examination, finds that the critical-historical spirit of our culture has so affected him that he can only make the former existence of myth credible to himself by means of scholarship, through intermediary abstractions."

This is what Nietzsche has sought to do in the *Birth*, to "take an aesthetic problem seriously,"[64] and everything is at stake. Myth unifies culture, saves the imagination from wandering, is central to the education of children. "Even the state knows no more powerful unwritten laws than the mythical foundation that guarantees its connection with religion and its growth from mythical notions." Against this Nietzsche counterpoises the contemporary situation:

[A]bstract man, untutored by myth; abstract education; abstract morality; abstract law; the abstract state; let us imagine [he asks] the lawless roving of the artistic imagination, unchecked by any native myth; let us think of a culture that has no fixed and sacred primordial site but is doomed to exhaust all possibilities and to nourish itself wretchedly on all other cultures.[65]

I take "abstract" here to signify the opposite of "mythical." I also take "mythical" to mean "not historical," that is, not subject to a narrative.

NIETZSCHE'S OMISSION OF A BOOK ON POLITICS

I have tried to establish two things. First, Nietzsche is available to a wide range of political appropriations, indeed perhaps to all. Second, to him the modern world appears to be politically impoverished. But with the exception of what he says here and there on political themes, Nietzsche does not write about political matters. Why not? His writings on politics are scattered, while this is not true of his concern with other topics. (It is simply wrong to see Nietzsche's works as a collection of more or less well-glued together aphorisms.[66]) Here the matter is quite different. While it is certainly the case that Nietzsche's books, especially those of the 1880s, are not written as treatises or essays, they do each have distinct subject matters. Taken as a whole, the books that occupy Nietzsche during the 1880s are indeed a fairly systematic attempt at investigating various realms of human affairs. *On the Genealogy of Morals* is about morality; *Beyond Good and Evil* is about *Wissenschaft*, knowing; the *Twilight of the Idols* is about authority; *Zarathustra* is about, among other things, worldly institutions. His autobiography, *Ecce Homo*, is, I think, about writing, and thus about the self and authorship. These books are, we are now tempted to say after looking at *The Birth of Tragedy*, Nietzsche's "transcendental deductions." But there is no book that does for politics what the others do for their subject matter.[67]

What is going on here? Over the 1870s and the early 1880s Nietzsche evolved an understanding that has come to be called "Nietzschean perspectivism." Most often this is interpreted as a kind of epistemological relativism – the doctrine that there is no intersubjectively valid way to determine which interpretation of a phenomenon is better than another. Such a reading, although understandable perhaps, seems to me quite beside Nietzsche's point. Nietzsche's doctrine of perspectivism does not, I think, imply that there are many "positions" from which one can see an entity, that I see in "my" way and you "yours," and, thus, that with a becoming toleration we should allow this diversity. It is rather an argument that who (or rather "what"[68]) one is is the result, and not the source, of claims to knowledge or action.[69]

Accordingly, Nietzsche's texts are not precisely transcendental deductions, that is, they do not ask "how is our knowledge of X possible?" Rather they seek to investigate what happens, in the modern (Western) world, to those who seek to make claims in these various realms of human affairs. Nietzsche asks: What kind of knower is constituted by any particular claim to knowledge in such matters? The subject is consequent to the activity, in Nietzsche's view, and not the activity's originator.

Why would Nietzsche then spend a decade investigating the various identities that the activities available to modern man have engendered? I think that he realized the logic of the genealogy of slave morality to be sufficiently strong that a simple call for living in the "mythical" such as the one of the *Birth* would not do. The texts of the 1880s are indeed "preludes" for a philosophy of the future. That is, they seek to show the reader to what degree s/he is in fact at the same time author, actor, and spectator in the various dramas of life: in morality, in knowledge, in authority, in social institutions and so forth. These texts show us the kind of hold that these activities have on us and, without freeing us from them, allow us the distance to them that true spectatorship permits.[70] With only a few changes – the focus on the "Germans," for instance – Nietzsche's project remains constant through much of his life.

We are now ready to understand why Nietzsche's texts lend themselves to such a variety of would-be appropriations. *The Birth of Tragedy* forms the model for the way that Nietzsche's texts work. Each of Nietzsche's texts works in two ways on its readers. It offers an opportunity for the reader to find himself or herself within it. In this sense it constitutes the readers as perfect spectators of a particular identity – being Greek, being an artist, being a slavely moral person, being a person of *Wissenschaft*. At the same time, it also impresses upon them the conventionality and ungrounded quality of that identity. Nietzsche has, I might say, taken the modern concern with identity – that is, the concern about one's capacity to make an identity one's own, to appropriate it for oneself by means of teleological narrative, a story with a goal – and turned it against itself.

Nietzsche's texts, therefore, are written in such a manner that if one seeks to find out what they "really mean," to appropriate them, one will only project one's own identity onto them. The reader will be like Aristotle's Oedipus, finding only himself, prisoner of a story told long ago, a last man, a last philosopher.[71]

Thus, it is not the case that Nietzsche simply omits writing a "transcendental deduction" of the political. Rather it would seem that the kind of book that he can write about morality, or about authority, or even about "becoming and being what one is," cannot be written about politics.

The reason for this comes from the triumph of slave morality, that is of the philosophy and ethics that Nietzsche identifies with the triumph of Socratism. Nietzsche reads Socrates and Plato as having eliminated the political as the root experience of life.[72] In *Twilight of the Idols*, for instance, Nietzsche claims to find in Thucydides a cure to Plato by his "unconditional will not to deceive [himself] and

to see reason in reality – not in reason, still less in 'morality'. . . .
The philosophers are the decadents of Hellenism, the counter movement against the old, the noble taste (against the agonal instinct,
against the polis . . .)".73 The polis is thus associated by Nietzsche
with "reality" as opposed to reason and morality. And for politics to
be possible the experiencing of reality has to be possible again.

From this it would seem that the problem with modernity is that
it lives in thought, not in reality, that it seeks solutions to problems
in thought and not in life. With the ancient Greeks, writes Nietzsche, "all became life. With us all stays at the level of knowledge."74

The Birth of Tragedy had established that the agonistic polis was
made possible by tragedy, by that double grasping of the world as
presence and illusion that Nietzsche calls *"übersehen."*75 The attempt to ground the world in "truth," in a philosophical argument,
destroys the world's reality, and thus destroys the possibility of
politics.

From this we see an answer to the question of why the attempt at a
political appropriation of Nietzsche's thought will always continue.
Politics first requires the ability to experience "reality," which for
Nietzsche is what the Greeks made available to themselves as
"myth." Failing such reality, the attempt to find politics will be abstract. "Our nerves," writes Nietzsche, "could not endure" the very
concrete reality of the Renaissance.76 The abstract world is anyone's
world, is no world at all. "Whoever thought he had understood something of me, had made up something out of me after his own image."
Thus for Nietzsche "all our political theories and state constitutions . . . are consequences, necessary effects of decline . . . our Socialists are decadents, but Mr. Herbert Spencer is also a decadent."77

Can politics then be a source of the ability to bear reality? This
question holds for all those who would appropriate Nietzsche to a
political theory. Bearing reality means acknowledging illusion, refusing to rely exclusively on the Apollonian, taking chaos upon one-
self.78 I tend to think that for most of Nietzsche's writing he does not
think that politics can do this. Thus, his texts are written so that the
attempt to appropriate them merely forces one to look at oneself,
without, however, affording one the cathartic relief of recognition. It
is only at the end of the same part of his life that Nietzsche began to
see another possibility and necessity for politics.

The letters written during the period between his collapse in Turin in December 1888 and his return to Germany for the asylum are filled with explicit politics. He is having the major political figures in Germany shot; he is ready to move into the seat of government in Italy; he is ready to "rule the world."[79] It is almost as if, having resisted explicit involvement in politics for most of his life, now, with one foot into the world of the unnamed, he finds politics. Perhaps there is a lesson here: Politics requires something of the Dionysian to be politics. Those who want a politics without the Dionysian would then not really want politics, but only the security of a story with an ethical ending.

Why then write texts which have as their political aim not to allow the reader to rest content with any meaning that she or he might want to find in them, that make it impossible successfully to appropriate them once and for all? What is the politics of writing in Nietzsche?

The answer is, I think, this. A text which has been appropriated is a text that no longer troubles me, that leaves who, if not what, I am quiet. It gives me assurance, perhaps in the way that Scripture for some gave assurance when it had been assimilated. Such assurance, such once-and-for-all-ness must always be wrong, because it claims to be always right; and assurance, Nietzsche knew, is the basis of domination. It turns fatally into a moralization of morality, into a justification for action in terms that escape this one world. Nietzsche's greatest fear is that we will have "thirty years of *Gloria*, with drums and fifes, and thirty years of grave-digging."[80]

There can then be no appropriation of Nietzsche for political theory. All that one can learn is to let uncertainty and ambiguity enter one's world, to let go the need to have the last word, to let go the need that there be a last word. In politics, Nietzsche can give us only the first word – but that may be more than we have now.

NOTES

1 For a fuller discussion see Tracy B. Strong, *Friedrich Nietzsche and the Politics of Transfiguration* (Berkeley: University of California Press, 1975), Chapter Seven.

2 FW 40; WKG V, pp. 81–82. (See abbreviation key at end of notes.)

3 WKG, IV$_2$, p. 557.

4 As Robert Pippin points out in his review of Bruce Detwiler, *Nietzsche*

and the Politics of Aristocratic Radicalism in American Political Science Review 86:2 (June 1992): 505–6, it is not at all clear that Übermenschen would need to command or "naturally" do so.

5 Der grieschiche Staat; WKG III₂, p. 266 (my italics).

6 See my Friedrich Nietzsche and the Politics of Transfiguration, pp. 186–217. The preceding paragraph draws on some material from these pages.

7 See my "Nietzsche's Political Aesthetics," in Michael Allen Gillespie and Tracy B. Strong, eds., Nietzsche's New Seas (Chicago: University of Chicago Press, 1988), pp. 153–74.

8 GT 12; WKG III₁, p. 82.

9 For a brilliant analysis, entirely supportive of what Nietzsche would have condemned, see Henry Kissinger, "Bismarck: the White Revolutionary," Daedalus XCVII (Summer 1968): 888–924.

10 I have in mind such thinkers as Michael Sandel, Benjamin Barber, and sometimes, Alasdair MacIntyre and Michael Walzer.

11 For a fuller consideration see my " 'What have we to do with morals?': Nietzsche and Weber on Ethics and History," History of the Human Sciences V: 3 (August, 1992): 9–18.

12 One would think here, for instance, of the conflict between Glaukos and Diomedes in Iliad, Book 6, lines 59–209.

13 Le Livre du philosophe (Paris: Flammarion, 1991), I 33, 45 (pp. 46, 52).

14 See Tracy B. Strong, The Idea of Political Theory (Notre Dame, Indiana: Notre Dame University Press, 1990), Chapter One.

15 See here, Philippe Lacoue-Labarthe, "History and Mimesis," in Looking After Nietzsche, ed. L. Rickels (Albany: State University of New York Press, 1990), pp. 209–31, which considers Nietzsche's relation to Rousseau.

16 This is Nietzsche's argument in Genealogy.

17 GM II, 8–16; WKG VI₂, pp. 321–40.

18 For a short discussion see the Epilogue to the expanded edition of my Friedrich Nietzsche and the Politics of Transfiguration (Berkeley: University of California Press, 1988).

19 The problem comes, as we shall see, with what one means by "reading," not with the false problem of "validity." There are exactly as many readings as there are readers, and it is very hard to make a reading. See the discussion of perspectivism in Alexander Nehamas, Nietzsche, Life as Literature (Cambridge, Massachusetts: Harvard University Press, 1985).

20 EH, Why I Write Such Good Books, 1; WKG VI₃, p. 298.

21 See Stanley Fish, Self-Consuming Artifacts (Berkeley and Los Angeles: University of California Press, 1974), Appendix.

22 The same is true of much of the work of Samuel Beckett. For a discus-

sion of a work of art requiring a response see Michael Fried, "Art and Objecthood," *Artforum* 5:10 (1967): 12–28; Stanley Cavell, "A Matter of Meaning It," in *Must We Mean What We Say?* (New York: Scribners, 1969); Tracy B. Strong, "How to Write Scripture: Words and Authority in Thomas Hobbes," *Critical Inquiry* 20 (Autumn 1993): 128–78.

23 See the discussion of the communist issue, for instance, in the early history of SDS in Jim Miller, *"Democracy Is in the Streets": From Port Huron to the Siege of Chicago* (New York: Simon and Schuster, 1987).

24 The greatest triumph of fascism is to have made us forget that it was very attractive.

25 The question on the Continent is somewhat different. In France, the approach to Nietzsche comes through the complexities of the increasing disaffection with Marx. It is no accident that the major impetus to Nietzsche studies in France was the attempt at a cultural revolution in 1968 (an event that Malraux with his usual hyperbolic insight proclaimed the end of Western civilization). In Germany, the publication of Heidegger's lectures in 1961 began the renewal of interest in Nietzsche; when once again in 1968 the French did what the Germans had been contemplating, the German revival took off. The Germans are, however, always braked by the memories of the 1930s. In the end I would argue that the dynamics are fundamentally the same across the Western world.

26 In the excellent work by R. Hinton Thomas, *Nietzsche in German Politics and Society, 1890–1918* (Manchester: Manchester University Press, 1983).

27 Cited in R. Hinton Thomas, *Nietzsche in German Politics and Society 1890–1918*, on p. 23 from Kurt Eisner, *Taggeist* (Berlin, 1902).

28 Literally the "bird of passage" movement, this was a late–nineteenth-century organization that promoted hiking and other outdoor activities and emphasized fraternity and German folk culture.

29 Geneviève Bianquais, *Nietzsche devant ses contemporains* (Monaco: Du Rocher, 1954).

30 John E. Seery and Daniel W. Conway, eds. *The Politics of Irony: Essays in Self-Betrayal* (New York: St. Martin's Press, 1992).

31 William Connolly, *Political Theory and Modernity* (Cambridge, Massachusetts: Blackwell, 1989), pp. 169–75; Mark Warren, *Nietzsche and Political Thought* (Cambridge, Massachusetts: MIT Press, 1988), p. 247.

32 Leslie P. Thiele, *Friedrich Nietzsche and the Politics of the Soul: A Study in Heroic Individualism* (Princeton: Princeton University Press, 1990), p. 180; see my review in *Journal of the History of the Behavioral Sciences* 28 (July 1992), pp. 269–71.

33 Keith Ansell-Pearson, *Nietzsche contra Rousseau* (Cambridge: Cambridge University Press, 1991), p. 223.

34 Allan Bloom, *The Closing of the American Mind* (New York: Simon and Schuster, 1987), p. 229.

35 Werner Dannhauser, *Nietzsche and the Problem of Socrates* (Ithaca: Cornell University Press, 1974).

36 See Jean-Luc Nancy, *"Dei Paralysis Progressiva,"* in Thomas Harrison, ed. *Nietzsche in Italy* (Stanford: Anma Libri, 1988), pp. 199–208.

37 See Ernst Nolte, *Three Faces of Fascism: Action Francaise, Italian Fascism, National Socialism* (New York: New American Library, 1969), epilogue.

38 Martin Heidegger, *An Introduction to Metaphysics* (1953), (New York: Anchor, 1961), p. 166.

39 Carl Schmitt, *The Concept of the Political*, trans. George Schwab (New Brunswick, New Jersey: Rutgers University Press, 1976); see Richard Wolin, "Carl Schmitt: The Conservative Revolutionary Habitus and the Aesthetics of Horror," *Political Theory* 20:3 (August 1992): 424–48; Chantale Mouffe, "Philosophie politique de la droite," *Esprit* (December 1993): 182–9; Stephen Holmes, *The Anatomy of Antiliberalism* (Cambridge, Massachusetts: Harvard University Press, 1993).

40 See my review of Victor Farias, *Heidegger and Nazism*, trans. Paul Burrell (Philadelphia: Temple University Press, 1989), "The Heidegger Case: On Philosophy and Politics," *American Political Science Review* 87:3 (September 1993): 775–6.

41 Walter Kaufmann, *Nietzsche: Philosopher, Psychologist, Antichrist.* 4th edition (Princeton, New Jersey: Princeton University Press, 1974).

42 *AC*, 43. Jesse Jackson had trouble with much less in the American presidential campaign of 1988.

43 For a critical but not unsympathetic reading, see Stephen F. White, *Political Theory and Postmodernism* (Cambridge University Press, 1990); see also Christopher Norris, *What's Wrong with Postmodernism: Critical Theory and the Ends of Philosophy* (Baltimore: Johns Hopkins University Press, 1990).

44 Jürgen Habermas, *The Philosophical Discourse of Modernity* (Cambridge, Massachusetts: MIT Press, 1989).

45 A completely devastating critique of Habermas's position has been accomplished by David Wellbury, "Nietzsche–Art–Postmodernism: A Reply to Jürgen Habermas," in Thomas Harrison, ed., *Nietzsche in Italy* (Saratoga, California: ANMA libri, 1988), pp. 77–100. A *minor* point in Wellbury's article is that Habermas is simply textually wrong about what Nietzsche says. Wellbury calls attention to two of the passages that serve as epigraphs to this essay.

46 *Le Livre du philosophe*, I, #26, p. 43.

47 One need simply start with my second epigraph. For a full discussion see

my *Friedrich Nietzsche and the Politics of Transfiguration* (Berkeley and Los Angeles: University of California Press, 1975 and 1988), Chapter Six.

48 There is nothing to add to David Wellbury's work on this matter. See Wellbury, op cit, p. 84.

49 See here Jürgen Habermas, *Knowledge and Human Interests* (Boston: Beacon Press, 1971), Chapter One.

50 GT 23; WKG III, 1, p. 144; WM 617.

51 GT. 4; WKG III, 1, p. 36 (K 47). See also GM II, pp. 137–9.

52 See GT 4. See also GT 21, WKG III, 1, p. 129, on the "third form."

53 Aristotle's view is delicately criticized by Nietzsche in GT 22.

54 For present purposes I am avoiding the question of whether or not this is a "correct" reading of Aristotle. Whether or not Nietzsche thought it to be, it is clear that it was a standard reading (and still is).

55 GT 23; WKG III$_1$, p. 141.

56 AC 30; WKG VI$_3$, pp. 198–9.

57 See William Connolly's recent work along these veins, especially, "Beyond Good and Evil: The Ethical Sensibility of Michel Foucault," *Political Theory* 21:3 (August, 1993): 365–90.

58 This is why Nietzsche refers to Socrates as having established reason as a "tyrant." See GD, The Problem of Socrates, 10; WKG VI$_3$, p. 66.

59 GT 12; WKG III$_1$, p. 81.

60 GT 8; WKG III$_1$, p. 58.

61 GT 12; WKG III$_1$, p. 87.

62 GT 5; WKG III$_1$, p. 43.

63 See the extended discussion in my "The Destruction of the Tradition: Nietzsche and the Greeks," in Tom Darby, Béla Egyed, and Ben Jones, eds., *Nietzsche and the Rhetoric of Nihilism: Essays on Interpretation, Language, and Politics* (Ottawa: Carleton University Press, 1989), pp. 55–69.

64 GT, Preface to Richard Wagner; WKG III$_1$, p. 19.

65 GT 23; WKG III$_1$, pp. 141–2.

66 For clear demonstration of the necessity of reading Nietzsche's works as work, see Alexander Nehamas, "Who are 'The Philosophers of the Future'?", in *Reading Nietzsche*, eds. Robert C. Solomon and Kathleen M. Higgins (New York: Oxford University Press, 1988), and Robert Pippin, "Irony and Affirmation in Nietzsche's *Thus Spoke Zarathustra*," in Gillespie and Strong, eds., *Nietzsche's New Seas*, pp. 44–71.

67 And to continue the analogy with Kant, nor is there one in Kant, except perhaps (significantly) for the *Critique of Judgment*. See Hannah Arendt, *Lectures on Kant's Political Philosophy*, ed. Ronald Beiner (Chicago: University of Chicago Press, 1982); Ronald Beiner, "Hannah Arendt and

Leo Strauss: the Uncommenced Dialogue," *Political Theory* 18:2 (May 1990): 238–45.

68 I owe to Alexander Nehamas the reminder that Nietzsche speaks of how one "becomes *what* one is" not "who" one is.

69 See Tracy B. Strong, "Texts and Pretexts," *Political Theory* XIII:2 (May 1985): 164–82.

70 To entertain a gnomic thought here: If the world is a stage, then the players are in fact imitations of the actions on that stage. This is part of Aristotle's point about *mimesis*.

71 *Le Livre du philosophe*, I, 87 (p. 73); see Tracy B. Strong "Oedipus as Hero: Family and Family Metaphors in Nietzsche," in *Why Nietzsche Now?*, ed. Daniel O'Hara (Bloomington: Indiana University Press, 1985), pp. 311–35.

72 Sheldon Wolin made such accusations against Plato thirty years ago. See his *Politics and Vision* (Boston, Little, Brown, 1960), Chapter Two.

73 GD, What I Owe to the Ancients, 2, 3; WKG VI$_3$, pp. 149–51.

74 *Le Livre du philosophe* 1, 47 (p. 53).

75 GT 8.

76 GD, Skirmishes 37; WKG VI$_3$, p. 131.

77 Ibid.

78 When T. S. Eliot speaks of shoring up "shards against our ruin," he takes the opposite stance.

79 See my "Nietzsche's Political Aesthetics," in Gillespie and Strong, *Nietzsche's New Seas*, pp. 153–74.

80 Alfred Bäumler, ed., *Der Unschuld des Werdens* (Kröner Verlag, 1956), vol. 2, pp. 478–9.

ABBREVIATION KEY

I have worked from the *Friedrich Nietzsche, Werke Kritische Gesamtausgabe* (Berlin. Bruyter, 1968ff) (WKG). The edition contains "divisions" (e.g. III) and volumes (given in subscript) Citations work with the following key:

AC – Der Antichrist – The Antichrist
EH – Ecce Homo
FW – Die Fröhliche Wissenschaft – The Gay Science
GD – Götzendämmerung – Twilight of the Idols
GM – Zur Genealogie der Moral – On the Genealogy of Morals
GT – Die Geburt der Tragödie – The Birth of Tragedy

Footnotes refer first to the work (e.g. GD) then to its internal division, if any (e.g. Skirmishes) then to the paragraph number (e.g. 37). This is followed by the page citation to the appropriate WKG volume.

Part III Nietzsche as Philosopher

5   Nietzsche's kind of philosophy[1]

That I still cleave to the ideas that I take up again in the present treatises today . . . , that they have become in the meantime more and more firmly attached to one another, indeed intertwined and interlaced with one another, strengthens my joyful assurance that they might have arisen in me from the first not as isolated, capricious, or sporadic things but from a common root, from a *fundamental will* of knowledge, pointing imperiously into the depths, speaking more and more precisely, demanding greater and greater precision. For this alone is fitting for a philosopher. (GM, P:2)[2]

A certain amount of historical and philological schooling, together with an inborn fastidiousness of taste in respect to psychological questions in general, soon transformed my problem into another one: under what conditions did man devise these value judgments good and evil? *And what value do they themselves possess?* Have they hitherto hindered or furthered human prosperity? . . .

Thereupon I discovered and ventured diverse answers . . . ; I departmentalized my problem; out of my answers there grew new questions, inquiries, conjectures, probabilities – until at length I had a country of my own. . . . Oh how *fortunate* we are, we men of knowledge, provided only that we know how to keep silent long enough! (GM, P:3)

I

The Nietzsche speaking here is the Nietzsche of 1887 – vintage Nietzsche, by any reckoning, commenting on the thinking that led up to *On the Genealogy of Morals*. In these passages and this whole Preface, one will find much that is of interest and importance in connection with the question of Nietzsche's kind of philosophy. The same is true of the other prefaces he supplied to his earlier and subsequent works (and, of course, of his post-*Zarathustra* works themselves).

It is in this last period, commencing with *Beyond Good and Evil*, that we unquestionably encounter "Nietzsche as philosopher." In these works and prefaces we find him doing and describing the sort of thing philosophy became for him. I consider it implausible (to say the least) to ascribe views to him about what philosophy is that are at fundamental variance with what he does in these works, and with what he says in these prefaces about what he is doing.

To be sure, Nietzsche has many critical things to say about philosophers and philosophy as they traditionally have been and continue typically to be. He also has much to say about truth and knowledge, reason and language, and interpretation and "perspective" that must further be reckoned with. But he makes much of the possibility of "new philosophers," of the sort he not only envisions and advocates but also himself attempts to be. And he makes much of a "philosophy of the future," of which more may be expected than the kinds of philosophical laboring and all-too-human interpreting he belittles and castigates.

Some take Nietzsche's critical remarks about "philosophers" as his last word on philosophy, and read these remarks as urging the abandonment and repudiation of philosophy in favor of other sorts of thinking, purged of all cognitive pretensions. This interpretation, in my view, fundamentally fails to do justice to Nietzsche's intentions and undertakings. It fails to take him seriously in the very matter about which he himself was most serious, above all during the last years of his productive life.

Nietzsche not only accepted but laid claim to the label "philosopher"; and he both preached and practiced something he did not hesitate to call "philosophy," which he deemed more deserving of this name than what generally passes for it. He further retained and claimed the term "knowledge" in this connection, even though he did emphatically reject the idea that anything attainable along these lines can ever be absolute, final, indubitable, or incorrigible. Moreover, he freely availed himself of the language of "truth" and "truths" – despite his rejection of "eternal truths" and the idea of truth as correspondence of thought with a "true world of being," and notwithstanding his views on language, "perspective," and interpretation.

These apparent tensions in his views lead some to suppose that Nietzsche was confused and inconsistent, or that he simply was unable to free himself of ways of speaking and thinking that his own views preclude and should have brought him to abandon. I suggest that these tensions should rather prompt a reconsideration of what his views actually were, or what they developed into in his post-*Zarathustra* writings.

Was Nietzsche "really" a philosopher? This has often been asked and negatively answered by those who have wanted to dismiss him as unwilling or unable to play by the rules of the game of philosophy as they themselves understood it. The same answer has more recently been given by others who embrace Nietzsche as a precursor of their own rejection of the traditional philosophical enterprise.

Nietzsche's kind of philosophy and philosopher admittedly differ enough from those of the mainstream to provide some grounds for those who contend that he departs from it. There may be some point to the debate about whether his departure is sufficient to warrant locating him outside of it. But this is not a very illuminating controversy. It may always be argued (as it was by Nietzsche himself) that the paradigms established by the mainstream are themselves too narrow or importantly misguided to settle anything of importance.

A more interesting and fruitful question concerns the character of the kind of philosopher and philosophy Nietzsche advocates and exemplifies, particularly during the last years of his productive life. In these writings we encounter the mature Nietzsche; and they provide the clearest examples of what philosophical inquiry meant for him. By examining them, one can most reliably ascertain Nietzsche's conception of philosophy and the philosopher. It will mark no small advance in the discussion of "Nietzsche as philosopher" if attention can be brought to bear primarily upon these instances of Nietzsche the philosopher at work.[3]

While these writings generally preserve something of the aphoristic form of Nietzsche's pre-*Zarathustra* works, they each have a greater coherence than may be readily apparent. In each of them he takes up a fundamental "problem" or related set of problems, which he proceeds to address in a variety of ways. On the most general level, they are all instances of his engagement in the twin basic tasks of his philosophical enterprise: *interpretation* and *evaluation*. These two tasks are not entirely separate operations, for each draws upon and contributes to the other, in a kind of dialectic. They may, however, be considered somewhat different "moments" of Nietzschean-philosophical inquiry, neither of which reduces entirely to the other. They may be likened to a pair of hands, which are used together to accomplish a united purpose. Their fundamental purpose is that of greater comprehension, involving both understanding and assessment.

While the "problems" Nietzsche addresses in these various works may be distinguished, they are not entirely unrelated. Their fundamental interconnection enables Nietzsche's treatment of each of them to shed light upon the others, either directly or indirectly. These problems spring from his basic concern with the *character and quality of human life*, as it has come to be and as it may yet become. The late works may be regarded as attempts to explore this basic question by approaching it from different angles, each supplementing the others in important ways. This required frequent stocktaking, reconsideration, and adjustment. The "perspectivism" Nietzsche espouses has a number of points and applications; and among them this *methodological* one is of great importance to the understanding of his philosophical practice.

Nietzsche's perspectivist approach is connected with the "experimental" character he ascribes to his kind of philosophical thinking. His treatment of problems is avowedly merely provisional and open-ended. The upshot of what he has to say about specific problems in any of these works is never complete and final; for it always remains open to revision when subsequent investigations are undertaken, involving yet other approaches that may shed further light upon them.

This does not mean that for Nietzsche nothing like genuine "comprehension" can ever be attained through such inquiry, and that all interpretive and evaluative efforts are exercises in futility. He repeatedly insists upon the distinction between the plausibility and soundness of various ideas, on the one hand, and their *"value for life,"* on the other (between their "truth-value" and their "life-value," as it were). Although some of his unguarded remarks may seem to suggest otherwise, he inveighs explicitly *against* the conflation of the two – even while *also* arguing that the *value* of all knowledge and truthfulness ultimately must be referred to their "value for life" for human beings, albeit human beings with differing constitutions and conditions of preservation, flourishing, and growth.

II

One who reads his books and prefaces with any care cannot fail to notice that Nietzsche constantly speaks of "problems," "questions," and "tasks." These terms recur over and over in his statements of what he is doing. It is not enough to observe that Nietzsche considers philosophy an interpretive affair, fundamentally involving reinterpretation and critical assessment of proposed interpretations. This is certainly and importantly true. But it is no less essential to observe that Nietzsche advocates and engages in such activities with respect to a variety of problems, questions, and tasks that he sets for himself, and that he would have like-minded philosophers join him.

As has often been observed, Nietzsche was not a systematic thinker and writer; but he was avowedly and quite evidently a *problem*-thinker. His early writings – *The Birth of Tragedy*, the "Truth and Lies" essay and the four *Untimely Meditations* – are all addressed to things he conceived as "problems" calling for consideration. The same is true of the books he published after *Zarathustra* – although in some cases it is the parts of the books, rather than the entire works, that are organized around "problems" on which he fixes attention. The books published in his "middle period" (*Human, All Too Human, Daybreak,* and *The Gay Science*) may appear to be exceptions. However, when he wrote new prefaces to them in 1886 (and again when he discussed them in *Ecce Homo*), he took pains to indicate the "problems" with which he had fundamentally been occupied in them.

This point is of no little importance for the understanding of Nietzsche's conception and practice of philosophy. He does seek to broaden and modify the range of "problems" which philosophers need to address, and he does suggest that they need to be dealt with in new ways. His repeated references to "problems" makes evident, however, that he does not propose to transform philosophy from a consideration of problems into something altogether different. He does resist the idea that philosophers ought only concern themselves with problems that can be dealt with by "arguments" of a purely logical, conceptual, or linguistic kind. Nevertheless, he clearly takes a variety of treatments akin to "arguments" to be called for in dealing with many issues.

What are Nietzsche's announced "problems"? An inventory of them reads rather strangely to one whose idea of a "philosophical problem" involves questions with some neatly distinguishable and articulable set of possible answers, which may be debated on the model of a scholastic disputation. Examples of such standard problems come readily to mind: for example, the problems of the existence of God, the reality of the external world, freedom of the will, the possibility of synthetic a priori knowledge, the derivability of "ought" from "is," and other such common fare of the traditional literature and textbooks of philosophy. Such problems characteristically resolve into sets of competing propositions which are then to be demonstrated to be true or false (or, sceptically, undecidable).

Nietzsche has little interest in such disputations. Indeed, he would have them abandoned, not only as idle but also as diversions from the genuine tasks of philosophy. Its real problems, for him, involve the identification and assessment of prevailing interpretations and evaluations, and the development and advocacy of more satisfactory alternatives. His inventory of problems loses its appearance of strangeness when this is recognized.

So, for example, Nietzsche calls attention to the "problems" of ascetic ideals, *ressentiment*, the bad conscience, the will to truth, and different forms of art, religion, and morality, as well as various forms of romanticism, rationalism, and nihilism. He makes much of the "problems" of art, science, truth, knowledge, morality, value, and "the type *Mensch* [human being]" more generally – under which may be subsumed the "problems" of consciousness and self-consciousness, logic and reason, the affects and their transformations, "herd" and "higher" humanity, and much else. All of these matters, according to Nietzsche, pose problems requiring (re)interpretation and (re)valuation, which he considers to be the main business of philosophy.

Nietzsche is not only a "problem" thinker, but a "case" thinker. His preferred way of approaching the larger problems with which he is concerned is to reflect on various "cases" of figures or developments he believes to be revealing with respect to them. These cases raise the problems with which he is concerned in vivid and concrete ways. Nietzsche was drawn to this "case-study" approach from his earliest works onward. *The Birth of Tragedy* affords a prime example: the case of the Greeks and their different art forms – and also the case of Socrates. The *Untimely Meditations* provide others: the cases of David Strauss, of Schopenhauer, of Wagner at Bayreuth, and of the new fashion of historical scholarship. The cases of the Greeks, Socrates, Wagner, and Schopenhauer continued to fascinate Nietzsche in his later life; and the cases of Christianity, Plato, Kant, Goethe, Napoleon, the new *Reich*, and a host of others were added to them. Nietzsche's pre-*Zarathustra* aphoristic works (*Human, All Too Human, Daybreak*, and *The Gay Science*) are full of small-scale case studies. In his post-*Zarathustra* works he undertook such studies on an expanding scale. *On the Genealogy of Morals, The Antichrist*, and *The Case of Wagner* are particularly obvious examples, with both *Beyond Good and Evil* and *Twilight of the Idols* also featuring a considerable number of cases.

Nietzsche's most common strategy in those works is to invoke a case to raise a problem, and then to examine it and employ it and other related cases to address the problem. The cases are (as it were) the witnesses he calls to the stand, the interrogation and interpretation of which serve to shed light upon the larger problems they exemplify or broach. They also serve the important function of keeping his treatments of problems from becoming lost in abstract reflections, and of keeping him (and us) mindful that these problems have real relevance to human life and experience.

There is another important sense in which Nietzsche's philosophy deals with "cases." As he practices it, philosophy involves the *making of cases* for and against various proposed interpretations and evaluations. Nietzsche does not for the most part present arguments of the customary sort.[4] But he recognizes the need to do more than merely say what he thinks, in order to make his criticisms stick and his own ideas convincing. On the attack, he typically seeks to *make cases against* certain ways of thinking. He proceeds by presenting an array of considerations to make us suspicious and aware of just how problematical these methods are, ultimately to deprive them of their credibility. He generally does not claim that the considerations he marshals actually *refute* his targets. Rather, he aims and purports to *dispose* of them. He attempts to undermine them sufficiently to lay them to rest, exposed as unworthy of being taken seriously – at least by those possessed of intellectual integrity.

When he turns to advancing alternatives, Nietzsche proceeds in a somewhat similar manner, presenting various other supporting considerations, both general and specific. None by itself may be decisive; but taken together these considerations are intended to be compelling. They allegedly establish his "right" to the view he is proposing, notwithstanding its novelty or one's initial reluctance to embrace it. Here, too, he is generally prepared to acknowledge that the cases he makes do not actually *prove* his points; and he couches his hypotheses and conclusions in tentative and provisional language. He even insists that they leave open the possibility of other interpretations and subsequent modification, as further considerations may be introduced. Nevertheless, he clearly supposes it possible to *make cases for* his interpretations and evaluations, whose positive upshot is strong enough to warrant confidence that he is at least on the right track. He suggests, for instance, that these are "*his* truths," to which others may not easily be entitled. One can read this as a challenge to *earn the right* to lay like claim to understand what he has grasped, rather than an admission that "his" truths are nothing but figments of his imagination.

Nietzsche's procedure may also be likened to what Sartre described in his *Search for a Method* as the "progressive-regressive method," the strategy of describing the present situation in its complexity, examining its history, and then conjoining these accounts in an informed analysis of the present. In Nietzsche's case, however, the movements of thought are even more complex. He constantly moves back and forth between the consideration of quite particular cases and phenomena, and more general reflections upon associated basic features or more fundamental traits of human life and human types – relating the former and the latter to shed light upon one another. He also constantly shifts his focus from some such phenomenon to others, from some human types to others, and from some features of human life more generally to others.

This strategy at first makes many of Nietzsche's books both before and after *Zarathustra* hard to follow; it is all too easy to become lost in the woods, failing to see their larger contours for all the trees. In a sense, Nietzsche *does* mean to keep us off balance. He tries to keep us from settling into any one line of thinking that would become a rut and lead us to neglect others that are no less germane to matters under consideration. Nietzsche suggests that his sort of philosopher must be a *dancer* rather than a plodder, adept at moving quickly from one stance to another, and so avoiding becoming frozen in any one of them and thus unable to bring a host of them into play.

The movement of philosophical thought for Nietzsche must be not only *progressive and regressive* by turns, but also perspectivally *horizontal* on the levels of both specificity and generality, in order to do anything approaching justice to the tangled complexity of human affairs. This is what I take to be the basic point of the following well-known (but seldom fully appreciated) passage in *On the Genealogy of Morals*:

But precisely because we seek knowledge, let us not be ungrateful to such resolute reversals of accustomed perspectives and valuations with which the spirit has, with apparent mischievousness and futility, raged against itself for so long: to see differently in this way for once, to *want* to see differently, is no small discipline and preparation of the intellect for its future "objectivity" – the latter understood not as "contemplation without interest" (which is a nonsensical absurdity), but as the ability *to control* one's Pro and Con and to dispose of them, so that one knows how to employ a *variety* of perspectives and effective interpretations in the service of knowledge.

Henceforth, my dear philosophers, let us be on guard against the dangerous old conceptual fiction that posited a "pure, will-less, painless, timeless knowing subject"; let us guard against the snares of such contradictory concepts as "pure reason," "absolute spirituality," "knowledge in itself": these always demand that we should think of an eye that is completely unthinkable, an eye turned in no particular direction, in which the active and interpreting forces, through which alone seeing becomes seeing *something*, are supposed to be lacking; these always demand of the eye an absurdity and a nonsense. There is *only* a perspective seeing, *only* a perspective "knowing"; and the *more* affects we allow to speak about one thing, the *more* eyes, different eyes, we can use to observe one thing, the more complete will our "concept" of this thing, our "objectivity," be. But to eliminate the will altogether, to suspend each and every affect, supposing we were capable of this – what would that mean but to *castrate* the intellect? (GM III: 12)

III

What exactly did Nietzsche write and publish, or prepare for publication, in the four years between *Thus Spoke Zarathustra* and his collapse? We do well to remind ourselves, for this provides a useful point of departure for our consideration of Nietzsche's approach to philosophy. First, he composed *Beyond Good and Evil*, a book proclaimed by its subtitle to be a "prelude" to something that Nietzsche sees fit to call "philosophy." This philosophy ("of the future") is evidently to diverge from common practice. On the other hand, it stands in some meaningful relation to that traditional enterprise sufficient to warrant his calling it by the same name. (Indeed, a reckoning with this tradition and enterprise is one of the book's first and continuing orders of business.)

Next, in rapid succession, Nietzsche composed a series of prefaces to works published previously – to both volumes of *Human, All Too Human, The Birth of Tragedy, Daybreak,* and *The Gay Science.* All of these retrospective prefaces were written in 1886, along with a Fifth Book added to a new edition of *The Gay Science* (published in the next year). Later in 1887, *On the Genealogy of Morals* appeared. Like the new prefaces and the Fifth Book of *The Gay Science, Genealogy* at once hearkens back to work begun earlier (as Nietzsche observes in its Preface) and also moves ahead, carrying this work further. The Fifth Book of *The Gay Science* clearly continues the project of that work, suggesting that Nietzsche's heralded "philosophy of the future" involves no turning away from the endeavor he called *fröhliche Wissenschaft* [gay science], but rather is to carry it further. *Genealogy* may likewise be regarded as an example of the kind of inquiry to be undertaken under both the banner of the free spirit and that of the future philosopher.

After *Genealogy*, there followed the works of 1888 – *The Case of Wagner, Twilight of the Idols, The Antichrist,* and *Ecce Homo* – all again looking both back and ahead. *The Case of Wagner* and *The Antichrist*, like *Genealogy*, have relatively specific targets. *Twilight*, by contrast, is more comparable to *Beyond Good and Evil* and *The Gay Science* in the breadth of the ground it covers. These works show us Nietzsche's final efforts at a *fröhlich-wissenschaftliche* "philosophy of the future" – or at least his prelude to it.

Nietzsche's productive life concluded with a reconsideration of the topics with which it had begun: with art and culture, truth and history, religion and ethics, philosophy and science, and with figures from Socrates to Schopenhauer and Wagner. Nietzsche also reflected upon his earlier works, both in his prefaces of 1886 and in *Ecce Homo*. In these late reflections he made increasing use of certain key notions – such as "the enhancement of life" and "will to power" – and brought several related central problems to the fore. These include, in particular, the problems of value and the assessment of values; morality; "the type *Mensch*" and our attained and attainable humanity; and, finally, knowledge and philosophy, as they have been and might be pursued. Nietzsche's post-*Zarathustra* works revolve around these large and fundamental problems. In the course of dealing with them, he arrived at his conception of philosophy in terms of the twin tasks of interpretation and evaluation. He took these tasks to involve the assessment of received interpretations and evaluations, but also reinterpretation and a basic "revaluation of values."

These tasks are quite evidently not only "deconstructive," but also, and more importantly, *constructive* for Nietzsche. Justice is not done to his kind of philosophy if the former dimension is stressed to the neglect or exclusion of the latter. One's own philosophical taste and disposition may run only to deconstruction or to analytic inquiry; but that should not blind one to the evidence that Nietzsche took such exercises as merely points of departure. Philosophy that aspires to nothing further is not much more than the mere "philosophical labor" that Nietzsche contrasted to "genuinely philosophical thinking." He would have been no more satisfied with such approaches than he was with neo-Kantianism, which he dismissed as "no more than a timid epochism and doctrine of abstinence – a philosophy that never gets beyond the threshold and takes pains to *deny* itself the right to enter – that is philosophy in its last throes, an end, an agony, something inspiring pity" (BGE 204).

Reflection upon the works of Nietzsche's last productive years also yields insight into his fondness for the notions of "perspective" and "perspectivism." These notions are commonly taken to have their primary place in Nietzsche's thought *within* the context of his treatment of perception, knowledge, and valuation. They are then extrapolated to apply to his conception of philosophy more generally. This may be to go at the matter in the wrong way, however, and to mistake the upshot of what he has to say.

Suppose we take Nietzsche at his word when he describes his efforts to approach certain phenomena – such as forms of art, morality, religion, society, and scientific and philosophical thinking – from "perspectives" from which they are not ordinarily viewed in order to achieve better comprehension. Suppose we further recognize that this not only is what Nietzsche sees himself as having been doing in his earlier works, but also is what he more self-consciously and deliberately undertakes to do in many of his later works.

Suppose we also take this to account for the fact that Nietzsche returns to such phenomena again and again, to take different looks at them. This is just what would appear necessary for increasing comprehension of them, if one agrees with Nietzsche that these phenomena are too complex and multiply conditioned to be adequately grasped by any single way of looking at them. This goal can be achieved only by taking collective interpretive account of what comes to light when phenomena are approached in many different ways, with eyes differently focused. This might well be called a "perspectival" kind of thinking – as Nietzsche himself calls it; but it would not signify the abandonment of the very idea of anything like comprehension as its aim. On the contrary: It would be quite compatible with an aspiration to comprehension, and indeed would be precisely what its pursuit would require.

Nietzsche's "perspectivist" pronouncements with respect to knowledge can and should be understood along similar lines. Understanding so conceived and attained may never be either certain or absolute. It may and presumably will always admit of improvement and of revision to take account of what comes to light as further different relevant perspectives are hit upon. The kind of comprehension afforded in this way may nonetheless still be deemed worthy of being called knowledge, even if (as Nietzsche suggests) its distinction from error will rarely be a simple black-and-white affair.

An illustration may be helpful. Consider for a moment Nietzsche's 1886 Preface to The Birth of Tragedy, where he describes what he was doing in that work. At the end of Section 2 he remarks: "how strange it appears now, after sixteen years – before a much older, a hundred times more demanding, but by no means colder eye which has not become a stranger to the task which this audacious book dared to tackle for the first time: *to look at science in the perspective of the artist, but at art in that of life*." And a little later, at the end of Section 4, he writes: "It is apparent that it was a whole cluster of grave questions with which this book broadened itself. Let us add the gravest question of all. What, seen in the perspective of life, is the significance of morality?"

In his Prefaces to *Human, All Too Human* and *Daybreak*, Nietzsche recognizes that these works had also been directed to further consideration of the same questions of perspective. He also expresses his dawning awareness of another and even more fundamental problem: "the problem of the order of rank." That, he says, is "*our* problem, we free spirits." (HATH I, P:7) This point is made again in his preface of the next year to *Genealogy*.

In two of his other early works, the "Truth and Lie" essay and the second *Meditation* on history, Nietzsche clearly undertakes to look at various kinds of "knowledge" in what again may broadly be called "the perspective of life," and more specifically in the context of what certain sorts of basic human needs require. Both early and late, he also turns his attention to such phenomena as Wagnerian and other forms of art, Christianity and other religions, the thinking of philosophers like Socrates, Schopenhauer, Plato, and Kant, various cultural and political tendencies, asceticism and *ressentiment*, and much else. What light can be shed upon them, he asks, and what light upon other related matters can be shed, by looking at such things from a variety of perspectives upon them, and then relating them to the larger contexts within which they have arisen, the interests they may serve and reflect, and their consequences for human life?

All perspectival assessments, for Nietzsche, ultimately culminate in what he calls "the perspective of life" and the related value problem of "rank." The larger reinterpretations and revaluations these notions make possible depend on many diverse and more specific perspectival analyses. This adoption and comparison of various perspectives is one of the most important applications of Nietzsche's "experimental" manner of philosophizing. Another of its applications is in connection with attempts to integrate and make collective sense of the results obtained when some phenomenon is considered from a variety of narrower and more limited perspectives. But

Nietzsche devotes at least as much effort to the search for specific "perspectives" from which something new may be learned, and to experimentation with such perspectives when he had hit upon them.

This, I would suggest, is what Nietzsche was already doing – more by predilection than by design – in his pre-*Zarathustra* works, as he recognized when he wrote his prefaces of 1886. It is also what he self-consciously undertook to do in his later works, from *Beyond Good and Evil* onward. At least partially motivating and warranting his "perspectival" methodology was his emerging conviction that the phenomena that concerned him were themselves conditioned and engendered by complex relations. This circumstance makes a perspectival approach at once necessary and possible. For we can gain insight into the relationally constituted natures of phenomena only by learning to look at them from perspectives attuned to these relations, with eyes become sensitive to them. (Hence the celebrated passage in GM III:12.)

IV

One consequence of Nietzsche's perspectival approach is that one must employ models and metaphors drawn from whatever resources are available in conceptualizing and articulating what may be discerned from the perspectives adopted. Indeed, these perspectives themselves are to no small extent framed only by means of such resources. This point may be usefully elaborated by way of a few remarks on what Alexander Nehamas has termed Nietzsche's "aestheticism," and the related "life as literature" thesis that Nehamas advances (the view that Nietzsche conceived of life on the model of literature).[5] Nehamas stresses that Nietzsche draws heavily and frequently upon resources from the domain of artistic-aesthetic activity and experience. In singling out literature and literary characters of a certain sort, however, it seems to me that Nehamas goes astray in two respects. First, Nietzsche avails himself at least as much of models and metaphors from *other* parts of the artistic-aesthetic domain as he does from this one. And second, this is only one of a fair number of domains upon which he draws in undertaking his perspectival experiments, and it is by no means exclusively privileged among them.

It is undeniable that Nietzsche often avails himself of notions like "text," "sign," and "interpretation," which certainly derive from discourse about literature. Such terms, however, have to do more generally with things written and otherwise expressed in language – matters very much on Nietzsche's mind throughout his career as philologist and as philosopher.[6] It is also undeniable that he often avails himself of notions having to do with arts *other* than literature, such as music, painting, architecture, and sculpture, along with the more general forms of human experience and phenomena to which *they* are related, as literature is to language. "Nietzsche's aestheticism" should properly be construed to refer to his tendency to think of life and the world on the models provided by the *various* arts – including but not uniquely privileging literature among them. (Indeed, while Nietzsche's heavy use of "interpretation" is evocative of literature, it is also importantly associated with music; and other, particularly *plastic*, arts are typically invoked by his prominent use of the notion of "perspective.")

Even in this more generalized version, however, the "aestheticism" thesis cannot be sustained if it means anything more than that the domain of the arts is *one of* the sources from which Nietzsche draws his models and metaphors. For he draws heavily and significantly upon a good many others as well. The biological sciences are a case in point, prompting some interpreters to make as much of Nietzsche's "biologism" as Nehamas makes of his "aestheticism." But biology (*cum* evolutionary theory) is no more exclusive among the sciences in this respect than literature is among the arts. Nietzsche draws upon the new physics and cosmology of his day, and even upon neurophysiology, in much the same way. He also takes models and metaphors from the social and behavioral sciences, from economics to psychology. One need only think of the extensive use he makes of notions such as "value," "social structures," and "affects" to appreciate this point. He further avails himself of resources drawn from other domains of discourse, including law, medicine, linguistics, and even theology.

My concern here is not merely to make the negative point that in this light little remains of the thesis of "Nietzsche's aestheticism," beyond the sound observation that the arts are one source of Nietzsche's models and metaphors. My larger point is a positive one – and it has an important bearing on how his "perspectivism" is to be understood. Nietzsche derives his models and metaphors from diverse sources, availing himself of the different ways of thinking variously associated with them, precisely in *order to play them off against each other*, and to avoid becoming locked into any one or particular cluster of them. They afford him means of discovering and envisioning an expanding repertoire of perspectives upon the matters with which he is concerned, and so of developing and sharpening what he calls the many and different "eyes" needed to contribute to a growing and deepening comprehension.

As Nietzsche utilizes and experiments with them, his models and metaphors are themselves modified, as are the provisional interpretations he frames by means of them. Connecting and integrating these models and metaphors requires both the "agility" and the ability to achieve the "comprehensive look" he asserts to be needful for the philosopher. It also requires the capacity and readiness to learn (cf. GS 335), and the conceptual and interpretive creativity that set such philosophers apart from both "dogmatists" and all mere "philosophical laborers." Essential also are uncompromising "honesty" and intellectual integrity, and what he is prepared to call "a *fundamental will* of knowledge, pointing imperiously into the depths, speaking more and more precisely, demanding greater and greater precision" (GM, P:2).

The upshot of these remarks is an indication of how Nietzsche's "perspectivism" is most fundamentally to be understood. It characterizes his strategy for teasing out aspects of the "truth" about the many matters that concern him. As he observes in his Preface to *Beyond Good and Evil*, truth has not yielded itself to philosophical dogmatists in the past, and it will continue to elude all those who approach it in a similarly heavy-handed and plodding, blinkered way. He would appear to have higher hopes, however, for his kind of philosopher and inquiry.

V

Another indication of what this "perspectivism" does and does not involve is provided by the language Nietzsche uses in referring to different sorts of perspectives. This language is frequently far from neutral with respect to these perspectives' epistemic status. For example, in speaking derisively of the "popular valuations and opposite values on which the metaphysicians put their seal," he suggests that they may well be "merely foreground estimates, only provisional perspectives, perhaps even from some nook, perhaps from below, frog perspectives, as it were, to borrow an expression painters use" (BGE 2). In the following sections of this work, and often elsewhere, Nietzsche contrasts such narrow, short-sighted, lowly, and merely "provisional perspectives" with others that would be broader, more far-sighted, better situated, and less problematic than the former. He constantly advocates making attempts to *position oneself* for a view – of things like values, moralities, religions, kinds of art, and ways of thinking typical of scholars, scientists, and metaphysicians – that will be more comprehensive, less superficial and naive, less skewed by all-too-human motivations, freer of the fashions and preoccupations typical of one's own time, and more honest than those most people and philosophers are willing to settle for, or are unable to rise above. In this connection Nietzsche frequently refers to the desirability of viewing things "from a height." A vivid example is to be found in the following passage from the 1887 Fifth Book of *The Gay Science*:

Thoughts about moral prejudices, if they are not meant to be [mere] prejudices about prejudices, presuppose a position *outside* morality, some point beyond good and evil to which one has to rise, climb, or fly. . . . That one *wants* to go precisely out there, up there, may be a minor madness, a peculiar and unreasonable "you must" – for we seekers of knowledge also have our idiosyncrasies of "unfree will" – the question is whether one really *can* get up there.

This may depend on manifold conditions. In the main the question is how light or heavy we are – the problem of our "specific gravity." One has to be *very light* to drive one's will to knowledge into such a distance and, as it were, beyond one's time, to create for oneself eyes to survey millennia and, moreover, clear skies in these eyes. (GS 380)

This last remark is well worth noting. It suggests the attainability, at least in some kinds of cases and under certain conditions, of a perspective ("create for oneself eyes") that Nietzsche takes to be privileged ("beyond one's time," "clear skies in those eyes") in relation to others, making possible a comprehensive and more discerning view of the matters under consideration. These conditions include not only strength but "lightness," together with a special sort of motivation (which he characterizes both here and elsewhere as "will to knowledge"). However problematic that motivation may be *in terms of its "value for life,"* and however mundane and maculate its genealogy may be, Nietzsche evidently does not take these circumstances to be such that nothing deserving of the name of knowledge can ever be attained.

Perhaps the attainability of such more elevated and comprehensive perspectives will not suffice to enable one to discern the basic features of all of reality (if indeed it has any such features). [7] But even if that is so, it would not follow that *there is nothing* of any significance to be comprehended. Nietzsche clearly considers the forms of morality that have arisen to admit of better-than-ordinary comprehension if approached in this manner and spirit. The same applies for him to a broad range of other such phenomena encountered within the compass of human experience. The domain that thus presents itself should be quite enough to keep Nietzsche's philosophers busy for a good while, with enough significance to sustain their interest (Cf. GM, P:3).

As long as Nietzsche remained the kind of Kantian he was in his earliest writings, or an ex-Kantian on the rebound, his comments about knowledge and its possibility have a distinctly negative character where most matters of both metaphysical and everyday interest are concerned. These remarks are frequently accompanied either by laments about what we cannot have, by brave words about our ability to get along without it, or by longings for something (possibly myths) that might replace it, psychologically if not cognitively. On the other hand, Nietzsche's comments from this period typically have a more positive and hopeful character in scientific contexts. Had he remained a quasi-nihilistic and quasi-positivistic neo-Kantian, his thinking and his kind of philosophy would have been of only modest interest. It would have been one rather complex variant of the post-Hegelian stance, reflecting and anticipating several familiar philosophical tendencies of the past century, which were subsequently carried further under diverse banners on both sides of the English Channel.

But I do not believe that Nietzsche stopped there. At first hesitantly, in the works of the years immediately prior to *Thus Spoke Zarathustra*, and then with greater boldness and assurance in his post-*Zarathustra* works, I see him as having extricated himself from this unsatisfactory predicament. Freeing himself from the limitations of his heritage, he found his way to a very different understanding and appreciation of the world, our existence, and the nature and possibility of knowledge.

In the final stage of his development, the character of Nietzsche's comments about knowledge and its compass changed. They became more affirmative as he reconsidered his earlier views. His respect for the sciences was in some respects not only preserved but deepened; yet his enthusiasm for them as privileged and paradigmatic domains of knowledge waned. Their limitations had long been apparent to him. He also came to be convinced that they did not represent the best that we can do in dealing with many of the matters with which he was concerned.

As Nietzsche reconsidered the "appearance-reality" distinction and relation (evident in his account of "How the 'True World' Became a Fable" in *Twilight of the Idols*), the notion of "knowledge" (beyond what the sciences by themselves can afford) received a new lease on life for him, in modified but nonetheless significant form. Rather like a latter-day Vico, he seized upon the idea that it is humanly possible to comprehend at least something of what has been humanly constituted. And "the world that concerns us" – which includes ourselves – consists of phenomena that are in various and very real respects "our doing."

Nietzsche thus in effect proposed to replace both the Holy Grail of an ultimate reality (whether conceived along the lines of a transcendent deity or as some other sort of "true world" of "being"), and the quest for it as the proper mission and picture of true knowledge, with different paradigms of reality and of comprehension. Suppose we take as our paradigm of reality the world of our activities and experience, and conceive of knowledge in terms of the comprehension of them of which we are capable. We then can consider how far we can expand the scope of these paradigms' application in the world in which we find ourselves, while devoting our main efforts to exploring what is to be encountered *within* the human realm, and to devising strategies most appropriate to its comprehension. Even if we cannot do much more than comprehend ourselves and things human, this will at least be something – and something quite significant and well worth achieving at that.

VI

In support of the interpretation I am advancing, I shall briefly consider a few of the remarkable series of prefaces Nietzsche composed in 1885–88, beginning with the famous Preface to *Beyond Good and Evil* (written in the summer of 1885). It begins with the strange question, "Suppose that truth is a woman – what then?" This question has occasioned a good deal of commentary, much of it critical of its seemingly sexist implications and sentiments. Nietzsche's point here, however, is an interesting and important one, and may be appreciated even if the sexism suggested by his way of putting it is not.

What I believe Nietzsche means to conjure up by this way of speaking is the idea that the "truth" of a good many things may be usefully likened more to the stereotyped figure of "woman" familiar to his contemporary readers than to its stereotyped male counterpart. Those who would pursue truth will fare better, he suggests, if they conduct their pursuit more along the lines of the correspondingly stereotyped way to win the heart of such a "woman" than if they proceed as though they were playing a different sort of game, of a stereotypically male nature.[8]

The kind of philosopher Nietzsche is here concerned to ridicule – the "dogmatist" – is rather like Henry Higgins in *My Fair Lady*, wanting the "truth" in these matters to be "more like a man." Were it so, truth could be dealt with in the direct manner of manly games in which the rules are simple and straightforward, with victories won by sufficiently forceful frontal assault. But this, for Nietzsche, is not how it is. The game to be played is a much trickier and more delicate business, in which such assaults are doomed to failure, and a sensitive mix of more indirect approaches is much more likely to be successful – even though success in achieving one's heart's desire is never complete and final, and one can never be certain of its attainment.

If this passage is read in this way, good and important sense can be made of it which accords very nicely with Nietzsche's "perspectival" strategy. There may be some domains of inquiry in which knowledge is to be differently conceived and differently won – logic, for example, or mathematics. Where most things human are concerned, however, Nietzsche is convinced that matters are not so simple. His first order of business, in this Preface to his "Prelude to a Philosophy of the Future," is to make this point through a vivid figure of speech guaranteed to get our attention. (Unfortunately, it can all too easily divert attention away from its point – as so often happens when he avails himself of such borrowed imagery.)

Nietzsche goes on to insist that we must rid ourselves not only of dogmatic ways of thinking and proceeding but also of the many old "superstitions" (like the "soul superstition") that have long been articles of faith, among philosophers as among the rest of us. To these critical injunctions he then adds a positive one. His "philosophy of the future" is to begin and proceed by recognizing "perspective, the basic condition of all life."

Here Nietzsche hearkens back to a theme from his second *Meditation* on history and other early writings, which from *Beyond Good and Evil* onward is moved to the fore and continually stressed. Human life, like all life, is for Nietzsche a *relational* affair. Particular creatures and types of creatures come to exist and preserve themselves – and can develop and flourish – only by way of the establishment of relations with their environing world. They interact with their world in ways that set up bounded relationships, expeditiously registering things that may make a difference to them, screening out those that do not. "Functional perspectives" thus are engendered, corresponding to and varying according to differing constitutions and situations.

The link between this conception of "perspective" and the perspectival strategy Nietzsche advocates, I would suggest, lies in his recognition that the key to comprehending anything is to learn to appreciate the relationships involved. The only way to do this, moreover, is by acquiring the eyes needed to discern these relationships in different cases. Far from associating the idea of "perspective" with the dissolution of the notion of "truth," Nietzsche here directly links the recognition of the former with the attainment of the latter, remarking that "when one spoke of spirit and the good as Plato did," this meant "standing truth on her head and denying perspective, the basic condition of all life" (BGE, Preface). An appreciation of the ways in which "all life" involves the establishment of and operation within "perspectives" is a step toward getting these matters right.

VII

Genealogy and its Preface of 1887 occupy a very special place in the last years of Nietzsche's mental life. In them Nietzsche speaks to us at the height of his powers, following the stock-taking previous year, in which he wrote his series of retrospective prefaces,[9] and prior to the frantic rush of the next and last. The Preface is dated "July 1887," and so it was written in the summer that might be considered Nietzsche's final "great noon," the summit of his philosophical ascent, before the sun of his life began its accelerating downward journey into night. What Nietzsche has to say about his kind of philosophy in this Preface is of surpassing importance and authority. If one reads and rereads it, and really *listens* to what he is saying and how he talks about his concerns and efforts, one will find strong support for the interpretation I am advancing.

"We are unknown to ourselves, we men of knowledge" (GM, P:1). With these opening words, Nietzsche indicates that knowledge is something with which he is concerned here. The book itself does indeed deal first and foremost with "morals" and their genealogy; but it deals with a host of other matters as well, to which he considers "the genealogy of morals" to be relevant. These include our own attained human nature and its prospects, and also the nature and prospects of those who are human "knowers."

Nietzsche's "genealogical" inquiries are often taken to have a kind of reductionist intent, as though he believed that the manner in which something originated *settled* all questions of its nature. In fact, however, while he does believe that one does well to *begin* by considering how something may have originated, he is equally insistent that this settles nothing on either score. For what is of decisive importance in both respects, he repeatedly insists, is what thereby has emerged and become possible. It is above all *by their fruits* – and not merely *by their roots* – that he would have us "know them," whether it is morals or "the type *Mensch*" or ourselves as "men of knowledge" that is at issue. And to this end, he suggests that a variety of questions must be posed and investigated from a variety of different perspectives.

In this Preface Nietzsche makes this point by way of yet another retrospective reflection – on the development of his own thinking about morality – beginning in the second section. Observing that he had long been interested in "the *origin* of our moral prejudices" (GM, P:2) and earlier still, in "the question of where our good and evil really originated" (GM, P:3), he then remarks that this interest eventually gave rise and gave way to other questions, both interpretive and evaluative: "*what value do they themselves possess?* Have they hitherto hindered or furthered human prosperity? Are they a sign of distress, of improvement, of the degeneration of life? Or is there revealed in them, on the contrary, the plenitude force and will of life, its courage, certainly, future?" (GM, P:3).

The passages cited at the outset of this essay, dealing explicitly with Nietzsche's view of philosophy, occur in these sections. Nietzsche judges that his early efforts left a good deal to be desired, as he proceeded "ineptly" but nonetheless with a determination, "as becomes a positive spirit, to replace the improbable with the more probable" – even if this may then often have been only to replace "one error with another," while he was "still lacking my own language for my own things" (GM, P:4). Quite clearly, however, the picture he paints of the kind of philosopher he was becoming is that of such a "positive spirit," seeking "the more probable" to the best of his ability.

As Nietzsche immediately goes on to observe, his concerns further extended to evaluation as well as interpretation. He summarizes the relation between these sorts of inquiry as follows:

Let us articulate this *new demand*: we need a *critique* of moral values, *the value of these values themselves must first be called in question* – and for that there is needed a knowledge of the conditions and circumstances under which they grew, under which they evolved and changed . . . , a knowledge of a kind that has ever yet existed or even been desired. (GM, P:6)

Nietzsche's genealogical inquiries are intended to provide this kind of preparatory "knowledge," and it is this further "demand" that his larger philosophical enterprise is (among other things) intended to meet. I say "among other things," because this "revaluation of values" is not the whole of it. His enterprise is also a response to other such "demands" that he elsewhere articulates, extending to a reckoning with the nature and significance of phenomena as diverse as the varieties of art, religion, social organization, science, and humanity itself – all of which Nietzsche touches upon in this book. And it further extends to questions pertaining to the character, scope, pursuit, and value of the varieties of humanly attained and attainable knowledge, as his opening remarks suggest.

Looking at these matters in the light of their relation to "morals" is not the only way to look at them, nor is it by itself decisive with respect to their nature or their significance; but this affords an illuminating perspective on them. Looking at them in other perspectives illuminates them in other ways – just as looking at moral phenomena in a variety of perspectives likewise is necessary to enable one to do anything approaching justice to them. And this is the very point Nietzsche makes next. Having recognized how profoundly problematic morality is, he writes:

> Let it suffice that, after this prospect had opened up before me, I had reasons to look about me for scholarly, bold, and industrious comrades (I am still looking). The project is to traverse with quite novel questions, and as though with new eyes, the enormous, distant, and so well hidden land of morality – of morality that has actually existed, actually been lived; and does this not mean virtually to *discover* this land for the first time? (GM, P:7)

I do not see how anyone can read this Preface, and take the Nietzsche one encounters in it seriously, without recognizing that the kind of philosophy to which he is committed aspires to *comprehension* in a strong sense of the term, and will settle for nothing less.

VIII

Before concluding, I would call attention to several passages in two of the brief prefaces Nietzsche supplied to the four works he completed with a final rush in 1888. They vividly show that his commitment to this conception of philosophy not only was sustained to the very end, but, if anything, became even stronger.

The greater part of his short Preface to *The Antichrist* consists of a description of the kind of reader for whom he is writing; but it serves equally well as a description of the kind of fellow philosopher he seeks and advocates.

> The conditions under which I am understood, and then of *necessity* – I know them only too well. One must be honest in matters of the spirit to the point of hardness before one can even endure my seriousness and my passion. One must be skilled in living on mountains – seeing the wretched ephemeral babble of politics and national self-seeking *beneath oneself*. One must have become indifferent; one must never ask if the truth is useful or if

it may prove our undoing. The predilection of strength for questions for which no one today has the courage; the courage for the *forbidden*; the predestination to the labyrinth. An experience of seven solitudes. New ears for new music. New eyes for what is most distant. A new conscience for truths that have so far remained mute. *And* the will to the economy of the great style: keeping our strength, our *enthusiasm* in harness.

In his last preface, to *Ecce Homo*, Nietzsche again takes up the same theme. He makes it clear at the outset that while *"overthrowing idols"* is *"part of my craft,"* it is not the whole of what he means by "philosophy." At the same time, it is not his intention merely to replace those overthrown by "new idols" of the same sort, wedded to some equally fictitious vision of the ideal. So he writes: "One has deprived reality of its value, its meaning, its truthfulness, to precisely the extent to which one has mendaciously invented an ideal world." His larger concern, beyond his war against all such "idols" and his "revaluation of all values" associated with them, is to recover what has been devalued and misinterpreted, and so to achieve a clearer and deeper comprehension of that upon which humanity's "health, its future, the lofty *right* to its future" depends (s.2).

In one of the most significant and remarkable passages in this Preface, Nietzsche describes his kind of philosophy very vividly, in language echoing and amplifying things he had been saying about it from *Beyond Good and Evil* (cf. 39) onward:

> Philosophy, as I have so far understood and lived it, means . . . seeking out everything strange and questionable in existence, everything so far placed under the ban of morality. . . .
>
> How much truth does a spirit *endure*, how much truth does it *dare!* More and more that became for me the real measure of value. . . .
>
> Every attainment, every step forward in knowledge, *follows* from courage, from hardness against oneself, from cleanliness in relation to oneself. . . .
>
> *Nimitur in vetitum* [We strive for the forbidden]: in this sign my philosophy will triumph one day, for what one has forbidden so far as a matter of principle has always been – truth alone. (EH, P:3)

IX

The interest and significance of these prefaces for the understanding of Nietzsche's view of philosophy should be clear. He would not have supplied them if he did not believe that they would help readers figure out what he is up to. His post-*Zarathustra* works themselves – from *Beyond Good and Evil* and the Fifth Book of *The Gay Science*[10] onward – show us his kind of philosophy in practice. If they are read with these prefaces in mind, they reveal a philosopher and a kind of philosophical activity rather different from the portraits often given of them by both his admirers and his detractors. Nietzsche's practice amply deserves the name "philosophy," and it is well worth taking seriously by philosophers today – for what it is and also for the examples it sets.[11]

In this essay I have attempted to show that the kind of philosophy Nietzsche called for and engaged in – especially during the final period of his productive life – is an interpretive and evaluative affair, of which good and important sense can be made. I have presented it as a *sense-making* activity, aimed at enhancing not only "life" but *comprehension* – not only despite but actually by way of its "perspectival" manner of proceeding. I shall conclude with a few general remarks on this score.

Interpretation and evaluation for Nietzsche are pervasive and indeed inescapable human activities that assume many forms and functions. Both are activities through which human beings *make sense* of things. Making sense of things is a feature of human life so central and basic that it may be deemed one of the hallmarks of our humanity. In a Nietzschean manner of speaking, one might go so far as to characterize *der Mensch* as "the sense-making animal."

Sense may be made of things in many different ways; and once made, this sense itself may become further grist for the mill of sense-making. In the course of human events, moreover, a variety of relatively distinct forms of sense-making have emerged and taken shape, each exhibiting manifold and changing varieties. Some of these we commonly subsume under such general rubrics as art, religion, morality, and science. All of these phenomena branch off in different directions from ordinary language and discourse (in which this impulse likewise is ever at work), and not infrequently feed back into them.

All of this sense-making does not occur in a vacuum, moreover, but rather within the varying and ever-changing context of human life. It is prompted and conditioned by a multiplicity of human needs, purposes and capacities – collective as well as individual, and physiological as well as psychological and social. Philosophy is another such sense-making activity, and likewise does not occur in a vacuum. As Nietzsche likes to remind us, it, too, has always occurred in the context of human life, and it always will. This goes for his kind of philosophy as well as for any other. All forms of philosophy are outgrowths, hybrids and cousins of other forms of sense-making, by which they may continue to be influenced. The exploration of this vast and complex domain, encompassing virtually all of what transpires in human life beyond the level of the merely physical and biological phenomena underlying it, is among the general tasks of Nietzsche's kind of philosophy.

The sense-making activities of interpretation and evaluation are fundamentally practical in their operation, even if they are not harnessed to immediately practical ends. They also are fundamentally *creative* in character, in that they do not passively mirror that of which sense is thus made. Instead, they *make something of it* – even though usually this involves little more than applying received ways of making sense to what is encountered.

These activities issue in and sustain ways of thinking and valuing that may come to be taken for granted by those who assimilate them. Nevertheless, it is only on a very superficial or provisional level of consideration that they may be accorded the status of "truths" and taken to deserve the name of "knowledge." The activities of interpretation and evaluation may also be limited to the humanly possible or conceivable. However, this does not doom all ways of making sense to perpetual parity, none of which may lay any stronger claim to the notions of "truth" and "knowledge" than any others, like the Hegelian "night in which all cows are black."

As the foregoing remarks imply, "truth" and "knowledge" can no longer be conceived in terms abstracted altogether from human sense-making activities. Once this point is grasped and accepted, however, one can proceed to differentiate among the various ways of thinking that aspire to "truth" and "knowledge." One can privilege those that take account of a wider range of attainable perspectives over others that are motivated by the promptings of narrower or "all too human" interests.

I consider it to have been Nietzsche's great merit to have battled his way clear of entanglement in more unenlightened and dogmatic ways of thinking, and risen to this challenge of confronting and transcending the philosophical "dark night of the soul" he came to associate with pessimism and nihilism. And even as he did so, he ventured out into the "new seas" with which he thus found himself confronted, learning as he went how to stay afloat and make headway upon them, beginning to chart them, and showing us how we might do likewise and continue their exploration. This is why, in my view, he does not mark the end of philosophy, but rather its coming of age. And this is also why what he offers us is indeed a "prelude to a philosophy of the future."

NOTES

1 Pun intended (in the spirit of that most wonderful remark in the first paragraph of the Preface to *Twilight of the Idols*). At the same time, I take the topic of the present essay very seriously (in the companion spirit of that paragraph's opening lines), and find quite disconcerting the common tendency to approach it in a manner all too playful and heedless of Nietzsche's injunctions to his readers (e.g., in the last section of his Preface to *On the Genealogy of Morals*). As he there observes, the spirit of the times would seem to be uncongenial to the "art of exegesis" and "rumination" his writings require if they are to be properly understood, and to attempts to deal with him accordingly.

2 In references to passages cited, I shall either simply give the section number (when the work in question is evident), or the standardly used acronym for the title of the English translation of the work plus the section numbers (when it is not). The translations followed are either those of Kaufmann or (in the case of *Human, All Too Human, Untimely Meditations,* and *Daybreak*) of Hollingdale.

3 The scholarly controversy over the status of a portion of these efforts – the extensive notebooks he kept during these years as well as previously – may be avoided by restricting attention to what he wrote for publication during this period. I do in fact believe that good use can and reasonably may be made of this *Nachlass* material in attempting to understand Nietzsche's thinking on a good many issues, including this one; but in order to finesse the vexing question of its status and reliability, nothing I shall say here will be based upon it. The case for my interpretation can be made well enough by reference to his published writings alone.

4 This reflects his early admiration for the intuitive "sooth-saying" of Heraclitus as opposed to the "rope-ladder reasoning" of Parmenides, as he puts the contrast in "Philosophy in the Tragic Age of the Greeks" – an unfinished and posthumously published essay written around the

time of *The Birth of Tragedy*. This essay, together with *Schopenhauer as Educator*, should be consulted by anyone interested in Nietzsche's early thinking about philosophy, which is of no little relevance to my topic here. See my "Nietzsche on Philosophy, Interpretation, and Truth," in Y. Yovel, ed., *Nietzsche as Affirmative Thinker* (Dordrecht: Martinus Nijhoff, 1986), pp. 1–19 (especially pp. 8–11), and my "Introduction" to William Arrowsmith's translation of *Schopenhauer as Educator* in his edition of Nietzsche's *Untimely Meditations* (New Haven: Yale University Press, 1990), pp. 149–61.

5 Alexander Nehamas, *Nietzsche: Life as Literature* (Cambridge, Massachusetts: Harvard University Press, 1985).

6 I would note in passing that there seems no good reason to believe that Nietzsche was preoccupied with those writings canonized as "literature" within this larger category, and that this raises further doubts about the soundness of Nehamas's "life as literature" thesis.

7 It may even be that Nietzsche would have us dispense with the very idea of anything of this sort. I remain convinced that he at least seriously entertained the idea that the world does possess a certain basic character, that it is possible for us to discern it, and that the interpretation of the world he offers in terms of "dynamic quanta" fundamentally disposed in a manner that may be expressed as "will to power" is a fair rendering of it. (See my *Nietzsche* [London: Routledge and Kegan Paul, 1983], Chapter IV.) But nothing I say here depends upon this.

8 One also should not fail to notice that in German the noun *Wahrheit* is feminine. It could well be that it was this circumstance that initially prompted Nietzsche to pose his opening question, as a fact of language suggesting the line of reflection he briefly pursues. This certainly would not be the only instance in which he plays with and capitalizes upon the lead offered by a linguistic point.

9 I urge interested readers to read all of Nietzsche's prefaces together with the basic question of this essay in mind.

10 For a corroborating discussion of this entire work, see my "Nietzsche's *Gay Science*, Or, How to Naturalize Cheerfully," in Robert C. Solomon and Kathleen M. Higgins, eds., *Reading Nietzsche* (New York: Oxford University Press, 1988), pp. 68–86.

11 See my *Nietzsche*, and my *Making Sense of Nietzsche* (Urbana and Chicago: University of Illinois Press, 1995).

6 Nietzsche *ad hominem:* Perspectivism, personality and *ressentiment**

That a psychologist without equal speaks from my writings, is perhaps the first insight reached by a good reader – a reader as I deserve him, who reads me the way good old philologists read their Horace. (Nietzsche, *Ecce Homo*[1])

Nietzsche repeatedly insisted on his importance first and foremost as a *psychologist,*[2] but this has not always been taken as seriously as it ought to be, especially by philosophers. Philosophers tend to insist on the truth of a belief, but psychologists are more interested in why one believes what one believes. "The falseness of a judgment is not for us necessarily an objection . . . The question is to what extent it is life-preserving."[3] Philosophical doctrines also carry with them a strong sense of universality and necessity, while psychological analyses remain inevitably bound to the particular contingencies of a personality or a people. But Nietzsche was suspicious of claims to universality and necessity, and he almost always preferred the witty, dazzling or even offensive psychological insight to a grand philosophical thesis. Writing about Socrates, he began, "In origin, Socrates belonged to the lowest class: Socrates was plebs. . . . he was ugly."[4] On Kant, he noted, "The instinct which errs without fail, *anti-nature* as instinct, German decadence as philosophy – *that is Kant!*"[5] On the "shabby" origins of morality as such he suggested, "The slave revolt in morality begins, when *ressentiment* itself becomes creative and gives birth to values."[6] And on German philosophy, he complains, "How much beer there is in the German intelligence!"[7] He saw himself and praised himself as a diagnostician, and his philosophy consists to a very large extent of speculative diagnoses, concerning the virtues and vices of those whom he read and read about, whose influence determined the temper of the times. His central strategy, accordingly, was the use of the *ad hominem* argument, a rhetorical technique often dismissed as a "fallacy," an attack on the motives and emotions of his antagonists rather than a refutation of their ideas as such. ("We know, we can still see for ourselves, how ugly [Socrates] was. But ugliness, in itself an objection, is among the Greeks almost a refutation."[8])

Nietzsche is often treated as one of those hermetic thinkers whose universe wholly consisted of his isolated self and his grandiose ideas about "modernity" and "culture" and "humanity" as such. But though Nietzsche's intellectual loneliness and over-reaching ambition is obvious, what is even more obvious is that he was not much prone to critical self-scrutiny even if he wrote not infrequently about himself and, on occasion, threw in a confession or a caveat for good measure. He did not usually write in grand generalizations, even if he had a philosopher's enthusiasm for abstract ideas, for example his fascinating thesis of "eternal recurrence," the notion that all things happen again and again, an infinite number of times. When Nietzsche did present such abstract theses, it was rather as a psychological test, not a metaphysical thesis. Although he was no "humanist" in the usual sense, he delighted in understanding and writing about *people*. His most brilliant and biting comments, observations, and essays involve a keen insight and understanding of people, whether as groups, types, or individuals. He wondered what made people "tick," and he rightly suspected that what they thought and said about themselves and their ideals was almost always misleading, mistaken, or just plain fraudulent. But nowhere is self-deception and hypocrisy more rife than in those aspects of life in which ordinary people as well as philosophers and theologians tend to make grand pronouncements about such lofty subjects as God, human freedom, and morality. Nietzsche's *ad hominem* arguments did not so much refute the doctrines of religion and morality as undermine them, by exposing the sometimes pathetic motives and emotions that motivated them. ("The moralism of the Greek philosophers from Plato on is pathologically conditioned."[9])

Nietzsche observed the people around him and read the great thinkers of the past. He reflected and speculated about the concealed motives and emotions that moved people to pontificate about "morals" and dogmatically defend sometimes incoherent beliefs in God, in divine justice, and in Heaven and Hell. He wanted to explain such perverse self-denying practices as asceticism and such seemingly "disinterested" enterprises as bookish scholarship. He wanted to understand what he called "the will to truth," and he wanted to get down to the true nature of such suspicious sentiments as pity, piety and much of what goes by the name of "love." Above all, he wanted to trace out the vicissitudes of that insidious and typically self-righteous set of emotions that give rise to what we call "morality," notably "*ressentiment*" and its far-reaching moral prejudices and principles. His thesis, now famous, was that what we call "morality" in fact originated in and now continues to be generated by a particularly "slavish" and "life-denying" set of values. Humility, for example, is such a value. It is the denial of pride, the refusal to acknowledge one's own talents, achievements, virtues. Thus the self-declared "pagan" philosopher David Hume chastized humility as a "monkish" virtue, and Aristotle, a genuine pagan, criticized it as a vice. Slavish values tend to deny joy and celebrate seriousness, decry risk and danger, and emphasize security. They encourage cautious reflection and reject or demean passion and "instinct." In short, they "say 'no' to life."

This "slave morality," however, does not think of itself as a particular psychological perspective, one way of looking at and living in the world. It rather presents itself as an "objective," essential and universal prescription, even a precondition for human life. Morality, while pretending to be based on the most noble of motives, even "pure practical reason" alone, in fact turns out to be motivated primarily by insecurity and resentment, even revenge. By uncovering such devious motives and emotions in others, Nietzsche tried and often succeeded in casting suspicion on their ideas and values. And by praising others (usually after they had been dead for centuries) he pointed the way to alternative ideas and values, whose motivation is not so suspect or subterranean. Unfortunately, Nietzsche's vitriolic style does not always make it evident whether it is suspicion or praise that is intended, whether he is condemning or admiring the genius of slave morality or when he is stating his pointedly ambiguous prejudices concerning Jesus or Socrates ("Above the founder of Christianity, Socrates is distinguished by the gay kind of seriousness and that *wisdom full of pranks* which constitute the best state of the soul of man. Moreover, he had the greater intelligence"[10] and "Socrates was the buffoon who got himself taken seriously."[11]) So, too, even when he seems to be advancing a moral thesis of his own, it is typically by way of a question or an allegory rather than an assertion.

In this essay, I want to look at Nietzsche and his philosophy from a somewhat unusual perspective. I want to look at Nietzsche both as perpetrator and as victim of *ad hominem* arguments. His works are full of such arguments, and, in turn, his critics and detractors have often used such arguments against him. (Allan Bloom writes, "Nietzsche, on the other hand, thought that writing a poem could be as primary an erotic act as sexual intercourse."[12]) I want to focus our attention on his psychological, sometimes very personal turn in philosophy. It is through this insistence that the personal cannot be taken out of philosophy that I want to look at Nietzsche's inimitable style and his thesis of "perspectivism," the view that *all* doctrines and opinions are only partial and limited by a particular point of view. (On philosophy and philosophers: "if one would explain how the abstrusest metaphysical claims of a philosophers really came about, it is always well (and wise) to ask first: at what morality does all this (does *he*) aim?"[13] On Kant's "theological instinct": "One more word against Kant as *moralist*. A virtue must be our own invention, our most necessary self-expression and self-defense: any other kind of virtue is merely a danger. . . . 'Virtue,' 'duty,' the 'good in itself,' the good which is impersonal and universally valid – chimeras and expressions of decline, of the final exhaustion of life . . . The fundamental laws of self-preservation and growth demand the opposite – that everyone invent *his own* virtue, *his own* categorical imperative."[14]) Finally, I want to look in particular at Nietzsche's justly famous *ad hominem* attack on "slave morality" and resentment, in order to appreciate just how complex and persuasive such arguments can be.

NIETZSCHE'S STYLE, AND NIETZSCHE'S PHILOSOPHY

. . . lest I break with my style, which is affirmative and deals with contradiction and criticism only as a means, only involuntarily . . . (Nietzsche, *Twilight of the Idols*[15])

I mistrust all systematizers and I avoid them. The will to a system is a lack of integrity. (Nietzsche, *Twilight of the Idols*[16])

Nietzsche is often accused of being "only destructive," of criticizing but not affirming, of destroying but not building. The case can be made, however, that Nietzsche's many *ad hominem* arguments do add up to an affirmative philosophy. To be sure, Nietzsche's philosophy is not a system in the Hegelian style, but it is a coherent point of view, a distinctive and often affirmative set of ideas.[17] Nietzsche's fragmentary and often aphoristic style makes his thought notoriously difficult to synthesize or summarize. Several of the grandest and best known of his ideas – eternal recurrence, the will to power and the *Übermensch* – are for the most part to be found in his unpublished notes and his literary tour de force, *Thus Spoke Zarathustra*. But if we loosen our demand for a unified philosophy and look instead to Nietzsche's *ad hominem* approach to a wide variety of issues, it becomes evident that he is indeed interested in many of the traditional issues that have challenged philosophers since ancient times – the nature of truth and of morality and religion, the genesis and structure of society, the locus of the self and its alleged freedom and rationality. It is clear that Nietzsche is not simply attempting to provide new answers to these old questions nor is he trying to reformulate the questions. He is rather trying to ascertain how such curious questions – and the concepts that provide their subject matter – could have arisen. It has thus been argued with some plausibility that Nietzsche is not so much a philosopher as an "anti-philosopher," who wishes to bring philosophy as we know it to an "end."[18] I think that this claim is too strong as it stands and assumes an overly narrow conception of what philosophy is and must be. Nietzsche's own approach to philosophy is peculiarly psychological, but we should not exaggerate the distinction between philosophy and psychology here, a distinction which Nietzsche sometimes suggests but would not endorse. Nietzsche is concerned not so much with the analysis and justification of philosophical concepts and doctrines but rather with an understanding of the type of people who would formulate such concepts and believe such doctrines. He does not focus on the concept or the doctrine alone, as many philosophers do. ("Paul thought up the idea, and Calvin rethought it, that for innumerable people damnation has been decreed from eternity, and that this beautiful world plan was instituted to reveal the glory of God ... What cruel and insatiable vanity must have flared in the soul of the man who thought this up first, or second."[19]) He does not

aim at eternal verities (except as targets), but neither is his philosophy nothing but an attempt to explode false truths and put an end to
fraudulent questions. It is not antiphilosophy but a more personal
approach to philosophy, in which philosophy and philosopher are
not so radically distinguished, in which it is the character of the
person – and not just the "correctness" of what he or she believes –
that counts. (*"The natural value of egoism.* Self-interest is worth as
much as the person who has it."[20])

This approach is reflected in (but it is emphatically not reducible
to) Nietzsche's provocative and highly personal "style." Nietzsche
does not just write philosophy, that is, record his thoughts and articulate his ideas and argument. Instead, he virtually *shouts* at us. He
cajoles us, teases us, confides in us. Even when Nietzsche is making
a pedestrian point, for example, in praise of honesty, the way he does
it is striking and memorable. But "Nietzsche's style" does not or
should not eclipse the ideas he is defending, and it is probably a
mistake to assume that the variety of styles reflects an inconsistent
or conscientiously self-undermining philosophy. Nietzsche's writing consists of ideas, often dazzling ideas, insights, and insults and
not just "tropes" and rhetoric, betraying a penchant for aphorisms
and the *bon mot* and a preference for hyperbole and first-person
pronouncements. He is, whatever else he may be, a profound philosopher. It is not as if Nietzsche were just playing with language and not
taking his own moral prejudices seriously.[21] If the older critics were
overly dismissive of Nietzsche's creative prose, many recent commentators are overly impressed by the fact that Nietzsche wrote in a
style so clearly unsuitable to most academic journals today.[22] But
style in philosophy is not just a matter of (admittedly unusual) literary sensitivity; it is first of all a style of thinking, an approach to life
and not just a way of writing. A style is not superficial but deep, not
word play but itself a worldview, a profound expression of *who one
is.* A style is itself a philosophy, or, to turn it around, philosophy is
first of all a matter of style. This must not be trivialized, particularly
in the case of Nietzsche. The point of Nietzsche's philosophy is how
to *live*, not how to write, and to confuse Nietzsche's verbal playfulness with his moral seriousness is simply to misunderstand him.[23]
("It may be necessary for the education of a genuine philosopher that
he himself . . . must have been critic and skeptic and dogmatist and
historian and also poet and collector and traveler and solver of rid-

dles and moralist and seer . . . but all these are merely preconditions of his task; it demands that he *create values*."[24])

Nietzsche's style is often that of the caricaturist, the prophet, the social critic, even the gossip. Approaching Nietzsche through his interest in the particular motives and emotions of other people may seem like a limited and even vulgar way of approaching his notoriously subtle philosophy. What about the grand skepticism that leads Nietzsche to declare, in a variety of ways, that there is no truth?[25] Where do the grand and famous themes of "eternal recurrence," the *Übermensch* and the will to power fit into this down-to-earth psychological approach? Isn't this pretty thin stuff on which to base a devastating critique of Christianity and Judaeo-Christian morality? But our propensity to believe (including, especially, to believe in truth) is itself a phenomenon to be explained, and that triad of famous Zarathustrian doctrines is best *not* interpreted as grand philosophical theses. Why is "truth" so important to us, and not only as philosophers?[26] What about the noble or the edifying lie? But why should we think that the answer to such disturbing questions lies in an abstract level of generality rather than a careful examination of ourselves as vulnerable human beings? Similarly, I think that the best interpretation of eternal recurrence is, in the phrase of Bernd Magnus, as an "existential imperative," a certain *attitude* towards one's life rather than a theory about the nature of time or a grand thesis about the meaning of existence.[27] How would one feel about the prospect of having to repeat this life, this moment, again and again and again? The *Übermensch* too is far better characterized as an attitude toward life and in terms of the presence (and absence) of certain emotions than as a metaphysical projection or a possible product of biological evolution. The *Übermensch* is whatever we want, in the most profound way, to be. The will to power is nothing if not Nietzsche's one attempt at an all-embracing if not ultimately convincing psychological hypothesis. How do we explain masochism, self-destructive behavior, righteous self-denial, the urge to martyrdom, wanton cruelty. The "desire for pleasure" fails on all of these counts. The desire for power gives us a much better understanding.

It is in contrast to the sometimes bloated pretensions of philosophy, theology, and metaphysical dogma that simple appeals to motives and emotion gain their force. In attacking Christianity and Christian morality, notably, Nietzsche does not remain on the same level of esoteric abstraction as his religious and moral antagonists. What he does instead is to *dig under them*. What could be more devastating against the boastful self-righteousness of some philosophers and theologians than an *ad hominem* argument that undermines their credibility, that reduces their rationality and piety to petty personal envy or indignation? What could be more humiliating than an accusation, against a morality that incessantly preaches against selfishness and self-interest, that it, too, is in fact not only the product of impotent self-interest, but hypocritical as well? And what could be a more effective argument against theism than ridiculing the ground from which such a belief has arisen? ("All men incapable of wielding some kind of weapon or other – mouth and pen included – become servile: for these Christianity is very useful, for within Christianity servility assumes the appearance of a virtue and is quite astonishingly beautified. – People whose daily life appears to them too empty and monotonous easily become religious: this is understandable . . ."[28])

That humiliation, of course, is Nietzsche's objective in his psychological guerilla war against Christianity and Judaeo-Christian bourgeois morality. Humiliation, if you like, is his style. He wants to shock us. He wants to disgust us. He wants us to see through the well-rationalized surface of traditional morality to the historical development and the actual human beings who lie behind it. Like Hegel, his great misunderstood predecessor, he holds that one only truly understands a phenomenon when one understands its origins, its development and its overall place in consciousness. But understanding a phenomenon, in this sense, does not always lead to further appreciation.

Nietzsche's theory of morality is suggested in his "middle works," *Daybreak* and *The Gay Science*, but first fully spelled out in *Beyond Good and Evil* (1886) and, especially, in his *On the Genealogy of Morals* (1887). He contends that what we call "morality" originated among the miserable slaves, the *Lumpenproletariat* of the ancient world (that is, the lowest classes of society, a term introduced by Marx). Morality continues to be motivated by the servile and resentful emotions of those who are "poor in spirit" and feel themselves to be inferior. "Morality," however brilliantly rationalized by Immanuel Kant as the dictates of Practical Reason or by the utilitarians as "greatest good for the greatest number," is essentially the devious strategy of the weak to gain some advantage (or at least not be at a disadvantage) vis-à-vis the strong. What we call morality, even if it includes (indeed emphasizes) the sanctity of life, displays a palpable disgust and "weariness" with life, an "otherworldly" nostalgia that prefers some other, idealized existence to this one. To show this, of course, is not to "refute" the claims of morality. Morality might still be, as Kant argued, the product of Practical Reason and as such a matter of universalized principles. It may in fact be conducive to the greatest good for the greatest number. But to see that such obsessions with rational principles and the public good are products and symptoms of an underlying sense of inferiority is certainly to take the glamor and the seeming "necessity" out of morality. To demonstrate this embarrassing truth is one of Nietzsche's primary aims, and his style is that of a vivisectionist – a disgusting, shocking profession if ever there was one. Cutting to the very heart of morality, he is the ruthless diagnostician, and his method of diagnosis is the *ad hominem* argument.

IN DEFENSE OF *AD HOMINEM* ARGUMENTS

Every philosophy is the philosophy of some stage of life. The stage of life at which a philosopher found his doctrine reverberates through it . . . Thus Schopenhauer's philosophy remains the reflection of ardent and melancholy *youth* – it is no way of thinking for older people. And Plato's philosophy recalls the middle thirties, when a cold and hot torrent often roar toward each other, so that a mist and tender little clouds form – and under favorable circumstances and the rays of the sun, an enchanting rainbow.[29]

One will notice that I wish to be just to the Germans: I do not want to break faith with myself here. I must therefore state my objections to them. . . . How much disgruntled heaviness, lameness, dampness . . . how much *beer* there is in the German intelligence! (Nietzsche, *Twilight of the Idols*[30])

An *ad hominem* argument, as everyone learns in any Introductory Logic or Basic Composition course, is an attack directed "against the person" instead of addressed to his or her thesis or argument. To so attack the person is to commit a common elementary fallacy, albeit "informal." Nevertheless, this fallacy is frowned upon almost as routinely as it is actually used, in philosophy as in politics and virtually every other human endeavor where people care more about winning the argument than obeying the rules of academic etiquette.

But are *ad hominem* arguments really fallacies? Or do they provide fair grounds for rejecting or at least being suspicious of the views or opinions of a person? The answer to the second question is, "of course they do," and the answer to the first is, at least, "not always." To recognize someone as a compulsive liar is to be suspicious, at least, of their most sincere-sounding pronouncements. To recognize that someone has a personal interest or investment in a case (e.g. a scientist hired by the Tobacco Institute to disprove the link between smoking and cancer) is good reason to be deeply suspicious of the supposed "objectivity" of the research, no matter how painstakingly pure the experimental methodology. It is true, of course, that such suspicions do not show such pronouncements or the conclusions of such research to be false. But the entanglement of truth and method, knowing and the knower, is such that the *ad hominem* argument is often – at least as a practical matter – conclusive. The thesis may in fact be true, but in the absence of arguments from other, less suspicious parties, we may be rightly no longer willing to listen.

It is often said that the problem with an *ad hominem* argument is that it reduces a (possibly good) thesis or argument to the faults and foibles of its promulgator, thus eliminating or eclipsing our search for the truth. A cheap argument ("he's drunk" or "she's just an undergraduate") may have this unfortunate effect, but a well-wrought *ad hominem* insight may explain what many pages or hours of analysis and textual exegesis will not. ("I seek to comprehend what idiosyncrasy begot that Socratic equation of reason, virtue, and happiness: that most bizarre of all equations, which, moreover, is opposed to all the instincts of the earlier Greeks."[31]) *Ad hominem* arguments expand, they do not limit, the field of philosophical argumentation. Instead of restricting the focus to mere thesis, antithesis and argument, the *ad hominem* approach brings in the motives, the intentions, the circumstances and the context of those who have a stake in the outcome. Or, in Nietzschean metaphor, *ad hominem* arguments make us look at the soil and the seed as well as the plant from which the flower grows. It also allows us to see what is *not* being said or argued, the limitations of a position as well as its possibilities. ("The Socratic virtues were preached because the Greeks had lost them."[32])

The truth is, even the most conservative philosophers leave some room for the legitimacy of *ad hominem* arguments. If one looks to see how the so-called *ad hominem* fallacy is qualified in the leading textbooks, one finds that certain uses of *ad hominem* arguments are not fallacies at all, notably, in cases in which there is an "expert." In his *Logic and Philosophy*, for example, Howard Kahane gives the usual definition, "an attack on the person rather than the argument."[33] But, he adds, it is not always a fallacy. Lawyers who attack the testimony of an expert witness and question his or her moral character, argue *ad hominem*, though not fallaciously.[34] But why should "expert" witnesses be the exception? An expert is presented (or presents him- or herself) as particularly knowledgeable in a certain field, and to throw doubt on either their knowledgeability or their objectivity will discredit their testimony and undermine their stated opinions. But insofar as anyone makes any pronouncement in any field, are they not presenting themselves as knowledgeable and so subject to similar suspicions, or even more so? Are not questions about their knowledge, their tendencies to lie or exaggerate, their being part of one interest group or another just as relevant and (sometimes) decisive? We suppose that an "expert" (in theory if not in practice) is defined (in part) by his or her "objectivity" and "disinterest" as well as his or her knowledge, but the fact that experts in a court of law are often hired and paid by one side or the other in an advocacy position obviously compromises their "disinterest" if not their "objectivity." Indeed, looking at academia (and not just academia) it becomes increasingly obvious that many "experts" increasingly define themselves not just in terms of their knowledge, much less in terms of objectivity, but rather on the basis of their well-known positions and entrenched antagonisms. (How readily one's position becomes comprehensible – whether or not it is also compromised – by the knowledge that "she's a deconstructionist" or "he's a libertarian.")

For those of us who do not claim to be "experts" but may nevertheless speak as such on any number of occasions, *ad hominem* arguments are often effective in putting us in our place ("how could you know anything about that?" and "you're just jealous"). But what can be most effective of all are the generic, global replies, "Oh, you think you know everything," "you have to find fault with everything," or "you can't accept anyone's opinions but your own." Raising questions about a particular judgment or opinion allows the speaker to alter his stance, or shift her emphasis, or qualify what's already been stated. But a generic, global put-down undermines the legitimacy of everything the speaker has said or might say. Thus Nietzsche seeks to dismiss the whole of morality on the grounds that it is born of *ressentiment*. ("While every noble morality develops from a triumphant affirmation of itself, slave morality from the outset says *No* to what is 'outside,' what is 'different,' what is 'not itself.' "[35]) So, too, Nietzsche supplements his "madman's" pronouncement of "the Death of God"[36] with his "historical refutation as the definitive refutation." ("In former times, one sought to prove that there is no God – today one indicates how the belief that there is a God could *arise* and how this belief acquired its weight and importance."[37])

Undermining an "expert" means showing that he is not to be trusted, even if his knowledgeability is not in question. But what are we to say, then, in a subject where it is by no means evident what "knowledgeability" would even mean – in ethics (as opposed to the technical study of ethical theories and arguments), in religion (as opposed to the scholarly study of theology or the history of religion) and in philosophy (as opposed to the scholarly study of the history of philosophy or the use of certain techniques of notation and argumentation)? Are there any "facts of the matter" in philosophy? Are the faithful necessarily more knowledgeable than the faithless? (Kierkegaard would certainly echo "no.") Does morality really require knowledge of anything more than "the difference between right and wrong" and the ability to deliberate in practical matters? In these fields in which there are no experts, one might say that everyone is an "expert," that is, our differences in knowledge as such are not particularly important but who we are and what we do is of considerable importance. A Christian should be judged on the basis of faith not theology. A moralist should be judged not by virtue of what he or she says but what he or she does. And a philosopher (here is the hard part) should be judged not just by his or her arguments and cleverness but by the integrity not only of his or her philosophy but also his or her feelings, actions and associations. ("Your association with an anti-Semitic chief expresses a foreignness to my whole way of life which fills me again and again with ire or melancholy . . . that the name of Zarathustra is used in every *Anti-Semitic Correspondence Sheet* has almost made me sick several times . . ."[38])

William Halverson gives us the standard view that "rational discussion requires that views be considered on their own merits, no matter who may happen to hold or express them. The fallacy of arguments against the person occurs when someone who wishes to oppose a certain view attempts to discredit the person who holds the view rather than assess the merits of the view itself."[39] Halverson does not bother to qualify or question the scope of the alleged fallacy, and in this we may take him to be providing us with the same old standard, traditional view. But he also gives us a particularly appropriate example: "Don't waste your time studying the philosophy of Nietzsche. Not only was he an atheist but he ended his days in an insane asylum."[40] Halverson goes on to distinguish *abusive* arguments – aimed at one's character or arousing negative feelings on the part of the audience, *circumstantial* arguments, aimed at the context and therefore probable personal motivation, and *tu quoque* or "you too" arguments, which shift the focus from the accused to the accuser. All three, of course, have been levied against Nietzsche [1. He was crazy. ("Abusive") 2. He lived in a family of Protestant women. ("Circumstantial") 3. And, wasn't *he* as filled with *ressentiment* as anyone?" ("*Tu quoque*")] If *ad hominem* arguments are acceptable in the court of philosophy, might they not apply with devastating effect on that self-appointed "expert" in moral psychology, Friedrich Nietzsche?

It can be argued that an *ad hominem* argument throws no light on the truth of a proposition (no matter who utters it) or the soundness of an argument (no matter who argues it). But propositions are put on the table only because they are uttered by someone in some context for some reason; and arguments are argued (except, perhaps, in a logic or debating class) only because someone (in some context, for some reason) wants to prove or establish something. Where the truth can be known or investigated quite independently (e.g. a claim about the possibility of "cold fusion," obviously intended to win the applause of the scientific community and the investment of the financial community), *ad hominem* arguments are something of a sideshow, at most a device to diminish attention to the promulgator and return the attention to the investigation itself. (The fact that such arguments are typically driven even if not initiated by resentment is quite irrelevant here.) But when there is no such available truth or proof (the typical ontological claim in philosophy), or when the argument is essentially incomplete, with no end of counter-examples and counter-arguments in sight, then *ad hominem* arguments become particularly appealing and appropriate. *Ad hominem* arguments are appropriate when an otherwise articulate philosopher keeps repeating an incomprehensible or most implausible thesis ("that Socratic equation of reason, virtue, and happiness: that most bizarre of all equations" [*Twilight,* "Socrates" #3]), when the argument doesn't quite make sense or cohere ("Carlyle: . . . constantly lured by the craving for a strong faith and the feeling of his incapacity for it." [*Twilight,* "Skirmishes" #12]), or when an argument is notoriously incompetent ("After all the first church, as is well known, fought against the 'intelligent' in favor of the 'poor in spirit.' How could one expect from it an intelligent war against passion?" [*Twilight of the Idols,* "Morality as Anti-Nature" #1]). Of course, there are bad *ad hominem* arguments too, namely those that are unsound (e.g. the speaker simply does not have the characteristic attributed to him) and those that invoke irrelevant features, that is irrelevant to the thesis or argument at hand, or simply luxuriate in their nastiness ("I cannot stand this motley wallpaper style any more than the mob aspiration for generous feelings. . . . How cold she must have been throughout, this insufferable artist! She wound herself like a clock – and wrote . . . And how self-satisfied she may have lain there all the while, this fertile writing cow . . ." [on George Sand, *Twilight,* "Skirmishes" #6]). In matters of science, *ad hominem* arguments may be of secondary importance, but in matters of morality, religion and philosophy, they are more often than not appropriate, for it is the *homo* that should concern us as much as the argument.

PERSPECTIVES AND INTERPRETATIONS: WHERE IS
THE "TRUTH"?

Our ideas, our values, our yeas and nays, our ifs and buts, grow out of us with the necessity with which a tree bears fruit – . . . evidence of *one* will, *one* health, *one* soil, *one* sun. (Nietzsche, *On the Genealogy of Morals,* Preface, 4)

What justifies an *ad hominem* argument is the essential connection between the thought and the thinker, the insistence that the quality or value of an idea depends in part on the person and the context. But it is not necessarily the person *as such* that is relevant to the argument, if by that we mean the person as a "bare particularity" or the person as the incidental bearer of an innumerable collection of aspects, properties, and relations. A person is related to an idea "insofar as . . . ," insofar as he or she is a Christian, or believes in God, or is a Republican, or an atheist, a male or a female, an American or an Amerasian. The fact that a philosopher smokes cigars is not relevant to her opinions on Aristotle or her religious beliefs. The fact that a philosopher drives a Lotus Elan may or may not be relevant to his opinions about the meaning of life or the finality of death, depending on what he believes that meaning to be and how he tends to drive. To put it a different way, a person is related to a thesis or an argument by virtue of his or her membership in a certain class, trivially, the class of those who promulgate that thesis or argument. Much less trivially, it is the class of those who are in a certain position, share a certain concern, utilize a certain apparatus or language. To take an obvious example, the arguments concerning the existence and nature of distant and mysterious astronomical phenomena depend upon access to certain very sophisticated, extremely expensive equipment and the evidence gained thereby. One can argue about such matters without the advantage of such equipment (Hegel's a priori argument for the necessity of there being only seven planets in our solar system being an embarrassing case in point), but once such equipment is available its use becomes essential to the issue. (An appropriate *ad hominem* argument, accordingly, would be that "So-and-so just doesn't know how to use the telescope. He keeps pointing it at his toe.") In religion, the class in question would be the class of believers, although what class that is will depend on the specificity of the issue in question. Disputes concerning papal infallibility will tend to include only Catholics (though others may readily voice their irrelevant opinions), while arguments concerning "who's a Jew" will include mainly Jews, Israeli politicians, and anti-Semites. Questions about the divinity of Christ will naturally include virtually every Christian, while Nietzsche's *ad hominem* arguments against the Judaeo-Christian tradition presuppose a certain antagonistic stance which understandably tends to alienate and offend believers. When Nietzsche comments that he is an atheist, "by instinct," it is this antagonistic perspective that he no doubt has in mind.[41]

So, too, all questions of morality depend on one's belonging to a culture. (Claude Lévi-Strauss: "When I witness certain decisions or modes of behavior in my own society, I am filled with indignation and disgust, whereas if I observe similar behavior in a so-called primitive society, I make no attempt at a value judgment. I attempt to understand it."[42]) If there are any universal rules or principles of morality, it is because we share a common context, minimally, the context of being "human." (The charge of "speciesism" looms here, an exaggerated estimation of the importance of human interests and a neglect of the interests of other species.) Morality depends upon context, and whether or not there are universal rules or principles of morality, one's view of what is and ought to be will depend on one's particular culture, background and experience, one's family and friends, one's class, one's health and financial position. So too more generally, the search for truth in philosophy depends on one's abilities, one's approach and one's viewpoint. The continuing search for a "method" in philosophy reflects the perennial desire for some definitive, direct access to the issues, but the proliferation of such methods (phenomenological and analytic, for example) only underscores the evident fact that philosophies differ as people and perspectives differ. *Who* one is (in the relevant sense) is a significant (though not sufficient) determinant of philosophical results. "Methods" are *post hoc* means of confirmation.

In other words, Nietzsche's use of *ad hominem* arguments has very much to do with his much-debated "perspectivism." That is, his view that one always knows or perceives or thinks about something from a particular "perspective" – not just a spatial viewpoint, of course, but a particular context of surrounding impressions, influences, and ideas, conceived of through one's language and social upbringing and, ultimately, determined by virtually everything about oneself, one's psychophysical make-up, and one's history. There is no perspective-free, global viewpoint, no "God's eye" view, only this or that particular perspective. There is, therefore, no external comparison or correspondence to be made between what we believe and truth "in itself" but only the comparison, competition, and differences in quality within and between the perspectives themselves. And as the charge that an *ad hominem* argument is a fallacy turns on this rejected assumption that there is such a ready distinction available, the comparison between what we believe and truth "in itself," Nietzsche's perspectivism is already a defense of his *ad hominem* method.

The perspectival metaphor actually leaves open the question of whether there is or might be some "truth in itself," which is the ultimate (even if never "unmediated") object of all perspectives.

Nietzsche's answer to this ultimately skeptical question is, all in all, equivocal. In *Beyond Good and Evil*, he famously claims, "there are no facts, only interpretations," and elsewhere he tells us, "there are no moral facts."[43] But this flamboyant relativism is typically misinterpreted; first, by leaping to the unwarranted conclusion that interpretation therefore has no basis and perspectives cannot be compared; and second, by similarly leaping to the conclusion that perspectivism leaves no grounds for evaluation. In its most vulgar form: "one interpretation is as good as any other." (To insist that something is an interpretation is not necessarily to say that it is not also true.) A perspective is always a perspective *of* something. It would make no sense to talk about perspectives if it didn't also make sense to compare and contrast perspectives in terms of that "something." It is an open (and sometimes unanswerable) question whether that "something" is the same in two very different interpretations. (Is the "gene" of classical genetics "the same" as some particular strands or particles of the complex protein called DNA? Is the body seen and described by an enraptured lover "the same" body examined by the physician?) So, too, an interpretation is always an interpretation *of* something. There is always that critical set of questions, about "fidelity" to the original, about "depth" and "insight," about being "strained" or simply implausible. And, of course, there are any number of practical and heuristic concerns which very quickly lead us to prefer some interpretations over all of the others. Perspectives and interpretations are always subject to measure, not by comparison with some external "truth," perhaps, but by evaluation in their context and according to the purposes for which they are adopted.

Loose talk about perspectives, as if they were nothing but potential viewpoints, leaves out the critical aspect of Nietzsche's perspectivism: The fact that a perspective is *occupied*. One might talk metaphorically, as Nietzsche does, about "looking now out of this window, now out of that one,"[44] but the image of a perspective as yet unoccupied belies the primary thrust of his argument. There is no separating the spectator from the spectacle, and in evaluating the one we inevitably evaluate the other as well. In the abstract, of course, one can blithely talk, on the one hand, about a possible perspective and, on the other, about the persons who might possibly occupy that perspective. But within a perspective, there is no such ready distinction between the particular person and the perspective itself. If my outlook is that of a Jew or a scholar or pessimist or a pervert, how much of that is *my* perspective and how much is *the* perspective of a Jew or a scholar or a pessimist or a pervert? And what an emaciated conception of self would one need in order to pretend that everyone could (or must) adopt exactly "the same" perspective? This is emphatically *not* to suggest that "everyone has his or her own perspective" or that there can be no comparing or contrasting one perspective with another. That is what an *ad hominem* argument is all about, not the substitution of merely offensive insult for serious consideration of the thesis in question but the serious consideration of the person through whom and perspective through which the thesis has come into question.

So, too, an interpretation is formulated and adopted by someone, and the quality or value of the interpretation depends, in part, on what we think of the interpreter. To be sure, a simple empirical observation ("the cat is on the mat") can be more or less confirmed without delving into the character of the speaker. But can any statement about value – whether it concerns the taste of the coffee or the desirability of a reduced capital gains tax – be adequately considered without asking whose it is? The *ad hominem* approach to philosophy asks, whose interpretation is this? If it is a claim about justice, is it that of virtuous Socrates or of brutish Thrasymachus? It is not incidental to the overall "argument" of *The Republic* that Thrasymachus is presented by Plato as a sarcastic thug while Socrates is the embodiment of virtue. Socrates' arguments are not really all that good or convincing, and Thrasymachus' political "realism" is not all that implausible. But by force of character and expansiveness of vision, Socrates wins the day (and Thraysmachus storms out in frustration). Other Platonic dialogues similarly show us a *character*, not just a sequence of arguments separated by a bit of drama. It is Socrates' virtue and charm, not his arguments, that persuade us.

Nietzsche was himself captivated by Socrates, whom he often called a "buffoon," a term of some endearment.[45] Not surprising, it is Socrates' character (also his looks) that attract Nietzsche's attention, even though Socrates is, for him as for us, a largely literary figure, created for us by Plato.[46] There is no easy separating the character from the position and, except by means of a fatal vivisection, teasing out the arguments away from the context. Elsewhere in the Platonic dialogues, character is also presented as an "argument." Cephalus, a rich but shallow old man, displays as well as presents his views in the *Republic*, as does Thrasymachus. In the *Symposium*, the characters of the scoundrel Alcibiades and the beautiful young poet Agathon are essential to their "speeches" about love. Socrates' character in the *Symposium* is shown to be overly aloof and somewhat insensitive, demonstrating something important about how we are to take the doctrines derived from his supposed conversation with the muse Diotima.[47] An interpretation is not just an abstract possibility; it is an embodied, sometimes impassioned viewpoint. It involves an engagement in which the dispassionate logic of the argument alone may be of little relevance and of minimal interest. Thus the rhetorical trick of some logicians, who easily demonstrate the infinite proliferation of interpretations and the inaccessibility of the mythical "*ur-text*," quickly breaks down in practice. Beneath the interpretations lie a person, and while we readily admit that a person may be "of two [or more] minds" about an issue, there is a real life stopping point that logic may not recognize.

Would it be reasonable to suggest that every interpretation, every perspective, is as good as any other? Only if interpretations and perspectives were considered in abstract isolation from any context in which they might be evaluated. But this is, sensibly enough, precisely what Nietzsche denies. There is *always* such a context, and it is defined in part by the character and circumstances of the person who holds the interpretation. Some interpretations and perspectives are superior to others because some people are better educated, more sensitive, more insightful than others. It is only the most decadent or lazy egalitarianism that would argue that "everyone has his own opinion" (i.e. "one opinion is as good as any other"), that all interpretations and perspectives are equal because all people are equal, no matter what else might be true of them. (The truth of even such minimal equality, of course, is one of the doctrines that Nietzsche wants most to call into question.) One could also argue that there will always be a plurality of interpretations and that, apart from some particular perspective or purpose, the choice between them is "undecidable." But this plausible suggestion has been absurdly expanded into the merely mathematical possibility that there might be an infinity of interpretations and perspectives and no "truth" or "facts" to distinguish between them. If we take into account the "truth" of our practical concerns and the "facts" of our social and biological embodiment, however, would or could there be any such myriad of conflicting interpretations that actually mattered to us? One should not become overly wedded to the distinctive American use of the term, but Nietzsche was nothing if not "pragmatic" in his views about value. It is what "makes a difference" that matters, not the abstract possibilities of difference as such.

What defines the context of our concern for knowledge and values alike is the inevitable "fact" of conflict. Typically, we only come to realize that we have a perspective, that what we believe is (only) an interpretation, when we run up against a different perspective or confront an alternative interpretation. We meet a person or enter a culture and find ourselves simply unable to understand what is going on. We get into a discussion and find ourselves in sharp disagreement, not about "the facts" (insofar as these are not also determined by our interpretations) but about the significance of those facts. Two knowledge claims contradict one another; two value systems clash in what might well become ideological warfare. But interpretations collide precisely because they claim to be interpretations of one and the same phenomenon, because they claim to share a context even though they have very different and incompatible implications for our lives. Perspectives can be recognized as perspectives just because they differ and they disagree. We thus demand criteria with which to evaluate our disagreement and order our perspectives. We will use "facts" if we can find them but in most philosophical matters we will more likely stand on our own sense of conviction and muster what arguments and rhetorical weapons we can to ward off doubt and prevent humiliating refutation (which, however, rarely undermines our faith in the doctrine at issue). In other words, we tend to justify our perspective(s) primarily on the basis of the singular fact that they happen to be our own. (" 'My judgment is *my* judgment': no one else is easily entitled to it – that is what such philosophers of the future may perhaps say of themselves."[48])

NIETZSCHE'S PERSPECTIVISM AND THE
PERSPECTIVES OF MORALITY

Wandering through the many subtler and coarser moralities that have so far been prevalent on earth, or are still prevalent, . . . I finally discovered two basic types and one basic difference. There are *master morality* and *slave morality*. . . . The moral discrimination of values has originated either among a ruling group whose consciousness of its difference from the ruled group was accompanied by delight – or among the ruled, the slaves and dependents of every degree. (Nietzsche, *Beyond Good and Evil*, 260[49])

Nietzsche's "perspectivism" is most at issue in his moral philosophy and the two perspectives most in question in Nietzsche's moral philosophy are the conflicting moral viewpoints of master and slave, respectively. Nietzsche denies that there any "moral facts," but what is most striking from a Nietzschean point of view is that neither master morality nor slave morality sees itself as a perspective, much less a mere interpretation. Both see themselves as "objectively true."

The master sees himself and his outlook as simply superior, although the standards according to which he is superior are, of course, his own, unexamined and self-fulfilling. The noble is his own moral paragon, or as the arrogant aristocrat sings in the comedy *A Funny Thing Happened on the Way to the Forum*, "I am my own ideal." The slave, on the other hand, is more interesting, for slave morality from its very inception is a *reaction* to master morality, bound to a theoretical framework and hungry for self-examination and justification. This emerges, first of all, in the incredible sense of self-righteousness that it generates, and, second, in the proliferation of theories and theologies that are brought in to support it. By contrast, a "theory" of master morality is virtually unthinkable. The closest one might come is Aristotle's *Ethics*, in which the Athenian virtues are simply described, together with a rich commentary of fine distinctions. Master morality is a perspective which, while never bothering to acknowledge itself as such, is *the* moral perspective, by virtue of the inherent and unquestioned superiority of its practitioners. But Aristotle's ethics, according to Nietzsche, is already "decadent," far removed from the Homeric virtues that Nietzsche sometimes seems to be defending.

So, too, the morality of the "slaves" is seen as the only moral perspective and so is not seen as a perspective either. But the slaves do see their antagonist, master morality, as a perspective, a false one, and the rigorous egalitarianism of slave morality entails the *immorality* of elitist master morality. Slave morality's emphasis on "inner goodness" as opposed to external fortune actually puts the masters, with all of their wealth and power, at a grave moral disadvantage.

"The act of *most spiritual revenge.*" It was the Jews who, with awe-inspiring consistency, dared to invert the aristocratic value-equation (good = noble = powerful = beautiful = happy = beloved of God) and to hang onto this inversion with their teeth, the teeth of the most abysmal hatred (the hatred of impotence), saying, "the wretched alone are the good; the suffering, deprived, sick, ugly alone are pious, alone are blessed by God . . . and you, the powerful and noble, are on the contrary the evil, the cruel, the lustful, the insatiable, the godless to all eternity, and you shall be in all eternity the unblessed, the accursed, and damned!"⁵⁰

The "masters" view the slaves as simply inferiors within their own moral perspective, denying or ignoring the peculiar ravings and rationalizations of slave morality, but because the slaves clearly see master morality *as* a perspective, they feel the need to defend the one perspective against the other. Slave morality is "reactive" in that it consists first of all in the rejection of another perspective, that of master morality. The subsequent evolution of ethical theory as a theory of "morality" and the attempt to define and defend morality against all objections and alternatives, is first and foremost the attempt to utterly discredit master morality. "Might makes right."

But is slave morality seen in turn as a perspective? It is, to be sure, viewed as an alternative, the *right* alternative to master morality. But is it an alternative *perspective?* The answer would seem to be an unqualified "no." Because it is "true," the slaves' perspective is not seen as a perspective. (Why does the notion of "perspective" not only imply "more than one" but also neutralize the claim of any one perspective to be the "right" one?) The whole history of morality from the Ten Commandments to Immanuel Kant's "categorical imperative" would seem to underscore the absolute nature of morality, and its internal logic would indicate that too. "Morality" means something like "trump" status. Thus we can appreciate how much the current phrase "the moral point of view" constitutes a remarkable retreat for the moral tradition. Morality cannot view itself as a perspective, a "point of view," but yet that is exactly what it is. What Nietzsche's critique of morality consists in is a refusal to share Kant's exclusive emphasis on the "a priori" aspects of the so-called logic of morality to include consideration of the empirical aspects of not only context but also of *character*. Nietzsche's question might be put, what kind of a person would adopt (and what sort of people actually have adopted) the kind of practical "logic" that Kant so incisively analyzes and, in a fashion, defends? What kind of philosophers would spend their lives analyzing (and "justifying") such a logic?

The linchpin of that logic, what some authors have taken to be the conceptual core of morality and moral judgments, is *universalizability*. Whatever one *ought* to do, anyone else (in sufficiently similar circumstances) ought to do so as well. The complications of this thesis (and, especially, of its parenthetical qualification) had been a matter of serious debate since Hegel,[51] but what Nietzsche points out is that the universalizability formulation presupposes a seemingly obvious falsehood, that all moral agents (at least *qua* moral agents) are essentially the same. Thus universalizability represents the exact antithesis of the *ad hominem* argument, since the whole point is to deny the relevance of personal differences and insist that we do not treat ourselves as exceptions to the moral law. (Kant warns us: "If we now attend to ourselves whenever we transgress a duty, we find that we in fact do not will that our maxim should become a universal law . . . we only take the liberty of making an exception to it for ourselves [or even just for this once]."[52]) So, too, it is supposed (although Kant himself would not argue in this utilitarian way) that since we are all in the same moral boat, the moral rules are ultimately to the advantage of everyone. But any rule with any substance, no matter how many people it benefits, will work to the disadvantage of someone. A "level playing field" works to the disadvantage of those who are skilled at climbing hills and leaping potholes. An easy grading system works against the interests of the best students, who have no opportunity to show their superiority. Slave morality, riding on the presumption that we are all in some sense of equal moral value, succeeds in protecting those who are vulnerable to harm and offense while inhibiting those who could protect themselves and harm and offend others. ("To make the individual *uncomfortable*, that is my task," Nietzsche notes.[53])

Of course, Nietzsche does not come out in defense of the virtues of harming and offending people (though on occasion he comes dangerously close to doing so, for example, in his apparent defense of cruelty[54]). But he does see in the universal restrictions of morality a genuine bias against those who would, could, and should assert themselves for the good of both themselves and their society. It has been argued since ancient times that those who rule and those who take the greatest risks for the sake of society (whether or not that is their personal goal) must sometimes ignore the moral inhibitions that are binding on ordinary citizens. And since the nineteenth century, at least, artists and intellectuals have often argued that they must remain "above" ordinary values if they are to be creative, culminating in the romantic cult of genius with which Nietzsche is associated. (E.g., "*My conception of genius*. Great men, like great ages, are explosives in which tremendous force is stored up. . . . What does the environment matter then, or the age, or the 'spirit of the age,' or 'public opinion'!"[55]) But what is also wrong with morality is what it hides and how it distracts us, even us ordinary citizens. By presuming an utterly minimal self and the importance of following a narrowly circumscribed set of universal, peculiarly "moral" rules, it removes all consideration of personal character and virtue (except, of course, as these may be redefined as the tendency to follow these rules).

Nietzsche is not an "immoralist" – as he occasionally likes to bill himself. He is instead the defender of a richer kind of morality, a broader, more varied perspective (or, rather, an indefinitely large number of perspectives) in which the gifts and talents of each individual count first and foremost. Nietzsche doesn't advocate immorality; he rather points out how minimal and inadequate is a morality of "Thou shalt not." Ultimately, it is a denial of life, a denial of our best talents, our energies, and our ambitions. It is not that we ought to break those standard moral imperatives against stealing, killing, and lying. It is rather that we should see how little and how pathetic it is just to obey such rules in the absence of any other virtues of character or excellence. How presumptuous it is for morality to give itself "trump" status at the expense of any number of other "nonmoral" virtues such as heroism, wit, charm, and devotion. Do we really want to celebrate the "good" man when we might have a great one instead?

Perspectivism in morals means that there is no one scale of values and no single way of measuring people and their virtues, but that does not mean that there is no comparing perspectives or that some perspectives cannot be seen as preferable to others. Of course, that preference will be based on the (kind of) people who occupy it and, of course, on the person whose preference it is. But when we compare the self-confident perspective of the master with the reactive perspective of the slave, do we really want to say that there is no reason to prefer one to the other? ("Submission to morality can be slavish or vain or selfish or resigned or obtusely enthusiastic or thoughtless or an act of desperation, like submission to a prince: in itself it is nothing moral."[56])

GENEALOGY AS *AD HOMINEM* ARGUMENT:
RESENTMENT AS A DIAGNOSIS OF MORALITY

While the noble man lives in trust and openness with himself (*gennaios* "of noble descent" underlines the nuance "upright" and probably also "naïve"), the man of *ressentiment* is neither upright nor naïve nor honest and straightforward with himself. His soul squints . . .

[The man of *ressentiment*] loves hiding places, secret paths and back doors, everything covert entices him as his world, his security, his refreshment; he understands how to keep silent, how not to forget, how to wait, how to be provisionally self-deprecating and humble. A race of such men of *ressentiment* is bound to become eventually cleverer than any noble race; it will also honor cleverness to a far greater degree. (Nietzsche, *On the Genealogy of Morals*[57])

Genealogy, I want to suggest, is something of a protracted *ad hominem* argument writ large. Genealogy is not mere history, a search for origins, verbal or material, but a kind of denuding, unmasking, stripping away pretensions of universality and merely self-serving claims to spirituality. Nietzsche presents it as if it were nothing but description, but his language shows it to be anything but that. Walter Kaufmann feels compelled to remind us that Nietzsche is not here defending master morality and attacking slave morality,[58] but once he has finished describing the difference in terms of "nobility" and "excellence" on the one hand and "misery" and "pathos" on the other, is there really anything left to say about "Nietzsche's preference" for one over the other? It is an *ad hominem* question: What sort of a person would want to be a slave and not a master?[59]

That lambs dislike great birds of prey does not seem strange: only it gives no ground for reproaching these birds of prey for bearing off little lambs. And if the lambs say among themselves: "these birds of prey are evil; and whoever is least like a bird of prey, but rather its opposite, a lamb – would he not be good?" there is no reason to find fault with this institution of an ideal, except perhaps that the birds of prey might view it a little ironically and say: "*we* don't dislike them at all, these good little lambs; we even love them: nothing is more tasty than a tender lamb."[60]

The argument of the *Genealogy*, briefly stated, is that what we call "morality" is in fact nothing other than the development of a special set of particularly pragmatic "prejudices" of an unusually downtrodden lot. The twin appeal to history and social psychology is designed to *account for* – rather than to *justify* – moral principles and moral phenomena. Part of that account is that morality consists of universal principles in order to impose some uniformity on a social world of individuals who are anything but uniform. It is the process that Nietzsche, after (but not following) Kierkegaard, calls "levelling." Who benefits from this procedure? Obviously those who are worst off, the weak, but also, and perhaps equally, the mediocre. The system works above all to suppress the drives and the energies of the superior, the strong, those who would rather make something of themselves that "morality" does not allow or, in any case, does not recognize.

A good example here is the idea (popular among students) that every student should get an "A." At first glance, that would seem to benefit everyone, but on a second and more careful look it penalizes the best students by neutralizing the worth of their grade. So, too, if what concerns us is greatness, heroism, and artistry, then morality is like giving an "A" to the merely obedient and ignoring higher ideals. From that perspective, morality appears not as a set of virtues but as an injustice. Again, this is not to say that for the sake of great ideals one ought to break the moral rules or abuse others. It is rather to say that most of the demands placed on us by morality are very minimal demands, hardly worthy of our attention but not therefore worth the cost of violating them either. The use of moral imperatives to insist on uniform equality and deny all nonmoral virtues, however, is a very different story. The nonmoral virtues are as important and, in some contexts (love, war, art and business, perhaps) they readily eclipse the moral virtues as the proper focus of attention. In this sense, at least, Nietzsche defends Aristotle's aristocratic "master" morality against Kant's universalizable slave morality.

Universality, according to Nietzsche, is thus not so much a logical feature of moral judgments, as philosophers from Kant to R. M. Hare have argued, but rather part of the strategy of the weak to deny the significance of the nonmoral virtues and impose their own morality on others. That, after all, is just what slave morality is all about: passing judgment on others in moral categories that may not be their own. "No wonder if the submerged, darkly glowering emotions of vengefulness and hatred exploit this belief for their own ends and in fact maintain no belief more ardently than the belief that the strong man is free to be weak and the bird of prey to be a lamb – for thus they gain the right to make the bird of prey *accountable* for being a bird of prey."[61] Even if universalizability were a (nontrivial) logical feature of moral language, of course, one could raise the question why someone would adopt such a logic and language and why they would try so hard to defend and *justify* it as Kant and others do. Grammar too has its purposes and the ultimate goal of moral language is to undermine those who would be your superiors. Even if it doesn't work, one has the subjective advantage of self-righteousness, knowing that one is "right" and "good" while they are "wrong" and "evil." The grammar of "ought" is political.

Master morality also passes judgment, but the judgments here are first of all *self*-directed, concerning one's own virtues. Aristotle provides us with a list of virtues (each of which is accompanied by two vices, one of excess and one of deficiency). To fail at virtue or (worse) succeed at vice is indeed blameworthy, but Aristotle makes it clear that the primary concern of his ethics is virtue and excellence rather than vice and wickedness. Slave morality, according to Nietzsche, is obsessed with the category of evil, and its virtues, as we have noted, are for the most part banal. For Aristotle, it is obvious that different virtuous men may nevertheless display different virtues in varying proportions.[62] The weapon of the weak, on the other hand, is a single scale of values that ignores or neutralizes virtues except for the minimal virtue of "obedience" – or worse, mere passivity – not doing wrong by not doing much of anything at all. ("Only the emaciated man is the good man."[63]) Whereas Aristotle's aristocrat shows himself to be virtuous by "being himself" and doing well what he does best, Kant's moral slave shows himself to be moral and to have virtue (in the singular only) by *not* doing anything that is forbidden by the Moral Law. (Thus it is far more common to universalize a negative commandment to abstain from certain actions than a positive prescription to do something. The law proscribes drowning someone, for example, but there are few laws that require a passerby to actually save someone who is drowning. Indeed, in most states, it is not a breach of law to sit fishing while watching a person drown, "without lifting a finger." The much-debated philosophical distinction between "killing" and "letting die," of course, is dependent on just the same dichotomy.[64]) To enforce the supposedly singular ("absolute") scale of values that morality commands, a metaphysical presumption is required that "every ego is equal to every other ego."[65] Nietzsche, on the other hand, is primarily interested in appreciating and defending interesting *differences*.

The point of genealogy is to demonstrate the plurality of human histories and the essential difference between the values of the weak and the virtues of the strong. If Nietzsche errs here, I would suggest that it is in the paucity of moral types he discovers, not their plurality, and it seems odd to me that "strength and weakness," which he too often conflates with "rulers and ruled," the politically advantaged and the socially disadvantaged, should constitute the definitive difference between them. (But cf. "I have found strength where one does not look for it; in simple, mild and pleasant people, without the least desire to rule – and, conversely, the desire to rule has often appeared to me as a sign of inner weakness."[66]) Social power does not dictate mastery or master morality, and slave morality is not unknown among those who rule. Nietzsche warns us again and again against confusing political power with strength and misfortune with weakness.[67] To the contrary, he often argues that what constitutes strength is the endurance of misfortune. (Cf. Nietzsche's famous declaration: "What does not destroy me makes me stronger.") What characterizes slave morality is not a set of social circumstances but a pathetic state of mind, a singularly "reactive" set of emotions. And this, he argues in his *Genealogy*, has given birth to what we call "morality." Morality is the product of a particular temperament, insidious emotion, and a specific set of historical circumstances. But the crucial argument, as always, is not aimed against morality or its putative justification as such; it is rather by way of a quasi-psychological question: *What kind of people would choose to live this way?*[68]

SLAVE MENTALITY: *RESSENTIMENT* AND
RESENTMENT[69]

> The slave revolt in morality begins when *ressentiment* itself becomes
> creative and gives birth to values. (Nietzsche, *On the Genealogy of
> Morals*[70])

The *ad hominem* focus of Nietzsche's genealogy of slave morality is a singular emotion, the emotion he calls "*ressentiment*."[71]
Slave morality, he tells us, is a defensive reaction to the values of
the more powerful. In revolt, it becomes creative. It gives birth to
values, contrary values, master virtues turned upside down to become vices, master misfortunes then turn into virtues. If the masters prize strength, then celebrate meekness. If they cherish wealth,
praise poverty. If they take advantage of their good fortune in life,
deny the moral relevance of fortune and insist on the importance of
the "soul" – whose worth is quite independent of the fortunes and
misfortunes of life. In contemporary terms, slave morality is the
self-righteous rejection of a success that one cannot hope to
achieve and a rejection of the values that define that success as
well. In emotional terms, this is the reaction of the emotion we
know as *resentment*, a vitriolic emotion that is always aimed out-
ward and whose presupposition is one's own oppression or inferiority. The *ad hominem* argument, quite familiar to us today, is that
the values that present themselves as ideal and objective in fact are
nothing but the expressions of bitter resentment, and should be
understood as such.

As a master philologist, Nietzsche traces the language of master
and slave morality back to the masters and slaves of ancient times. He
suggests that our most cherished values originated not among those
who were the best and brightest of their times, but among those who
were the most oppressed and impoverished. The dominant emotion
in the evolution of morality, in other words, was not pride in oneself
or one's people, but a defensive prejudice against all of those who
succeeded and achieved the happiness that one could not oneself
achieve. The ancient Hebrews and then the early Christians, Nietzsche argues, simmered with resentment and concocted a fabulous
philosophical strategy against their ancient masters. Instead of seeing
themselves as failures in the competition for wealth and power, they
turned the tables ("re-valued") their values and turned their resent-

ment into self-righteousness. Morality is the product of this self-righteous resentment, which is not nearly so concerned with living the good life as it is with chastizing those who do live it. In its extreme form – asceticism – it is the active denial of the good life, the ultimate outlet of resentment as self-righteous self-denial.

Morality is neither justified nor undermined by its origins, however. The motives which drive one's action do not necessarily undermine their value. But it is not only Nietzsche who tries to tie the rightness (or wrongness) of an action to its source and its intentions. It is very much in agreement with Kant, for example, that Nietzsche asks, is acting "in conformity with" the moral rules sufficient to be moral? And the answer, for both of them, is clearly "no." One has to be properly motivated as well; one has to have the right intentions. As Kant puts it, one has to act for the sake of duty and duty alone, motivated by reason and not our inclinations. But even Kant freely admits that the actual motives of our behavior may be unknown to us. Among those inclinations may well be such self-absorbed and bitter emotions as resentment. Thus Nietzsche's *ad hominem* argument emerges within the Kantian scheme: Insofar as "moral behavior" is motivated by resentment, it is thereby despicable. Kant's (complementary) argument is that insofar as our action is motivated by duty, it has "moral worth." Of course, Nietzsche couldn't care less about "moral worth," nor would he agree what is to count as an "inclination"? Why are respect for the moral law and the urge to do one's duty not, for Kant, inclinations? Nietzsche, who would reject the very distinction between reason and the inclinations, would argue that the motive of resentment may be just as relevant to the evaluation of morality as the intention to do one's duty, but with very different results.

It is unclear for Kant whether resentment would undermine or simply be irrelevant to moral worth, assuming (as both Kant and Nietzsche do) that motivation is complex and both respect for one's duty and resentment of others are possible motives. Nietzsche, perhaps, would deny that there is any such motive as a sense of duty for its own sake; but he would clearly insist that the presence of such a motive cannot eclipse, but should rather be explained in terms of, the sentiments that accompany it. (It should be noted, however, that Nietzsche uses the word "duty" himself, not as an essential ingredient in Kantian morality but as part of a much older noble sense of self, such as when he suggests that the strong have a duty to help the weak.[72])

What is wrong with resentment? Why does pointing out *ad hominem* that someone is acting (or theorizing) out of resentment undermine their authority? Resentment cannot be despicable merely because it is an inclination or a feeling, for all acts, according to Nietzsche, are motivated by the inclinations – our desires, passions, and emotions. Indeed, it is action supposedly motivated solely by reason that he finds most suspicious (and he therefore suspects that resentment may be the actual motive). The problem with resentment cannot be its lack of "objectivity" either, since Nietzsche denies that *any* authority is based on objectivity. Neither is the problem the apparent egoism of resentment, for Nietzsche often observes that all acts are essentially egoistic; the question is rather, "whose ego?" One might well object to the hypocrisy of claiming to be selfless while defending rules that are clearly to one's advantage, but it is not as if deceit as such is a vice. Indeed, Nietzsche (like Machiavelli) sometimes seems to quite admire it and practices it in his work with some consistency. Nor can the problem be that resentment (like vengeance, to which it is closely related) is notoriously self-absorbed and obsessive. All passions and virtues are in some sense self-absorbed and obsessive, according to Nietzsche, and that (as opposed to the "disinterestedness" of reason) is one of their virtues.

Resentment undermines claims to authority, according to Nietzsche, because it is essentially pathetic. It is an expression of weakness and impotence. Nietzsche is against resentment because it is an ugly, bitter emotion which the strong and powerful do not and cannot feel. Strong personalities who are politically or economically oppressed may also experience the most powerful feelings of resentment, but in them that emotion may even be a virtue. The difference, Nietzsche says, is that they act on it. They do not let it simmer and stew and "poison" the personality. There is also petty resentment, and sometimes Nietzsche makes the case against resentment in these terms. Resentment is an emotion that does not promote personal excellence but rather dwells on competitive strategy and thwarting others. It does not do what a virtue or a proper motive ought to do – for Nietzsche as for Aristotle – and that is to inspire excellence and self-confidence in both oneself and others.

A simple but useful example of this particularly vicious and unvirtuous aspect of resentment is a simple footrace. There are two ways of winning such a race. One is to run faster than everyone else and in doing so inspire those you beat to greater effort and faster speeds too. (It is not unusual, when a runner breaks a world record, for those behind her to clock their best times ever too, and sometimes even to break the old world record themselves [a fraction of a second too late, however, to make it into the record books themselves].) The other way to win is to trip your opponents, greasing the track, perhaps, and through your deceptive strategy degrade the race, demean the skill, and trade virtue for a cheap victory. It is clear what Nietzsche would object to here. If the moralist replies that the rules of morality are formulated precisely to prevent the strategy described here, the Nietzschean response is that the universal rules of morality are themselves just such a strategy, a strategy for inhibiting the best.

Nietzsche's protracted *ad hominem* argument, his "genealogy" of morals, is not a simple undermining of morality, and though his language shows this only grudgingly he admires the genius of the slave "revaluation of values" as much as he condemns that strategy as the desperation of the weak. True, there are "life-denying" aspects of slave morality. The universalization of morality ignores— if it does not inhibit–the exercise of the virtues. But it is just too simple to say, as is often said, that Nietzsche wants to get rid of morality or that he wants to get rid of slave morality and replace it with a new, improved, updated version of master morality. What Nietzsche wants to do is to get rid of Kantian conceptions of morality and those features of morality which depend upon universalizability and our undifferentiated equality as moral agents. He wants to replace these with an ethics of the virtues not unlike Aristotle's, a compromise between the spirituality we have developed over two thousand years of Christianity and the rather barbarian master morality of Homeric Greece. The role of *ad hominem* arguments – and genealogy in general as an *ad hominem* argument writ large – is to demonstrate the viciousness as well as the inferiority of the minimalist character of the "moral point of view." This may not "refute" either morality or resentment but it does expose one pretentious form of resentment whose primary purpose is to deny or inhibit the virtues and enjoy a judgmental self-righteousness at the expense of action and enthusiasm.

ECCE HOMO: "NIETZSCHE WAS MAD, WASN'T HE?"

> But I think the ultimate argument against [Nietzsche's] philosophy, as against any unpleasant but internally self-consistent ethic, lies not in an appeal to facts, but an appeal to the emotions. (Bertrand Russell, *A History of Western Philosophy* ["Nietzsche"][73])

> ... all my writings are fishhooks: perhaps I know how to fish as well as anyone? – If nothing was caught, I am not to blame, *There were no fish.* (Nietzsche, *Ecce Homo* [commenting on *Beyond Good and Evil*][74])

The great irony, of course, is that more than any other philosopher Nietzsche himself has long and often been dismissed on the basis of just such *ad hominem* arguments. "Nietzsche was mad. Therefore ... ," and he is dismissed from the discussion. Of course, one quite proper response to his own victimization by *ad hominem* arguments is that "he asked for it," and, indeed, he often did. But the charge today does not have the bite it once had. Alexander Nehamas, for instance, has reconstructed Nietzsche in such a way that the "*ad hominem*" is shifted from the sickly, lonely writer Friedrich Nietzsche to the self-created author, "Nietzsche."[75] This literary creation "Nietzsche" emerges, not surprisingly, as something of his own ideal, and the *ad hominem* argument finds itself strangely without a target. A very different response to Nietzsche, not necessarily to Nietzsche's advantage, has issued out of the oddly persistent French obsession with the virtues of madness, which has led some *au courant* Parisian neo-Nietzscheans (e.g. Georges Bataille and, only slightly saner, Gilles Deleuze) to suggest that Nietzsche was a great philosopher *because* he was mad.

Needless to say, neither the dismissive nor the glorifying argument is very persuasive, though of Nehamas's reconstruction there is much more to say. Indeed, he may be exactly right about Nietzsche's own intentions. Nevertheless, the virtue of an *ad hominem* argument is that it displays not only an author's manifest intentions but the deeper, usually unpublished secrets that explain those intentions. In Nietzsche's case, the not very well kept secret is that he was an utterly miserable human being, "nice" enough to be sure, but hardly a hero, much less an ideal.[76] But if in his "real life" Nietzsche was (quoting Nehamas) "a miserable little man" with a witty mind and occasional quiet blasts of ecstasy, in his writings, he displays all of the clinical symptoms of psychosis, even in his earliest works. Nietzsche often explodes in mad hyperbole and overstatement and displays frequent megalomania and lapses of common sense. But then again, none of this is rare in armchair philosophers who have the most impeccable clinical credentials.

Worst of all, perhaps, Nietzsche displays incredible enthusiasm (all of those exclamation points!), and this alone would be sufficient in most academic contexts to invite chastizing comments in the faculty common room. But enthusiasm is hardly the fatal flaw in intellectual character that would allow an *ad hominem* argument to succeed in getting a philosopher dismissed from the Western intellectual tradition. Outside of philosophy, pronouncements to the effect that "there is no truth" and declarations such as "let us remove the concept of sin from the world" might indeed be certifiably insane. But, within philosophy, they are all in a day's conversation.

Nietzsche was, beyond dispute, a somewhat pathetic oddball, but for my purposes here, I just want to ignore those rather clumsy and clinically unproven *ad hominem* arguments directed so often against Nietzsche and his work. I find no evidence that he was mad when he wrote most of his books. Even if it is true, as C. G. Jung argued in his seminars, that the faultlines of Nietzsche's eventual madness were already present as neurosis throughout his career, I do not think that Nietzsche's life needs to interfere with a proper appreciation of his insights.[77] The question is, can we get this knife to cut one way but not the other? How can we even begin to legitimize Nietzsche's use of *ad hominem* arguments against others without finding that we have already dismissed him as some sort of a crank who is not to be taken seriously? In the immortal words of Edward G. Robinson's "Little Caesar," "he can dish it out, but can he take it?"

If the reader detects a certain inconsistency here it is not one for which I intend to apologize. Rather, it reflects an ambivalence towards my subject that I share with Nietzsche and his own use of *ad hominem* arguments. An *ad hominem* argument evaluates a thesis and its arguments in the light of the person, but to so look at the person does not mean that one ignores the thesis and the arguments, but only that one refuses to look at the thesis and arguments alone. Moreover, to diagnose a motive is not necessarily to dispute the genius through which it is expressed. To find pathos in the philosopher is not therefore to dismiss the philosophy. *Ad hominem* arguments don't have to be dismissive. The more we look at the thinker rather than only the thoughts, the more we may find to admire, even through his or her foibles and frailties. In his several attacks on Socrates, to take the most dramatic example, Nietzsche's ultimate admiration and even envy of his ancient Athenian hero's ironic genius and his ability to turn his rather obnoxious personality into a powerful weapon emerge quite clearly, giving rise to interminable and ultimately pointless disputes about whether Nietzsche ultimately "liked" or "didn't like" Socrates. Nietzsche "saw through" Socrates, but in doing so he made his great predecessor's accomplishments all the more remarkable.

More to the point of this essay, Nietzsche's well-known critique of morality in terms of its underlying motive of *ressentiment* is in fact far more ambivalent and multifaceted than it is usually thought to be.[78] Far from simply rejecting "slave morality," Nietzsche finds much to admire in both its origins and its possibilities. True, both his attacks on Socrates and his attacks on much of morality and many religious moralists are often vicious, *ad hominem* in the worst sense, and uncompromising, displaying no sign of ambivalence whatsoever (e.g., "Socrates was ugly"[79] and "the intestinal morbidity and neurasthenia which has affected priests at all times"[80]). But Nietzsche was not easily given to praise. Nor was he the sort of philosopher who felt comfortable with "on the one hand . . . on the other hand" accounts of his own opinions and prejudices, no matter how often he urges us now to adopt this perspective, now that one. Not surprisingly, therefore, his writing abounds in the most libelous *ad hominem* arguments. A more careful reading, however, requires cutting through that aspect of his "style" to see some of the most important ambiguities of Nietzsche's philosophy emerging by way of context and contrast. An *ad hominem* argument can bring out virtues as well as vice, and a more complete portrait of a philosopher should make us think more of him, not less.

It was Nietzsche who insisted a philosopher, first of all, should be an *example*. It is a fair question, therefore, to ask how well Nietzsche himself would fare, not just his literary *persona* or his much-distorted historical image. There is quite a difference between the ironic genius portrayed (in the first person) in *Ecce Homo* and the Nietzsche whom his sometime companion Lou Salomé described as "quiet, pensive, refined and lonesome." On the one hand there are all of those volumes celebrating Homeric warrior virtues and the love of life, and on the other there is poor Nietzsche, lying lonely and sleepless, thinking about suicide as a way to get through the difficult night. There are all of those pages unmasking *ressentiment* in some of the greatest minds in Western thought, but they are self-evidently animated by the same unmistakable resentfulness and envy in their unloved and unappreciated author. Indeed, even so enthusiastic a defender of Nietzsche as Alexander Nehamas feels compelled to contrast the author's writings to the "miserable little man" who wrote them. To be sure, Nietzsche hardly displayed in himself the virtues he makes us envision. Does his work suffer for us thereby?

It is not altogether implausible to suggest that Nietzsche's works were neither substitutions nor projections of himself, but rather a kind of rage against his solitude and suffering – and against those who sought to conceal or deny their own suffering. Thus the relation between the author and his texts is not, despite the persona, one of self-expression but rather of antagonism and dialectics. Could it be that Nietzsche, far from declaring himself one of "the few" who were the hope of the future, was rather more like Jean-Jacques Rousseau, quite explicit about his own unhappiness, outspoken in his perversity, concerned to envision and promote a world in which there would be no more people like himself. Quite the contrary of self-glorification, Rousseau's works (excepting his *Confessions*, of course) argue for a world filled with people *not* like himself, not so unhappy, not so corrupted. True, Nietzsche sometimes addresses the "philosophers of the future," who will, he hopes, read him. But does it follow that he sees himself as one of them, like them, an untimely precursor of them? I think not. Nietzsche's poignant argument is against himself and against the petty bourgeois moralistic world that produced him. *Amor fati*, on this interpretation, is Nietzsche's ultimate self-irony; if only he *could* accept his life as it is, not wish for another one, or a new age, or a new breed of philosophers, or an *Übermensch*. ("My formula for greatness in a human being is *amor fati*: that one wants nothing to be different, not forward, not backward, not in all eternity. Not merely to bear what is necessary, still less conceal it . . . but *love* it."[81]) Philosophy as wishful thinking.

I believe that Nietzsche wanted to live like that. His pathetic life was the test for that "love of fate." He failed the test. But then again,

Nietzsche often told us how important it was to turn your weaknesses into virtues and advantages. (The Greeks turned their suffering into beauty, Nietzsche tells us, and Napoleon compensated for his stutter by making it even worse.) Nietzsche *used* his resentment. Nietzsche made resentment his style – with its tarantula-type attack and the quick retreat, the ferocious diatribe in the safety of one's private hole – and his target, with obvious irony, was other people's resentment. It is through this perverse holistic picture of the failed philosopher and his heroic philosophy that we can best appreciate Nietzsche. And it is in the similarly holistic picture of human insecurity and resentment and the absolute commandments that people impose on themselves that we might best appreciate the rather striking phenomenon that we call "morality."

CONCLUSION: CONFESSIONS AND MEMOIRS: A PLEA FOR THE PERSONAL IN PHILOSOPHY

> Gradually it has become clear to me what every great philosophy so far has been: namely, the personal confession of its author and a kind of involuntary and unconscious memoir. (Nietzsche, *Beyond Good and Evil*[82])

Nietzsche's philosophy is "the personal confession of its author," whether or not it is "involuntary" or "unconscious." It would be a crass inconsistency for him to claim otherwise (though he could, I suppose, try to capitalize on the "so far" in his comment and claim himself as the first exception). Nietzsche's philosophy is not merely a confession, of course. (No great philosophy could be.) It is, however, irreducibly *personal*. In every case, Nietzsche argues, philosophy expresses the outlook of the philosopher and defines (sometimes misleadingly, sometimes fraudulently) his or her engagement with the world and relations with other people. Thus a critique of the philosophy entails criticism of the philosopher, and vice versa. But to read philosophy as "memoir," to read Nietzsche's own philosophy as "expression" if not "confession," is not a reason to ignore the philosophy, nor does it mean that soundness and persuasiveness of argument are not *de rigueur* as well.

An *ad hominem* argument, properly understood, appreciates not only the profundity of an idea and the effect of an argument but their source and author as well.[83] It thus involves a rich conception of the self, as opposed to the minimal, emaciated, and merely "transcendental" self – "unencumbered" by emotions, desires, personality, or character – presupposed by so many philosophers from Descartes and Kant to John Rawls. Nietzsche presumes a substantial self which cannot be distinguished from its attributes, attitudes, and ideas, and he holds an equally tangible conception of ideas and arguments, not as abstract propositions but as part and parcel of the personality(ies) that promulgate them. Thus the first person voice is not, for him, a mere presentational device, a rhetorical anchor (as in Descartes' *Meditations*) for a chain of thoughts that could (and were intended to be) entertained by anybody. Nietzsche's continuing emphasis on his own uniqueness – one of his more obnoxious stylistic obsessions – is important not for its megalomania but for its more modest message that there is always a particular person behind these words, these books, these ideas.

Philosophy, according to Nietzsche, is first of all personal engagement, not arguments and their refutations. The concepts of philosophy do not have a life of their own, whether in some Platonic heaven or on the blackboards of the philosophy lounge. They are from the start culturally constructed and cultivated and insofar as they have any meaning at all that meaning is first of all personal. This does not mean that they are private, much less personally created but that they are personally *felt*, steeped in and constitutive of the character of the person in question. So much for the alleged *ad hominem* "fallacy." The fallacy, to the contrary, is supposing that a philosophy or its arguments can be cut away from their moorings in the soul of the individual and his or her culture and treated, as they say, under the aspect of eternity. That is precisely what Nietzsche refuses to do.

NOTES

* Portions of this essay, which were previously presented at NANS, have now appeared in "Nietzsche, Postmodernism and Resentment" in Clayton Koelb, *Nietzsche and Postmodernism* (S.U.N.Y., 1990), in Chapter 6 of my *Passion for Justice* (Addison-Wesley, 1990) and in "One Hundred Years of *Ressentiment*: Nietzsche's '*Genealogy of Morals*'" in Richard Schacht, ed. *Nietzsche, Genealogy, Morality* (University of California Press, 1994).

1 Nietzsche, *Ecce Homo* III, 5 (Viking Portable Nietzsche [WK] p. 266).
2 Friedrich Nietzsche, *Beyond Good and Evil*, trans. W. Kaufmann (New York: Random House, 1967), I, 23.

3 Friedrich Nietzsche, *Beyond Good and Evil* 4. Cf. "What is needed is that something must be held to be true, not that it is true." (Friedrich Nietzsche, WP 507).

4 Friedrich Nietzsche, *Twilight of the Idols*, trans. W. Kaufmann (New York: Viking, 1954), "The Problem of Socrates" 3.

5 Friedrich Nietzsche, *Antichrist*, trans. W. Kaufmann (New York: Viking, 1954), "The Problem of Socrates" 11.

6 Friedrich Nietzsche, *On the Genealogy of Morals*, trans. W. Kaufmann (New York: Random House, 1967), I, 10. The adjective "shabby" comes from *Will to Power* trans. R. J. Hollingdale and W. Kaufmann (New York: Random House, 1968), 7.

7 Friedrich Nietzsche, *Twilight of the Idols*, "Germans," 2.

8 Friedrich Nietzsche, *Twilight of the Idols*, "The Problem of Socrates," 3.

9 Friedrich Nietzsche, *Twilight of the Idols*, "The Problem of Socrates," 10.

10 Friedrich Nietzsche, *The Wanderer and His Shadow*, trans. W. Kaufmann (New York: Viking, 1954), 86.

11 Friedrich Nietzsche, *Twilight of the Idols*, "The Problem of Socrates," 6.

12 Allan Bloom, *The Closing of the American Mind* (New York: Simon and Schuster, 1987), p. 231.

13 Friedrich Nietzsche, *Beyond Good and Evil* I, 6.

14 Friedrich Nietzsche, *Antichrist* 11.

15 Nietzsche, *Twilight of the Idols*, viii, 6 (WK 511).

16 Nietzsche, *Twilight of the Idols*, I, 26 (WK 470).

17 The coherence of Nietzsche's ideas is an issue that has provoked a remarkable amount of commentary, from Karl Jaspers' thesis that Nietzsche thoroughly contradicts himself to the now-popular "postmodern" theses (tediously single-minded themselves) that Nietzsche speaks in several voices, from several perspectives, and there is no single "Nietzsche." To which one can only reply, "of course." Nevertheless, several voices can sing in harmony, and several perspectives can converge on a single set of targets and admit of similar origins. On Nietzsche's "affirmative" philosophy, see, e.g., the various essays in Yirmiyahu Yovel, ed. *Nietzsche as Affirmative Thinker: Papers Presented at the Fifth Jerusalem Philosophical Encounter, April 1983* (Dordrecht: Nijhoff, 1986) and Alexander Nehamas, op. cit., pp. 221–34.

18 Bernd Magnus, "Nietzsche and the Project of Bringing Philosophy to an End," *The Journal of the British Society for Phenomenology* 14 (October 1983): 304–20.

19 Friedrich Nietzsche, *The Wanderer and His Shadow* 85.

20 Friedrich Nietzsche, *Twilight of the Idols* "Skirmishes" 33.

21 Richard Rorty, notably, has defended the "playful" Nietzsche in opposi-

tion to the serious philosophical Nietzsche ("one of the worst of the various Nietzsches"), but why, apart from certain internal skirmishes within the philosophy profession, should one feel compelled to see these two as opposed? See his *Contingency, Irony and Solidarity* (Cambridge: Cambridge University Press, 1989).

22 Some of the older, harsher critics include Brand Blandshard and Bertrand Russell. The new commentators include a small army of postmodernists and deconstructionists, but perhaps still exemplary is Paul de Man, for example, "Nietzsche's Theory of Rhetoric," *Symposium*, Spring, 1974. Three excellent discussions of Nietzsche's style are Arthur Danto, "Some Remarks on Nietzsche's *The Genealogy of Morals*," in Solomon, Higgins, eds., *Reading Nietzsche* (Oxford University Press, 1988), Alexander Nehamas, *Nietzsche: Life as Literature* (Harvard, 1985) and Bernd Magnus, Stanley Stewart, and Jean-Pierre Mileur, *Nietzsche's Case: Philosophy as/and Literature* (Routledge, 1993).

23 In a recent debate (the focus was Alexander Nehamas's *Nietzsche: Life as Literature*), both Nehamas and Bernd Magnus argued at some length against the idea that Nietzsche in any sense tried to tell us "how to live." I responded then, as I hold here, that Nietzsche's passionate prescriptions and his impact cannot otherwise be understood. "Telling someone how to live," of course, does not have to involve specific prescriptions, "don't ever tell a lie" or "change your underwear daily," but may consist wholly of general exhortations. "Be yourself" (or "become who you are") is, in the right circumstances and for the right readers, not an annoying vacuity but a profound, even life-changing bit of advice. So, too, "don't feel guilty," may not be anything like "don't ever tell a lie," but for some people, it may be the most important admonition they will ever receive.

24 Friedrich Nietzsche, *Beyond Good and Evil* 211.

25 For instance, WP 540.

26 I have pursued this topic in my "What a Tangled Web: Deception and Self-Deception in Philosophy" in Michael Lewis and Caroline Saarni, eds., *Lying and Deception in Everyday Life* (New York: Guildord Press, 1993), pp. 30–58.

27 Bernd Magnus, *Nietzsche's Existential Imperative* (Bloomington: Indiana University Press, 1978).

28 Friedrich Nietzsche, *Human-all-too-Human* trans. R. J. Hollingdale (Cambridge: Cambridge University Press, 1986), 115.

29 Friedrich Nietzsche, *Mixed Opinions and Maxims*, 271.

30 Friedrich Nietzsche, *Twilight of the Idols* viii, 1–2 (Kaufmann, *Viking Portable* p. 507).

31 Friedrich Nietzsche, *Twilight of the Idols*, The Problem of Socrates, 5.

32 Friedrich Nietzsche, *Twilight of the Idols*, "What I Owe to the Ancients" 3.
33 Howard Kahane, *Logic and Philosophy*, 2nd ed., p. 240.
34 Michael Scriven (*Reasoning* (Prentice-Hall, 1976), p. 228) seems to agree with the exception for "experts," and with the legal context again in mind he distinguishes the "reliability, consistency and credibility" of a witness, three concerns where criticism of his or her moral character may be "appropriate." But why, again, should it be that with an "expert witness" *ad hominem* arguments are tolerable, but not in general? Paul Feyerabend, no doubt, would be quite happy with this bit of antiauthoritarian discrimination, but why should experts be singled out for *ad hominem* abuse? Why should legitimate *ad hominem* arguments be confined to the courtroom and excluded, presumably, from the philosophy seminar?
35 Friedrich Nietzsche, *Genealogy* I, 10.
36 Friedrich Nietzsche, *Gay Science* 125, cf. 343.
37 Friedrich Nietzsche, *Daybreak* I, 95.
38 Friedrich Nietzsche, letter to his sister, Christmas, 1887 (in Kaufmann, *Viking Portable*, pp. 456–7).
39 William Halverson, *A Concise Logic*, p. 58.
40 Ibid.
41 Friedrich Nietzsche, *Ecce Homo* (trans. W. Kaufmann, with *Genealogy*) II, 1.
42 Claude Levi-Strauss, Interview, 1970, quoted in R. Solomon, *A Handbook for Ethics* (Harcourt Brace, 1995) p. 9.
43 Friedrich Nietzsche, *Will to Power* 481, *Beyond Good and Evil* I, 22, IV, 108.
44 Friedrich Nietzsche, *Will to Power* 410.
45 Friedrich Nietzsche, *Twilight of the Idols*, II, 4. He says the same of himself (*Ecce Homo* IV, 1) and of Shakespeare (*Ecce Homo* II, 4).
46 On the "real" Socrates, see Gregory Vlastos, "The Paradox of Socrates," in Vlastos, ed., *The Philosophy of Socrates* (New York: Doubleday, 1971), pp. 1–4.
47 See, for example, Vlastos, "The Individual as Object of Love in Plato's Dialogues" in *Platonic Studies* (Princeton: Princeton University Press, 1973), pp. 1–34; Martha Nussbaum, "The Speech of Alcibiades," *Philosophy and Literature* 3, 2 (1979): 131–69.
48 Friedrich Nietzsche, *Beyond Good and Evil* 43.
49 Friedrich Nietzsche, *Beyond Good and Evil* 260.
50 Friedrich Nietzsche, *Genealogy* I, 7.
51 As early as his Jena lectures at the beginning of the (nineteenth) century, G. W. F. Hegel rejected the formalism of Kant's morality. He openly rejects formal "morality" in favor of a more situated "custom-ethics" in

both his *Phenomenology of Spirit* in 1807 and his *Philosophy of Right* in 1821.

52 Immanuel Kant, *Groundwork of the Metaphysics of Morals*, trans. Paton (New York: Harper and Row, 1964), p. 91. Original German edition p. 424.

53 Friedrich Nietzsche, *Notes*, 1875, vii, 216 in Kaufmann, *Viking Portable* p. 50.

54 Friedrich Nietzsche, *Genealogy*, Second essay, 6, 7.

55 Friedrich Nietzsche, *Twilight of the Idols*, "Skirmishes" 44.

56 Friedrich Nietzsche, *Daybreak* 97.

57 *On the Genealogy of Morals* I, 10, 11.

58 Kaufmann *Nietzsche: Philosopher, Psychologist, Antichrist*, p. 302.

59 But cf. Kafka's "Couriers": "They were offered the choice between becoming kings or the couriers of kings. The way children would, they all wanted to be couriers" (from *Parables and Paradoxes* (Schocken, 1958); reprinted in Solomon, *Existentialism* (Random House, 1974), p. 167.

60 *On the Genealogy of Morals* I, 13. Cf. Bob Dylan's line about the pathetic character who is "bent out of shape by society's pliers" and "gets you down in the hole that he's in." ("It's Alright Ma (I'm only bleeding)," *Bringing it All Back Home*, Columbia Records, 1965).

61 *On the Genealogy of Morals* I, 13.

62 Aristotle's "decadent" concessions to morality may already be noted in his rather unconvincing defense of "the unity of the virtues," the thesis that a good man must and will have *all* the virtues. This is a thesis that Nietzsche, naturally, rejects utterly.

63 Nietzsche, *Antichrist* 47.

64 See, for example, Peter French, *Responsibility Matters* (Lawrence: University Press of Kansas, 1992).

65 *Will to Power* 364.

66 *Daybreak* 413, quoted in Kaufmann, p. 252.

67 I have discussed Nietzsche's conceptions of strength and weakness at length in my "One Hundred Years of *Ressentiment*: Nietzsche's *Genealogy of Morals*," in R. Schacht, ed. *Nietzsche, Genealogy, Morality*.

68 Alexander Nehamas: "In order to refute [Nietzsche's perspectivism] we must develop a view that . . . does not promote a particular kind of person and a particular kind of life – a view that applies equally well to everyone at all times and in all contexts. The task may be possible, but simply saying that it can be done is not the same as doing it. Alternatively, we must show, in the same detail in which Nietzsche revealed the presuppositions of the views he attacked, that his efforts were a failure." *Nietzsche: Life as Literature*, p. 68.

69 Portions of this section have been adapted from my essay in Richard Schacht (op.cit.).

70 Nietzsche, *On the Genealogy of Morals* I, 10.

71 It is worth noting that the French term is much broader than the German or the English, signifying deep feeling in reaction to an offense or a disappointment. Arthur Danto has suggested that it may be the feeling itself that is the critical sign of weakness, taking an offense "personally" and brooding over it as opposed to exercising one's aristocratic prerogative as a matter of course.

72 *Antichrist* 57.

73 Bertrand Russell, *A History of Western Philosophy* ["Nietzsche"] (New York: Simon and Schuster, 1945).

74 Nietzsche, *Ecce Homo*, "Beyond Good and Evil," 1.

75 Alexander Nehamas, *Nietzsche: Life as Literature*, p. 68.

76 Lou's description here: "quiet, pensive, refined and lonesome." (in Solomon, ed. *Nietzsche* [New York: Doubleday, 1973]).

77 Jung's Seminars on Zarathustra: Jung, Carl G., *Nietzsche's "Zarathustra,"* ed. James L. Jarrett (Princeton: Princeton University Press, 1988).

78 See my "One Hundred Years of *Ressentiment*: Nietzsche's *Genealogy of Morals*."

79 *Twilight*, op. cit.

80 *Genealogy* I, 6.

81 Nietzsche, *Ecce Homo* II, 10 (WK 258).

82 Nietzsche, *Beyond Good and Evil* I, 6.

83 I find it fascinating that Nietzsche is often credited as a major contributor to the "death of the author" movement, promoted by such well-known and successful authors as the late Michel Foucault and Roland Barthes. This is a major theme of Nehamas's recent work, and, indeed, Nietzsche did play around considerably with narrative identities and "masks." But, when all is said and done, I cannot think of a philosopher who was more conscientiously an *author* who could be identified with a very real flesh-and-blood writer.

7 Nietzsche, modernity, aestheticism

A long line of philosophers, from Plato to Aquinas, from Descartes to Kant, from Hegel to Heidegger, have composed their works at least partly out of concern with the broader social and cultural events of their time. Yet, for a variety of reasons, it is Nietzsche who is most often read as addressing directly the issues and problems created by his historical period. In particular, we regularly concentrate on his views on what is tendentiously referred to as "the problem" of Modernity. Some see him merely as a diagnostician of that problem; others also find in his work a solution to it; still others consider him as one of its most telling and poignant parts. It might therefore not be inappropriate to approach Nietzsche by means of an examination of his attitude toward Modernity and its "problem" in the hope that we might thereby reach an understanding of some of his general philosophical ideas.

Consider, then, the following statement by Allan Bloom, who describes Nietzsche as both diagnostician and creator of various of the ills of contemporary life. "Prior to Nietzsche," Bloom writes, "all those who taught that man is a historical being presented his history as in one way or another progressive. After Nietzsche, a characteristic formula for describing our history is 'the decline of the West.' "[1] What I particularly want to draw attention to in this passage is Bloom's emphasis on the notions of progress and decline. My reason is that it is a commonplace that Modernity is essentially characterized by a belief in an overcoming of tradition as the result of radical progress in scientific, technological, economic, social, and perhaps even moral practices. But this commonplace does not stand alone.

On the contrary, it is tempting to contrast this social, progressive, optimistic understanding of Modernity with another, much less positive though equally commonplace attitude toward it, perfectly encapsulated in the aesthetics and general philosophy of Modernism. In Modernism we find both the love of innovation and the rejection of the authority of tradition, but also, and at the same time, a questioning of the value of progress, a critique of rationality, a sense that premodern civilization involved a wholeness and unity that have now been irreparably fragmented.[2] This double stand is acutely described by Stanley Cavell, who writes that Modernism represents a moment

in which history and its conventions can no longer be taken for granted; the time in which music and painting and poetry (like nations) have to define themselves against their pasts; the beginning of the moment in which each of the arts becomes its own subject as if its immediate artistic task is to establish its own existence. The new difficulty which comes to light in the modernist situation is that of maintaining one's belief in one's own enterprise, for the past and the present become problematic together. I believe that philosophy shares the modernist difficulty now everywhere evident in the modernist arts, the difficulty of making one's present effort become a part of the present history of the enterprise to which one has committed one's mind, such as it is.[3]

Such an aesthetic and philosophical predicament – the sense that secure foundations are still required but can no longer be found – is not at all opposed to the social and political optimism of Modernity. Cavell's own reference to "nations" hints at their interconnection, and Jürgen Habermas has written extensively about them as two aspects of a single movement. Having abandoned an uncritical reliance on tradition, particularly on religion, in order to find grounds legitimating its various practices, Modernity, Habermas claims, "can and will no longer borrow the criteria by which it takes its orientation from the model supplied by another epoch; *it has to create its normativity out of itself.* . . . The problem of grounding modernity out of itself first comes to consciousness in the realm of aesthetic criticism."[4] What Cavell describes primarily as a predicament of modernist art, therefore, is just an expression and an emblem of a more general problem. This is the problem of finding reasons or criteria for establishing one's identity, one's values, and the legitimacy of one's enterprise as valid without appeal to anything that is located outside that identity, those values, or that enterprise. But can anything we do be of any value if all external or objective standards of value – traditional, religious, or rational – have become suspect?

Asking this question brings us directly into the center of Nietzsche's philosophical concerns, for this is one of the issues most immediately raised by Nietzsche's pronouncement that "God is dead" and by his apparent despair over the devastating consequences of that idea (see *The Gay Science*, sec. 125). As Bloom, again, writes, "Longing to believe, along with an intransigent refusal to satisfy that longing, is, according to him, the profound response to our entire spiritual situation."[5]

Faith in progress, in the overwhelming value of the new, the experimental, the innovative, and the modern does not lead by itself to the impasse on the existence of which Habermas and Bloom, despite their many other differences, agree. For though the past may no longer be considered a source of standards of value, one might well believe that the future can play that role. This faith, which it is equally commonplace to associate with Modernity, springs from the idea that modernist progressivism is the secularization of the Christian doctrine of the millennium. History is still supposed to end, though not through the Second Coming of Christ; it now is supposed to tend toward more "worldly" goals like the perfectly just society, the Spirit's reaching the state of Absolute Knowledge, or the total elimination of human suffering.

Yet faith in the existence of such all-embracing goals is difficult to maintain in the light of the evidence of history. And as this faith begins to erode, the impasse we have been discussing begins to arise: Standards of value are eliminated one after the other; the very idea of progress is undermined from within. As Gianni Vattimo has written,

Modernity is that era in which being modern becomes a value, or rather, it becomes *the* fundamental value to which all other values refer. . . . This formula. . . . coincides with the other, and more widely disseminated, definition of modernity in terms of secularization . . . as faith in progress. . . . But faith in progress, understood as a kind of faith in the historical process that is ever more devoid of providential and meta-historical elements, is purely and simply identified with faith in the value of the new.[6]

Without the notion either of a first origin or of a final destination, the idea of progress is left without content. What is new cannot be better because it leads further away from a bad beginning or closer to a good end: It can, at best, be better because it is new.

The problem is this. Once the value of tradition has been called into question, we cannot appeal to the fact that, say, a practice belongs to a tradition as a reason for valuing it. On the contrary, the traditional now becomes something to be avoided. On the other hand, the absence of a final goal to which the practice can be seen to lead seems to deprive us of the only other rational grounds for valuation. Neither an appeal to origins nor an appeal to ends can supply the legitimation many of us may feel we need for our preferences and actions. The absence of origins and goals deprives all change of any direction, and without direction the evaluation of change becomes at least problematic, if not impossible.

The idea that direction is lacking brings us once again back to Nietzsche, whose madman, in his proclamation of the death of God, bewails:

Who gave us the sponge to wipe away the entire horizon? What were we doing when we unchained the earth from its sun? Whither is it moving now? Away from all suns? Are we not plunging continually? Backward, sideward, forward, in all directions? Is there still any up or down? Are we not straying as through an infinite nothing? (GS, 125)

The problems of the erosion of the authority of tradition and of the grounding of value, which Nietzsche raises here in metaphorical terms, occupied him in different guises and from various points of view throughout his life.

We find these problems raised in literal terms in the three passages that follow. Each passage describes a predicament which is stronger than, and depends upon, the difficulty preceding it. The first concerns simply the low esteem in which tradition is held in Modernity:

What is attacked deep down today is the instinct and the will of tradition; all institutions that owe their origins to this instinct violate the taste of the modern spirit. - At bottom nothing is thought and done without the purpose of eradicating this sense for tradition. One considers tradition a fatality; one studies it, recognizes it (as "hereditary"), but one does not *want* it. The tension of the will over long temporal distances, the selection of the states and valuations that allow one to dispose of future centuries - precisely this is antimodern in the highest degree. Which goes to show that it is the disorganizing principles that give our age its character. (*The Will to Power*, 65)

Nietzsche does not stop with this observation. In addition, in a note which reads like a summary of one of the most central points of his earlier essay *On the Uses and Disadvantages of History for Life*,[7] he writes that suspiciousness of tradition and the past is of a piece with resignation about the new and the future:

The mistrust of our previous valuations grows until it becomes the question: "Are not all 'values' lures that draw out the comedy without bringing it closer to a solution?" Duration "in vain," without end or aim, is the most paralyzing idea, particularly when one understands that one is being fooled and yet lacks the power not to be fooled. (WP, 55)

If history is no longer available as a source of values, it might be thought that reason could play that role. Perhaps it could be demonstrated that our values are based on rational principles which transcend historical contingencies. But the possibility of such a demonstration, Nietzsche writes, is foreclosed. A rational examination of reason cannot be undertaken because "the intellect cannot criticize itself, simply because it cannot be compared with other species of intellect and because its capacity to know would be revealed only in the presence of 'true reality,' i.e., because in order to criticize the intellect we should have to be a higher being with 'absolute Knowledge' " (WP, 473).[8]

Taken together, these three passages produce the following picture. Reason has revealed the inadequacy of tradition: the putatively divine, or in some other way authoritative, origins of various institutions are not sufficient to justify them. The idea that such a justification might be provided by the existence of an inexorably progressive path toward final perfection is equally unacceptable: neither a single beginning nor a unitary end can provide a sense to the events that surround us. But in revealing the inadequacy of history, reason has also itself lost the ability to provide the means for the evaluation of our institutions because any such evaluation is bound to be circular. Reason can provide a rational evaluation of such institutions only if it can be rationally demonstrated that it has the ability to do so; but such a demonstration will inevitably have to be based on the very principles which need to be justified.

What Nietzsche calls "Nihilism," the condition he often identifies as the central feature of Modernity, is brought about by a threefold realization. First, having sought "a 'meaning' in all events," having come to believe "that something is to be *achieved* through the process," we come to lose faith in the existence of such a meaning and to realize "that becoming aims at *nothing* and achieves *nothing.*" Second, having "posited a totality, a systematization, indeed any organization in all events," we come to understand that the various aspects of the world and of history do not form a coherent pattern of their own, we see that "there is no such universal!" Finally, having posited a stable world of being by appealing to the enduring principles of which we can rationally criticize and evaluate the world of becoming, we come to discover that the former "is fabricated solely from psychological needs, and how one has absolutely no right to it." In short, Nietzsche concludes, "the categories 'aim,' 'unity,' 'being,' which we used to project some value into the world – we *pull out* again; so the world looks *valueless*" (WP, 12).

This appears to be (and has been taken as) one of the most penetrating diagnoses of the predicament of Modernity. But Nietzsche in addition seems to offer an acute, impassioned, and vicious critique of modern institutions, particularly of science and morality (which he often associates with one another).[9] He seems to know what Modernity is, and to despise it. He wants to leave it behind, or (if "behind" is not always the appropriate spatial metaphor) to place himself somewhere else altogether: "New ways I go, a new speech comes to me; weary I grow, like all creators, of the old tongues. My spirit no longer wants to walk on worn soles." (*Thus Spoke Zarathustra*, II.1)

This view of Nietzsche's attitude toward Modernity, which is not totally implausible, has underwritten an influential approach toward his thinking as a whole. It is an approach which has been given forceful expression by Habermas, who interprets what he takes as Nietzsche's uncompromising rejection of Modernity as a radical rejection of rationality as well. Nietzsche, Habermas writes, confronts reason with its "absolute other,"[10] and

enthrones taste, "the Yes and No of the palate," as the organ of a knowledge beyond true and false, beyond good and evil. But he cannot legitimate the criteria of aesthetic judgment that he holds on to because he transposes aesthetic experience into the archaic, because he does not recognize as a moment of reason the critical capacity for assessing value that was sharpened through dealing with modern art – a moment that is still at least procedurally connected with objectifying knowledge and moral insight in

the processes of providing argumentative grounds. The aesthetic domain . . .
is hypostatized instead into the other of reason. (p. 96)

This irrationalist interpretation of Nietzsche[11] involves two further
assumptions, both controversial: first, that Nietzsche considers aesthetic judgment irrational and, second, that he reduces all judgments
to aesthetic ones. This is an issue to which we shall return. For the
moment, we should note that Habermas believes that Nietzsche also
urges a return to conscious myth-making, in which he supposes him
to find the only hope for our decadent, declining culture:

Authentic culture has been in decline already for a long time; the curse of
remoteness from origins lays upon the present; and so Nietzsche conceives
of the gathering of a still dawning culture in antiutopian terms – as a
comeback and a return. . . . What is *older* is *earlier* in the generational
chain and nearer to the origin. The *more primordial* is considered the more
worthy of honor, the preferable, the more unspoiled, the purer: It is
deemed better. (p. 126)

Personally, I am convinced that this interpretation of Nietzsche
cannot even be reconciled with the views expressed in *The Birth of
Tragedy*, the most "nostalgic" of his works. Despite its call for a
return to the "tragic" values of Greece, this book does not thereby
privilege whatever is earlier or "more primordial": Greek tragic culture, the reemergence of which Nietzsche here predicts and glorifies,
was itself, as he well knows, a late development; Nietzsche describes
it explicitly as the taming of more primitive, purely Dionysian
("Bacchic") elements through their intermingling with the Apollonian strains of Greek culture (see especially section 2).[12] Furthermore,
in *Philosophy in The Tragic Age of the Greeks*, which dates from the
period when *The Birth of Tragedy* was composed, Nietzsche writes in
a manner which belies directly the combination of aestheticism and
archaism which Habermas attributes to him: "Everywhere, in all
beginnings we find only the crude, the unformed, the empty and the
ugly. . . . Everywhere, the way to the beginning leads to barbarism"
(sec. 1). And in a famous passage in *Daybreak*, he attacks without
qualification the importance often attributed to beginnings and thus
rejects in anticipation Habermas's interpretation: "*The more insight
we possess into an origin the less significant does the origin appear:*
while *what is nearest to us,* what is around us and in us, gradually
begins to display colours and beauties and enigmas and riches of

significance of which earlier mankind had not an inkling" (sec. 44; cf. GM, I.6).

Nietzsche does not therefore in any way glorify origins. Furthermore, he does not, again contrary to Habermas's reading, believe that "authentic culture has been in decline." In fact, it is doubtful that he believes, in general terms, in decline at all. Just as the origin is the other face of progress, to deny progress, as we have seen Nietzsche do, is not at all to affirm decline. The idea of decline, too, provides a meaning, a goal and a message, even if its message is not a happy one. It supplies sense and support in that it presupposes that a unified and purposeful story (though one with a sad ending) can in the end be told about us all: The notion of decline depends on the three categories rejected in the passage from WP, 12 which we discussed above as surely as the notion of progress. For it still presupposes the existence of what Jean-François Lyotard (1984) has called a "metanarrative," and is therefore itself part and parcel of modern and modernist thought.

Neither progress, then, nor decline; no salvation and no downfall. That this is Nietzsche's position is suggested by his asking the first question prompted by such a realization: "Can we remove the idea of a goal from the process and then affirm the process in spite of this?" (WP, 55). Despair at the absence of a goal is what Nietzsche calls "passive" nihilism, a "decline and recession of the power of the spirit"; the ability to affirm the process nevertheless is "active" nihilism, a "sign of increased power of the spirit" (WP, 22).

But the second question prompted by this realization may raise more fundamental philosophical issues: If the idea of a goal is indeed removed from a process, in what sense are we left with a single process at all, since it seems reasonable to suppose that there is no way of specifying a process apart from the goal toward which it leads? It is by following those issues that we will be able to articulate Nietzsche's essentially equivocal relation to "Modernity" and trace its connections to his general approach to philosophy.

Vattimo has written that "by depriving progress of a final destination, secularization dissolves the very notion of progress itself" (p. 8). More radically, as I have just suggested, the idea that there is a process there at all itself begins to break down. And though Vattimo does not make this second connection explicit, he definitely hints at its direction when he goes on to claim that the "dissolution of history" in contemporary historiography "means, first and foremost,

the breakdown of its unity and not that it is simply come to an end."
Nietzsche's "nihilistic" denial of an all-encompassing goal, and of
the existence of the values that such a goal could underwrite, results
in the fragmentation of the unities designated by terms like "the
world," "the West," or, for that matter, "Modernity."

But, as always, Nietzsche's attitude regarding these issues is considerably more complex and equivocal than this description may suggest. To deny an overall goal, a unitary process, is not to abandon
oneself to the sheerly blind contingency which Richard Rorty sometimes seems to envisage as the only alternative once the ideal of "a
neutral and universal metavocabulary" in which every story can be
told consistently with every other is abandoned.[13] Nietzsche maintains a double relation to any grand narrative, including, in particular,
the philosophical tradition itself. He undermines that tradition,
though he knows he cannot completely reject it; he looks beyond it,
though he knows that he cannot see anything fundamentally different there. This double relation makes it impossible to classify him,
following Heidegger, as "the last metaphysician"; following Vattimo,
as "an extreme example of the consciousness of modernity in the
subjective meaning of the genitive, not in the objective one" (p. 98);
or, following Rorty, as an "ironist theorist" committed to the idea
that "something (history, Western man, metaphysics – something
large enough to have a destiny) has exhausted its possibilities" (p.
101). Conversely, it makes it equally impossible to classify him, following Deleuze, as the originator of a radically, foundationally different mode of "nondialectical" thought:

We do not replace the ascetic ideal [Deleuze writes], we let nothing of the
place itself remain, we want to destroy the place, we want another ideal in
another place, another way of knowing, another concept of truth, that is to
say a truth which is not presupposed in a will to truth but which presupposes a *completely different will.* (p. 99)

Both approaches are too simple, pushing Nietzsche toward an unequivocal extreme where he does not belong. Nietzsche, as we have
seen, denies *the* goal, but not goals; how could he, when he writes,
"The formula of my happiness: a Yes, a No, a straight arrow, a *goal"*?
(*The Twilight of the Idols*, I. 44).

Consider now this passage from *The Will to Power* (25), which
seems at first sight to suggest that all goals are to be totally rejected:

On the genesis of the nihilist. – It is only late that one musters the courage for what one really knows. That I have hitherto been a thorough-going nihilist, I have admitted to myself only recently: the energy and radicalism with which I advanced as a nihilist deceived me about this basic fact. When one moves toward a goal it seems impossible that "goallessness as such" is the principle of our faith.

"Goallessness as such" (or, better, "goallessness in itself," "*die Ziellosigkeit an sich*")[14] does not imply that goals do not exist any more than the fact there is no "thing in itself" implies that there are no things or the fact that there is no "real world" implies that there is no world. What it does imply is that goals exist only insofar as they are established by individuals and, perhaps, by cultures (though Nietzsche, who delighted in the latter idea in his early works, became increasingly pessimistic about it later on). But goals, like values and processes, are not already there in the world to be discovered – they are not "in themselves": they are to be made.

But "making," like "discovering," is again too unequivocal a term to use in this context. It involves too much of a contrast – a contrast, moreover, which, to the extent that it has been historically associated with the distinction between the arts and the sciences, is essential to Modernity and forces a choice between nonexistent alternatives. It is a choice which seems so natural that even those who are suspicious of it are always in danger of asking us to make it: The ironist, Richard Rorty writes, for example, "thinks of final vocabularies as poetic achievements *rather than* as fruits of diligent inquiry according to antecedently formulated criteria" (p. 77, my italics; see also pp. 76, 80). But note that to contrast "poetic achievement" so directly with "diligent research" is to agree with Plato when, in the *Ion*, he argued that in contrast to generals and charioteers, poets and rhapsodes proceed not by "craft" but by inspiration, and simply to reject his preference for the former. The merits of these positions are not my concern. But I do wonder whether a simple reversal of Plato's evaluative scheme can indeed, as it is intended to do, carry us beyond "philosophy."

Extreme distinctions of this sort force us to be either for or against choices which are much too complex for such simple reactions; they enjoin us to be either part of or outside institutions and practices which do not allow such wholesale commitments. Indeed, they mislead us into thinking that the objects they concern are unitary in a way which makes such wholesale attitudes necessarily appropriate. And it is precisely of such distinctions and of the all-encompassing unities they presuppose that Nietzsche, as his famous discussion of oppositions in *Beyond Good and Evil* I.2 shows, was so deeply suspicious.[15]

It is reasonable now to ask on what basis, if distinctions of this sort are absent, can choice and preference be based? Doesn't the situation we described above deprive us of all ability to take sides, and isn't choice just such a taking of sides? It is now, finally, that we can see why the arts, and aesthetics in general, are so absolutely crucial to Nietzsche's thought. Let me begin by quoting Allan Megill:

> In the nature of things ... one has no ground for choosing one mode of behavior over another, for morality is not a question of "the nature of things." ... How, then, does one choose between competing modes of behavior? Nietzsche's answer is that choice ultimately has to be made on aesthetic grounds. (p. 31)

Now this statement is ambiguous. It may mean that the choice of a particular mode of behavior is *like* an artistic decision concerning, say, the adoption of a particular style.[16] But it may also mean that the choice of a mode of behavior is *itself* an artistic decision, focusing only on the aesthetic features of the course of action in question. The first alternative concerns the basis on which choices and decisions are made: It holds that artistic decisions provide the model for all action. The latter refers to the very content of the decision itself: It holds that all decisions are straightforwardly artistic. And though the two interpretations are probably interconnected, my own view is that the former is more likely to be correct.[17]

In turning to the arts, and among many other points that are relevant to Nietzsche's thought, we should focus our attention on one of the most important facts established by their historical investigation. This is that artistic "creativity" is far less free and far more constrained by time and history than the Platonic-Romantic tradition has ever tempted us to suppose. "Poetic achievement" and "diligent research" are far from the polar opposites we have seen Richard Rorty take them to be.

It is an allusion to just this fact that emerges out of one of Nietzsche's most powerful statements in *On the Genealogy of Morals*: "If a temple is to be erected," he writes, "*a temple must first be destroyed;* that is the law – let anyone who can show me a case in which it is not fulfilled!" (II.24). The image here is worth pursuing at some length. Temples, both as religious and as architectural edifices, always replace earlier competitors. They are often built on the very spot the defeated religion (or the earlier patron) had laid claim to, both in order to express the new temple's victory over the old one and, more practically, in order to have the material of the earlier temple close to hand. Greek temples, for example, are built on mountain tops or on promontories. Even in the few cases when they are found in "the midst of a jagged rocky gorge," as Heidegger writes, they are built to be visible from a large distance: they do not harmonize with their environment, they don't so much allow its elements to fall into place around them – they *occupy* it.[18]

Yet the destroyed temple inevitably exacts a partial victory: both its design and its materials tend to be used in the construction of its replacement. Early Christian churches, for example, maintain much of the structure of late pagan temples and at least partly consist of the very same stones, their ornamented face turned inward and thus both hidden from the faithful and also, unwittingly, from the dissolution of time. No temple, in short, is so radically new. The very notion of originality, contemporary art historians are claiming, cannot be taken for granted:

Modernism and the avant-garde are functions of what we could call the discourse of originality, and . . . that discourse serves much wider interests – and is thus fueled by more diverse institutions – than the restricted circle of professional art-making. The theme of originality, encompassing as it does the notions of authenticity, originals, and origins, is the shared discursive practice of the museum, the historian, and the maker of art. And throughout the nineteenth century all these institutions were concerted, together, to find the mark, the warrant, the certification for the original.[19]

Though Nietzsche's untimely, presciently ironical attitude toward Ezra Pound's modernist slogan, "Make it new!," is not a call for the return to the archaic, as Habermas believes, neither is it a denial that change, development, or even originality, suitably understood, is possible. Once again, just as the fact that the "real" world does not exist does not obliterate the world, so the impossibility of "absolute" originality does not abolish originality: On the contrary, it places it within a structure and within history, which is where, after all, it has always belonged.[20] Still, Nietzsche's reliance on the idea of "overcoming" (*überwinden*), especially in *Thus Spoke Zarathustra*, may suggest that his thought on the issue is inconsistent. The point is well stated by Vattimo:

> Modernity is defined as the era of overcoming and of the new which rapidly grows old and is immediately replaced by something still newer. If this is indeed the case, as Nietzsche claims, then no way out of modernity can be found in terms of an *overcoming* of it. . . . overcoming . . . is a part of modernity itself. (pp. 76–7)

But even Zarathustra, the great proponent of overcoming, knows that one cannot leave everything behind. With a direct reference to the scene in the Prologue in which a clown jumps over a tightrope walker and causes him to fall to his death, Zarathustra later says: "There are many ways of overcoming: see to that *yourself*! But only a jester thinks: 'Man can also be *skipped over*' " (Z III.12.3).[21] Once history has been fragmented, once the necessity of relying on models and materials from earlier periods has been established, where is absolute novelty going to come from and where can it lead? The notion of total originality is as "other-worldly" as any of the ideas Nietzsche characterizes by that term.

The fragmentation of history implies that the wholesale criticism of one's time or institutions, which Habermas, for example, considers essential to rational discussion, is impossible. The very desire to engage in such a sort of universal criticism seems to me to be one of the central features of Modernity itself – which we may almost define as a period obsessed with the desire to state, once and for all, what its essence is, either to affirm or to abandon it altogether. And if we are to agree with Milan Kundera that the modern era is inaugurated by Cervantes's great novel, then it will be doubly appropriate to characterize this desire as perfectly quixotic.[22]

But because absolute originality and the absolutely new are not to be identified with originality and the new, I cannot agree with Vattimo when he claims that "the dissolution of the value of the new . . . is the meaning of the post-modern. . . . From architecture to the novel to poetry to the figurative arts, the post-modern displays, as its most common and most imposing trait, an effort to free itself from the logic of overcoming, development, and innovation" (p. 105). Innovation has not been abandoned at all. In any case, the effort to gain such radical freedom, to leave Modernity so far behind, would itself constitute yet another modernist episode. Postmodern art has taken to heart the lesson that reappropriation, rearrangement, rethinking are all ways of creating new things – and that there are no rules for establishing in advance when such combinations will be successful. That much postmodern art engages simply in rearrangement without accomplishing much that is in any way original [23] is not a feature of postmodern art itself but of inferior postmodern art, which, in its lack of even relative originality and history only repeats the history of all inferior art – which is to say, of most art. Where modernist architecture, for example, was, in its effort to avoid any references to the past, often stark and impersonal, postmodernist buildings, in their proliferation of such references, commonly end up being both fussy and boring.

The fragmentation to which we have been referring so far raises a number of complex problems both in itself and in relation to Nietzsche. Richard Rorty considers it as the result of the realization that there is no overarching neutral vocabulary in which all the world's problems can be given a nontendentious statement and a clear solution acceptable to all. It may then seem to follow, as Rorty urges, that intellectuals, as intellectuals, are to retreat to the essentially private concern which he calls "self-creation," avoiding any desire to produce a narrative that claims to tell the story of anything larger than themselves. This, of course, need not prevent those intellectuals who are also "liberals" from devoting themselves to reducing cruelty in the world and to giving to all the opportunity to create without interference something out of themselves, if they can and if they want. But this, Rorty insists, is a different enterprise. Private projects of self-creation have no direct implications (in fact, they have no implications at all, in his view) for public projects directed at changing how people live.

Rorty contrasts Nietzsche with Proust, who he believes saw himself as *just* the product of the specific accidents of his life. But Nietzsche, according to Rorty, displays a divided attitude. On the one hand, he is one of those philosophers who, on a personal level, "define their achievement by their relation to their predecessors rather than by their relation to the truth," those philosophers who just try to make something out of themselves that is simply different from what anyone else has done so far. "Nietzsche," Rorty writes, "may have been the first philosopher to do consciously what Hegel had done unconsciously" (p. 79 with n. 2). On the other hand (and here the contrast with Proust becomes crucial),

the vocabularies Nietzsche discusses . . . are linked dialectically, related internally to one another. They are not a chance collection but a dialectical progression, one which serves to describe the life of somebody who is not Friedrich Nietzsche but somebody much bigger. The name Nietzsche most often gives to this big person is "Europe." In the life of Europe, unlike that of Nietzsche, chance does not intrude. (p. 100)

Rorty relies on a particularly "firm distinction between the private and the public" to support his division of philosophers and his general approach to the role of intellectuals as well. In contrast to Habermas, he writes, who sees "Hegel through Foucault and Derrida as destructive of social hope," he himself considers "this line of thought as largely irrelevant to public life and to political questions. Ironist theorists like Hegel, Nietzsche, Derrida, and Foucault seem to me invaluable in our attempt to form a private self-image, but pretty much useless when it comes to politics" (p. 83).

But on what grounds can we maintain such a strong distinction between the private project of making something out of ourselves and the public goal of changing the lives of others, for better or worse? A person, as Rorty insists throughout *Contingency, Irony, and Solidarity*, is a "network" of attitudes, beliefs, and desires, and these form various subsets each of which connects the same person to a variety of different groups whose own identity, in turn, cannot be easily separated from that of the individual in question. Everything one is, and in respect of which one changes, has (in different degrees, to be sure) effects on the nature of those groups; and changes in such groups, conversely, have similar effects on the individuals who compose them.

Nietzsche, who believed that things are the sums of their effects (WP, 551) and who wrote that the soul might be characterized as the "social structure of the drives and affects" (BGE, 12), was well aware of this. Contrary to Rorty's claim, he did not "want not just the effable and relative beauty of rearrangement but the ineffable and absolute sublimity of the Wholly Other . . . . The ironist theorist cannot imagine any successors, for he is the prophet of a new age, one in which no terms used in the past will have application" (pp. 101–102). This description might be true of Hegel or Heidegger. But it is not true of Nietzsche, whom Rorty reads under Habermas's influence. The author who writes that "only the day after tomorrow belongs to me; some are born posthumously" (*The Antichrist*, Pref.), who composes *A Prelude to the Philosophy of the Future* and who announces that "a new species of philosophers is coming up" (BGE, 42) wants both readers and successors – though his successors are to be of an unusual sort, as the following dialogue demonstrates:

A: "What? You want no imitators?"
B: "I do not want people to imitate my example; I wish that everybody would fashion his own example as *I* do."
A: "So?" (GS, 255)

The reason for this is that Nietzsche is perfectly aware that in making something out of oneself, even if one tries to do so in the most private of terms, one also changes (if one writes books that get to be read) what many others will think and do as well. And what others do, which determines what they are, will also determine much else besides – for example, what in the future will or will not count as cruelty, and what therefore it will be that "liberals" will have to fight against. What we take ourselves to be is essentially connected to how we propose to treat one another: The public and the private intermix and philosophy, for better or worse, often has political implications.

In his discussion of Nietzsche, Rorty writes that "the goal of ironist theory," a goal which is also his own, is "to understand the metaphysical urge, the urge to theorize, so well that one becomes entirely free of it" (pp. 96–7). Does Nietzsche pursue that goal? Not surprisingly, perhaps, my answer to this question is that he does not, and that the desire to become "entirely free of the metaphysical urge," though perhaps a desire which drove Heidegger, is too naive and unequivocal to be Nietzsche's. In *The Gay Science* (sec. 344), Nietzsche concludes that even he should be counted among the "metaphysicians" he has so often attacked: "Even we seekers after knowledge today, we godless anti-metaphysicians still take our fire, too, from the flame lit by a faith that is thousands of years old, that Christian faith which was also the faith of Plato, that God is the truth, and that truth is divine." Now it might be argued that since Nietzsche introduces this statement with the view that "it is still a *metaphysical faith* upon which our faith in science rests," he is only attributing such a faith to those who, unlike him, still have "faith in science." The issue is extremely complex, but I believe that we cannot in the end exclude Nietzsche from among the metaphysical antimetaphysicians he describes here. "Faith in science" (*die Glaube an die Wissenschaft*) is not simply a belief that the truths of the natural science are privileged; more broadly, it is the view that the value of truth is unconditional, that "*nothing* is needed more than truth," as Nietzsche writes earlier in this section. If this is so, then we must take very seriously the question with which the section ends: "But what if this [sic., the idea that truth is divine] became more and more incredible, if nothing should prove to be divine any more unless it were error, blindness, the lie – if God himself should prove to be our most enduring lie?"

This question is crucial partly, and simply, because it is a question. Nietzsche does not spell out his answer to it, and we cannot just assume that he believes that in that case we would be "liberated" from metaphysics. But the question is also important because it gives rise to the following speculation. Suppose that it is indeed "proven" that God is our most enduring lie, that the truth is not of unconditional value, that, in other words, it is *false* that we should always accept what is true. Would we then just give up that view? If we did, we would do so, presumably, because the view is false. And that would involve us, once again, in believing that we should not always believe the truth (whatever exactly that is supposed to mean) because it is *true* that we should not. In other words, we would still be motivated, in that particular belief – "godless" and "antimetaphysical" as it may be – by the same faith in truth which this belief was supposed to be supplanting. The faith in truth simply cannot be eliminated, and Nietzsche's question, in my opinion, is intended to force us to think through this conundrum ourselves.[24]

The conundrum is difficult to avoid because Nietzsche refuses an easy "pragmatist" identification of truth with usefulness.[25] For example, Richard Rorty, who accepts this identification and who thinks that Nietzsche, in some of his moods, did too, writes that, in those moods, Nietzsche urges us "to simply erase from our minds such notions as 'truth,' 'error,' 'appearance,' and "reality." These notions can be replaced by notions like 'beliefs advantageous for certain purposes, but not for others' and "a description of things useful for certain kinds of people, but not for others."[26] The difficulty with this reading of Nietzsche is that it attributes to him a general *theory* of truth, relying on usefulness as a rival for the more traditional notion of correspondence. But Nietzsche does not offer such a theory. In particular, he refuses to identify truth with usefulness: "A belief, however necessary it may be for the preservation of a species, has nothing to do with truth" (WP, 487). How could he, when he also writes the following: "How is truth proved? By the feeling of enhanced power – by utility – by indispensability – in short, by advantages (namely, presuppositions concerning what truth *ought* to be like for us to recognize it). But that is prejudice: a sign that truth is not involved at all – " (WP, 455). In fact, Nietzsche refuses to offer any theory of truth at all. It is true that his statement that "the criterion of truth resides in the enhancement of feeling of power" (WP, 534) is often interpreted as his "theory" of truth. But, I believe, the effect of this passage is exactly the opposite. Nietzsche is explaining why people *accept* certain ideas as true, independently of whether these ideas are in fact true or not. If Nietzsche has any theory concerning truth, it is not a theory about what truth is, but a theory about why people tend to believe certain views over others. This is a very different matter.

But if Nietzsche has no theory of truth, it may now be asked, how can he possibly say that Christianity is a "lie," or that his own genealogical account is an instance of a "plain, harsh, ugly, repellent, unchristian, immoral truth" (GM, I.1)? How can he consider anything as true or false? This question poses a real problem only for those who think that a term can be used correctly only if we have a general theory about its use and application. But this "Socratic" assumption is not justified. We do not need to be able to explain what feature makes all our true theories true in order to be able to claim that the theory of relativity is true partly because it explains the observations concerning the perihelion of Mercury better than its competitors, any more than we need to be able to give a general account of justice in order to know if returning a murderous weapon to its insane owner is just.

The issue is important and has implications beyond the interpretation of Nietzsche. Rorty vacillates on the question whether philosophers should offer theories of truth. In the passage I quoted above, he seems to me to offer just such a theory, however rudimentary. In

Contingency, Irony and Solidarity, however, he takes a more radical approach, arguing that "our purposes would be served best by ceasing to see truth as a deep matter, as a topic of philosophical interest, or 'true' as a term which repays 'analysis' " (p. 8). But then he also writes that "the difficulty faced by a philosopher . . . like myself . . . is to avoid hinting that [my] suggestion gets something right, that my sort of philosophy corresponds to the way things really are" (p. 8).

Note, first, that these last two claims are not equivalent. To say that a view gets something right is or should be very different from arguing that it corresponds to the way things really are. The latter is not an argument at all, but an *explanation* (if one wants to give one) why that view is true. The *argument* ("suggestion") for the truth of the view in question is simply the set of specific, nongeneralizable reasons on account of which it is better than its particular competitors. Second, given that these two statements are not equivalent, there is no reason why we should try to avoid the former: Rorty, in fact, argues for the superiority of his "ironist" approach over that of the realists, and does so on specific grounds. It is only, in my opinion, his residual commitment to the Platonist view that particular applications of "true" must be underwritten by a general account of the nature of truth that prevents him from acknowledging his belief in particular truths and his reliance on argument.[27]

For these reasons I cannot accept Vattimo's optimistic assessment: "Even if God dies because he must be negated in the name of the same imperative demand for truth that was always considered one of his own laws, the meaning of an imperative demand for truth itself is lost together with him" (p. 24). The loss of the demand for truth is what I, for one, cannot possibly find in Nietzsche. What he is honest enough to acknowledge is that even the search for "small," specific truths, and belief in them, may spring from the same motive that brought Plato to the deification of Truth as a whole which we saw him denounce above. And it is just because of his unsettling vacillation on this issue that I am tempted to think of him, perhaps paradoxically, as a postmodern thinker *avant la lettre,* in the sense that he has abandoned the desire for complete liberation and innovation that presupposes the existence of a single, all-encompassing system in which one is located and from which one can therefore exit. In my view, Nietzsche realizes that "Modernity" does not designate a single thing just as he realizes that the same is true of many, if

not of all, of our most general terms. It is precisely because of the
complexity of the phenomena involved that Nietzsche writes that
"we set up a word at the point at which our ignorance begins, at
which we can see no further, e.g., the word 'I,' the word 'do,' the
word 'suffer' " (WP, 482). All criticism is therefore immanent: Modernity cannot be criticized, or justified, as a whole and there is no
radically new place (or time) beyond it. But the complexity of both
individuals and social structures, which Nietzsche devoted his life
to revealing, ensures that there will always be *some* place to stand
and from which specific criticisms and specific defenses can be issued: This will not be a place from which everything could be seen,
of course; a place from which everything might be seen would have
to be nowhere; but, in fact, nothing (which is all that "everything"
refers to) can be seen from nowhere.

Far from being a symbol and hero of Modernity, for good or ill,
Nietzsche, despite his talk of "us moderns," has deep doubts about
the very existence of such a distinct period. More than any other
thinker before him (and with greater suppleness than some of his
contemporary followers), he realized both the continuity and the
immense complexity of our intellectual history from the Greeks to
today. Its gleaming monuments and piles of rubble surround us and
every new monument creates its own rubble.

Nietzsche's attitude, then, is in my opinion the real source of
what Vattimo calls "weak thought" (*pensero debole*), much more so
than Vattimo concedes. But Nietzsche's approach is also both more
critical and more optimistic than Vattimo suggests in regard to his
own idea when he writes that

when the origin has revealed its insignificance, as Nietzsche says, then we
become open to the meaning and richness of proximity [cf. *Daybreak*, sec.
44, quoted earlier] .... We become capable of playing those language games
which constitute our existence upon the sole basis of our belonging to a
particular historical tradition, which we have to respect in the same way in
which we feel respect for monuments, tombs, traces of past life, or even
family memories. (p. 177)

Tradition, however, is to be described in more living images as well.
It does not only constitute a past that is gone, as all of Vattimo's
metaphors suggest, but our present as well. It is, of course, to be
respected; but if respect is the only appropriate attitude toward it,

then perhaps Habermas's identification of postmodernism with neo-conservatism is not unjustified. But our present, along with the monuments, tombs, traces of past life or even family memories that have made us what we are, can also be criticized and changed; and Nietzsche provides both reasons and strategies for that purpose.

Vattimo writes that the postmodern is a matter "of living completely the experience of the necessity of error and of raising oneself for an instant above that process; or . . . of living the errant in the light of a fundamentally different attitude" (p. 171). I am as suspicious of the idea of "a fundamentally different attitude," whatever that can be, as I am of the idea that Nietzsche's aestheticization of experience has shown, as many believe, that "there is no such thing as truth."

Taking artistic activity as our paradigm for understanding our interaction with the world and with one another, as Nietzsche does, does not at all imply that all our interactions involve falsification. The notion of falsification is not directly applicable to the arts in the first place. But the artistic model does imply that we can no longer lay claim to a clear-cut distinction between what is perfectly real and what is purely fictional.

It is true that artistic styles change and that no single style can claim to represent the world as it really is. But, as long as one employs a particular style (and this is something we necessarily always do) one cannot distance oneself from it, and see the very respects in which that style is conventional. For to do this, one must have already developed another style the conventional elements of which will remain necessarily invisible and which will therefore supply the standards of naturalness, truthfulness, and accuracy in terms of which the previous style will have to be evaluated. There is no way around it: Something always has to be taken for granted, and a conditional dogmatism, perfectly captured by Nietzsche's aesthetic model, is our fate.

"Conditional dogmatism" is another term for Nietzsche's perspectivism. Alasdair MacIntyre characterizes the latter as the view that because everything we know and believe is the product of a tradition and not of some undistorted access to an independent reality, it is impossible to say that what we actually believe can be true. For, according to MacIntyre's understanding of perspectivism, what we believe is supposed to be the product of one tradition to which there are always significant alternatives, with as great a claim to truth and accuracy, and which are therefore immune to criticism (p. 352). MacIntyre then proceeds to criticize perspectivism on the grounds that it

fails to recognize how integral the conception of truth is to tradition-constituted forms of enquiry. It is this which leads perspectivists to suppose that one could temporarily adopt the standpoint of a tradition and then exchange it for another, as one might wear first one costume and then another, or as one might act one part in one play and then a quite different part in a quite different play. But genuinely to adopt the standpoint of a tradition commits one to its view of what is true and false and, in so committing one, prohibits one from adopting a rival standpoint. (p. 367)

But, as I suggested above in my discussion of conditional dogmatism and as I have argued in detail elsewhere,[28] the latter part of MacIntyre's statement describes *exactly* Nietzsche's view of how one is related to one's perspective or tradition. In what is now a common error, MacIntyre identifies perspectivism with relativism. He refuses to attribute to Nietzsche the more sophisticated view he himself accepts and ignores Nietzsche's warning against those "historians of morality (mostly Englishmen)," who are either too impressed with the fact that the "tame nations" agree on some basic principles and infer that those principles are therefore unconditionally binding or who, conversely, "see the truth that among different nations different valuations are *necessarily* different and then infer from this that *no* morality is at all binding" (GS, 345). "Both procedures," absolutism and relativism (Nietzsche concludes), "are equally childish."

MacIntyre's position, however, is not in all respects similar to Nietzsche's. For MacIntyre, too, tends at times to totalize the traditions with which he is concerned, to attribute too great a unity to them. This is at least suggested by his description of how various traditions encounter crises and rivals; he writes, in this connection, that "the rationality of tradition requires an acknowledgment by those who have hitherto inhabited and given their allegiance to the tradition in crisis that the alien tradition is superior in rationality and in respect of its claims to truth to their own" (p. 365). But traditions are seldom confronted in this wholesale manner, and we need a considerably more fine-grained analysis of how specific parts of one tradition can be revised in light of elements of another. Traditions are confronted in their totality only in times of war, and rationality then has relatively little to do with which one emerges victorious.[29]

Nietzsche's attitude toward Modernity, therefore, is complex and divided. He attributes to it a complexity which it never has been willing to acknowledge of itself:

As in the realm of stars the orbit of a planet is in some cases determined by two suns; as in certain cases suns of different colors shine near a single planet, sometimes with red light, sometimes with green light, and then occasionally illuminating the planet at the same time and flooding it with colors – so we moderns are determined, thanks to the complicated mechanics of our "starry sky," by *different* moralities; our actions shine alternately in different colors, they are rarely univocal – and there are cases enough in which we perform actions *of many colors*. (BGE, 215)

In this, it is emblematic of his attitude toward most everything and does, indeed, lead us to the heart of this thought. Even though, for example, he writes, "I call Christianity the one great curse, the one great innermost corruption, the one great instinct of revenge, for which no means is poisonous, stealthy, subterranean, *small* enough – I call it the one immortal blemish of humanity" (A, 62), he also considers it as "the means through which the European spirit has been trained to strength, ruthless curiosity, and subtle mobility" and claims that "this tyranny, this caprice, this rigorous and grandiose stupidity has *educated* the spirit" (BGE, 188). Absolute rejections, like absolute distinctions, are very much what he constantly, absolutely tried to avoid. And underneath this all is his aestheticism, which allows him to make choices knowing all the while that they cannot be binding on everyone and to recognize that everything in the world is beyond good and evil, that everything in the world, like everything art touches, can become part of a great work.[30]

NOTES

1 Bloom (1987), p. 196.
2 This distinction permeates the erudite and engaging study of Modernity in Calinescu (1987). It is, however, pertinent to note that people of all eras, even of those which were subsequently held up as the paradigms of greatness, have tended to perceive their times as periods of confusion and fragmentation: "Mihi degere vitam / Impositum varia rerum tur-

bante procella" [My lot is to live in the midst of varied and disturbing storms], Petrarch, for example, wrote in his *Africa* (IX, 451–2).

3 Cavell (1969), p. xxii.

4 Habermas (1987), pp. 7, 8.

5 Bloom (1987), p. 196.

6 Vattimo (1989), pp. 99–100.

7 The essay is the second of Nietzsche's *Untimely Meditations*. I have discussed this particular point and its later development in *The Genealogy of Morals* in Nehamas (1994).

8 This problem, of course, is precisely what Habermas's theory of "communicative action" is intended to resolve. I will suggest later on why such a solution seems to me unnecessary.

9 This connection is made explicitly in the Fifth Book of *The Gay Science* and in the Third Essay of *The Genealogy of Morals* (GM).

10 Habermas (1987), p. 94. Further references to this work parenthetically in the main text.

11 Another proponent of such an irrationalist account is Alasdair MacIntyre (1988). An adherent of Nietzsche's perspectivism, as MacIntyre construes the latter, "must not engage in dialectical argument with Socrates, for that way would lie what from our point of view would be involvement in a tradition of rational enquiry, and from Nietzsche's point of view subjection to the tyranny of reason. Socrates is not to be argued with; he is to be mocked for his ugliness and bad manners . . . The use of aphorism is itself instructive. An aphorism is not an argument" (p. 368). To bolster this last claim, MacIntyre appeals to Gilles Deleuze's (1983) characterization of aphorism as "a play of forces." But even if this unsatisfactory characterization of the aphorism is accepted, the fact remains that aphorisms are only a very small part of Nietzsche's dialectical arsenal (an arsenal which, if we are to be more fair to MacIntyre than he is to Nietzsche, must be admitted to include the mockery – but also the praise – of Socrates); see Nehamas (1985), ch. I. Nietzsche does, in fact, often argue, though he considers as elements of argument practices which MacIntyre's "Socrates," in contrast to the Socrates of Plato, who uses rhetoric as well as logic, would not accept.

12 See also Megill (1985), p. 30: ". . . in any culture that has become sufficiently self-conscious about its behavior to articulate moral theories, the very notion of naturalness will have become so distant as to be all but useless, except as propaganda."

13 This is one of the central ideas of Rorty (1989). I will return to Rorty's views below. I have examined them in detail in Nehamas (1990).

14 See Colli and Montinari (1980), band 12, p. 408.

15 Nietzsche's attitudes toward traditional philosophical distinctions have

been widely discussed. But the issue deserves further attention and detailed study. Attention must be paid, in this connection, both to the structure of and to the subjects addressed in various of Nietzsche's works. These include *The Birth of Tragedy, On the Uses and Disadvantages of History for Life, Human, All Too Human, Daybreak, The Gay Science,* and *Beyond Good and Evil.* Each of these books begins with a section devoted to the presentation of a number of oppositions. But whereas his early works, notably the first two in the list above, discuss oppositions like that between the Dionysian and the Apollonian or between the historical and the unhistorical sense which Nietzsche seems to believe are irreducibly opposed to one another and can only be reconciled by some sort of proper combination, the later works eventually try to show that the oppositions they concern are deceptive. The literary and philosophical implications of Nietzsche's practice, and of his change of approach, are important but, unfortunately, I cannot discuss them in more detail on this occasion.

16 In neither case, of course, need such a decision be a fully conscious event.

17 For this reason, I cannot quite accept the criticisms of Pippin (1991), who writes that the position I have attributed to Nietzsche is that "of an aesthete or *littérateur*": I think that by this Pippin means to attribute the second of the two alternatives I list above to me. I agree with his view that if that were all that Nietzsche claimed, his position (and any interpretation that attributed only this view to him) would be incomplete. But I do not believe that this is the view attributed to him in Nehamas (1985).

18 Heidegger (1977), p. 124.

19 Krauss (1988), p. 162 and passim.

20 Nietzsche, in my opinion, was as suspicious of the notion of absolute originality as he distrusted the Romantic idea of the genius with which originality had traditionally been connected. For a discussion of Nietzsche's view on genius, see Pletsch (1991).

21 In this respect, Nietzsche's notion of *überwinden* seems to me much less different than Heidegger's concept of *verwinden* than Heidegger himself and Vattimo, following him, believe.

22 Kundera (1986).

23 See Danto (1986), pp. 114–15.

24 The closing sections of the Third Essay of *On the Genealogy of Morals* raise exactly the same problem (and refer to the discussion of *The Gay Science*). Nietzsche writes there (sec. 24) that "the will to truth requires a critique – let us thus define our own task – the value of truth must for once be experimentally *called into question.*" But this is not a project he

actually undertakes. Nor, more importantly, does he answer the question whether such a critique can be undertaken in anything other than the very name of truth itself, thus perpetuating the very will it is intended to put into question. Richard Rorty asks what the sense of "truth" I have in mind is in the phrase "in . . . the very name of truth itself." The sense is that in which Nietzsche himself undertakes the project announced in the first section of the First Essay of the *Genealogy*, in his appeal to the "English genealogists" to follow him and "to sacrifice all desirability to truth, *every* truth, even plain, harsh, ugly, repellent, unchristian, immoral truth. – For such truths do exist. – " In other words, Nietzsche believes that a critique of a certain view presupposes that the view being criticized is false; he does not reject Christianity simply because he finds it distasteful, but because he believes that it is false (among many other faults he finds in it). But he also comes to realize that such a project perpetuates the faith in truth which constitutes the "kernel" of Christianity, and that he cannot extricate himself from his history. This is the paradox that keeps haunting him, and which we cannot avoid by means of a casual rejection of the notion of truth altogether, or with an identification of the true and, say, the useful.

25 I argued against Arthur Danto's approach to this question in *Nietzsche: Life as Literature*, pp. 52–5. I shall here discuss some of the views of Richard Rorty.

26 Rorty (1991), p. 62.

27 I have given a more detailed version of this argument in Nehamas (1990), pp. 107–11.

28 Nehamas (1985), ch. II. Stanley Fish has also been arguing for a view similar to this; see Fish (1980), Fish (1985), and Fish (1990). The main difference between Fish's position and mine, which I claim can also be found in Nietzsche, is that though Fish allows that a single individual can belong to a number of different "interpretive communities," he does not seem to believe that such communities are permeable, and that the standards functioning in one can enable an individual who belongs to it to criticize it by appealing to the standards of some of the other communities of which it is also a member. His view, therefore, makes criticism and revaluation more difficult to account for, and less subject to rational discussion.

29 MacIntyre's (1990) more recent attack against what he describes as "Nietzschean genealogy," which he contrasts unfavorably with his version of "Thomistic tradition" deserves separate and extended treatment. One of his central points is that genealogical moral enquiry deprives itself of any notion of a coherent, unified subject which can tell the story of its life and assume responsibility for it, whereas the organizing principles provided by the traditional virtues allow the Thomist traditionalist to

supply such a narrative. MacIntyre's view is in general subtle and intriguing, but we should note, provisionally, that it depends on a contrast which is not itself as subtle as other elements in his position. "The genealogist," MacIntyre writes, "follows Nietzsche in dismissing any notion of *the* truth and correspondingly any conception of *what is* as such and timelessly as contrasted with what seems to be the case from a variety of perspectives.... Where the Thomist understands texts in terms of a relatively fixed, even in analogically related and historically developing, set of meanings and genres, the post-Nietzschean genealogist envisages an indefinite multiplicity of interpretative possibilities, so that the speaker or writer is no more tied down by the given determinateness of his or her utterances than by what the genealogist takes to be a fictitious relationship to the truth" (p. 205). But, as I have insisted, abandoning the notion of "the" truth is not at all equivalent to accepting only "what seems to be the case"; it is, rather, to deny the very contrast on which MacIntyre depends ("With the true world we have also abolished the apparent one" [TI, 4]). As to MacIntyre's claim that genealogy is not committed to the truth of the narrative which it is, in each case, in the process of telling, the discussion above, I hope, suggests why I believe it to be unacceptable.

30 I am grateful to Richard Rorty for his comments on an earlier version of this paper.

BIBLIOGRAPHY

Bloom, A. (1987) *The Closing of the American Mind*. New York: Simon and Schuster.

Calinescu, M. (1987) *Five Faces of Modernity*. Durham, NC: Duke University Press.

Cavell, S. (1969) *Must We Mean What We Say?* New York: Scribner's.

Danto, A. C. (1986) "The End of Art." In *The Philosophical Disenfranchisement of Art*, pp. 81–115. New York: Columbia University Press.

Deleuze, G. (1983) *Nietzsche and Philosophy*. Trans. H. Tomlinson. New York: Columbia University Press.

Fish, S. (1990) *Doing What Comes Naturally*. Durham, NC: Duke University Press.

(1985) "Consequences." In *Against Theory*, ed. W. T. J. Mitchell, pp. 106–31. Chicago: University of Chicago Press.

(1980) *Is There a Text in this Class?* Cambridge, Mass.: Harvard University Press.

Habermas, J. (1987) *The Philosophical Discourse of Modernity*. Trans. F. Lawrence. Cambridge, Mass.: The MIT Press.

Heidegger, M. (1977) "The Origin of the Work of Art." In *Basic Writings*, ed. D. F. Krell. New York: Harper and Row.

Krauss, R. E. (1988) "The Originality of the Avant-Garde." In *The Originality of the Avant-Garde and Other Modernist Myths*, pp. 151–70. Cambridge, Mass.: The MIT Press.

Kundera, M. (1986) "The Depreciated Legacy of Cervantes." In *The Art of the Novel*, pp. 3–20. New York: Grove Press.

Lyotard, J. (1984) *The Post-Modern Condition: A Report on Knowledge*. Trans. G. Bennington and B. Massumi. Minneapolis: University of Minnesota Press.

MacIntyre, A. (1988) *Whose Justice? Which Rationality?* Notre Dame, Ind.: University of Notre Dame Press.

(1990) *Three Rival Versions of Moral Enquiry: Encyclopedia, Genealogy and Tradition*. Notre Dame, Ind.: University of Notre Dame Press.

Megill, A. (1985) *Prophets of Extremity: Nietzsche, Heidegger, Foucault, Derrida*. Berkeley: University of California Press.

Nehamas, A. (1985) *Nietzsche: Life as Literature*. Cambridge, Mass.: Harvard University Press.

(1990) "A Touch of the Poet: On Richard Rorty." *Raritan Quarterly*, 10:101–25.

(1994) "The Genealogy of Genealogy: Interpretation in Nietzsche's *Second Meditation* and in *The Genealogy of Morals*." In Richard Schacht (ed.), *Nietzsche, Genealogy, Morality*. pp. 269–283. Berkeley: University of California Press.

Nietzsche, F. (1980) *Sämtliche Werke, Kritische Studienausgabe*. Ed. G. Colli and M. Montinari. Berlin: de Gruyter. 15 vols.

(1954a) *The Antichrist*. Trans. W. Kaufmann. New York: Viking Press.

(1954b) *The Twilight of the Idols*. Trans. W. Kaufmann. New York: Viking Press.

(1954c) *Thus Spoke Zarathustra*. Trans. W. Kaufmann. New York: Viking Press.

(1966) *Beyond Good and Evil*. Trans. W. Kaufmann. New York: Random House.

(1967) *The Birth of Tragedy*. Trans. W. Kaufmann. New York: Random House.

(1968) *The Will to Power*. Ed. W. Kaufmann. Trans. W. Kaufmann and R. J. Hollingdale. New York: Random House.

(1969) *On the Genealogy of Morals*. Trans. W. Kaufmann and R. J. Hollingdale. New York: Random House.

(1974) *The Gay Science*. Trans. W. Kaufmann. New York: Random House.

(1982) *Daybreak: Thoughts on the Prejudices of Morality*. Trans. R. J. Hollingdale. Cambridge: Cambridge University Press.

Pippin, R. B. (1991) *Modernism as a Philosophical Problem*. Cambridge, Mass.: Blackwell's.

Pletsche, C. (1991) *Young Nietzsche: Becoming a Genius*. New York: The Free Press.

Rorty, R. (1989) *Contingency, Irony and Solidarity*. Cambridge: Cambridge University Press.

(1991)"Nietzsche, Socrates and Pragmatism." *South African Journal of Philosophy*.

Vattimo, G. (1989) *The End of Modernity*. Trans. J. R. Snyder. Baltimore: Johns Hopkins University Press.

8   Nietzsche's alleged farewell: The premodern, modern, and postmodern Nietzsche

According to a widely discussed recent book by Jürgen Habermas, Nietzsche's thought represents the "entry into post-modernity"[1]; Nietzsche "renounces a renewed revision of the concept of reason and *bids farewell* to the dialectic of enlightenment."[2] In Habermas's unique narrative, this "farewell" to the hopes of the Enlightenment is seen as the decisive European "turning point" that sets the direction for the divergent "postmodernist" paths of Georges Bataille, Jacques Lacan, and Michel Foucault on the one hand, and Heidegger and Derrida on the other. According to Habermas's somewhat tendentious history, the European dissatisfaction with the Enlightenment comes down to the failed attempt of Hegel and the post-Hegelians at a "dialectical" reformulation and completion of such hopes, and a "Nietzschean" inauguration of "irrationalism" and therewith a complete rejection of such hopes.

Such a popular, now nearly standard characterization of Nietzsche as the decisive "post-" or "counter-Enlightenment" thinker is painted in very broad strokes by Habermas.[3] However, for all the scholarly problems with Habermas's characterizations, there is certainly something right in treating so much recent, influential European philosophy as "neo-Nietzschean,"[4] and perhaps even in the extraordinary claim that "Friedrich Nietzsche is today the most influential philosopher in the Western, non-Marxist world."[5]

There is also something quite apposite in Habermas's pairing of Hegelian and Nietzschean dissatisfactions with modernity, an opposition that surfaces too in other influential writers, like Gilles Deleuze.[6] I would, however, introduce that whole matter somewhat differently. First, one should note the way in which both Hegel and Nietzsche directly engage, and either radically transform or appear to reject, the great problem of all post-Cartesian or modern philosophy. The problem that began in Descartes – how to justify the adoption of a new, rigorous method – quickly became the perennial modern problem: some sort of comprehensive *self-reassurance* about the modern orientation itself; at once the academic problem of epistemological skepticism and the cultural and political problem of legitimate authority.

In the face of the spectacular scientific errors of the premodern tradition, and the collapse of the Christian religion and its political authority into sectarian warfare, we now needed some comprehensive reassurance about the new resolve to treat only the mathematizable properties of nature as substantial or real, the resolve to replace contemplation as the *telos* of inquiry with mastery, the resolve to begin political reflection with the natural individual. The nearly pathological sense of insecurity that prompts Descartes's radical doubt and methodological resolve, and the great narrowing of what will count as reliable in the empiricist tradition, speak to such a pretheoretical need. (As moderns, we could at least resolve to restrict ourselves to foundations that we *can* reassure ourselves about; the immediate, the incorrigible, what is a safe foundation because not "due to us"; or what was wonderfully, even religiously, named later: "the given.")

The first crisis in this attempt at reassurance, the crisis that produced Hegel and Nietzsche, was the book aptly titled *The Critique of Pure Reason* and its attack on the early modern strategies of reassurance as still dogmatic and uncritical. Eventually Kant's own suspicions of dogmatism were turned against him, his accounts of transcendental necessity, a fixed table of categories, a "natural" architectonic of reason, etc. The "critical spirit" had begun to devour itself and the project of reassurance was in trouble again.[7] Hence the nineteenth-century crisis with which Habermas begins his account: either a wholly new form of such reassurance – a Hegelian narrative of what sanctioning principles or justificatory criteria *it has turned out* we could not seem to do without (and so, implicitly, an appeal to some social model of collective self-reassurance), or, apparently, a spectacularly new beginning, an attempt to imagine a form of life *wholly* without reassurance, in which the very search for such consolation, philosophy itself, was best understood as a slavish failure of nerve, not the one thing always needful.⁸ This, I would suggest, is the issue most at stake in Nietzsche's alleged "farewell."

All of which, however, is not to deny the fact that the very idea of "a modernity problem," now so popular and influential, is also tremendously controversial and quite possibly wrong-headed from the start. Many of the current participants in the postmodernity discussion often simply assume the highly debatable presupposition that modernity *is* in some sort of "crisis"; that all of the standard "grand narratives" used to legitimate the self-understanding of Enlightenment modernity, from Whig progressivism to positivist self-congratulation to Blumenberg's up-to-date, sophisticated strategy,⁹ are deeply flawed, products all of a comprehensive self-delusion. Without such an assumption, the Enlightenment, whether understood traditionally as the final achievement of human maturity ("autonomy") and as the discovery of a certain, truth-producing methodology, or more pragmatically as simply our collective best bet for a better future life, may simply still be incomplete on its own terms, in need of no dialectical overcoming or bold farewell. ("We just need more time.")

But for anyone who rejects this appeal to "delayed fulfillment" as an explanation for the persistent lack of fit between the original promise of the Enlightenment and the contemporary payoff, the centrality of Nietzsche's thought for all so-called post-Enlightenment reflection is clear and makes all the more compelling an attempt to understand in detail what we might call Nietzsche's own historical self-consciousness, the modernity problem he called "nihilism." There are, after all, all sorts of ways to say good-bye. If that is indeed what he is doing, what, I want to ask, is distinctive about Nietzsche's supposed "farewell"?¹⁰ And what exactly does he take himself to be leaving behind?

I raise this issue by examining the three obvious historical categories relevant to Nietzsche's understanding of this problem: His complex relation to modernity itself (or the question of his own "modernism"); the common suspicion that his attack on modern self-satisfaction must betray an atavism, a premodern celebration of aristocratic politics and the heroic virtues of nobility and strength; and the recent fascination with his supposed postmodernism, his attempt to write, propose and affirm, without consolation and without "revenge," to play, perhaps even to anticipate the attempt to write *"sous rature"* ["under erasure," i.e. disavowing in one sense what one is asserting in another].

I. MODERNITY AS A "PHYSIOLOGICAL SELF-CONTRADICTION"

It is relatively uncontroversial to begin by noting that there clearly *is* some sort of historical, even typically modern, apocalyptic dimension to Nietzsche's work, evident in some of his titles: *Daybreak*, *Beyond Good and Evil*, *Twilight of the Idols*, *The Anti-Christ*, and in his announcing the "age of the *last* men" and the possibility of an "overman" in *Thus Spoke Zarathustra*. Long before he was thought of as a metaphysical or postmodernist thinker, Nietzsche became internationally famous as a kind of cultural prophet, for proclaiming that we have arrived at the "afterglow of European civilization," that "nihilism stands at the door," that the "highest values have devalued themselves," and so forth.

This emphasis on the Nietzschean jeremiad is fair enough, in spite of several necessary qualifications. In the first place, the idea of a "farewell to the Enlightenment" in Nietzsche must acknowledge the tendentious nature of some of Nietzsche's characterizations of modernity. He tends to highlight certain thinkers and phenomena, particularly Locke, Rousseau, Hume, Kant, Whig progressivism, democracy, socialism, Darwinism, Wagner and Schopenhauer, mass culture, conformism, and to underplay (although he notes) his affinity with a much different strain in modernity represented by the likes of Machiavelli, Hobbes, Spinoza, materialism, the Gothic or darker sides of romanticism, aesthetic modernism itself.[11]

Secondly, and much more importantly, the canonical treatment of Nietzsche as an anti-Enlightenment thinker can be confusing, since "the Enlightenment" or "modernity" is not itself of central importance in Nietzsche's treatment of major contemporary institutions. Indeed, Nietzsche's remarks on the modernity issue tend to pull in two different directions. On the one hand, the problem he calls nihilism, while certainly of relevance to the major institutions of modernity – natural science, liberal democracy, skepticism, religious tolerance, and so forth – is a crisis he discusses within a *much* broader historical context, one that identified "Platonism" and

"Christian humanism" as the major targets of interest. Somewhat puzzlingly, for Nietzsche, modern politics is in many ways as Christian as feudal politics (perhaps even more so); modern scientists are *priests*, they pursue the "ascetic ideal" as vigorously if not as self-consciously as do recognizable priests, and modern "free thinkers" express as much *ressentiment* as their more devout brethren.

Yet, on the other hand, for Nietzsche there is something *distinctive* about the post-Enlightenment period in Western history, something not merely a repetition of Platonism and Christianity. Modernity represents some sort of epochal, unique "twilight," or "decline," or "degeneration," or "exhaustion," to use his frequent descriptions. At the heart of Nietzsche's theory of modernity is a complex, elusive characterization clearly meant to confront the optimism and self-satisfaction still prominent in much of modernity's self-under-standing: the modern age is, uniquely, *the advent of nihilism.*[12]

These claims for both the *repetitive* and the *distinct* nature of the modern epoch can be summarized this way. On the one hand, Nietzsche's account, particularly when compared with the numerous, post-Hegelian theories of modernity, is rather tame, and does not take much, by comparison, out of the theoretical notion of "the modern." He stresses instead the continuity between Enlightenment thought and the prior tradition, but he often notes that modernity is mostly distinctive in its smug *confidence*, its ambition to complete the ancient "will to truth" and the identification of the "good in itself." It is this modern insistence on a successful resolution of Platonic and Christian "incompleteness" that makes the failure of such an attempt ("nihilism") more prominent and more significant. Modernity's dream of Enlightenment is so extreme, and, according to Nietzsche, fails so utterly, that it helps reveal this dreamlike illusion in all post-Platonic thought, and it allows us a distinct opportunity to understand that failure. Hence Nietzsche's images of modernity are physiological images of a final or decisive exhaustion and sickness, "symptoms" that finally allow a correct diagnosis, or poetic images (bows that have completely lost their "tension") that make the same point.

To begin to sort out these claims, we first need more details from the surface, the more accessible features of Nietzsche's attack on modern culture. For the most part, and somewhat surprisingly, this surface attack, the expression of Nietzsche's "farewell," concerns the *self-understanding* of the modern enterprise. In keeping with the unusually idealistic maxim he had announced in *Beyond Good and Evil*, that the "greatest events" of an age are its "greatest thoughts" (BGE, p. 227),[13] Nietzsche's analysis of the major institutions of modernity is directed to the "Christian-moral *interpretation*," the "thought" claimed to be responsible for the nihilism crisis (WP, p. 6). And "what does nihilism mean? *That the highest values devalue themselves.* The aim is lacking; 'why' finds no answer" (WP, p. 9). Somehow the Christian "faith in morality," its "cultivation of 'truthfulness' " (ibid.) has undermined the possibility of affirming a "goal," has itself "devalued" the values that make such an affirmation possible.[14] As expressed in *Thus Spoke Zarathustra*,

Humanity still has no goal.
But tell me my brothers, if humanity still lacks a goal – is humanity itself not still lacking too? (TSZ, p. 60)

Indeed, humanity as a self-overcoming creature is lacking. Because "man will no longer shoot the arrow of his longing beyond man," or "will no longer give birth to a star," we are confronted with the "most contemptible," the "last man," "who makes everything small," who says "we have invented happiness" and "blinks" (TSZ, p. 17).

The way in which the "Christian-moral interpretation" has *itself* created this state of "goallessness" is among the most interesting, most obscure, and certainly most neglected of Nietzsche's claims. The unmistakable pride with which Nietzsche, or let us say, the official Nietzsche, unmasks self-delusions, points to the hidden, low origins of the high, and so forth, is everywhere matched by what appears to be an insistence that *he* is not doing anything. He is pointing out to us what *we* have done to ourselves, what we are beginning to require ourselves to face, now. There is little doubt, to return to the Hegelian alternatives of such importance for Habermas, that Nietzsche means his project to be as much a phenomenology as a genealogy, and that he recognizes the methodological and self-referential problems generated by a naive faith in a "scientific" genealogy.

This large problem, which we might call Nietzsche's puzzling, common reliance on *the first person plural*, itself suggests connections with Hegelian themes introduced earlier. Nietzsche (more like Schopenhauer, Wittgenstein, Husserl, less like Kierkegaard,

Heidegger, Derrida) actually knew very little with any sophistication about the grand philosophical tradition he battled with. Had he, his own approach to the *aporiai* of modernity would have immediately suggested his common cause with the revolution effected by the Introduction to the hated Hegel's *Phenomenology of Spirit*. It was that work which first proposed that all institutions, even scientific practices, philosophic schools, moral institutions, were to be treated as themselves *"appearances," "shapes of Spirit,"* or cultural practices.[15] Their possibility and adequacy were not to be unlocked by some exogenous method, or tool, or genealogical procedure, or research paradigm (themselves all mere "appearances"). There is no such external point of view, and so "we," ourselves inheritors and products of such self-transformations, must understand how such institutions and practices have come to assess themselves, what sort of reassurance they have achieved, how satisfying they have turned out to be, how they have led to "us." That is all there can be to understanding and assessing ourselves, at least for many of the "post-Kantians."[16]

Since Nietzsche himself is well known for insisting that all philosophy or theory is continuous with, an expression of, or a strategy wholly internal to, "life," (a "confession" of its author) – that it cannot be an external tribunal, with "life" as some *object* of study[17] – it should not be surprising that Nietzsche should need to restrict his account of modern failures and possibilities to "who *we* have become," "what *we* face," et cetera. He has of course misled many readers on this point by means of his many personae or masks: as "philosopher of the future," "genealogist," "philologist," a man "philosophizing with a hammer," et cetera; and that raises rhetorical issues I shall address below. For now we need only note the similar strains in Hegel's and Nietzsche's reliance on this "we," at once neutral, descriptive, and yet also critically, contentiously narrative. (Hence also the similar ambiguities in a claim about the supposed modern *"self*-contradiction.")

The official account of such a self-undermining is relatively straightforward and relies heavily on an understanding of the influence of Christianity, especially its morality of selflessness, its mistrust of all partiality in practical reasoning. By "training the instincts" in a certain way, we tied the possibility of valuing or esteeming, to transcendence, the "good" and "the true" in itself. By doing so, we insured that, when such criteria begin to lose their contingent social authority, the result would have to be nihilism, a sense that, where there had been value, there now could only be *nihil*, nothing. And nihilism is what produces what Nietzsche calls in the *Twilight of the Idols* a state of "physiological self-contradiction" (TI, p. 95), apparently some sort of "double-bind" state in which we must still actually direct our conduct, choose, exclude, affirm, and so forth, but, given our Christian inheritance, and what we now understand to be the conditions of such esteeming, we cannot with any confidence.

It was the Christian elevation of intention and so honesty, self-transparency, to the forefront of moral evaluation, which somehow assured that a relentless inner logic would take over in such a required self-examination, and that the true intentions of the pitying, humanistic egalitarian would have to emerge, overcoming all "sentimental weakness." This inner logic would have to reveal to the person in whom it operates that life itself is everywhere partial, interest-driven, self-promoting. "Life itself is essentially appropriation, injury, overpowering of what is alien and weaker; suppression, hardness, imposition of one's own forms, incorporation and at least, at its mildest, exploitation" (BGE, p. 203).[18]

But such a self-revelation only renders *moral* values nil, and this fact will also play an important role in the nature of Nietzsche's supposed "farewell" to modernity. That is, Nietzsche frequently exploits the point we are now stressing: that the historical crisis of nihilism is as contingent as its Christian origin, that "modern pessimism is an expression of the uselessness of the *modern* world – not of the world of existence" (WP, p. 23). Accordingly, "our modern world" has an "ambiguous character," "the very same symptoms could point to *decline* and to *strength*." Nihilism could be a "sign of a crucial and most essential growth, of the transition to new conditions of existence," or "genuine nihilism" (WP, p. 69). Nietzsche does not discuss in this context what would have to occur for a genuinely new condition of existence to emerge historically (not just as a mere hope, or merely for the individual, Nietzsche). However, that issue appears to be the major theme of his most difficult work, *Thus Spoke Zarathustra*.[19]

This general story then forms the basis for a wide-ranging discussion of many modern phenomena, including Nietzsche's attention to the complex dimensions, even paradoxes, of his own phenomenology. Nietzsche clearly realizes, especially throughout *Thus Spoke*

Zarathustra, that by far the most telling "manifestation" of nihil-ism is its *nonmanifestation*, the thoughtlessness with which this deflationary moment is actually *embraced*. " 'What is love? What is creation? What is longing? What is a star?' thus asks the last man, and he blinks" (TSZ, p. 17).

This misinterpretation of enervation, the decline of the instincts and collective goallessness, as the "achievement of freedom," is char-acteristic of modern mass society ("herd morality") according to Nietzsche in *Beyond Good and Evil*, (#202) and in the "Criticism of Modernity" in *Twilight of the Idols*.

The entire West has lost those instincts out of which institutions grow, out of which the *future* grows: perhaps nothing goes so much against the grain of its 'modern spirit' as this. One lives for today, one lives very fast – one lives very irresponsibly: it is precisely this which one calls 'freedom'. (TI, p. 94)

We interpret the "loss of instincts out of which institutions grow" *as* our institutions.[20] In what has by now become a familiar Tocque-villean warning about modern democracy, Nietzsche suggests that such modern ideas as respecting individual worth, attempting to think universally, putting oneself in the position of the other ("pity"), merely betray an anxiety about possible domination by the strong, a fear of (inevitable) inequality, and so reflect a desire to be safely and anonymously absorbed into a herd. Nietzsche interprets the new modern idols, like the state of humanity or reason, not as genuine goals, capable of commanding a genuine instinctual alle-giance, but as counterfeit, filling the teleological void by a tranquiliz-ing normality, and as symptoms of the degeneration of man into a creature who can only will to do "what all others do."

It is this sort of Nietzschean dissatisfaction with modernity, with its language of failure, crisis, and self-contradiction, which has natu-rally suggested to many the *antimodernism* long associated with Nietzsche. It has, given the tenor of his contempt, an atavistic pre-modernism, the specter of the familiar "premodern" Nietzsche of traditional interpretations, the elitist, patriarchal "blond beast" en-thusiast, the Nietzsche who simply celebrates the absence of con-sensual or even minimally communal life, promoting not a social unity (always "the herd"), but a stern "order of rank" created ("bred") and maintained from above.

2. PREMODERN ORIGINS

For those who read Nietzsche this way, much of the motivation for Nietzsche's farewell to the modern tradition appears to stem from his famous analysis of "the origins" of the Platonic, otherworldly, Christian, life-denying perspective at the heart of modernity's internal decay, an interpretation given in one of his most exciting and accessible books, *On the Genealogy of Morals*. This is the story that has seemed to many to celebrate the premodern, and to encourage a kind of return.

The story Nietzsche tells about such origins has become very well known; it is a kind of staple in undergraduate survey courses and history of ethics textbooks. Culturally, the still dominant (but tottering) moral distinction is between "good and evil." This is a distinction between an act motivated by selfless, altruistic motives, an act done for the sake of the good in itself, or, more broadly, an act in which one's own good is never primary but measured in concert with the good of the other's,[21] and an egoistic act, one asserted with complete indifference to others or the act's effect on others.

To understand this distinction, and the nature of its appeal, we must understand it as a "reaction" to a very different distinction, one already in place, from which it degenerates. That earlier "aristocratic" distinction is between the good and the "base" or "bad" (*Schlecht*), a distinction that is virtually the mirror image of the good/evil standard. This dichotomy divides acts and characters that are noble, beautiful, or fine (*kalos*), from the ugly and common; acts done with the supreme self-confidence of the agent, with the agent's own sense of a worthiness simply to *decree* how he shall act, and those done in weakness and self-doubt, requiring the reassurance or consolation of an eternal value or rational criterion or the approval of others. In Nietzsche's typological account, the good/evil distinction, so central to modern political and moral life, represents a "reaction" by the "slave" type to such confident, aristocratic legislation. The whole Socratic and Christian point of view, he contends, should be considered the "slave revolt in morality," a revolt fueled by *ressentiment* against the powerful by the powerless.

Further, in order for the slave to deny consistently the worth or significance of the very real power exercised by the master over him, a metaphysical and moral system begins to unfold. This system makes possible the justification of an inner, private world, and a metaphysics wherein intentions, and intentions alone, can determine what an agent is truly responsible for, and wherein soul, or a true self, can be distinguished from the "external" body so obviously subject to the will of the master. In the Second Essay of *On the Genealogy of Morals*, this genealogy of the subject is continued. Nietzsche tries to account for the variety of ways a subject would have to come to think of himself, how he would have to train himself to be, in order to complete successfully the slave revolt. Nietzsche reads all of post-Christian metaphysics as a practical strategy, the construction of an edifice within which the illusion of strength, of *unassailable* power, or of "the will" itself, could be defended and esteemed.

In the last essay of *Genealogy*, Nietzsche generalizes his account of morality and the moral understanding of subjectivity and focuses on many of the issues we are interested in. The basic moral phenomenon in question, Nietzsche claims, should be broadly construed as an "ascetic ideal," an ideal which, while most visible in the priest or moralist, is, as he tries to show throughout, also pursued by philosophers, artists, and scientists. It is a paradoxical ideal, one that requires a subtle interpretation of its meaning. For the ascetic priest, in all his manifestations, encourages us to "turn against life," to deny life itself, view it as a "wrong road," a "mistake that is put right by deeds" (OGM, p. 117). This "monstrous mode of valuation," apparently grossly self-destructive, has produced an "ascetic planet," "a nook of disgruntled, arrogant, and offensive creatures filled with a profound disgust at themselves, at the earth, at all life, who inflict as much pain on themselves as they possibly can out of pleasure at inflicting pain – which is probably their only pleasure" (ibid.).

We have, however, made ourselves into such a "life-inimical species" "*in the interest of life itself,* that such a self-contradictory type does not die out" (ibid.). What must be denied at all costs and overcome by postulating a better, different life to come, by good works, a "narcosis" of the spirit, and so forth, is what Nietzsche variously calls the reign of mere chance in the universe, pure becoming, and, especially, the unredeemable character of suffering (all the deepest concerns of the "slave" or the slavish, the type we now call "bourgeois").

But the self-preserving strategy seems to have played itself out. The illusions under which it prospered have been exposed. Where there used to be monasteries, churches, even salons and museums – testimonials to the sanctity and primacy of the inner citadel of will and intention – there are now "really" only madhouses and hospitals, concessions to the modern view of the always conditioned, arbitrary, contingent character of such "unowned," chaotically formed inner lives. On the other hand, much of the modern exposition of itself, much of this "modern spirit" itself, *is still as committed to the ascetic ideal as what it exposes.* And this charge is what raises all the interesting questions about Nietzsche's alleged "farewell."

When Nietzsche asks about these supposed modern "counter-idealists," deniers of the ascetic ideal, "nay-sayers and outsiders of today," he is uncompromising: ". . . all these pale atheists, anti-Christians, immoralists, nihilists; these skeptics, ephetics, hectics of the spirit . . . ; these last idealists of knowledge in whom alone the intellectual conscience dwells and is incarnate today – they certainly believe they are as completely liberated from the ascetic ideal as possible" (p. 148–50). They are wrong, though, these self-proclaimed "free spirits," because *"they still have faith in truth"* (OGM, p. 149–50).

And it is this attack on modernity's critics (really starting in the beginning of OGM with the discussion of the English genealogists) which immediately turns upside down any reading of Nietzsche himself as a sort of Darwin or Freud, proposing some resigned reconciliation with the natural or primitive being we truly or originally are. Nietzsche cannot be read as some sort of armchair anthropologist or ethnologist puncturing the pretensions of the modern Western tribe. He strictly distinguishes his own voice from that of the predominant skeptical, secular institution of modernity, modern science. It still derives its "flame from the fire" of Plato's divine truth and from Christianity. It still encourages an ascetic enterprise, one tied to the need to *secure* mankind from contingency, to reassure him *by means of truth.* (Nietzsche also shows none of the hope of say, Freud, that such a naturalist or materialist enlightenment will be progressive, will produce some new, reduced-expectation form of social cooperation. His attitude towards such "leveling" Christian hopes for peace and cooperation are clear throughout.)

This sort of attack on "the ascetic ideal," on any sort of scientific genealogy, then raises the obvious questions: In *what* sense has a great "devaluation of values" in modernity been *shown*? In what sense has a "transvaluation" been prepared for? If Nietzsche does not claim to have discovered premodern or less corrupted origins, what has he proposed?

Put the problem this way, in his terms. We can safely restate at least this much of what Nietzsche claims to be doing: Nietzsche famously proclaimed that, by "abolishing the true world, we have *abolished* the apparent." We are, at least, not skeptics who must resign ourselves to the phenomenal, and the *inaccessibility of the real* amid the play of interpretations. Everything about this issue looks different when the assumptions behind the "will to truth" have been exposed and undermined. This is a difficult point for Nietzsche to state properly, since his favorite metaphors for leading one's life without delusion invoke the images of "masks" and the task of "interpretation." These terms naturally involve the logic of originals and texts, even as Nietzsche insists that there *is* only "masking" in human action; no texts, only interpretation.[22]

But it is also at least clear that, even if this paradoxical play on the "essential" character of the "appearances" could be clearly understood, it would not end the problem of gathering up and holding together, "reading," the *phenomena* rightly, *as* they show themselves. Nietzsche may, as is often said, be trying simply to "legislate," to create or will the authority of his own narrative with the force of a great *auteur*, but this would simply raise the stakes *for him*; it just puts in starker relief the problem of *his own* reassurance that he *is* legislating or creating, not merely imitating or following. (In Hegel's terms, self-consciousness is not a mere species of self-perception. It is always originally only an orientation, a self-regarding which projects one's activities forward, and so is always unstable, challengeable by others, redeemed – reassured – more by future activity, or what one does, or by others, than by some "depth" of present insight. The Nietzschean actor can likewise claim no privileged access to a unitary, true self, no original, privileged confidence concerning his own self-interpretation. He has available to him no simply decisive interpretive frame or context within which to understand the various dimensions of his own doings and sufferings.)

The familiar Nietzsche who responds to such doubts and questions with aristocratic indifference, or by proclaiming some aesthetic reassurance, is only a preliminary or surface Nietzsche. The more interesting Nietzsche is not at all divinely immune to such an internal tension, and not indifferent to what such doubts might require.

3. POSTMODERN PROSPECTS

To discover what Nietzsche does think of himself as doing, we need to attend again to some of the odd rhetorical details of his self-presentation, especially the peculiarities of Nietzsche's style, his way of raising these issues. When we do, we can see that this crucial issue of Nietzsche's self-understanding, and therewith the nature of his proposal for a form of (supposedly) "postmodern" life, is hardly straightforward.

To return to a phenomenological problem raised above, the *Genealogy* oddly begins with Nietzsche identifying *himself* with those who would be the object of attack in the third section, the "men of knowledge" who *still* believe in the ascetic ideal: "We are unknown to ourselves, we men of knowledge" (OGM, p. 15). (In the passages quoted above from the Third Essay, Nietzsche's remarks are often made in the first person plural. Just as in the Preface, he writes, with some sort of irony, as "we men of knowledge," and refers, with even more irony, to a type some commentators associate with a Nietzschean ideal, the "free spirits.")[23] In the Preface, however, Nietzsche not only refers ahead to his claim about the wholly practical, even Christian motives of any quest for knowledge (he quotes Matthew as a way of explaining "our" view of "salvation"), but he also claims, as he begins a book that professes to discover "the" origins of the moral point of view, that "we are *necessarily* strangers to ourselves," that "we *have* to misunderstand ourselves," "we are not men of knowledge with respect to ourselves" (ibid.).

The creation of such an odd rhetorical voice for the work is not the only peculiarity of its form, but it is enough to raise a number of thematic as well as interpretive problems. In particular, it returns us to Nietzsche's claims about modernity's "devaluation of *itself*," its "*self*-contradiction," and the nature of Nietzschean interpretation. If Nietzsche *is* identifying himself with the "men of knowledge" ascetics identified in the Third Essay, then not only would Nietzsche, somewhat bizarrely, be accusing himself of the futile, self-

destructive pursuit of an ascetic ideal, he would clearly be contradict-
ing his own genealogy of the "will to truth" in, among many other
places, the first chapter of *Beyond Good and Evil*. If, as is much
more likely, the identification is ironic, if he is trying to parody the
form of the work (a scientific genealogy) even as he makes use of it,
and so to forestall our interpreting the work as a "new" form of
knowledge, then the obvious question returns again: what *is* he
doing and why the irony? Are we now engaged in the indirection,
ellipsis, the self-canceling "play" of "postmodern" discourse?[24]

Some of the reconstruction suggested above begins, I think, to answer that question. Nietzsche is assuming that the modernity crisis,
nihilism, is a wholly historical crisis, one that originates within the
self-understanding of modernity, *because* of the pursuit of modern
ideals. Presumably, then, Nietzsche would be proposing that the *Genealogy* should be read as the "dawning" self-understanding *of* "we
men of knowledge," or "free spirits." The *Genealogy* is then to a large
extent the self-revelations of "we modern men" (still not fully
"known to ourselves") who "are the heirs of the conscience-
vivisection and self-torture of millennia."

Nietzsche's irony, the absence of a complete identification with
such "scholars," is something he himself remarks on, elliptically
and evasively, in *Ecce Homo*. He calls the *Genealogy* "uncannier
than anything else written so far," and tells us that it is a "beginning
calculated to mislead: cool, scientific, even ironic, deliberately foreground, deliberately holding off" (EH, p. 313, my emphasis). His
irony appears to be a result of his sensing the *incompleteness* of the
self-revelation concerning the contingency of moral institutions.
"Men of knowledge," still convinced that traditional claims about
the possibility of valuing hold, conclude that the consequences of
their unmaskings would be will-lessness. Since man "would rather
will nothing than not will," they also convince themselves of the
"*truth*" of their claims about "nothingness," taking pride and solace
in their courage and their science, but ending up a mere "decaying,
self-doubting present" (p. 96). This is the step Nietzsche will not
take, the move to what he calls "weak" or "passive nihilism."

This hesitancy is evinced by stylistic devices which are, as far as I
know, ignored in the Nietzsche literature.[25] In the First Essay, Nietzsche mysteriously switches narrative voices, and suddenly (in section #9) speaks in the persona of a plebeian, "free spirit" democrat,

who complains that the genealogist's worries are irrelevant. The mob has won; why worry about origins? Nietzsche explains this frustrated interruption as an understandable response to *his* (Nietzsche's own) "silence" (even though we are now nine sections into the book). He simply notes that, whoever the character presenting the genealogy, it is not, or not wholly, Nietzsche. *He* has had "much to be silent about" (OGM, p. 36). And at the conclusion of the Second Essay, Nietzsche oddly again mentions his own "silence" at points in the narration, suggesting that he is both presenting a genealogy, and distancing himself from its surface claims to truth or a historical correctness ("But what am I saying? Enough! Enough! At this point it behooves me only to be silent" [p. 96]).[26]

Of course, Nietzsche's account of origins is still far from unproblematic. This is so even if it is construed as some sort of ironically qualified phenomenology, not grounded in a theory tied to the "will to truth," but a representation and radical extension of our own "dawning" historical perspective and its current fate. He must still be able to make the proper distinctions and draw the appropriate conclusions within, let us say, his phenomenology of *the genealogy we have begun to write for ourselves.*

Here the obvious problems emerge for someone like Habermas. If this whole issue of Nietzsche's "farewell" comes down to his reliance on some form of radically historical hermeneutics, then, Habermas has often asked in a number of contexts, in essays on Nietzsche, Horkheimer and Adorno, and Gadamer,[27] what constitutes a possible resolution of *disputes* about such issues, disputes about who "we" really are? Without some account of the conditions of such interpretive activity, some standards or measure to separate the wheat from the chaff, then, the charge would go, the question involved in a possible farewell to the Enlightenment is begged. And this in turn provokes the obvious Nietzschean counter-charge (one evident in much of the furious French and Francophile response to Habermas's book): that is the very possibility of such a reliance on transcendental (or "quasi-transcendental") conditions, identified by reason with some sort of necessity as governing *any* possible dialogue, which is being challenged by genealogy. Any suspicion about the "all too human" origin of an insistence on such a possible reassurance would unfairly be foreclosed from the start, if we also needed some original rational reassurance that *the suspicion were warranted.* It would then be Habermas who begs the question by presupposing the necessity of such "criteria" from the start.[28]

However, I would like to conclude by suggesting that the situation need not be left at this kind of "begging the question" stand-off. For Nietzsche's radically "internalist" version of any assessment of socially sanctioned practices, his denial that philosophy could have "life" as an "object" and his insistence that philosophy is always itself the expression of a form of life, should mean, quite consistently, that Nietzsche has no abstract, meta-level response to the kind of justification demanded by Habermas. As the details of the above summary of his position make abundantly clear, he has a proposal, a possible interpretation of what the demand for objective consensus within post-Platonic, Christian modernity means for us. As we have seen, Nietzsche is proposing an interpretation of the contingent social meaning of modern attempts at rational, or universally binding consensus, collective reassurance. This interpretation is straightforwardly based on the notions of *ressentiment*, weakness, pity, and the contingent facts of European social history. It should therefore be possible to examine, in a way internal to Nietzsche's own assumptions, that interpretation and its implications for the question of the authority of Nietzsche's claims.

At least, it is possible to begin an examination of such an issue here and to suggest a last, internal problem in Nietzsche's account (i.e. one subject to no question-begging charge). As we have seen in several contexts (to focus now on the issue of most relevance to Habermas, and the whole Hegel-Nietzsche issue introduced above), Nietzsche regards any commitment to an ideal of some sort of intersubjective acceptability for one's "evaluations" as a "sign" of weakness, and a latent expression of fear of those who need no such support. It is a requirement that arises, that makes sense, only within a certain sort of social arrangement and historical experience. Such "pitying" concerns for others' views is to be contrasted with those who simply "seized the right to create values" out of a "pathos of distance" (OGM, p. 26). (See also BGE, section #261, and the "characteristic right of masters to create values" p. 209.) Bodying forth such a sense of their "distance" from others, "The 'well-born' *felt* themselves to be the 'happy'; they did not need to establish their happiness artificially by examining their enemies, or to persuade themselves, *deceive* themselves, that they were happy" (OGM, p. 38).

For all of the rich complexity of Nietzsche's historical and psychological interpretation, it is *this* basic, somewhat crude contrast between "self-assertion" and the "weakness" of social dependence that forms the core of all his claims about a great deal of the insufficiencies of modernity, modernity's origins in the premodern, and the new, "postmodern", distinctly self-assertive type for which he hopes. And, even when all the methodological and stylistic subtleties of Nietzsche's approach have been conceded, there are still serious, unresolved tensions in Nietzsche's account.

Consider in conclusion one small passage in the *Genealogy* where many of these issues can be brought to a very fine point, and consider again the issue of Nietzsche's interpretation of the social meaning of the typically modern need to rely on a universally binding justification, the needs of the reactive, ascetic Enlightenment type. In Section #10 of the First Essay in the *Genealogy*, he begins his concluding comments by noting first that the counter-ideal, Nietzsche's "noble creator," would be "incapable" of "taking his enemies seriously" for very long. This creator acts, with premodern glory and postmodern possibility, nobly, in supreme indifference to others, without the "pity" characteristic of modern humanism. But then a curious dialectic, for want of a better word, takes over the passage. If, Nietzsche reasons, one *is* indifferent to one's enemies, to the "others" who oppose one's evaluations, then one can be *supremely* indifferent, can forget one's slights and be in the best position, not simply to ignore, but actually to *forgive* one's enemies. But then, as Nietzsche seems to get carried away, if one's relations to enemies are not determined by *ressentiment* and fear, then one can not only forgive, one can actually enjoy one's enemies, indeed, "here alone genuine 'love of one's enemies' is possible" (p. 39). And finally, as we have moved very far from "not taking one's enemies seriously," "How much reverence has a noble man for his enemies! – and such reverence is a bridge to love. – For he desires his enemy for himself, as this mark of distinction; he can endure no other enemy than one in whom there is nothing to despise and very much to honor" (ibid.).

This remarkably disintegrating passage comes very close to associating the possibility of the master's self-esteem, his "distinction," the issue Nietzsche worries so much about in modernity, with "recognition" by the other. (Why else would a Master "*desire* his enemy for himself"?) Such a notion would seem to link the possibility of the creation of value with a "self-consciousness" about the presence of others and a conflict with *their* "creation." And Nietzsche's rather abrupt shift in tone in describing this conflict, from "indifference" to "love," suggests an important ambiguity in his account of modernity.

As we have seen, Nietzsche's most frequent description of the modern situation is that Western Europe has become a "mass" or "herd" society. Stimulated by the secularism of modern social life and the theoretical attitude of modern science and philosophy, the dawning awareness of the contingency of traditional religious, metaphysical, and moral ideals has begun to make such ideals unavailable as bases of social cohesion and order. A vacuum has been created, and in its confusion and panic, "modernity" fills that vacuum with a sterile, timid conformism. At some points. Nietzsche even goes so far as to say that institutions like modern physics, with its assumptions about "nature's conformity to law" or "equality before the law," is itself a "naively humanitarian emendation and perversion of meaning" that makes "abundant concessions to the democratic instincts of the modern soul" (BGE, p. 30; cf. also section #14).

However, even if there is something true about this picture of modernity, in the now rather standard claim that modern societies must face the prospect of collective evaluation and action without reliance on grand views of the cosmos, God, or the "good in itself," some of Nietzsche's own texts begin to suggest that this prospect does not mean that the alternatives open are some form of premodern heroic individualism (with its accompanying aristocratic code of war and primitive honor), or modern conformism, with its bourgeois ideals of security and prudence. The problem of a *collectively self-determined ideal*, one *based* wholly on the absence of natural ends or natural hierarchy, is as typical and difficult a modern problem as anything else. Nietzsche tends to focus attention on such forms of modern sociality as contract, or a collective insuring of the basest, most "slavish" form of self-affirmation – self-interest. But there are many other accounts, motivated by a skepticism about metaphysics or realism as deep as Nietzsche's, that all attempt to account for a cooperative social existence and political ideals without such a narrowing of the issue of self-determination. (Examples include those philosophers who represent alternatives to both modern natural right and rational egoist traditions, or the "rational will" theorists. Rousseau, Kant, Fichte and Hegel all come to mind.)

Indeed, Nietzsche himself seems to concede in the passage above that one can never *be* radically independent or wholly "active." Given simply the presence of others and so the possibility of conflicting interpretations of what one is doing, and given the simple possibility of *self*-deceit, one is always "*self*-reactive," despite Nietzsche's talk of an "active forgetting," or a "kind of second innocence." And given this concession, it is not hard to see how the conflict he points to could be historically transformed; it need not be permanently violent or unresolvable. Surprisingly, the passage at least suggests an account of the *social* basis of an ultimately necessary appeal to a universal or mutually agreeable reassurance (perhaps a final mutual recognition of those who have come to regard themselves as equals or "Masters") that this is only *originally* and not finally fearful and "slavish." (This basis is familiar to readers of Hegel's *Phenomenology of Spirit*.)

This is not, of course, Nietzsche's theory. The above expressed "desire" (*verlangen*) for the enemy as the master's mark of "distinction" (*Auszeichnung*) is directly contradicted by a typical passage in *Daybreak*, attacking any desire for "distinction" (*Streben nach Auszeichnung*) as necessarily leading to the dreaded "ascetic ladder of rank" (D, #113, p. 113). For the most part, moreover, Nietzsche keeps up the fiction of Master morality as wholly autochthonous and socially indifferent.

However, this passage in the *Genealogy* is not the only place in the corpus where this fiction of a wholly self-reliant or self-created master is undercut. A great deal in *Thus Spoke Zarathustra* is simply incoherent unless such things as the apparently unbreakable link between Zarathustra and his disciples, even between him and the grim city of the Many-Colored Cow, the status of Zarathustra's equivocal "love of man," and his constant wandering between solitude and community are all reconceived in ways that would finally undermine any heroic ideal of independence or the "pathos of distance."[29] Zarathustra is one of the least traditionally heroic, least independent of the personae in all of Nietzsche's work. He talks rather than fights, and worries frequently about how he is reflected in the souls of his disciples. The work itself begins and ends with a dramatic rejection of solitude or indifference, with Zarathustra leaving his cave.[30]

All of which introduces a much larger topic. Nietzsche's confusing remarks undermining his own antimodern ideal, his suggestions that the noble man cannot live an independent life and must seek worthy enemies to "love," does not by itself go very far, or suggest much more than a social elite of mutually worthy antagonists. But the tensions in Nietzsche's account can help throw a different light on his response to the modernity crisis. These tensions can begin to undermine the simplicity of any picture of Nietzsche as a pre- or postmodern thinker.

If, that is, it turns out to be impossible for Nietzsche to promote coherently some contrasting, wholly active, noble ideal by which the modern failure is to be measured, then we will have good, even Nietzschean reasons for rejecting an interpretation of much of the post-Socratic and modern tradition as "slavish." First, whether that claim represents a discovery of Nietzschean genealogy or "our" own disenchantment with Enlightenment optimism, the noble-base, active-reactive contrast as its core turns out to be an unstable one. Its boundaries are hardly as fixed or as obvious as Nietzsche sometimes suggests. Nietzsche himself seemed to realize that Christian self-subjection can be a brilliant strategy for mastery, and that, as in the classical account of tyranny, mastery can be a form of slavery.

This result should suggest that the modern demand for some sort of methodological self-reassurance is misread if understood as a bourgeois or slavish failure of nerve, a timid conformism. That problem arises *necessarily* once a vast distrust of our pretheoretical experience, our "natural," "lived" orientation, the "human experience of the human," begins. It arises automatically once we think of ourselves as requiring a secure or honest or reliable way to *reestablish* some connection with that lost world and with other agents. That Nietzsche himself inherits this modern sense of loss, and so necessarily, in spite of himself, inherits all the problems and implications of the self-critical form of modern self-consciousness, helps to confirm Heidegger's otherwise baffling remark that Nietzsche is a Cartesian.[31]

The absence of any distinct pre- or postmodern ideal suggests that the issue of Nietzsche's "rejection" of or "farewell" to modernity is badly posed. At least in many passages (those more consistent overall with his whole project), Nietzsche clearly regards himself, to use again Heidegger's phrase, as the "culmination" (*Vollendung*) of modernity. Somewhat in spite of himself and his explosive rhetoric, he does not intend to free himself from "our" modern problems of reflection, and the social consequences of "our" legacy. Thus, on this reading, the unresolved tensions in Nietzsche's account, or the position of his Zarathustra, homeless both when in isolation and noble indifference and when wandering among the mankind to whom he finds himself inextricably attached, are not evidence of any revolutionary turn. Instead, they represent the still unresolved problems of the resolutely self-critical modern age itself. Nietzsche is not bidding modernity farewell; he is the first, finally, and uncompromisingly, to understand its implications and to confront its legacy.

NOTES

For comments and criticisms, I am grateful to Michael Gillespie, Tracy Strong, Andrew Feenberg, Deborah Chaffin, George Kateb, and Alexander Nehamas. I owe a special debt to my friend Robert Rethy.

1 Jürgen Habermas, *The Philosophical Discourse of Modernity*, trans. Frederick Lawrence (Cambridge, Mass.: The MIT Press, 1987), p. 85.
2 Ibid., p. 86. I pause here to note the obvious: that a sensitive account of the very terms "modernity" or "the Enlightenment" would be required before this sort of discussion could properly get off the ground, especially in the face of critics who deny there is any such decisive or epochal moment in history, or who think the phenomena are too diverse to be discussed together. There is however a conventional understanding of the terms current in much contemporary discussion, and I shall rely on such assumptions in what follows. The same could also obviously be said about the widespread use of the term "postmodernism." Of the polysemous uses of that term, there is at least one general problem clearly of relevance to Nietzsche: the claim that the great dualities or oppositions of modern social and intellectual life, between reason and unreason, good and evil, normal and insane, free and unfree, are all arbitrarily drawn, not internally or objectively defensible, and so that any exercise of social power based on appeal to the legitimacy of such distinctions is groundless. See also my discussion in *Modernism as a Philosophical Problem: On the Dissatisfactions of European High Culture* (Oxford: Blackwell, 1991), pp. 1–8; 148–67.

3 The issue of Heidegger's relation to Nietzsche is itself complex enough
   for a book length study. In his lecture series in the 1930s, and 1940s,
   Heidegger proclaimed that Nietzsche's "fundamental metaphysical position is the end of Western philosophy" itself, and that it "performs the
   grandest and most profound gathering – that is, accomplishment – of all
   the essential fundamental positions since Plato in the light of Platonism." So for Heidegger, what is important is that Nietzsche's thought
   is a "consummation," not a "farewell." Martin Heidegger, *Nietzsche.*
   Volume II. The Eternal Recurrence of the Same, trans. David Farrell
   Krell (New York: Harper and Row, 1984), p. 204 and p. 205. Cf. Chapter
   Five of *Modernism as a Philosophical Problem,* and my "Nietzsche,
   Heidegger, and the Metaphysics of Modernity," in *Nietzsche and Mod-*
   ern German Thought, ed. Keith Ansell-Pearson (London: Routledge,
   1991), pp. 282–310.
4 As does, e.g., Charles Taylor in "Overcoming Epistemology," in *After*
   Philosophy: End or Transformation? (Cambridge: MIT Press, 1987), p.
   482ff.
5 Stanley Rosen, "Nietzsche's Revolution," in *The Ancients and the Mod-*
   erns (New Haven: Yale University Press, 1989), p. 189. Cf. also Leo
   Strauss, *Natural Right and History* (Chicago: University of Chicago
   Press, 1953), p. 253, and Alasdair MacIntyre, *After Virtue* (Notre Dame:
   Notre Dame University Press, 1984), p. 114.
6 Gilles Deleuze, *Nietzsche and Philosophy,* trans. H. Tomlinson (New
   York: Columbia University Press, 1983).
7 Cf. *Modernism as a Philosophical Problem,* op. cit., pp. 46–79.
8 This way of thinking about their respective dissatisfactions with the
   modern tradition suggests many other affinities. Both, for example, are
   often understood to have rejected any "transcendent" or metaphysical
   standpoint in philosophy (it was actually Hegel who first announced
   that the "religion of modern times" held that "God is dead"), and so to
   have understood philosophy as continuous with and an expression of
   "life," whether understood in terms of some historical "spirit" or as
   "will to power." And, somewhat paradoxically, for all their differences,
   by so positioning themselves so far outside the tradition, both are supposed to have fallen into some sort of trap or paradox. The idea is that we
   can see in both how, deprived of metaphysical transcendence, the subjective certainty of Cartesian method, or Kant's transcendental necessity,
   they fall prey to a dangerous sort of affirmation. Hegel is supposed to be
   a philosopher of radical "reconciliation" (*Versöhnung*), affirming the
   real as rational; Nietzsche's great injunction is, "No revenge!" ("*Keine*
   Rache!"), especially no revenge against time and so, finally, an uncritical
   affirmation of the "eternal return of the same." See the helpful essay by

Daniel Breazeale, "The Hegel-Nietzsche Problem," *Nietzsche-Studien* 4 (1975): 146–64.

9 Hans Blumenberg, *The Legitimacy of the Modern Age*, trans. Robert Wallace (Cambridge: MIT Press, 1983). See also my "Blumenberg and the Modernity Problem," *Review of Metaphysics*, vol. 40 (1987): 535–57.

10 It is also true that conceiving of the problem in terms of such an abstract opposition leaves out a number of other options, and is itself incomplete without a wider discussion of the historical context within which the whole "Enlightenment problem" developed. This latter detail would have to include the theological-romantic challenges of Jacobi, Hamann, and Herder, among others, the Idealist appropriation and transformation of such a reaction, and the "left-right" post-Hegelian discussions. To raise the issue of modernity in Nietzsche in a manageable way, though, we shall have to start with this admittedly crude distinction.

11 To complicate matters, he *does* frequently express great admiration for the clarity of style, the coolness of thought, in French eighteenth century "psychology," itself in many ways typically "modern."

12 Clearly this is meant to be a historical as well as a critical comment, and this fact raises the difficult issue of Nietzsche's view on history. Cf. *On the Advantages and Disadvantages of History for Life*, p. 8, pp. 24–6, with *Twilight of the Idols*, p. 35. See also notes 3 and 4 in my "Nietzsche and the Origin of the Idea of Modernism," *Inquiry* 26 (1983), p. 175, for a fuller discussion and fuller references to other treatments of Nietzsche's notion of history.

13 This paragraph, #227, besides bringing Hegel to mind, also represents a Nietzschean analog to Hegel's famous "Owl of Minerva" passage. Here, the light from a star, a "great thought" in this case, perhaps the thoughts of the philosophers of the future, takes many years to reach an observer, and until then we deny that there is such a star. Philosophy, in other words, is always and necessarily untimely. Although Nietzsche's dissatisfactions with modernity appear in many works, he tells us in *Ecce Homo* that we should look to *Beyond Good and Evil* "in all its essentials" for a "critique of modernity" and some "pointers" to contrary "noble, yes-saying type," EH, p. 310.

14 One of the terms Nietzsche uses most frequently to describe our discovery about "the Christian interpretation" is that it is "counterfeit" (*Falschmünzerei*). See GS, p. 308.

15 Cf. the famous account of science itself as an "*Erscheinung*," why science itself "must *free itself* from this seeming (*Scheine*)" and how the *self-education* of "consciousness" results from this, all in Hegel's *Phänomenologie des Geistes* (Hamburg: Felix Meiner, 1952), pp. 66 and 67; *Hegel's Phenomenology of Spirit*, trans. A. V. Miller (Oxford: Oxford Uni-

versity Press, 1979), pp. 48 and 50. Why these phenomena should have to be treated this way is a longer story, but, I would claim, involves similar issues in both Hegel and Nietzsche, and derives from the Kantian revolution. See Chapter Five of my *Hegel's Idealism: The Satisfactions of Self-Consciousness* (Cambridge: Cambridge University Press, 1989).

16 There is little in Nietzsche's self-understanding which connects him to the critical or post-Kantian tradition. But there is much in Nietzsche's work that evinces such a connection *malgré lui*, particularly the problems which develop when Kant's attack on the possibility of realism is accepted, but the possibility of a transcendental or a priori method is rejected. Indispensable in understanding this connection: W. Müller-Lauter, "Nihilismus als Konsequenz des Idealismus," in *Denken im Schatten des Nihilismus*, ed. A. Schwan (Darmstadt: Wissenschaftliche Buchgesellschaft, 1975), pp. 113–63; and Otto Pöggeler, "Hegel und die Anfänge des Nihilismus-Diskussion," *Man and World* 3 (1970), pp. 143–99. I develop this point in Chapter Four of *Modernism as a Philosophical Problem*.

17 This point is made very clearly in TI: "When we speak of values we do so under the inspiration and from the perspective of life: life itself evaluates through us *when* we establish values. . . . " (p. 45).

18 At least, *sometimes* Nietzsche claims that this realization (that morality itself is not just rendered difficult by such "baser" motives, but is itself an expression of such motives) all results *from* attempting to achieve the ideals of the moral point of view. In other places, as in his most polemical attacks on Christianity in *The Anti-Christ*, Nietzsche assumes the role of an enraged prophet, bringing a message violently denied by the community, "philosophizing with a hammer" (AC, #24–44). In somewhat less polemical works, like *Beyond Good and Evil*, he also underplays this notion of "values *devaluing themselves*," and seems to write as if *he* is devaluing them, thanks to some special insight, or psychological or metaphysical discovery.

However, in numerous other passages and throughout his unpublished notes, he says very clearly that it is "morality" that discovers its teleology, "recognizes" its "inveterate mendaciousness" (WP, p. 10). For a very typical passage on how the concept of truthfulness within *Christian* morality "triumphed over the *Christian* God" see GS, p. 307.

19 I defend such a reading at length in "Irony and Affirmation in Nietzsche's *Thus Spoke Zarathustra*," in *Nietzsche's New Seas*, ed. Michael Gillespie and Tracy Strong (Chicago: University of Chicago Press, 1988), pp. 45–71.

20 Cf. also *The Gay Science*, p. 304.

21 Nietzsche clearly does not think modern forms of utilitarianism are

distinctive in this regard. While they may not judge the act by reference to the intention of the individual agent, the overall evaluation of the act still invokes some sort of ideal of selflessness, that the act is unworthy unless it can be shown to benefit the many, not just the agent. See, especially, BGE, #201. Moreover, "The Utilitarians are naive" (WP, #291) since they mistakenly believe that they can identify both the consequences of an act and "what is useful."

22 An important essay on the history of Nietzsche's use of the notions of *Schein* and *Erscheinung*, especially sensitive to the internal tensions developing in Nietzsche's later understanding of the "true" world and the "apparent": Robert Rethy's "*Schein* in Nietzsche's Philosophy," *Nietzsche and Modern German Thought*, op. cit., pp. 59–87.

23 Part Two of BGE makes frequent use of the expression "we free spirits" even as Nietzsche struggles to dissociate such a class from all "goodly advocates of modern ideas" (p. 55).

24 Cf. Peter Dews, *Logics of Disintegration: Post-Structuralist Thought and the Claims of Critical Theory* (London: Verso Press, 1987), pp. 200–42.

25 This is not to say that the general issue of Nietzsche's literary style has not assumed major importance in contemporary commentary. See the essays in *Nietzsche's New Seas*, op. cit., *Reading Nietzsche*, ed. Robert Solomon and K. Higgins (Oxford: Oxford University Press, 1988), and especially *Nietzsche: The Body and Culture*, by Eric Blondel, trans. Sean Hand (Stanford: Stanford University Press, 1991).

26 There is a very interesting reference to the value of silence in Nietzsche's discussion of Socrates' last days in GS, #340.

27 See especially J. Habermas, "The Entwinement of Myth and Enlightenment: Re-reading *Dialectic of Enlightenment*," *New German Critique*, 26 (1982), p. 28.

28 Nietzsche is famous for his apparent indifference to Habermas's question, and does seem inclined to the response sketched above: "Supposing that this also [Nietzsche's claim about the totality of interpretation, the absence of "text"] is only interpretation – and you will be eager to make this objection? – well, so much the better" (*BGE*, p. 31). And in *Thus Spoke Zarathustra* " 'This is *my* way; where is yours?' – thus I answered those who asked me 'the way'. For *the* way – that does not exist" (*TSZ*, p. 195).

29 Cf. "Irony and Affirmation in Nietzsche's *Thus Spoke Zarathustra*," op. cit.

30 This also raises the question of how to understand Nietzsche's "politics," especially what he later referred to as "great politics." On that issue, the interpretation I am suggesting here would lead in a direction

other than the received alternatives on that theme. (Many commentators take their bearings from the "aristocratic politics" of Nietzsche's early phase, where the task of politics is, essentially, the production and cultivation of geniuses, higher types, aesthetically understood. Others follow what appear to be the more antipolitical suggestions of some works, where Nietzsche seems, more like the Stoics, to be encouraging a "politics of self," or of self-experimentation and, perhaps, a kind of cosmic resignation.) On many of these issues, I have been helped by the work of Henning Ottmann. See especially his *Philosophie und Politik bei Nietzsche* (Berlin: de Gruyter, 1987).

31 Martin Heidegger, *Nietzsche*, volume IV, *Nihilism*, trans. Frank Capuzzi (San Francisco: Harper and Row, 1982), Section 19, pp. 123–35. A fuller treatment of this point would raise a number of other issues: how we should understand the historical provocation which led to such a loss; whether the Hobbesean and Cartesian reaction was appropriate to the provocation; if somehow inappropriate, whether a form of philosophy (premodern, classical, fundamental) which does not share such assumptions is possible without being "uncritical."

REFERENCES AND ABBREVIATIONS

The Anti-Christ, trans. R. J. Hollingdale (Baltimore: Penguin, 1968) (AC)
Beyond Good and Evil, trans. Walter Kaufmann (New York: Vintage, 1966) (BGE)
Daybreak, trans. R. J. Hollingdale (Cambridge: Cambridge University Press, 1982) (D)
The Gay Science, trans. Walter Kaufmann (New York: Vintage, 1974) (GS)
On the Advantage and Disadvantage of History for Life, trans. Peter Preuss (Indianapolis: Hackett, 1980)
On the Genealogy of Morals, trans. Walter Kaufmann and R. J. Hollingdale (New York: Vintage, 1969) (OGM)
Thus Spoke Zarathustra, trans. Walter Kaufmann (New York: Viking, 1966) (TSZ)
Twilight of the Idols, trans. R. J. Hollingdale (Baltimore: Penguin, 1968) (TI)
The Will to Power, trans. Walter Kaufmann (New York: Vintage, 1967) (WP)

Part IV Nietzsche's Influence

9 Nietzsche in the twentieth century

In his autobiographical writing *Ecce Homo* of 1888, Nietzsche makes a statement about his success as an author that has baffled many of his readers ever since. After chiding the Germans for not understanding his notion of *Übermensch*, for aligning him with Darwinism, and for absolutely misinterpreting his *Beyond Good and Evil*, Nietzsche continues:

This was said for the benefit of the Germans; for everywhere else I have readers – nothing but first-rate intellects and proven characters, trained in high positions and duties; I even have real geniuses among my readers. In Vienna, in St. Petersburg, in Stockholm, in Copenhagen, in Paris, in New York – everywhere I have been discovered; but not in the shallows of Europe, Germany. (EH, 262)[1]

Nietzsche's claim to such exquisite readers is usually dismissed as the tortured self-appraisal of an author painfully aware of the low success rate of his writings or even as a sign of megalomania foreshadowing his impending mental breakdown in January of 1889.[2]

Only recently has one attempted to take this statement literally and come to amazing discoveries. If we simply look at the title page of one of Nietzsche's published texts, *The Gay Science*, for instance, we see the cities to which Nietzsche refers listed for branches of his publishing house Ernst Schmeitzner, namely, H. Schmitzdorff in St. Petersburg (5 Newsky Prospekt), C. Klincksieck in Paris (11 Rue de Lille), Loescher & Co. in Rome (307 Via del Corso), E. Steige in New York (22–24 Frankfort Street), and Williams & Norgate in London (14 Henrietta Street, Covent Garden). Yet Nietzsche's statement was meant not only to indicate that these firms affiliated with Schmeitzner were able to distribute his published writings in these cities, but to point to actual readers known to him either through direct contact or reference by others.

The continuing Nietzsche reception of over one hundred years now can easily be divided into two main phases separated by the end of the Second World War in 1945. During the first half of our century, along with the last decade of the nineteenth, Nietzsche's extraordinary dominance in European intellectual life was primarily literary and owed much to his poetic imagination. Gabriele d'Annunzio, the French Symbolists, and Stefan George elevated Nietzsche to the rank of a prophet, to the mythical anticipation of a new human being. André Gide saw Nietzsche as a deeply ambivalent figure caught between the overflowing, immoral celebration of life and the decadent, disillusioned nausea of existence.

Thomas Mann interpreted Nietzsche in relation to irony, the intellectualizing, psychologizing, and literary radicalization of our mental and artistic life. Gottfried Benn, the expressionist poet, saw the quintessence of Nietzsche in the statement "fanatics of *expression* 'at any price,' " which according to Benn had led to a language that can desire and accomplish nothing but to scintillate, demonize, and anesthetize. Nietzsche's impact on European literature and the other arts was widespread and extended from the Russian Symbolists, including Vyacheslav Ivanov, Andrei Belyi, and Valerie Brysov, to such diverse authors as August Strindberg, Georg Brandes, William Butler Yeats, Walt Whitman, Robert Musil, and Hermann Hesse. Gustav Mahler, Frederick Delius, and Richard Strauss responded musically to Nietzsche, and George Bernard Shaw brought the *Übermensch* as the "superman" to the London stage as early as 1903.

In contrast to this many-sided literary reception, the response to Nietzsche within the discipline of philosophy was originally surprisingly narrow and provincial during the first half of the twentieth century. To be sure, the Nietzsche interpretations developed by Max Scheler and Karl Jaspers were major philosophical accomplishments not only in the realm of Nietzsche scholarship but in the broader sense of a widening of the concept of philosophy itself. Heidegger began his Nietzsche lectures in 1936, continuing them until the end of the war in 1945. Yet Heidegger did not publish his lectures until 1961, when they clearly became a work of the postwar period. Scheler's and Jaspers' impact was decisively impeded during the

Nazi period, and their writings also did not come to full fruition until after World War II.

We can perhaps say that as much as interest in Nietzsche during the first half of our century was oriented toward literature and an artistic culture, this shifted after 1945 to philosophical questions and problems. Yet we have to add that during World War II and especially afterwards, interest in Nietzsche abated and a great silence began to spread around him. The impulse for a renewed study of Nietzsche came from the United States with Walter Kaufmann's interpretations and translations of Nietzsche as a "philosopher, psychologist, antichrist," and soon spread to Italy, France, and eventually Germany. While the emphasis here is on philosophical or theoretical questions and problems, we can hardly call this new attention to Nietzsche a philosophical preoccupation or a discovery of Nietzsche as a philosopher in traditional terms. The intellectual atmosphere into which he is thrust is one where the genre distinction between philosophy and literature has become uninteresting or even meaningless. More important, however, is that Nietzsche is seen as having initiated this transgression, even producing the postmodern turn itself.

EARLY VIEWS OF NIETZSCHE AND THE COMPILATION OF *THE WILL TO POWER*

At the beginning of this process we notice two Nietzsche images that are certainly not the first in chronological terms, but stand out because of their comprehensive character and by anticipating in their opposition a basic tension in Nietzsche interpretation throughout the twentieth century. These are the books *Friedrich Nietzsche: The Man in His Works* by Lou Salomé of 1894 and *The Life of Friedrich Nietzsche* by his sister Elisabeth Förster-Nietzsche, which appeared in two volumes in 1895 and 1897.

Both writers had a profound knowledge of Nietzsche as a person and author. Lou Salomé had earlier published sections of her book in magazines, and Nietzsche, knowing of her intention to write about him, provided her with information concerning his life and thought that she used throughout her book. Erwin Rohde, one of Nietzsche's closest friends, said that "nothing better or more deeply experienced and perceived has ever been written about Nietzsche."[3] Elisabeth Förster-Nietzsche had of course known her brother throughout her life, but she also became the inheritor of his literary estate and, as the organizer of the Nietzsche Archives in Weimar, had access to the vast materials of his unpublished philosophical fragments, including his correspondence. These two women had perhaps a better knowledge of Nietzsche than anyone else at that time, and their accounts are without a doubt of special significance for the emergence of the early images of Nietzsche.

Lou Salomé came from a Russian family of Huguenot descent. Her father was a general under Czar Alexander II, and she had come to Western Europe to obtain a university education. Zürich was one of the first universities to admit women, and Lou Salomé frequented intellectual circles in Switzerland and northern Italy also familiar to Nietzsche. When they met for the first time in April 1882 in Rome through their mutual friend Malwida von Meysenbug, Lou Salomé was twenty-one and Nietzsche was thirty-seven years old. Their friendship had some amorous overtones, Nietzsche even proposing marriage, but was mostly of an intellectual nature and revealed a certain didactic, self-revelatory intent on the part of Nietzsche.

Through manipulations and intrigues Elisabeth Förster-Nietzsche made certain that this relationship ended a few months later. The high point occurred on May 5, 1882, at Lake Orta, near Stresa, when the two hiked up Monte Sacro and Nietzsche revealed to Lou Salomé afterwards "the most enchanting dream of my life, that I owe to you." It was probably on that mountain that Lou Salomé gave Nietzsche her poem *Life Prayer*, a soliloquy personifying and addressing life as from friend to friend, expressing her gratitude for everything she has received from it, pleasure and pain, joy and suffering. Written in a composed style, the poem concludes on a touching note by imploring Life not to withhold anything from her: "If you have no more happiness to give me, / Well then! *you still have your pain.*"[4]

Nietzsche was about to conclude *The Gay Science* at that time and had already articulated some of the main themes of *Thus Spoke Zarathustra*. It was certainly the poem's life-affirming attitude that appealed to him as he began writing *Zarathustra* and inspired him to the musical composition *Hymn to Life* based on Lou Salomé's text. He considered this composition a "symptom of my condition during that year when the yes-saying pathos *par excellence*, which I call the

tragic pathos, was alive in me to the highest degree." He did not fail
to remember this particular inspiration for his *Zarathustra* when he
described the origin of this work in his *Ecce Homo* and said of Lou
Salomé's poem: "Whoever can find any meaning at all in the last
words of this poem will guess why I preferred and admired it: they
attain greatness. Pain is *not* considered an objection to life" (EH,
269–97).

Lou Salomé's book on Nietzsche is neither a biography nor a psychological study, but is nevertheless closely related to the personality and individuality of Nietzsche. She wants to show how Nietzsche's peculiarity mirrors itself in his writings, in the way a poet
shapes his own unique world through words, metaphors, and correspondences. *Mihi ipse scripsi*, "I have written for myself," is a motto
she finds recurrently in Nietzsche's letters, especially following the
completion of one of his books, but she is also aware of the deeply
ambiguous character of this statement because of the "reclusiveness
of all of his thoughts and the manifold, living husks that clothe
them." When the "premier stylist of his period" speaks in these
terms about himself he seems to indicate that "he has succeeded
like no one else in finding the creative expression for each of his
thoughts and their finest shadings." Yet we soon realize the dissimulating character of Nietzsche's text, his operation through masks
and different personae that veils his own nature while he is commu-
nicating it.

Lou Salomé claims to have discussed this particular style of communication with Nietzsche himself in October, 1882 (LS, 4). We also
realize that the task of the biographer is to explicate the thinker
through his life, whereas her task appears as exploring Nietzsche
through his style, not so much through *what* he said, but *how* he
said it. Indeed, she turns away readers "wishing to discern the significance of Nietzsche as a theoretician" or "academic philosopher":
"For the value of his thoughts does not lie in their originality of
theory, nor does it lie in that which can be established or refuted
dialectically. What is of value is the intimate force which speaks
through one personality to another personality" (LS, 5). In a remarkable display of familiarity with all of Nietzsche's writings, including
his poetry, Lou Salomé substantiates most of her claims with quotes
from Nietzsche and cites in this instance: "Gradually, it has become

clear to me that every great philosophy up to the present has been the personal confession of its author and a form of involuntary and unperceived memoir" (BGE, 6).

Masking, veiling, and dissimulating constitute the first feature noticed by Lou Salomé in Nietzsche's writings, one closely related to his loneliness. A certain "taciturn solitude" was the first impression one received from him (LS, 9). Even Nietzsche's thoughts resemble a skin "which reveals something but conceals even more" (BGE, 32). She saw the compelling reason for this "inner aloneness and reclusiveness," however, in his physical suffering, a suffering revealing a close connection between the life of the mind and the life of the body and with Nietzsche, "the value of suffering for the gain of knowledge" (LS, 13). Nietzsche attempted to interpret his period of declining health and physical suffering as "a story of recovery" (LS, 23), but Lou Salomé sees a deeper interrelatedness of the healthy and the pathological in Nietzsche: "Here then, health is not something overtowering which converts the pathological into an incidental instrument for its own purposes; instead, health and pathology represent indeed a unique split of the self and mutuality within one and the same intellectual life" (LS, 24).

This "mysterious interconnection between the healthy and the pathological" is simultaneously the source of what she considers the "essential Nietzsche problem," basically a religious problem, approached by an "intellectual being" who was truly a "religious genius" (LS, 24). His person typifies the "inner dynamics of our time, the 'anarchy within instincts' of creative and religious forces that so energetically desire satiety that they cannot be content with the crumbs that fall from the table of modern knowledge" (LS, 29). The "great and moving feature" in Nietzsche's thought is for Lou Salomé this "insatiable and passionate demand" that comes to the fore "in every new turn of expression" and reveals itself as a "series of tremendous attempts to solve his problem of modern tragedy" (ibid.).

There are many other interesting aspects in the Nietzsche image developed by Lou Salomé. She originally formulated the division of Nietzsche's intellectual development into three periods, not so much in the sense of distinctly different phases, but more as "Nietzsche's transitions" (LS, 31). This distinction soon caught on and often served to condemn the third period as one of excessive polemics, uncritical exuberance, and intoxicated utterances. Ferdinand

Tönnies is a case in point for that attitude. Originally a great admirer of Nietzsche, he maintained his appreciation for the artist and aesthetician in the first period and critical philosopher in the second by completely dismissing the third period "as a witches' sabbath of thoughts, exclamations and declamations, outbursts of anger, and contradictory statements," although these writings too occasionally show "many luminous and brilliant appearances of wit."[5] Lou Salomé did not share this aversion to Nietzsche's late writings, but also saw them as texts that shifted towards the excessive, the exuberant, and instilled her with fear and awe. Nietzsche's thinking expresses itself in ever more general, but also more radical demands – *Übermensch*, eternal recurrence of the same, revaluation of all values. His entire line of thought assumes a self-destructive course for which madness was the natural outcome (LS, 148).

Lou Salomé included several photographs of Nietzsche in her book dating from the time following his mental collapse and showing him in the state of madness. She thought that it was "during this time that his physiognomy, his entire exterior, appeared to be most characteristically formed" (LS, 9). Quite predictably, this book met with the sharpest enmity among the representatives of the Nietzsche-Archives, especially Peter Gast, who had begun the first critical edition of Nietzsche's writings including some unpublished fragments.

Lou Salomé's bitterest enemy, however, was Elisabeth Förster-Nietzsche, who one year after the appearance of this book, published the first volume of her Nietzsche biography in which she refuted virtually everything that Lou Salomé had maintained. In this counter-image Nietzsche appears as healthy, a hero of thought, a conqueror of freedom, an advocate of life, and the pronouncer of new and daring doctrines. One point that particularly intrigued Elisabeth Förster-Nietzsche was Lou Salomé's assumption of a deeply rooted decadence that formed an integral part of Nietzsche's personality. Not only in her book, but especially in the influential periodical *Die Zukunft*, she launched a broad attack on these views and declared Nietzsche's illness as a completely exterior matter unrelated to his personality and caused by poor diet, wrong medication, overextension, and a sudden stroke within an otherwise robust state of health.

The most important facet of Elisabeth Förster-Nietzsche's image-making, however, concerns Nietzsche's text, the compilation of *The Will to Power*. From 1895 on, six years after the beginning of her brother's intellectual incapacity, Elisabeth Förster-Nietzsche owned all the rights to Nietzsche's immense unpublished notes, his entire literary estate. Upon her insistence, several editors, who also participated in the first edition of Nietzsche's works (the Naumann edition, 1895–1901), compiled an allegedly central work from the fragments of the late years by using Nietzsche's own earlier content outlines for its compilation. Nietzsche's proposed outlines for the selected notes were never consistent, however, and the ensemble of notes selected had to be reduced considerably to make them into a somewhat coherent work. In effect, Nietzsche's editors created a "book" by picking and choosing a small fraction of notes, revising many of them, and then arranging them from a planned outline Nietzsche had himself abandoned. This is the origin of *The Will to Power*, which in its first edition of 1901 contained 483 aphorisms and in its second of 1906, 1,067 aphorisms. A great deal of Nietzsche research during the first half of the twentieth century rests on this text made widely available through a popular inexpensive edition by Alfred Bäumler.

One of Elisabeth Förster-Nietzsche's major motivations for the compilation of *The Will to Power* was the desire to produce a philosophical masterwork or centerpiece for a writer whose other publications had been received as too self-contradictory and aphoristic, too "literary" and poetic for such a demand. The guiding assumption certainly was that a great philosopher would naturally leave behind a masterpiece presenting his philosophy systematically. This text distinguishes itself from Nietzsche's previous writings in that it undertook a profound revaluation of everything on the basis of one dominant principle – will to power, eternal return, or both. Nietzsche's previous writings lacked such a central philosophical principle. Instead of a linear and systematically coherent way of thinking, Nietzsche had tried out a multiplicity of "perspectives" and developed his ideas by constantly shifting from position to counterposition without arriving or aiming at a final result, a firm solution.

The Will to Power served to rescue Nietzsche from the reproach of a "poet-philosopher" and suggested that he had hidden his "true philosophy" in his published writings, that his real arguments were to be found in the texts of *The Will to Power*. As a result, *The Will to Power* came to dominate the whole of Nietzsche's oeuvre and depreciate the writings he himself had published or designated for publication.

FIRST INTERPRETERS

Georg Brandes, the famous Danish literary critic, should be credited for having accomplished the first major discovery of Nietzsche. In April and May of 1888 he delivered five public lectures on Nietzsche in Copenhagen before a constantly growing audience. Sections of these lectures appeared in the newspaper *Politiken* and became the basis for the comprehensive essay "Friedrich Nietzsche: An Essay on Aristocratic Radicalism," which appeared in August, 1889, in the periodical *Tilskueren* and in 1890 in German in the *Deutsche Rundschau*.[6] Brandes had been corresponding with Nietzsche since November 26, 1887. Nietzsche had sent him his *Beyond Good and Evil* and, somewhat later, *Toward the Genealogy of Morals*. While not understanding everything, Brandes realized that a "new and original spirit" emanated from these writings and particularly appreciated Nietzsche's "disdain of ascetic ideals, the utter rejection of democratic mediocrity, and your aristocratic radicalism." When Brandes concluded his lectures on Nietzsche, an ovation by a large audience ensued, and on May 23, 1888, he told Nietzsche: "Your name now, I can say without exaggeration, is very *popular* in all intelligent circles of Copenhagen, and *known*, at least, in all of Scandinavia."

The discovery of Nietzsche occurred at precisely this time, only a few months before his breakdown, and Brandes played a major part in it. He was a critic who saw his task not only in exploring established works, but especially in discovering new ones, and he had a particular talent for sensing just what his contemporaries wanted to hear. When Nietzsche died in 1900, Brandes wrote a brief reminiscence of him, recalling the time ten years before when his fame rose to such an unsurpassed height, his writings were translated in all main languages and became known all over the world:

For all those of the older generation who had already paid attention to Nietzsche when he conducted a hard and embittered battle against the absolute indifference of the reading public, the enormous velocity with which he then suddenly obtained world fame had something most astonishing. No contemporary author has experienced anything comparable. Within five, six years, Nietzsche's manner of thinking (now reasonably understood, now misunderstood, now involuntarily caricatured) became the dominating force in a great part of the literature of France, Germany, England, Italy, Sweden, and Russia. Without a doubt, no one during the decade from 1890 to 1900 has made such an impression and found so much attention as this Northern German son of a pastor who by all means wanted to be taken for a Polish aristocrat.[7]

In his Copenhagen lectures and essay on Nietzsche's "aristocratic radicalism," Brandes focuses on those writings exhibiting Nietzsche's critique of his time, of shallow optimism, and his reaction against the "herd." In Nietzsche's striving for individualism, Brandes discovers a correspondence to Kierkegaard. Eventually, however, Brandes turns to *Toward the Genealogy of Morals* because this text critiques on a much deeper level by questioning the validity and self-assurance of our moral world and deriving it from long subterranean processes.

Brandes is by no means an uncritical interpreter of Nietzsche and occasionally shows his attempt to distance himself from what must have appeared extravagant to him. When Nietzsche lashes out against cultural progress, human happiness, and welfare morality, Brandes objects that the goal of any welfare morality is of course to procure for humanity as much pleasure and as little pain as possible. When Nietzsche insists on the intertwinement of pleasure and pain, he displaces, according to Brandes, the problem to the highest intellectual level ignoring that the lowest and most common pain or "displeasure" is hunger, physical disabling, excruciating work destructive to health, and that there are no rapturous enjoyments that could compensate for such sufferings. In other words, Nietzsche does not really argue against the welfare principle in morality; his argumentation is on a completely different level. What distinguishes Nietzsche's argumentation from any other in this realm is the predominant psychological interest in his subject matters, the brushing aside of all "facts," which makes them more visible in themselves and permits him to discuss these themes with unheard-of passion, but simultaneously withdraws his claims from any scientific or rational control.

Perhaps the designation "aristocratic radicalism" is best suited for characterizing the approach taken by Brandes toward the new philosophy. There is a certain admiration in these words, deriving from Nietzsche's striving for independence in the sense of the motto "Become what you are." Aristocratic radicalism or individualism would certainly not be the appropriate designation for a writer like Brandes himself, however. Brandes dealt with Tolstoy, Shakespeare, Goethe, and Voltaire in his critical work, along with the more contemporary German writers such as Hauptmann, Sudermann, and Wedekind, and the Vienna circle around Schnitzler and Hofmannsthal. His social consciousness was quite well developed, and Nietzsche's outbursts against the love of others and social responsibility must have appeared strange to him. Yet he was able to recognize beyond such features one of the great minds of his time:

In the literature of contemporary Germany, Friedrich Nietzsche appears to me to be the most interesting author. Although hardly known in his own country, he is a mind of important rank who deserves that we study, discuss, refute, and appropriate him. Among other good qualities, he has the ability of conveying atmosphere and setting thoughts in motion.

This original receptiveness to Nietzsche, even from a socialist or communist position, can be noticed in many other instances at the turn of the century, especially in prerevolutionary Russian forms of Marxism, in the attempts by authors like Anatoly Lunasharski, Alexander Bogdanov, and Maxim Gorky to create a "Nietzschean Marxism" or a "Socialist Nietzscheanism." The common ground for such endeavors is obviously the battle against the existing order of bourgeois-Christian society and the striving for a new form of humanity, a "new man." The hardening toward Nietzsche in socialist ideology also occurred already prior to the new century. It was Franz Mehring who in a series of articles interpreted Nietzsche's thought as the philosophy of exploitative capitalism and coined a designation for him that can be seen as an intensification of the formulation created by Brandes (the philosopher of "aristocratic radicalism"), namely, the "philosopher of capitalism."[8] From here it was not far to Georg Lukács' "the philosopher of fascism" and the complete closure of Eastern Europe to Nietzsche until just recently.[9]

Brandes had told Nietzsche that his lectures had made him not only very popular in intellectual circles of Copenhagen but also in other Scandinavian countries as well, especially in Sweden. Nietz-

sche's appeal certainly consisted primarily in his challenge to tradition, and Brandes, with an eye for his public, had strongly emphasized this aspect in his lectures. Brandes also attempted to create
direct contacts between Nietzsche and Scandinavian authors. Strindberg had begun to read Nietzsche in 1888, and Brandes wrote to
Nietzsche on April 3, 1888: "If you read Swedish, I should like to
draw your attention to the only genius of Sweden, August Strindberg. When you write about women, you are very similar to him."
Strindberg sent Nietzsche his works and Nietzsche responded on
November 27, 1888, to the tragedy *Fadren* with deep emotion. He
was surprised beyond all expectations to become acquainted with a
work expressing his own notion of love – "in its means, war, in its
basis, dead hatred of the sexes" – in such a "grandiose manner."

Nietzsche's appearance in England, especially in London, around
1900, has been characterized as one of the greatest popular successes
a modern philosopher has ever experienced.[10] This success was not
based on a particular doctrine, a scientific discovery, but simply on
the challenge his critique of Christianity and bourgeois morality
constituted to Victorian morals and the help he provided to those
seeking to subvert this system. The terrain for Nietzsche was well
prepared by George Eliot's centering morality in the human being,
Walter Pater's religion of art, and Oscar Wilde's assumption that we
can attain perfection through art.

And then there was Fabianism, the Fabian Society, a socialist organization of intellectuals proclaiming the emancipation of the working class and equality of women. Here again, Nietzsche, in spite of
his attacks on democracy and the social movement of his time,
found easy access to a group of people with a highly developed social
consciousness. The most prominent member of the Fabian Society
was of course George Bernard Shaw, who helped develop the Fabian
Nietzscheanism and even integrated this type of Nietzscheanism
into his own "Shavian" style of life. This is a highly complex, original, and also ironic form of Nietzscheanism, which leaves us completely uncertain as to whether Shaw wanted to develop and further
Nietzsche's thoughts or use Nietzsche to allow his own thoughts to
profit from the wave of Nietzscheanism in England.

The central motto for this reception of Nietzsche by a socialist
individualist consists in the simple word *Übermensch*, superman,

which also functions in the title of Shaw's philosophical comedy of 1903, *Man and Superman*.[11] Nietzsche had used the term mostly in the sense of self-transcending, self-overcoming, but also occasionally combined it in an ironical twist with the idea of breeding the *Übermensch*. In the chapter "On Child and Marriage" of *Zarathustra*, he derives sexual love between the partners from the desire to beget the *Übermensch*. This idea is dominant in Shaw's usage of the notion but cleverly combined with his own social program. In the dedicatory letter of his comedy to Arthur Bingham Walkley, Shaw explains that we have to replace man by the superman. His nurse had been fond of remarking "that you cannot make a silk purse out of a sow's ear," and he had come to believe that she was right. The more he saw of the "efforts of our churches and universities and literary sages to raise the mass above its own level," the more he had become convinced that "progress can do nothing but make the most of us all as we are" and that we must "either breed political capacity or be ruined by Democracy" (MS, XXIV): "Promiscuous breeding has produced a weakness of character that is too timid to face the full stringency of a thoroughly competitive struggle for existence and too lazy and petty to organize the commonwealth co-operatively" (ibid.)

In order to bring this problem to consciousness, Shaw put these ideas into a Don Juan comedy utilizing the characters of the old Seville Don Juan story, but reorganizing them according to contemporary requirements. The new Don Juan is a "political pamphleteer" inspired by the "politics of the sex question" (MS, XXVI): "Instead of pretending to read Ovid he does actually read Schopenhauer and Nietzsche, studies Westermarck, and is concerned for the future of the race instead of for the freedom of his own instincts" (MS, XIII). His pamphlet is given in full at the end of the comedy with the title *The Revolutionist's Handbook*.

Another important change in the old Don Juan story, as it is perhaps best known to us from Mozart's opera *Don Giovanni*, concerns the role of woman in the relationship between the sexes. In Shaw's comedy Don Juan is no longer "the victor in the duel of sex" (MS, XII). Whether he ever has been, can be readily doubted, but at least in more recent history the "enormous superiority of woman's natural position in this matter is telling with greater and greater force" (ibid.). So in the politics of the sex question, the task of begetting superman slips to the woman, while the man writes pamphlets about it. Shaw's comedy, of course, exploits this situation to the utmost:

The woman's need of him to enable her to carry on Nature's most urgent work, does not prevail against him until his resistance gathers her energy to a climax at which she dares to throw away her customary exploitations of the conventional affectionate and dutiful poses, and claims him by natural right for a purpose that far transcends their mortal personal purposes. (MS, XIII)

This too is a characteristically Nietzschean idea. In *The Gay Science* he said: "Animals do not think about females as men do; they consider the female the productive being" (GS, 128).

The result is a highly complex drama to which Nietzsche might have provided the impetus, but in which he is soon absorbed and outdone by Shaw's dramatic imagination. The convoluted work consists of a long and witty introductory letter exposing the entire problematic and followed by four acts, the full performance of which would require six hours. Don Juan Tenorio is John Tanner and Doña Anna, Ann Whitefield, but John Tanner has become "the quarry instead of the huntsman" (MS, XVIII). The other figures of the fable have also changed correspondingly, Octavio, for example, becoming Tavy Robinson ("Ricky-ticky-tavy"). While sleeping and dreaming, these personalities return to their historical or mythological identities in the third act, disputing with the Devil and the Statue about the progress of humanity, and the fourth act concludes with the union of John Tanner and Ann Whitefield. Tanner's incessant speech-making gains him the epithet "brute" by Violet, another character, wherefore Ann reassures her future husband, "Never mind her, dear. Go on talking."

The work concludes with the comprehensive "The Revolutionist's Handbook" by John Tanner, M.I.R.C. (Member of the Idle Rich Class) presenting his views on humanity, progress, breeding, and superman, deemed the "vital purpose" of the human race. It is in this context that Nietzsche occurs in Shaw's text, not the prophet of superman, however, but only as some philosopher whose insufficient conception of the idea is now to be fully developed. Nietzsche also makes an appearance in the third act when the Devil tells the statue that among the latest arrivals in Hell was "that German Polish madman" who "raked up the Superman," although the idea was "as old as Prometheus" (MS, 137). While Nietzsche is kept at a distance from John Tanner's conception of superman, we cannot tell whether Shaw himself accepts these notions. He does not "disclaim the fullest responsibility" for Tanner's opinion nor for those of the other characters, but as opinions occur here, they occur "for the dramatic moment" (MS, XXVI). *Man and Superman* therefore appears to be a highly ironic dramatization of a Nietzschean theme very much en vogue at the turn of the century.

THE FRENCH RECEPTION OF NIETZSCHE

Of all European nations, France was always of special importance for Nietzsche and that country where he wanted to be read the most. This predilection for France derived from what Nietzsche considered as France's "cultural superiority over Europe" (BGE, 193), the talent of the French for "converting even the most calamitous turns of spirit into something attractive and seductive" (BGE, 131), and having found "a halfway successful synthesis of the north and south" (BGE, 194). On this basis, Nietzsche expected from France "an advanced understanding and accommodation of those rarer and rarely contented human beings who are too comprehensive to find satisfaction in any fatherlandishness and know how to love the south in the north and north in the south – the born Midlanders, the 'good Europeans' " (BGE, 195).

When he reports in *Ecce Homo* that people in Paris were amazed by "toutes mes audaces et finesses," he is referring to Hippolyte Taine who had used this expression with regard to Nietzsche's *The Antichrist* and simultaneously declared that because of these qualities, the text was too difficult for him to translate. Taine referred Nietzsche to Jean Bourdeau, the editor of the *Journal des Débats* and *Revue des Deux Mondes*, who indeed began to write about Nietzsche at the time of his mental breakdown. Bourdeau's essays solicited a great number of articles and translations of Nietzsche, but this early reception also had negative nuances, since Bourdeau had depicted Nietzsche as a philosopher of brutal force, and other critics took issue with Nietzsche's hostility toward Wagner. Nietzsche's discovery occurred at the height of a fervid Wagnerianism in Paris.

It is against this background that one of the most significant Nietzsche images of these early years, that of André Gide, should be seen. Gide's emergence as an author coincided with the French discovery of Nietzsche during the last decade of the nineteenth century. Initially closely associated with French symbolism, Gide must have become acquainted with Nietzsche in the circle around Mallarmé. Yet the first noticeable trace of Nietzscheanism in Gide can be detected only when he turned away from symbolism as too cerebral a form of poetry and embraced vitalism or a worship of this earth that he wanted to touch and step onto with his bare foot. This is the origin of *Les nourritures terrestres* of 1897 (*Earthly Nourishment*), his lyrical prose composition exhorting a young disciple, Nathanael, to follow impulse and abandon himself to sensation. "Nathanael, I no longer believe in sin," is the motto of the text, which clearly exhibits a Zarathustrean atmosphere.

Yet to demonstrate the presence of Nietzsche in this text is of greater difficulty than one would expect. First of all, Gide strongly and consistently denied that he had any knowledge of Nietzsche when he wrote *Les nourritures terrestres* and claimed that his acquaintance with Nietzsche occurred at a much later date.[12] This denial, which has been refuted, reveals Gide's distancing himself from an author he considered dangerous and with whom he did not want to be too closely identified.

A similar attitude can be noticed in the text of the prose poem itself, which if read as an unrestrained praise of life and worldliness, soon presents difficulties. The style appears stilted, the atmosphere theatrical, the whole intolerable. The theme is the liberation of the self from constrictive systems – Puritanism, morality, tradition, family – and the attainment of a vital fullness of life, an immediacy of experience, and an abandoning of the intellectual or the merely symbolic. All we actually receive from the author, however, is an intellectual image of spontaneity, a theory, a philosophy of immediacy, a stylized vitalism that has been thought and systematized.[13]

By integrating the desirability and unattainability of pure vitalism into one and the same text, Gide gave us not only vitalism but also its critique. He himself maintained a distance from pure vitalism and kept the oscillation between vitalism and that Puritanism so characteristic of his entire oeuvre. If Nietzsche is present in *Les nourritures terrestres*, the message of Zarathustra is not only reshaped, but simultaneously criticized.

This last point can be clarified by turning to another, much later book by Gide, the novel *Les caves du Vatican* (*Lafcadio's adventures*) of 1914, famous for its depiction of a "gratuitous act" without premeditation, without any intention, advantage, or purpose, performed on impulse and possibly to gratify a desire for sensation. Lafcadio, the handsome young Nietzschean immoralist protagonist, had acted several times in a "gratuitous" way. Once at the risk of his life, he had rescued two little children from a burning house in Paris, but to show that the gratuitous act has nothing to do with morality, he also once acted differently while on a train to Rome. Opposite to him in his compartment was a bourgeois fellow, pedantically dressed, sweating a little, and constantly fumbling with his nose.

Counting to ten, Lafcadio opened the door of the car and pushed the man to death just as if he had chased away a fly. When his friend is later arrested for the deed, Lafcadio takes full responsibility, however, indicating that there really is no gratuitous act. Gide's depiction of the murder is so stylized, so stereotypical and artificial that we are aware of seeing not real life at all, but literature. One can write about the gratuitous act, but not live it, for writing about it already demonstrates that it is unreal.[14] Immoralism, like vitalism, requires counteraction, a corrective, an oscillation to its opposite, for it to become real and emerge from caricature.

We could say that such oscillation and counteraction would indeed be an excellent form of Nietzscheanism, yet Gide did not think so. He assumed that Nietzsche was an unrestrained force of instinct, of vital power and life that had to be curbed and controlled by Gide's own Puritanism. He admitted to Nietzsche's influence starting in only 1898, when he began work on his Nietzschean novel *The Immoralist*. Even then Nietzsche was a disturbing, rather than furthering force: "When I discovered him, I wrote *The Immoralist*. Who will ever believe me how much of an annoyance he was?"[15]

Gide was nevertheless grateful to Nietzsche for his devastating critique of morality and traditional values, which saved him a lot of time and kept his work free of "those theories which have perhaps prevented Nietzsche from achieving artistic production on his own." In 1898 Gide also wrote his own essay on Nietzsche occasioned by the French translation of *Beyond Good and Evil* and *Zarathustra*. The essential aspect of this Nietzsche interpretation is Gide's contention that Nietzsche was a destroyer, as Jean Bourdeau had maintained.

Gide says: "He undermines, not out of satiety, but rather full of captivating anger – noble, radiant, superhuman, like a young conqueror who tramples walls through his disgust with satiety, the comfortable and above all with that which debases, stupefies, and lulls."[16]

Gide believes that in order to grasp Nietzsche one has to abandon oneself fully to him, but this is only possible for those minds prepared by a sort of "inborn Protestantism or Jansenism." Here again it becomes obvious that Gide realized only the vital side of Nietzsche, not his tragic, reflective, skeptical, intellectual dimension. The reason for this Nietzsche image is evident, since the latter components of Nietzsche's personality found expression in theory and philosophy, whereas Gide was more concerned with poetry and art. Philosophy would only spoil his art, he thought and said: "The work of the philosophers is necessarily monotonous."

This was Nietzsche's central problem according to Gide, for whom he became "his own captive." He appears like a "lion in the cage of a squirrel": "There is no more tragic example than this antirationalist who wants to prove something. He is an artist, but he does not create – he proves with passionate obstinacy. He negates reason and reasons. He negates with the fervor of martyrs." Nietzsche's own lament: "It should have sung, this soul" (BT, Preface), could have served as a motto for Gide's Nietzsche critique. Other figures soon replace Nietzsche for Gide, especially Goethe and Dostoevsky. The famous Dostoevsky lectures of 1922, however, still maintain a strong relationship to Nietzsche, in that Nietzsche's unresolved problems lead to their artistic solution in Dostoevsky and Gide himself. These are mainly related to the interpretations of Christianity and Christ, which according to Gide, show that the philosopher is shipwrecked on the intricacy of these problems, whereas the artist's creative energy is able to unravel them.

THE GERMAN RECEPTION OF NIETZSCHE

Since the beginning of the last decade of the nineteenth century, Nietzsche's presence looms large on the German scene of letters, and one could boldly say there is hardly any author who at one time or another did not have his moment of experiencing Nietzsche. Hugo von Hofmannsthal, Stefan George, Frank Wedekind, Hermann

Hesse, Rainer Maria Rilke, and Bertold Brecht exemplify a more decisive and lasting impact of Nietzsche upon their work. There are three authors, however, Thomas Mann, Gottfried Benn, and Robert Musil, whose work not only showed a high degree of receptiveness to Nietzschean ideas and themes, but also responded critically to Nietzsche, furthering an understanding of his thought as one of the great events of the twentieth century.

Thomas Mann's occupation with Nietzsche was a lifelong process evidenced not only by a considerable number of theoretical texts, but above all by his creative work, his narrations, especially the late novel *Doctor Faustus* of 1947. The main motif of Mann's Nietzsche image is that of a "martyr of thought," a "saint of immoralism," who died the "martyr's death on the cross of thought." There is an aura of exclusivity, of nobility, of an extraordinary and paradigmatic human fate surrounding Mann's Nietzsche. Yet Mann also saw disturbing features in Nietzsche and felt entitled to denounce them as signs of an antihuman barbarism. Nietzsche's paroxysms of an *Übermensch*, an eternal recurrence, a will to power, appeared dull, obtuse, and simply below Nietzsche's intellectual level to him.

Nietzsche's proclamation of the primacy of life and its elevation to the last criterion of value, however, were taken by Mann as an important challenge to his own position, one worth taking it up and refuting as part of his life's work. Mann's Nietzsche image can perhaps best be illuminated by his refutation of this central Nietzschean issue, the superiority of life above all else, the "self-denial, the self-betrayal of the intellect in favor of life," as Mann puts it, or "that ruthless Renaissance estheticism, that hysterical cult of power, beauty, and life" (RNM, 13).[17] Like André Gide, Mann sees in Nietzsche a source of vitalism and vital power that is enormously resourceful for a type of poetry that has become cerebral and removed from life. This cult of life, however, is in need of a corrective provided by Mann's critical approach to it, two instances of which are most revealing. The first occurs in the *Reflections of a Nonpolitical Man* of 1918 and the latter in the lecture "Nietzsche's Philosophy in the Light of Recent History," which Mann delivered in 1947 at the Pen-Club in Zürich.

The Prologue to the *Reflections of a Nonpolitical Man* provides in quintessential form Mann's understanding of Nietzsche and his own reaction to him:

From an intellectual-poetic viewpoint, there are two brotherly possibilities produced from experiencing Nietzsche. The one is that ruthless Renaissance estheticism, that hysterical cult of power, beauty, and life that found favor for a while in a certain literary school. The other is called *irony* – and here I am speaking of myself. With me, the experience of the self-denial of intellect in favor of life became irony – a moral attitude for which I know no other description and designation than precisely this one: that it is the self-denial, the self-betrayal of the intellect in favor of life. (RNM, 13)

The thrust of this statement appears obvious: Nietzsche is seen as representing the position of a "self-denial of intellect in favor of life." This philosophical position releases enormous potentialities for poetry because it provides artistic creation with the infinity of life. The infusion of the experience of the Dionysian is comparable to the rise of romanticism in literature, when old sterile forms of poetic expression were replaced by new and more vigorous ones.

Yet there are two ways of responding to Nietzsche. One would be to simply mirror "that ruthless Renaissance estheticism, that hysterical cult of power, beauty, and life" already expressed in Nietzsche's own writings. This was done by a "certain literary school" at the beginning of the century, presumably by the early forms of German expressionism. The other consists in a more thoughtful response, in irony, in Mann's own approach. He too embraces "the self-denial, the self-betrayal of the intellect in favor of life," but he defines life "with a different, lighter, and more reserved nuance of feeling," a type of feeling that signifies lovableness, happiness, power, grace, the pleasant normality of lack of intellect, and of nonintellectuality."

In this mood of irony, in other words, the self-denial of intellect "can never be completely serious, completely accomplished." Irony seeks to "win for the intellect," but only indirectly, never by "placing itself seriously and actively in the service of desirability and of ideals." After all, irony is a "completely personal ethos, not a social one," it is "not a means of improvement in the intellectual-political sense," and in the last analysis "does not believe in the possibility of winning life for the intellect" (NPM, 13–14).

The antagonism of life and intellect, as Mann had inherited it from Schopenhauer, thus receives decisive modifications through Nietzsche. Mann readily conceded to Nietzsche that life, health, and vigor are supreme desirabilities, especially for the pale and decadent artist. In this sense, Mann made the antagonism of health and sickness, life and intellect the central theme of his work. If we ascribe Nietzsche to the side of life, we immediately see his importance for Mann's creative work. Yet with the intrusion of irony, this antagonism is no longer stable, and we realize a mental reservation toward either side – a mental reservation expressing itself in a mutual courting, wooing, and mediating: for the intellect from the side of life, and for life from the side of the intellect.

This attitude, however, implies decisive corrections of Nietzsche's position, as Mann sees it. Life is not that intoxicated Dionysian force as Nietzsche depicts it, but assumes the more moderate and disciplined nuance of proficiency as in the early representatives of the merchant house of Buddenbrooks before decay and decadence had set in. Mann considers it erroneous to view the intellect as the domineering force in our times and feel obliged to come to the rescue of life. The opposite is rather true. It is equally mistaken to construct an opposition between life and morality. Morality supports life and enables us to assume our position in life.

In *Tonio Kröger* the protagonist discusses the eternal antinomy of life and intellect with the artist Lisaweta and comes to the same conclusions. "Lisaweta, I love life," he exclaims, but immediately modifies this statement: "don't think of Cesare Borgia or any drunken philosophy that has him for a standard-bearer." He cannot imagine how one might adore the "extraordinary and demonic" as ideal and then continues:

No, life as the eternal antinomy of mind and art does not represent itself to us as a vision of savage greatness and ruthless beauty; it is the normal, the respectable, and admirable that is the kingdom of our longing: life in all its seductive banality – a longing for the innocent, the simple, and the living, for a little friendship, devotion – for the bliss of the commonplace.

When Mann delivered his speech on "Nietzsche's Philosophy in the Light of Recent History" before the Pen-Club in Zürich in 1947, the situation had changed decisively and no longer permitted him the attitude of an ironic mediation between life and intellect as an appropriate answer to Nietzsche.[18] The "nonpolitical" atmosphere of the period after the First World War had been replaced by a deep engagement and political involvement by Mann in anti-Nazi activities. He had become a citizen of the United States and had watched the collapse of the Hitler empire, which fused in a strange vision for him with Nietzsche's mental breakdown in 1889.

All this finds apocalyptic expression in Mann's novel *Doctor Faustus*, a Nietzsche novel, which he wrote more or less parallel to these events. The novel appeared in 1947 and was accompanied by a "novel of the novel," the *Origin of Doctor Faustus* in which all these biographical and intellectual relationships are explained. "Nietzsche's Philosophy in the Light of Recent History" of the same year clearly belongs to these texts as a third form of expression. It is Mann's final statement of account as far as Nietzsche is concerned, where Nietzsche is definitely relegated to the past to free the future from his fateful impact.

Right at the start, Mann sets the tone for this account. When Nietzsche's mental breakdown became known at the beginning of 1889, those who knew the "stature of the man" might have mourned like Ophelia: "O, what a noble mind is here o'erthrown." Indeed, we search the history of literature in vain for "a more fascinating figure than that of the hermit of Sils Maria." Yet this is a fascination, Mann adds, "closely akin to that which through the centuries has emanated from Shakespeare's melancholy Dane" (NP, 14). Nietzsche was "a phenomenon of vast cultural scope and complexity, a veritable résumé of the European spirit." Yet the emotion Mann experienced as a "fascinated 'observer' and reader of the following generation" of Nietzsche was "a combination of reverence and pity," more precisely "tragic pity for an overburdened soul, a soul upon whom too many charges have been laid – one only called for knowledge, not really born for it and, like Hamlet, shattered by it" (NP, 142). Upon this "delicate, fine, warmhearted soul in need of love," the "coldest solitude, the solitude of the criminal" was imposed. This mind, "by origin profoundly respectful, shaped to revere pious traditions," became dragged by the hair "into a posture of wild and drunken truculence, of rebellion against all reverence": "This mind was compelled to violate its own nature, to become the mouthpiece and advocate of blatant brute force, of the callous conscience, of Evil itself" (NP, 142).

To realize the "fantastical nature of this development, its complete unpredictability," one has to look at the origins of Nietzsche's mind. From all we know about his beginnings, we picture "a man whose high intellectual endowments and unexceptionable propriety would seem to guarantee a respectable career on a distinguished plane" (NP, 143). Instead we see someone "driven forward into pathless wastes," like a mountain-climber who has reached "the point of no return where he can move neither forward nor backward." If we ask what it was that drove Nietzsche upward into these pathless wastes and brought him to a "martyr's death on the cross of thought," we have to say that it was his destiny, his genius.

But for this type of genius, there is another name, and that is disease. Mann makes it clear that this is not meant to "devaluate the creative achievements of a thinker, psychologist, and master of language who revolutionized the whole atmosphere of his era," but has to be taken in that specific sense in which a Dostoevsky, a Nietzsche are sick (NP, 144). He refers to Nietzsche's early affliction of syphilis in a Cologne brothel during his student days in Bonn and sees in this infection that type of fateful predestination of Nietzsche's intellectual life that offered the world "the heartbreaking spectacle of self-crucifixion" (NP, 146).

We have seen that Mann especially admired the early phase of Nietzsche when everything still appeared to be in order and cohesion. Next to this, Nietzsche was "a great critic and philosopher of culture, a European prose-writer and essayist of the first rank." This talent of his reached its height at the time when he wrote *Beyond Good and Evil* and *Toward the Genealogy of Morals* (NP, 148). A clear misappropriation of his mission and a beginning dissolution of Nietzsche's stature is noticed by Mann in *Thus Spoke Zarathustra* and its ambition to be poetic, religious, and prophetic. He says about it:

This faceless and bodiless monstrosity, this drum major Zarathustra with laughter's crown and roses upon his disfigured head, his 'Become hard!' and his dancer's legs, is not a character; he is rhetoric, wild verbiage and puns, a tormented voice and dubious prophecy, a phantom of pitiable grandezza, often touching and usually embarrassing, an abortion bordering on the verge of the ludicrous. (NP, 149)

Similarly, Mann sees Nietzsche's style in a process of continuous deterioration. To be sure, his style remains "musical," but it "gradually degenerated from the rather old-fashioned scholarly discipline and restraint of the humanistic German tradition into unhealthy sophisticated and feverishly gay super-journalism, which in the end he adorned with the cap and bells of a comic jester" (NP, 151).

More principally, however, Mann depicts Nietzsche's later intellectual biography as the "history of decay" of one single idea, namely, the idea of "culture," the highest accomplishment of human life. Originally, with the proposition that life can be justified only as an aesthetic phenomenon, Nietzsche represented that tragically ironic wisdom which, for the sake of culture, "holds science within bonds" and defends life against the "pessimism of the calumniators of life" (the "apostles of an afterlife") and against the "optimism of the rationalists and reformers who preach their fables of justice and happiness on this earth for all men" (NP, 152).

Yet, already in *The Birth of Tragedy* Nietzsche assumes a combative posture toward Socrates, the "theoretical man." Later, he "sang hymns to strength and beauty," professed the "amoral triumph of life," and "defended life against all the mind's attempts to cripple it," although even then, he "paid unexampled homage to suffering" (NP, 158). His life was certainly both "inebriation and suffering – a highly artistic combination," or in mythological terms the "union of Dionysus with the Crucified One." His "immoralism" was the "self-destruction of morality out of concern for truth," a kind of "excess and luxuriance on the part of morality" (NP, 159). We have to realize that all these subtle ideas "stand back of the atrocities and the drunken messages of power, violence, cruelty, and political trickery into which his idea of life as a work of art, and of an unreflective culture governed by instinct, degenerated so brilliantly in his later writings (NP, 159).

There are basically two errors that according to Mann "deranged Nietzsche's thinking and gave it its fatal cast." The first relates to the "relative power of instinct and intellect on this earth" and expresses itself in the absurd proposition "to defend life against mind": "As if there were the slightest danger of too much intellectualism on earth!" (NP, 162). The second error is the "utterly false relationship into which he puts life and morality when he treats them as antagonists" (NP, 162). Mann says:

The truth is that they belong together. Ethics is the prop of life, and the moral man a true citizen of life's realm – perhaps a somewhat boring fellow, but highly useful. The real dichotomy lies between ethics and aesthetics. Not morality, but beauty is allied to death, as many poets have sung. How could Nietzsche not know this? (NP, 162)

Nietzsche once said: "There is no fixed point outside of life from which it would be possible to reflect upon existence; there is no authority before which life might be ashamed." Mann asks: "Really not?" and refers to "the spirit of man, humanity itself assuming the form of criticism, irony, and freedom, allied with the judging world." To Nietzsche's proposition: "Life has no judge above itself," he responds that in man "nature and life somehow go beyond themselves," that in him "they lose their innocence" and acquire mind as "life's self-criticism" (NP, 161).

This humane self-realization lets us throw "a pitiful glance at Nietzsche's 'hygienic doctrine' of life" and also leads to the last point in Mann's argumentation. In his earlier and saner days, Nietzsche had mobilized his doctrine of life against the "disease of historicism," but as time went on, his attitude became one of a "maenadic rage against truth, morality, religion, humanitarianism, against everything that might effect a reasonable taming of life's savagery" (NP, 161). When Nietzsche predicts "monstrous wars and cataclysms" or begins his hymn to the "blond beast" of prey, we are filled with alarm "for the sanity of the noble mind which is here raging so lustfully against itself" (NP, 165). It would be pointless, however, and sheer stupidity "to respond to all these shrill, tormented challenges with scorn" or with "moral indignation." What we have before us is "a Hamlet figure, the tragedy of insight exceeding strength," and the feelings experienced in front of this tragedy are "those of awe and pity." Mann says:

And the grotesqueries of his doctrine are so permeated by infinitely moving lyrical grief, by such painful longing for the dew of love to fall on the parched, rainless land of his solitude, that any scorn or repugnance we may feel for this *Ecce Homo* is quickly checked. (NP, 167)

Mann rejects in particular any direct affiliation of Nietzsche with the Nazis in the sense of a "forerunner, co-creator, and ideologue of European and world fascism" (NP, 167). He would like to "reverse cause and effect in this matter" and not maintain "that Nietzsche created fascism, but that fascism created him," that this intellectual "was so delicate a recording instrument that he sensed the rise of imperialism and the fascist era of the Occident" and was "like a quivering needle pointing to the future" (NP, 167).

The problem of Nietzsche, however, remains the close relationship of aestheticism and barbarism. There will always be "something spurious, irresponsible, unreliable, and passionately frivolous" in his philosophical effusions. With an element of deep irony, we will be able to understand "his raging denial of intellect in favor of the beauty, strength, and wickedness of life" as the self-lashing of a man who suffered profoundly from life. Nietzsche not only offers us an art, he also requires a special art to read him. In a letter to Carl Fuchs of 1888, he advises the critic not to judge for or against him, but to characterize him with neutrality. "It is completely unnecessary, and even undesirable," he says, "to take my side. On the contrary, a dose of curiosity mingled with ironical resistance as of someone confronted with a strange plant, would seem to be a far more intelligent attitude toward me – Forgive me! I have just written a few naïve remarks – a little recipe for getting yourself happily out of an impossible situation." "Has any writer ever warned against himself in so strange a manner?" Mann asks, and remembering Nietzsche's curses upon the "theoretical man," comes to the conclusion that "he himself was this theoretical man *par excellence*" (PN, 174): "His thinking was sheer virtuosity, unpragmatic in the extreme, untinged by any sense of pedagogic responsibility, profoundly unpolitical. It was in truth without relationship to life, to that beloved life which he defended and hailed above all else" (PN, 174). Above all, his philosophy was not a "cold abstraction," but an "experiencing, suffering, and sacrificing for humanity." Although he was driven "to the snow-covered peaks of grotesque error," Nietzsche will stand for coming generations, as well as for the generation of Thomas Mann, as "a frail and honorably tragic figure illumined by the lightening of these times of upheaval" (PN, 177).

The full impact of this Nietzsche image becomes noticeable when we see it in relation to Mann's novel *Doctor Faustus* paralleling the downfall of Germany toward the end of World War II with the mental breakdown of the composer Adrian Leverkühn, a Nietzschean figure, symbolizing the greatness and dangers of the German mind. The novel concludes with the paragraph:

Germany, the hectic on her cheek, was reeling then at the height of her dissolute triumphs, about to gain the whole world by virtue of the one pact she was minded to keep, which she had signed with her blood. Today, clung round by demons, a hand over one eye, with the other staring into horrors, down she flings from despair to despair. When will she reach the bottom of the abyss? When, out of uttermost hopelessness – a miracle beyond the power of belief – will the light of hope dawn? A lonely man folds his hands and speaks: 'God be merciful to thy poor soul, my friend, my fatherland.'[19]

TWENTIETH-CENTURY PHILOSOPHICAL DISCUSSIONS

The discovery of Nietzsche in the academic discipline of philosophy assumed a much slower pace and was obviously impeded by the untraditional character of his thought and his unconventional way of expressing himself. The designation "poet philosopher" was certainly no great compliment for Nietzsche, as it implied fuzziness of thought, inconsequential argumentation, and lack of intellectual rigor. The other designation often employed for Nietzsche, "philosopher of life," refers to a philosophical school or trend of the time.

Max Scheler characterized the philosophy of life as a "philosophy out of the fullness of life, out of the fullness of the experience of life" and illustrated this attitude with Dilthey, Bergson, and Nietzsche.[20] Dilthey saw the most characteristic feature of a philosophy of life in an attempt "to interpret the world on its own terms," which required an emphatic approach to the world, a type of recognition achieved by projecting oneself into the object "as the interpreter relates to a work of art." The "interpretation of the world on its own terms" became for Dilthey "the motto of all free spirits" over the course of the nineteenth century. Following the decline of the Hegelian system, this interpretation was developed further by Schopenhauer, Feuerbach, Richard Wagner, and Nietzsche.[21]

This was the type of philosophical school to which Nietzsche was relegated by academic philosophers during the first decades of our century. Raoul Richter, Hans Vaihinger, Georg Simmel, and Ludwig Klages interpreted him with greater or lesser success as a philosopher of life and focused on his relationship to and difference from former philosophers, especially Schopenhauer. Georg Simmel's lectures on *Schopenhauer and Nietzsche* of 1907 are a particularly good example of this interpretation of Nietzsche.

Altogether, however, this is the type of Nietzsche interpretation that Heidegger mentions quite disdainfully at the beginning of his

Nietzsche lectures (HN1, 5).[22] These interpreters did not know what to make of Nietzsche and related him to something they knew and comprehended, namely Schopenhauer and the philosophy of life. Heidegger, in contrast, wanted to show "that Nietzsche moves in the orbit of the question of Western philosophy" and that he knew what it meant "to be at home in genuine questioning" (HN1, 4, 6). The first two comprehensive Nietzsche interpretations to take cognizance of the striking originality and intellectual rigor of Nietzsche's philosophizing derive from the two leading existential philosophers in Germany and originated at about the same time. Whereas Heidegger intended to relate Nietzsche to the unbroken tradition of occidental philosophizing, Jaspers wanted to reveal the astonishing newness and originality of his thought. Karl Jaspers published his book in December of 1935 and gave it the title *Nietzsche: An Introduction to the Understanding of His Philosophical Activity.*[23] In 1936, Heidegger had begun a series of lecture courses and seminars on Nietzsche, which he did not publish, however, until 1961 and then simply entitled them *Nietzsche.*

Jaspers' particular approach to Nietzsche manifests itself in the first sentences of his Preface to the first edition of his *Nietzsche* of 1935 and can be characterized as a search for an appropriate manner of dealing with this philosopher. Reading Nietzsche seems easy: "Whatever passage one happens upon can be understood immediately, almost every page that he has written is interesting, his judgments are fascinating, his language is intoxicating, and even the briefest reading is rewarding." Soon, however, the reader becomes "disturbed" by encountering a "great variety of judgments that are seemingly binding upon no one," and he finds it "insufferable that Nietzsche says first this, then that, and then something entirely different." What Jaspers proposes in that situation is indeed the core of his entire Nietzsche interpretation:

We must abandon mere reading of Nietzsche for a study that amounts to an appropriation achieved by occupying ourselves with the totality of the intellectual experiences which make him so representative of our age. He then becomes symbolic of the destiny of humanity itself as it presses onwards toward its limits and its sources (JN, XI).

This is surely not an uncritical approach to Nietzsche. Among Nietzsche's writings, especially in those "on the verge of insanity,"

Jaspers notices disturbing "aberrations." Originally, he had planned a chapter of quotations collected as evidence of these aberrations, of Nietzsche's "mistaken naturalistic and extremist pronouncements." The result, however, was "devastating," and Jaspers omitted this chapter "out of respect for Nietzsche." From the point of view of understanding what Jaspers intended to convey, "such aberrations are seen to amount to nothing": "The essence of his life and thought is so utterly magnificent that he who is able to participate in it is proof against the errors to which Nietzsche momentarily fell victim and which at a later date could provide phraseological materials to be used by the National Socialists in support of their inhuman deeds." Jaspers sees Nietzsche as "perhaps the last of the great philosophers of the past" and hopes "that his prophetic earnestness will prevail over mere semblance." It is this severe demand and complexity of Nietzsche that motivated the Nazis eventually to abandon Nietzsche "without further ado" (JN, XIII–XIV).

Jaspers' book is divided into three parts – "Nietzsche's Life," "The Basic Thoughts of Nietzsche," and "Nietzsche's Way of Thinking" – all of which were innovations for the understanding of Nietzsche at that time. In these sections he unfolds a fascinating image of the philosopher, the central feature of which is Nietzsche's persistent questioning of every self-enclosed form of rationality as a new kind of modernity in his philosophizing. This is the thrust of Jaspers' analyses of Nietzsche's "philosophical activity" in terms of infinite reflection, masks, self-dissembling writing, groundless thought, and an infinitely self-completing dialectics that brings all apodictic statements into question through the consideration of new possibilities.

In *Reason and Existence* of 1935,[24] Jaspers had tried to integrate these aspects of Nietzsche's thought into his own philosophy of existence. In the famous introduction to this text, Jaspers portrayed Nietzsche's and Kierkegaard's works as prime examples of two important arguments against the basic tendency of Western thought to transform everything nonrational or counter-rational into rationality and to ground reason on its own basis. To illustrate this thesis, Jaspers divided the intellectual history of the West into two periods: one marked by the domination of the logos and the admonition "Know Thyself," which culminated in Hegel; and the other characterized by a radical disillusionment with the self-confidence of reason, the dissolution of all boundaries, and the collapse of all authority, a period that began with Kierkegaard and Nietzsche. With their claim that human knowledge is nothing but interpretation, their seductive willingness to indulge in concealment and masks, and their dizzying call for a truthfulness that continually calls itself into question, they represent "modernity somersaulting over itself." They offer "no teachings, no basic position, not a world view, but a new, basic manner of thinking in the medium of infinite reflection, a reflection conscious that, as reflection, it can no longer gain a foundation."

In a later study of the fifties, "On Nietzsche's Importance in the History of Philosophy," Jaspers again insisted on the uniqueness of Nietzsche's thought in its processional, indeterminable character.[25] Nietzsche's work was "a heap of ruins," Jaspers claimed, animated by a factual, not a methodologically developed dialectics. He ranked him together with Marx and Kierkegaard as one of the three thinkers who no longer permitted themselves "claims to the absolute" in the tradition of the Western mind. They were questionable in what they prophesied but magnificent in view of the unrest into which they have placed us: "They stand at the entrance door to modern thought. They did not point out the right way, but illuminate in an incomparable manner."

Heidegger, in sharp contrast to Jaspers' view of Nietzsche, seems to be motivated by the question whether the philosopher's aphoristic and fragmentary text, which apparently rejects final principles and systematic coherence, nevertheless can be read in the style of traditional metaphysics. Heidegger's *Nietzsche*, a compilation of his lectures and manuscripts from 1936 to 1945 published in 1961, presents the most comprehensive, self-enclosed interpretation of Nietzsche yet produced. Heidegger limits his interpretation to one single philosophical principle, the will to power, and derives all particular themes in Nietzsche from that principle. This principle, however, does not appear simply in the concept of "the will to power," but emerges only if we think the apparently irreconcilable thoughts of "the will to power" and "the eternal recurrence of the same" together, and in such an intensive way that "in terms of metaphysics, in its modern phase and in the history of its end, both thoughts think the selfsame" (HN3, 163).

At this point we should recall that Alfred Bäumler, in his Nietzsche interpretation of 1931, had rigorously insisted that the will to power constituted the central thought of Nietzsche's philosophy.

The works published by Nietzsche himself comprised a mere "foreground philosophy" for Bäumler, a dizzying phosphoressence of Yes and No, an irresponsible display of opinions. Only in his unpublished fragments, that is, in the compilation of his unpublished fragments known by the title *The Will to Power*, do we encounter a consequential line of thought centered in the will to power in the sense of an overpowering of the weaker by the stronger.

Bäumler introduced the notions of the hidden, but authentic, and an openly displayed, but inauthentic philosophy into Nietzsche and practically devalued Nietzsche's published writings in favor of the posthumous work *The Will to Power*.[26] In his book of 1934, *Nietzsche's Philosophy of the Eternal Recurrence of the Same*,[27] Karl Löwith also concentrated on Nietzsche's central "philosophical doctrine," in contrast to all those who had written on Nietzsche *and* some other topic, such as Romanticism (Karl Joël), his "psychological accomplishments" (Ludwig Klages), Schopenhauer (Georg Simmel), or politics (Alfred Bäumler). Löwith assumed that the task of the philosopher was to bring to light a central thought as the organizing principle of philosophy. To Löwith the structural principle of Nietzsche's thought was the doctrine of the eternal recurrence of the same, and this raised Nietzsche, Löwith believed, from a mere cultural critic and writer of aphorisms to a true philosopher.

Heidegger went far beyond the claims made by Bäumler and Löwith. First, he decided that Nietzsche's central thought was not actually present in his writings, or present only in an unthought, unelaborated way, and had to be realized through our efforts, through hermeneutics and a "better understanding." Heidegger was perfectly aware of the fabricated character of *The Will to Power* and referred to it in dismissive statements about "the so-called major work" (HN3, 10) that contains a "mixing" of passages "from many different periods" (HN3, 13). From this, however, arose for Heidegger the obligation to make the effort to think the central thought inscribed into the configuration "the will to power."

In order to accomplish this realization, a double effort is necessary. We must intensively fuse together the apparently irreconcilable concepts of the will to power and the eternal recurrence of the same, so that they are seen as two aspects of one and the same concept. In classical terminology, the will to power is the essence (*essentia*) of all things, whereas the eternal recurrence of the same is its existence (*existentia*). In the language of transcendental philosophy, the will to power is the thing in itself (*noumenon*) and the eternal recurrence of the same is appearance (*phainomenon*). In Heidegger's own terminology of "the ontic–ontological difference," which refers to the fundamental difference between Being and beings, the will to power stands for Being, and the eternal recurrence of the same stands for the multiplicity of beings (HN3, 168).

As Heidegger joined the will to power and the eternal recurrence of the same to one and the same thought, he tried to "complete" Nietzsche's thinking and to the end the Western project known as "metaphysics." Fused together, these two thoughts become a "*sole thought*" (HN3, 10), and with this thinking Nietzsche fulfills "the essence of modernity; now, for the first time, modernity comes into its own." Ultimately, "in the essential unity of the two thoughts, the metaphysics that is approaching consummation utters its final word" (HN3, 163).

This finality, however, should be seen in an ambiguity characteristic of all Heidegger's essential terms. For him, Nietzsche's philosophy is the completion of Western metaphysics. This thinking expresses not only the end of philosophy, its *eschaton*, but also its apocalypse as the unveiling of its meaning or, better, as the revelation of its meaninglessness. The concept of subjectivity in Western metaphysics, which reaches its highest expression in the will to power, is revealed as madness in the cycle of the eternal recurrence. For Heidegger, Nietzsche's philosophy is therefore "not an overcoming of nihilism," but "the ultimate entanglement in nihilism." Through this entanglement "nihilism first becomes thoroughly complete in what it is": "Such utterly completed, perfect nihilism is the fulfillment of nihilism proper" (HN4, 203).

The texts in which Heidegger conducts this important task, the ensemble of his Nietzsche lectures from 1936 to 1946, arose from a time of apocalyptic events in Germany. In those years, Heidegger achieved a new understanding not only of Nietzsche's thought, but also of his own philosophical position. The "question of Being," which dominated his thinking throughout his life, had evolved from the phenomenological, hermeneutic or existential "analysis of *Dasein* [Being]" in *Being and Time* to a "history of Being," that is, a history of the interpretation of Being over the course of Western metaphysics. The theme of a "forgottenness of Being" now applied more and more to the great metaphysical thinkers of the West who through their giving a name, a final word to Being, had obliterated Being's manifold structure.

The main figures of this "history of Being" include Plato, who interpreted Being as "idea"; Descartes and Kant, who transformed "idea" into "perception" and "transcendental subjectivity"; and Hegel and Nietzsche, who analyzed the notion of subjectivity and its constituents. Hegel came to the elevation of rationality in its speculative-dialectical form as the decisive principle, whereas Nietzsche arrived at the notion of *brutalitas* and *bestialitas* (will to power) as the unconditioned essence of subjectivity (HN4, 147–8). With this position, however, a historical moment has been reached "in which the essential possibilities of metaphysics are exhausted" (HN4, 148). Plato, who began this history, and Nietzsche, who ended it, appear as the two pillars of Western metaphysics. The rapid, catastrophic collapse of Hitler's Reich, the articulation of the will to power as the basic thought of Nietzsche's philosophy, and the conclusion of Western metaphysics in Heidegger's history of Being converge at this point in a unique and unsettling way.

In a more concrete description of the origin of the will to power, Heidegger notices that at about the time Nietzsche was writing *Daybreak* (1881), "a light dawns over Nietzsche's metaphysical path" (HN3, 188). Plans, sketches, attempts, and alterations from this time are not "signs," not "programs" of something uncompleted, "but records in which unmooted yet unmistakable paths are preserved, paths along which Nietzsche had to wander in the realm of truth of being as such" (HN3, 189). During this time, in 1881 or 1882, Nietzsche wrote in his notebook: "The time is coming when the struggle for world domination will be carried on – it will be carried on in the name of *fundamental philosophical doctrines*" (HN3, 190). One can say that it was Heidegger's goal to reconstruct these fundamental philosophical doctrines – which would ultimately determine the struggle for world domination – from Nietzsche's aphoristic and fragmentary text and to uncover their "hidden unity," however incoherently and obliquely Nietzsche may have formulated them.

In the essay "The Word of Nietzsche: God is Dead," Heidegger presents a concise summary of his Nietzsche interpretation and pays special attention to the critical, destructive character of Nietzsche's writing expressed most prominently in the theme of the death of God.[28] This assessment is also for Heidegger the most concise and consequential summary of the meaninglessness of previous Western metaphysics. According to Heidegger, Nietzsche revealed the meaninglessness of this event but was unable to bring himself out of it. The opening he had created was immediately blocked by the acceptance of the will to power and the eternal recurrence of the same, which prevented him from uncovering the truth of Being.

Despite all his revaluation of metaphysics, Nietzsche therefore remained "in the unbroken path of the tradition." With the interpretation of Being as will to power, however, Nietzsche realized the most extreme possibility of philosophy. He had inverted Platonism, which for Heidegger represented the essence of traditional metaphysics, although this reversal remained metaphysical as a form of inverse Platonism. As metaphysics, philosophy had entered its last phase. Heidegger was able to let Nietzsche emerge as the last great philosopher of the age of the subject, even of the entire phase called metaphysics. Through his own notion of a history of Being, his *Nietzsche* considerably gained in interest and became one of the great philosophical texts of our time.

We can also say that the post–World War II occupation with Nietzsche consists to a great extent in responding directly or indirectly to the challenge emanating from Heidegger's *Nietzsche*. During and just after the war, the world had become silent about Nietzsche. It was certainly the merit of Walter Kaufmann to have opened the debate about Nietzsche anew when in 1950 he published his *Nietzsche: Philosopher, Psychologist, Antichrist*.[29] Kaufmann's goal was not a debate with a specific author like Heidegger. He wanted to show to the world that Nietzsche was "a major historical event" and that his ideas "are of concern not only to the members of one nation or community, nor alone to philosophers, but to men everywhere." As far as the will to power was concerned, it was Kaufmann's contention "that the will to power *is* the core of Nietzsche's thought, but inseparable from his idea of sublimation." Kaufmann introduced the will to power as an apolitical principle of personal, existential self-overcoming and self-transcendence. This became a most influential image of Nietzsche during the fifties, sixties, and seventies. Yet a complete picture of Kaufmann's influence on the study of Nietzsche in North America can emerge only through a consideration of his translations of Nietzsche, which are accompanied by introductions and commentaries.

The most effective refutation of the will to power as the core of Nietzsche's writings occurred in postwar Germany, although this move was originally unrelated to Heidegger and more concerned with editorial problems. Already during the thirties, serious doubts arose about the authenticity of *The Will to Power*, first among editors at the Nietzsche Archives. They attempted a reconstruction of the original texts in their full length and in chronological order, but their editorial plans were never carried out. One of them, Karl Schlechta, wrote extensively about the inauthenticity and fabrication of *The Will to Power* after World War II, but had no access to the original manuscripts preserved in Weimar, in East Germany at that time.[30]

Access to Nietzsche's manuscripts was granted in the early sixties to two Italian scholars, Giorgio Colli and Mazzino Montinari, who published their *Critical Edition of the Complete Works* in 25 volumes as well as their *Critical Edition of the Complete Letters* in 16 volumes, based on the manuscript holdings of the Nietzsche Archives in Weimar. After Colli's death, these editions were carried out by Montinari alone. His main accomplishment was to produce the complete edition of all of Nietzsche's unpublished fragments; the sections from which *The Will to Power* was compiled appear in the last three volumes of the Montinari edition. They bear the unsensational title *Unpublished Fragments: 1885 to 1889* and appear in chronological order from April, 1885, to January, 1889. The new edition demonstrates with overwhelming evidence the transitory and tentative character of "The Will to Power" as a literary or philosophical project. The idea that Nietzsche broke down mentally while desperately trying to finish his master work is a myth. After having discussed the last sequence of books published by Nietzsche himself, Montinari laconically adds: "The rest is *Nachlass* (unpublished text)."[31]

This new textual situation has given rise to two groups of Nietzsche interpreters who try to deal with the "new Nietzsche" as he emerges anew from these critical editions. The first is a German group of scholars around *Nietzsche-Studien*, an international and annual periodical which has appeared in the same publishing house as the new Nietzsche edition, Walter de Gruyter in Berlin. The activities of this group manifest themselves in occasional symposia such as *Friedrich Nietzsche and the Nineteenth Century* (1978), *Friedrich Nietzsche in the Twentieth Century* (1981/82), *Basic Questions of Nietzsche Research* (1984), or in different kinds of collaborative work such as the *Commemorative Volume for Mazzino Montinari* (1989). The volumes of *Nietzsche-Studien* are accompanied by a series of *Monographs of Nietzsche Studien*.

Altogether one can say that this German center of a reinterpretation of Nietzsche is strongly oriented toward the new textual situation created by Montinari through his critical editions of Nietzsche. In a similar way, the Italian project "La biblioteca e le letture di Nietzsche" attempts to cope with the new Nietzsche as he is emerging from these new editions, but combines this project with the attempt, already pursued by Montinari, of establishing the manifold sources from which Nietzsche's text originated.

The designation "the new Nietzsche," however, finds its most pronounced expression in the great variety of writings on Nietzsche coming from France. Indeed, the notion "the new Nietzsche" is often replaced by names such as "the French Nietzsche" or "Nietzsche from France." The French translation of Heidegger's *Nietzsche* was already available at an early date, and much of the French work on Nietzsche can be seen as a refutation of Heidegger's interpretation by insisting on the metaphorical character of Nietzsche's writings, his style, his irony, and his masks.

Maurice Blanchot, for instance, argued that we can certainly organize Nietzsche's contradictions coherently, especially if we arrange them in a hierarchical, dialectical, or Hegelian manner.[32] But even if we assume such a continuous discourse as the background for Nietzsche's discontinuous writings, we sense Nietzsche's dissatisfaction with that. His discourse is always already a step ahead of itself. He exhibits and formulates his philosophy in a completely different language, a language no longer assured of the whole, but consisting of fragments, points of conflict, division. According to his own account, Blanchot wrote these notes on fragmentary writing in the margins of certain books about Nietzsche that appeared around 1969 by writers such as Michel Foucault, Gilles Deleuze, Eugene Fink, Jean Granier, and Jacques Derrida. We could add the names of Sarah Kofman, Bernard Pautrat, Philippe Lacoue-Labarthe, but will concentrate on Foucault and Derrida to illustrate this phase of Nietzsche reception.

Nietzsche was without a doubt the central figure in Foucault's discourse analyses and pervades his text in such a decisive manner that his presence cannot be limited to particular topics, such as power. Rather, Foucault's entire text can be seen as a reenacting of Nietzsche in our time, an actualization of Nietzsche toward the end of the twentieth century. Two examples will have to suffice to show the deep affinity of Foucault to Nietzsche. In a paper on "Nietzsche, Freud, and Marx," presented at a philosophy conference already in 1964,[33] Foucault sketched out a hypothetical project of a universal encyclopedia covering all interpretative techniques from the Greek grammarians to the present day. Nietzsche, Freud, and Marx would constitute a particular chapter in this work and mark a decisive rupture in the history of the sign. They drive us into an "uncomfortable" hermeneutic situation. Their interpretive techniques have shock effects. They neither increased the number of signs nor created new meanings; rather, they changed the relationships among signs, ordered them in more complicated ways, placed mirrors among them, and thereby gave them new dimensions (NFM, 184).

Interpretation, in this new situation, has become an infinite task. The further we proceed, the nearer we approach a dangerous zone in which interpretation is not only rejected as interpretation but disappears as interpretation. Foucault writes: "There is no longer anything foundational underlying interpretation; each sign that lends itelf to interpretation is no longer the sign of an object, but already the interpretation of another sign" (NFM, 189). He draws attention to Nietzsche's *Toward the Genealogy of Morals* and its etymology of "good and evil" or "good and bad" – words that are nothing but interpretations and become signs only through interpretations. Foucault suggests: "Perhaps this primacy of interpretation over the sign is the decisive feature of modern hermeneutics" (NFM, 190).

Another approach to Nietzsche's sign theory is suggested in Foucault's famous essay of 1971 "Nietzsche, Genealogy, History."[34] Whereas history views events from the perspective of the endpoint, teleologically and with an anticipated meaning, genealogy concentrates on the contingency of events, the episodes of history, the details and games of chance outside any preconceived finality (NGH, 76). Genealogy deals with "emergence," "origin," "descent," and "birth," in the sense of the origins of morality, asceticism, justice, or punishment (NGH, 77–8).

According to Foucault, such genealogical analyses by Nietzsche, particularly those in *Toward the Genealogy of Morals*, reveal something completely different from the external appearance of things. Such analyses demonstrate that there is no secret, atemporal essence of things lying behind them; their secret is that perhaps they have no essence, or that their essence is constructed piece by piece, out of forms foreign to them. Analyses of origin make us "identify the accidents, the minute deviations – or conversely, the complete reversals – the errors, the false appraisals, and the faulty calculations which gave birth to those things that continue to exist and have value for us" (NGH, 81). It is obvious, however, that in this text Foucault not only outlines Nietzsche's unconventional conception of history, but simultaneously describes his own research program.

The image of the "new Nietzsche" has perhaps nowhere found a more diversified and ambitious expression than in the writings of Jacques Derrida. Nietzsche occurs in almost all of Derrida's writings and always at crucial points. Nietzsche, as explored by Derrida, offers a new kind of communication, one that resists temptation to posit fixed doctrines or ultimate meanings but persists in the endless deciphering of its own terms. Derrida highlights Nietzsche's turn toward infinite interpretation, or the affirmation of the world as play, and shows how the style in which such thinking manifests itself must be plural.

Yet in his insistence on these attitudes, Derrida necessarily challenges Heidegger's interpretation of Nietzsche as the thinker of the most condensed notion of modern metaphysics, the "will to power." Derrida views Heidegger's reading of Nietzsche as an extreme type of truth-oriented, unifying, and systematizing hermeneutics that because of its own attachment to metaphysics, misconstrues the multiple subtleties of Nietzsche's text in a highly reductionist manner. Indeed, Derrida disputes Heidegger in each of his writings, and the confrontation is always, directly or indirectly, bound up with Nietzsche. The most important aspect of these confrontations lies not just in the spectacle of a contest in Nietzsche interpretation and Nietzsche philosophy, but in the ongoing attempt to press the limits of philosophy and writing. Drawn into the debate as if he were a contemporary, Nietzsche heralds a kind of critical thinking that has become more urgently our own: the critique of thought, an auto-critique of philosophy.[35]

Derrida also brings Nietzsche to the threshold of postmodernity, but to explore this relationship would require another chapter. Three book titles will have to suffice to indicate this direction of Nietzsche's reception in the contemporary world. These are: Richard Rorty, *Contingency, Irony, and Solidarity* (Cambridge University Press, 1989), Alexander Nehamas, *Nietzsche, Life as Literature* (Harvard University Press, 1985), and Bernd Magnus, Stanley Stewart, and Jean-Pierre Mileur, *Nietzsche's Case, Philosophy as/and Literature* (New York: Routledge, 1993). It would be hard to find a common denominator for these studies. One theme, however, common to all of them, is the overcoming of the traditional genre distinction between philosophy and literature in Nietzsche's writings. His text is seen in such a way that the old question "Is it philosophy or is it literature?" appears to be no longer relevant.

NOTES

1 References to Nietzsche are to the following sources. References are to aphorisms and not to page numbers:

AC   Friedrich Nietzsche, *The Antichrist*: See TI
BGE   Friedrich Nietzsche, *Beyond Good and Evil*, trans. Walter Kaufmann (New York: Random House, 1966).
BT   Friedrich Nietzsche, *The Birth of Tragedy and the Case of Wagner*, trans. Walter Kaufmann (New York: Random House, 1967).
CW   Friedrich Nietzsche, *The Case of Wagner*: See BT.
DB   Friedrich Nietzsche, *Daybreak*, trans. R. J. Hollingdale (Cambridge: Cambridge University Press, 1982).
EH   Friedrich Nietzsche, *Ecce Homo*: See GM.
FN   Friedrich Nietzsche, *Kritische Studienausgabe*, ed. Giorgio Colli and Mazzino Montinari, 15 vols. (Berlin: de Gruyter, 1980).
GM   Friedrich Nietzsche, *On the Genealogy of Morals; Ecce Homo*, trans. Walter Kaufmann and R. J. Hollingdale (New York: Random House, 1969).
GS   Friedrich Nietzsche, *The Gay Science*, trans. Walter Kaufmann (New York: Random House, 1974).
HH   Friedrich Nietzsche, *Human, All Too Human, A Book for Free Spirits*, trans. R. J. Hollingdale (Cambridge: Cambridge University Press, 1986).
TI   Friedrich Nietzsche, *Twilight of the Idols; The Anti-Christ*, trans. R. J. Hollingdale (New York: Penguin Books, 1968).

UM   Friedrich Nietzsche, *Untimely Meditations*, trans. R. J. Hollingdale (Cambridge: Cambridge University Press, 1986).

ZA   Friedrich Nietzsche, *Thus Spoke Zarathustra. A Book for All and None*, trans. Walter Kaufmann (New York: Viking Press, 1966).

References to Nietzsche's correspondence are given by date according to the following editions:

Nietzsche Briefwechsel, Kritische Gesamtausgabe, ed. Giorgio Colli and Mazzino Montinari (Berlin: de Gruyter, 1975–84).
Selected Letters of Friedrich Nietzsche, trans. Christopher Middleton (Chicago: University of Chicago Press, 1969).

2   This is the approach to Nietzsche by Analecto Verrecchia, *La Catastrofe di Nietzsche a Torino* (Torino: Einaudi, 1978).

3   Lou Salomé, *Nietzsche*, trans. with an introduction by Siegfried Mandel (Redding Ridge: Black Swan Books, 1988), IX. In the following "LS."

4   LS, LIV.

5   Ferdinand Tönnier, *Der Nietzsche Kultus* (Leipzig, 1987), III, VI, 25.

6   Quoted from Georg Brandes, *Menschen und Werke, Essays* (Frankfurt: Rütten and Loening, 1895), 137–225: "Friedrich Nietzsche. Eine Abhandlung über Aristokratischen Radicalismus."

7   Georg Brandes, *Gestalten und Gedanken, Essays* (München: Albert Langen, 1903), 337–40.

8   Franz Mehring, *Zur Philosophie und Poesie des Kapitalismus*, in: Franz Mehring, *Gesammelte Schriften* 13, 159–66. See also his *Lessing-Legende*, in *Gesammelte Schriften*, Vol. 9.

9   Georg Lukács, *Die Zerstörung der Vernunft* (Berlin, 1954), also in a separate publication with a special preface: *Von Nietzsche zu Hitler oder Irrationalismus und die deutsche Politik* (Frankfurt: Fischer, 1966).

10 Patrick Bridgewater, "English Writers and Nietzsche," in Malcolm Pasley, ed., *Nietzsche, Imagery and Thought* (Berkeley: University of California Press, 1978), 220–58.

11 See on the following George Bernard Shaw, *Man and Superman, A Comedy and a Philosophy* (New York: Dodd, Mead, and Company, 1943). In the following "MS."

12 See on the following Renée Lang, *André Gide und der deutsche Geist* (Stuttgart: Deutsche Verlagsanstalt, 1953). This is an enlarged and improved version of Renée Lang, *Andre Gide et la pensé allemande*.

13 See on this William H. Holdheim, *Theory and Praxis of the Novel. A Study of Andre Gide* (Geneva: Droz, 1968).

14 See William H. Holdheim, *Theory and Praxis of the Novel*.

15 Renée Lang, *André Gide und der deutsche Geist*, 98-149.
16 André Gide, *Lettres à Angèle*, in *Oeuvres Complètes* (Paris: N.R.F.) BD.3, 182.
17 Thomas Mann, *Reflections of a Nonpolitical Man*, trans. Walter D. Morris (New York: Unger, 1983). In the following "RNM."
18 Thomas Mann, "Nietzsche's Philosophy in the Light of Recent History," in Thomas Mann, *Last Essays*, trans. Tania and James Stern (New York: Knopf, 1959), 141-77. In the following "NP."
19 Thomas Mann, *Doctor Faustus. The Life of the German Composer Adrian Leverkühn as Told by a Friend*, trans. H. T. Lowe-Porter (New York: Knopf, 1948).
20 Max Scheler, "Versuche einer Philosophie des Lebens. Nietzsche–Dilthey–Bergson," in Max Scheler, *Vom Umsturz der Werte* (Bern: Francke, 1955).
21 Wilhelm Dilthey, *Gesammelte Schriften* (Göttingen: Vandenhoeck and Ruprecht, 1959), 4, 528-9, 210-11.
22 Martin Heidegger, *Nietzsche*, trans. David Farrell Krell, Joan Stambaugh, Frank A. Capuzzi. 4 vols. (San Francisco: Harper and Row, 1979-87). In the following "HN."
23 Karl Jaspers, *Nietzsche. An Introduction to the Understanding of His Philosophical Activity*, trans. Charles F. Wallraff and Frederick J. Schmitz (Chicago: Gateway 1966). In the following "JN."
24 Karl Jaspers, *Vernunft und Existenz* (Munich: Piper, 1973).
25 Karl Jaspers, "Zu Nietzsches Bedeutung in der Geschichte der Philosophie," in Karl Jaspers, *Aneignung und Polemik: Gesammelte Reden und Aufsätze*, ed. Hans Sauer (Munich: Piper, 1968). 389-401.
26 Alfred Bäumler, *Nietzsche der Philosoph und Politiker* (Leipzig: Reclam, 1931).
27 Karl Löwith, *Nietzsches Philosophie der ewigen Wiederkehr des Gleichen* (Stuttgart: Kohlhammer, 1956).
28 Martin Heidegger, "The Word of Nietzsche: 'God is Dead'," in Martin Heidegger, *The Question Concerning Technology and Other Essays*, trans. William Lovitt (New York: Harper and Row, 1977), 53-114.
29 Walter Kaufmann, *Nietzsche, Philosopher, Psychologist Antichrist* (4th edition: Princeton University Press, 1974).
30 Karl Schlechta, "Philologischer Nachbericht," in Friedrich Nietzsche, *Werke in drei Bänden*, ed. Karl Schlechta (Munich: Hanser, 1954-6), 3, 1383-1432.
31 Mazzino Montinari, "Textkritik und Wille zur Macht," in Mazzino Montinari, *Nietzsche lesen* (Berlin: de Gruyter, 1980).
32 Maurice Blanchot, "Nietzsche et l'ecriture fragmentaire," in Maurice Blanchot, *L'entretien infini* (Paris: Garnier, 1969), 47-63.

33 Michel Foucault, "Nietzsche, Freud, Marx," in *Cahiers de Royaumont: Philosophie*, no. 6 (1967), 183–92. In the following "NFM."

34 Michel Foucault, "Nietzsche, Genealogy, History," in Michel Foucault, *Language, Counter-memory, Practice* (Cornell University Press, 1977), 139–64. In the following "NGH."

35 Derrida's most important texts on Nietzsche are Jacques Derrida, *Spurs: Nietzsche's Styles*, trans. Barbara Harlow (University of Chicago Press, 1978); Jacques Derrida, *Otobiographies, L'Enseignement de Nietzsche et la politique du nom propre* (Paris: Galilée, 1984); Jacques Derrida, "Interpreting Signatures (Nietzsche/Heidegger)," in *Dialogue and Deconstruction, The Gadamer-Derrida Encounter*, ed. Diane P. Michelfelder and Richard E. Palmer (State University of New York Press, 1989). See also my book *Confrontations: Derrida, Heidegger, Nietzsche*, trans. Steven Taubeneck (Stanford University Press, 1991).

10 Nietzsche's French legacy

In Memoriam: Sarah Kofman
1934–1994

What charity and delicate precision those Frenchmen possess!
Even the most acute-eared of the Greeks must have approved of
this art, and one thing they would even have admired and
adored, the French *wittiness* of expression . . . (*The Wanderer
and His Shadow*, 214)

The moment Germany rises as a great power, France gains a new
importance as a *cultural power*. A great deal of current spiritual
seriousness and *passion* has already emigrated to Paris; the question of pessimism, for instance, the Wagner question, virtually
every psychological and artistic question, is speculated on with
incomparably more subtlety and thoroughness there than in Germany . . . (*Twilight of the Idols*, "What the Germans Lack," 4)

As an *artist* one has no home in Europe, except Paris . . . (*Ecce
Homo*, "Why I Am So Clever," 5)

That we find, approximately a century after his productivity ended,
commentators referring to French "Nietzscheanism"[1] is a development that we can imagine would have pleased Friedrich Nietzsche.
On several occasions, Nietzsche remarked that he felt more at home
with the French, their culture and their language, than with Germans.[2] More than once, he regretted having to write in German
rather than in a more fluid, playful, musical language like French.[3]
And more than once, he felt his spiritual kin to reside west of the
Rhine, preferring the philosophical companionship of Montaigne,
Voltaire, and La Rochefoucauld to that of Leibniz, Kant, or Hegel.[4]

323

Whatever the reasons for Nietzsche's fond feelings for the French, there can be no doubt that for the past three decades, Nietzsche's texts have been received more enthusiastically in Parisian intellectual circles than anywhere else. In the following few pages, I would like to chart this reception, highlighting some of the significant moments in its evolution and some of the paradigmatic forms it has taken.

To begin, let me situate contemporary French thought by offering a somewhat simplified sketch of the last half century of French philosophy in which we can locate three successive developments. The first, existentialism, is associated most closely with the works of Jean-Paul Sartre and Maurice Merleau-Ponty. Drawing its inspiration first from Husserl and Heidegger, and later from Marx, existentialism in its phenomenological or Marxist forms dominated the French philosophical scene during the forties and fifties. Inspired by Ferdinand de Saussure's work in linguistics, the second development, structuralism, emerged in the late fifties and came into prominence in French circles in the early sixties. United by a profound distrust of phenomenology and its privileging of subjectivity, structuralists like Claude Lévi-Strauss, Jacques Lacan and Louis Althusser drew on the methodology of Saussurean linguistics and applied it to their respective investigations of the "human sciences" of anthropology, psychoanalysis and political economy. The structuralist rediscovery of Freud and Marx along with Heidegger's retrieval of Nietzsche[5] set the stage for the third development in French thought – poststructuralism.[6] While there are many ways to characterize the relationships between poststructural French philosophy and its structural and existential predecessors, one of the most obvious differences between them is the appearance of Nietzsche as an important reference for virtually all those writers who would be characterized as poststructuralist.[7]

   To help understand the various appearances of Nietzsche within poststructural French thought, we can organize these appearances into two groups. In the first, we can situate those works in which Nietzsche's texts, and his philosophy in general, appear as the "object" of interpretation. These works reflect contemporary philosophical approaches in various degrees and primarily take the form of traditional scholarship: they offer interpretations of Nietzsche's philosophy, often focusing on the major Nietzschean themes of eternal recurrence, will to power, nihilism, *Übermensch*, and so on. In the second group, we can locate those writers who "use" Nietzsche in developing their own philosophical voices. In the works of these writers, Nietzsche appears as a reference point, someone whose works or ideas have inspired his descendants to develop them into forms that are useful for their own philosophical-critical ends. Their goals are not to offer "interpretations" of Nietzsche's philosophy, although that may in fact result from their productions; rather, they use those Nietzschean motifs they find advantageous in the development of their own critical projects.[8] To begin our examination of Nietzsche's French reception, we will survey the range of Nietzsche scholarship within this first group of Nietzsche interpretations, making our own "use" of Michel Foucault as an example of the second group to set the scene in which these interpretations appeared.[9]

INTERPRETING NIETZSCHE

Approximately fifteen years after Georges Bataille's influential *Sur Nietzsche*[10] and immediately following the publication of Heidegger's two-volume *Nietzsche* in 1961, the French interest in Nietzsche increased dramatically, and the next two decades saw a wide range of new approaches to Nietzsche interpretation. In 1962, Gilles Deleuze's *Nietzsche and Philosophy*[11] appeared as the first major interpretation to follow Heidegger's. Two years later, an international philosophy conference on Nietzsche was held at Royaumont, with such figures as Deleuze, Foucault, Henri Birault, Jean Wahl, Gabriel Marcel, Jean Beaufret, and Karl Löwith in attendance. The next ten years saw books dealing exclusively or primarily with Nietzsche by, among others, Jean Granier, Maurice Blanchot, Pierre Klossowski, Jean-Michel Rey, Bernard Pautrat, Pierre Boudot, Sarah Kofman, and Paul Valadier;[12] special issues on Nietzsche by several of France's leading journals,[13] and a second major conference, at Cerisy-la-Salle in 1972, addressing the theme "Nietzsche aujourd'hui," with many of France's leading philosophers in attendance.[14]

This proliferation of Nietzsche interpretation in the 1960s and 1970s exhibits two basic trends of poststructural French philosophy. First, following the structuralists, these interpretations reflect the passage away from the existentialists' preoccupation with Hegel, Husserl, and Heidegger. Although the "three H's" continue to influence contemporary French philosophers, the problems which engage these philosophers are framed by another influential triumvirate: the "masters of suspicion" – Nietzsche, Freud, and Marx. Second, these interpretations reflect a heightened awareness of the *style* of philosophical discourse, bringing questions of literary *form* to bear on the *content* of philosophical issues. To understand the particular, and often peculiar, claims made by Nietzsche's French interpreters, therefore, it will help to survey first Nietzsche's place in the general intellectual context in which these interpretations appeared.

Broadly viewed, these interpretations can be situated around three basic themes that dominated the French scene: the hermeneutics of suspicion; the reflection upon the nature of language; and the critique of metaphysical humanism. The early work of Michel Foucault provides an excellent example of the conjunction of these themes and Nietzsche's French reception. At the Colloquium at Royaumont in 1964, Foucault presented a paper entitled "Nietzsche, Freud, Marx."[15] In these three thinkers, Foucault detects a profound change in the nature of the sign and the way signs in general are interpreted. Foucault sees this change breaking the ground for the modern epoch, as the representative function of the sign gives way to a view of the sign as already a part of the activity of interpretation. This is to say, signs are no longer viewed as the reservoir of some deep, hidden meaning; rather, they are surface phenomena which confront interpretation with an infinite task:

Interpretation can never be brought to an end, simply because there is nothing to interpret. There is nothing absolutely primary to interpret because at bottom everything is already interpretation. Each sign is in itself not the thing that presents itself to interpretation, but the interpretation of other signs.[16]

In Marx's talk of phenomena as "hieroglyphs," Freud's view of the dream as always already an interpretation, and Nietzsche's theory of masks and the essential incompleteness of the interpretive act, Foucault locates a movement away from the "hegemony of the sign" as a univocal relation between a signifier and a signified toward the properly hermeneutical view of the sign as always already interpreted and interpreting. The hermeneut must be suspicious, therefore, because the naive view of the sign as a simple relation of signifier and signified obscures relations of domination (Marx), neurotic desire (Freud), and decadence (Nietzsche).

The other two themes, the reflection on the nature of language and the critique of humanism, are both raised by Foucault in *The Order of Things*, a work in which Nietzsche figures prominently as the precursor of the *episteme* (or conceptual framework) of the twentieth century. This *episteme* erupted with the question of language as "an enigmatic multiplicity that must be mastered."[17] It was "Nietzsche the philologist" who first connected "the philosophical task with a radical reflection upon language,"[18] and insofar as the question of language is still the single most important question confronting the contemporary *episteme*, Foucault traces the roots of this *episteme* back to Nietzsche.

Similarly, Foucault discovers in Nietzsche the first attempt at "the dissolution of man":

Perhaps we should see the first attempt at this uprooting of Anthropology – to which, no doubt, contemporary thought is dedicated – in the Nietzschean experience: by means of a philological critique, by means of a certain form of biologism, Nietzsche rediscovered the point at which man and God belong to one another, at which the death of the second is synonymous with the disappearance of the first, and at which the promise of the superman signifies first and foremost the imminence of the death of man.[19]

When speaking of the "disappearance" or the "death" of "man," Foucault means something quite specific: "man" functions in this context as a technical term, the analysis of which takes place at the transcendental levels of the biological and historico-cultural conditions which make empirical knowledge possible. "Man" thus names the being who serves to center the increasingly disorganized representations of the classical *episteme* and who, as such, comes to be the privileged object of philosophical anthropology.[20] The passage quoted above, relating Nietzsche to the uprooting of anthropology, follows by one page a reference to Kant's formulation of anthropology as the foundation of philosophy.[21] These references to Nietzsche and to Kant appear in a section entitled "The Anthropological Sleep," and it is clear that Foucault sees Nietzsche waking the modern *episteme* from its anthropological slumber in much the same way that Kant saw himself awakened from his own dogmatic slumber by Hume.[22]

While "man" as a foundational concept has been privileged in the discourse of the human sciences since Kant, Foucault foresees the end of man's reign as such a foundation. He locates the announcement of this end in Nietzsche's doctrine of the *Übermensch*, for the *Übermensch* will overcome nihilism only by overcoming humanity. This point is crucial for understanding Foucault's situating Nietzsche at the beginning of the end of man. For Foucault, Nietzsche offers us a philosophy of the future, and that future will belong not to man but to the *Übermensch*. The *Übermensch* thus makes its appearance in Nietzsche together with the "last man": both are introduced for the first time in Zarathustra's "Prologue."[23] This last man is literally the last of "man," and Foucault interprets the *Übermensch* as something which breaks with the tradition of metaphysical humanism.

With this in mind, we can understand the significance of Foucault's final reference to Nietzsche in *The Order of Things*, where he couples Nietzsche's death of God with the death of man. Viewing Foucault's "death of man" in Nietzschean terminology, we find the death of man to be the death of the "last man," the death of the murderer of God. Foucault here recalls that in *Thus Spoke Zarathustra* ("The Ugliest Man"), God is reported to have died of pity upon encountering the last man, and he writes:

Rather than the death of God – or, rather, in the wake of that death and in profound correlation with it – what Nietzsche's thought heralds is the end of his murderer; it is the explosion of man's face in laughter, and the return of masks; it is the scattering of the profound stream of time by which he felt himself carried along and whose pressure he suspected in the very being of things; it is the identity of the Return of the Same with the absolute dispersion of man.[24]

Foucault applauds Nietzsche's announcement of the disappearance of "man" as the standard-bearer of an all-too-serious anthropocentrism for opening the postmodern *episteme*, one that will no longer view "man" as the privileged center of representational thinking and discourse. And with Nietzsche's dispersion of man, Foucault locates a return of the project of a unification of language. The conclusion of Foucault's project in *The Order of Things*, which he characterizes as "archaeological," is thus inscribed within Nietzsche's eternal recurrence of the same – what recurs is the problem of language as a multiplicity to be mastered.

Foucault's focus on the reflection on language, on the new status of the sign as always already interpreted, on the problematic status of human subjectivity, and his linking these three foci to Nietzsche provide us with a good beginning for exploring the proliferation of French Nietzsche interpretation in the late sixties and seventies. While it is impossible to categorize these interpretations as adhering to a single "central" view of Nietzsche's philosophy, we will orient our examination around the "question of style" as one question with which many of these interpretations are concerned.²⁵ By the "question of style" I mean the relation between the "content" of Nietzsche's thinking and the manner in which this content is set forth, and under this somewhat generic term can be placed a number of important questions addressed by Nietzsche's French interpreters. The "question of style" as a focal point in the interpretation of Nietzsche's text was first raised explicitly by Bernard Pautrat in *Versions du soleil*²⁶ and it operates as well in Foucault's citing Nietzsche as the first to engage in the philosophical task of a "radical reflection upon language"²⁷; in Derrida's raising "the question of writing" ("*c'est la question du style comme question de l'écriture*" ²⁸); and in Lacoue-Labarthe's "question of the text": "Without [Nietzsche], the 'question' of the text would never have erupted, at least in the precise form that it has taken today."²⁹

In addressing the question of style, these interpreters attend to the *way* that Nietzsche writes as much as to what he is writing. Taking as their point of departure the Nietzschean insight into the inseparable unity of philosophical form and content,³⁰ these interpreters bring to light an array of Nietzschean themes hitherto overlooked by many of his most careful and comprehensive commentators.³¹ By means of an attentiveness to his theory and use of language, rhetoric, philology, metaphor, myth, and the strategic use of different literary genre (aphorism, polemic, narrative, autobiography, essay, treatise, poem, dithyramb, letter, note, etc.), Nietzsche's French interpreters explore a range of new interpretive possibilities. Although we cannot examine here all of these interpretive possibilities, it will be instructive to examine briefly the works of Deleuze, Granier,

Pautrat, and Kofman to give a sense of the sorts of interpretations that a focus on the question of style can generate.

Gilles Deleuze, in *Nietzsche and Philosophy*, directs himself against what he regards as a misguided attempt to strike a compromise between the Hegelian dialectic and Nietzsche's genealogy. Where Hegel's thinking is always guided by the movement toward some unifying synthesis, Nietzsche, in contrast, is seen to affirm multiplicity and rejoice in diversity.[32] Deleuze comes to view the entirety of Nietzsche's corpus as a polemical response to the Hegelian dialectic: "To the famous positivity of the negative Nietzsche opposes his own discovery: the negativity of the positive."[33]

Focusing on the qualitative difference in Nietzsche between active and reactive forces, rather than the merely quantitative distinction between amounts of power, Deleuze argues that the *Übermensch's* mastery is derived from her or his ability to negate *actively* the slave's reactive forces, even though the latter may often be quantitatively greater. In other words, whereas the slave moves from the negative premise ("you are other and evil") to the positive judgment ("therefore I am good"), the master works from the positive differentiation of self ("I am good") to the negative corollary ("you are other and bad"). There is, according to Deleuze, a qualitative difference at the origin of force, and it is the task of the genealogist to attend to this differential and genetic element of force which Nietzsche calls "will to power."[34]

Thus, whereas in the Hegelian dialectic of master and slave, the reactive negation of the other has as its consequence the affirmation of self, Nietzsche reverses this situation: the master's active self-affirmation is accompanied by and results in a negation of the slave's reactive force. By tracing the interplay of affirmation and negation in Nietzsche's typology of active (artistic, noble, legislative) and reactive (*ressentiment*, bad conscience, the ascetic ideal) force, Deleuze concludes that the *Übermensch*, Nietzsche's metaphor for the affirmation of multiplicity and difference as such, is offered in response to the conception of human being as a synthesized unity provided by the Hegelian dialectic.

Jean Granier, in his six-hundred-plus-page study *Le problème de la vérité dans la philosophie de Nietzsche*, draws on the hermeneutical insights of Heidegger and Ricoeur as he explores the relationship between Being and thinking in Nietzsche's text. According to Granier, "will to power" designates the manner in which Nietzsche sees "the essence of Being as Being-interpreted [*l'essence de l'Etre comme Etre-interprété*]."[35] Insofar as Being is always already interpreted, Granier sees Nietzsche avoiding the apparent antinomy between the relativity of knowledge and the absoluteness of Being. For Granier, relativism and absolutism are two complementary poles of one and the same ontological operation: the will to power as knowledge. Granier locates the relativistic pole, which he calls "vital pragmatism," in Nietzsche's perspectivism and his view of truth as a useful and necessary error. The absolutist pole Granier calls "intellectual" or "philological probity." This probity demands absolute respect for the text of Being and commands us "*to do justice to nature, to reveal things as they are in their own being.*"[36] It is within this essential paradox of the will to power as creative, perspectival pragmatism and as respectful of and truthful to Being that Granier locates Nietzsche's "revolutionary" contribution to the philosophical treatment of the problem of truth. He suggests that Nietzsche, insofar as he is able to avoid both a relativistic and a dogmatic view of knowledge, may best be viewed as presenting a "meta-philosophical" account of interpretation. This is to say, in addition to the first-order interpretations of Nietzschean perspectivism, there is a second-order interpretation of the phenomenon of interpretation itself. This second-order interpretation of interpretation is put forward in a meta-language which can be evaluated neither in terms of the ideals of the interpreter (relativism) nor in terms of its absolute correspondence with "the facts" (dogmatism). Rather, this interpretation of interpretation, remaining true to the "duplicity of Being" (i.e., the identity Being = Being-interpreted), seeks to explain the phenomenon of interpretation in a way that will disqualify neither of the complementary poles whose presence is required if the truth is to be.[37]

Taking as its point of departure Nietzsche's theory of language and metaphor, Bernard Pautrat, in *Versions du soleil*, offers an "oriented description" of Nietzsche's text that seeks to provide a "new version" of Nietzsche's philosophy. This description is oriented around two axes:

on the one hand, once recognizing that Nietzsche's thought cannot exceed the limits established for it by natural language in connection with Western metaphysics (with Platonism), we must take an exact inventory of these limits, indicating the complete metaphoricity of language, unfolding all the rhetoric within – this will be the task of a theory of signs of which Nietzsche's writings, as early as *The Birth of Tragedy*, convey the insistent mark; but, on the other hand, it would suffice to awaken the metaphorical power of language in general for "the work of Nietzsche" to be marked by a different exposition, [thereby] liberating style, figures, that labor of writing not reducible to the simple transmission of a philosophical sense.[38]

Around these two axes, Pautrat organizes an examination of the family of solar metaphors in Nietzsche's text, setting them up in relation to two other philosophical "heliologies": Plato and Hegel. Whereas Plato's system is guided by the sun as ideal and Hegel's system is directed toward the complete illumination which only the sun can provide, Pautrat sees Nietzsche's heliology avoiding the helio-logocentrism of these two sun-worshipers. This is to say, in Nietzsche's solar system the emphasis is placed not on the center, the sun, but on the circulation which surrounds it, the eternal return of light and darkness. Both midday and midnight play a role in Nietzsche's thinking and the appearance of light is always accompanied by shadows. By focusing on the fluidity with which Nietzsche uses language, appropriating concepts when necessary and then discarding or forgetting them when no longer useful, Pautrat examines Nietzsche's theories of metaphor and language and the ways he utilizes these theories as concrete manifestations of Nietzsche's theoretical insight into the world as a play of becoming.

The question of Nietzsche's literary style is also a major theme in Sarah Kofman's reading.[39] Arguing that Nietzsche's use of metaphors is not merely rhetorical but "strategic," *Nietzsche et la métaphore* offers several examples of the sorts of genealogical deconstructions that a focus on style can generate. For Kofman, Nietzsche's metaphors are not merely literary devices devoid of philosophical import. Rather, the way Nietzsche uses metaphors reinforces one of the major themes in his philosophy: the affirmation of the play of becoming. Like many of Nietzsche's French commentators, Kofman makes much of Nietzsche's Rhetoric lectures[40] as well as the writings gathered together by the Musarion editors as the "Philosopher's Book,"[41] in particular, the little essay "Truth and Lies in an Extra-moral Sense" in which we find the oft cited definition of truth as a "mobile army of metaphors, metonymies, and anthropomorphisms."[42] She points out that Nietzsche situates metaphor at the origin of language and truth. Concepts are, in his view, simply congealed metaphors, figurative descriptions whose metaphorical nature has been forgotten. In forgetting the metaphoricity at the origin of concepts, their figurative sense comes to be taken literally. This petrification of the concept as literal description of "reality" ultimately gives rise to the illusion of truth as eternal and unchanging, and Kofman sees this view of truth as fixed and universal as one of the hallmarks of a philosophical tradition that Nietzsche endeavors to deconstruct.

Taking the tendency of metaphors to solidify into concepts as one of Nietzsche's basic insights, Kofman suggests we avoid focusing on any single Nietzschean metaphor as privileged, fundamental, or foundational. Conscious of the inherent danger in language of restricting the fluidity and mobility of sense (Μεταφορά-Übertragen = transference), Kofman claims that Nietzsche refrains from an enduring commitment to any one particular metaphorical expression. Even the metaphor of "metaphor," so prevalent in Nietzsche's early writings, comes to be discarded and, Kofman argues, is later reappropriated as "perspective" or "interpretation" or "text."[43] This strategy reveals Nietzsche's desire to free culture of its dogmatic tendency towards one-dimensional thinking. In other words, whereas Nietzsche will eventually place an explicit value on pluri-dimensional thinking, on seeing the world from a multiplicity of perspectives and with more and different eyes (cf. GM III 12; also GS 78, 374), this value has been exhibited through his writing in the way he shifts from metaphor to metaphor.

Among the "families" of metaphor examined by Kofman are those drawn from architecture[44] and the senses,[45] the inversion of Plato's cave and sun metaphors in *Zarathustra*, Nietzsche's uprooting of Descartes's "tree of knowledge," and the utilization of various figures from Greek mythology.[46] In each case, Kofman shows that Nietzsche's style of writing, the *way* he uses metaphors, provides an important clue for understanding what is at issue in his philosophy. In so doing, Kofman claims that Nietzsche does not so much create new metaphors as "rehabilitate" those metaphors which the tradition has already adopted. In other words, Nietzsche's strategy is to reiterate the habitual metaphors of the tradition in a way that brings their conceptual insufficiencies to light.[47]

This reiteration of metaphor emerges in Kofman's text as a concrete illustration of the Nietzschean transvaluation: within his strategic rehabilitation of the tradition's metaphors, the values implicit in these traditional metaphors are *revalued*. Nietzsche's use of metaphor itself exemplifies this transvaluation insofar as the use of metaphor within philosophical discourse had been *devalued*. By focusing on Nietzsche's use of metaphor, Kofman demonstrates that the appearance of metaphor in Nietzsche's text is not gratuitous; rather, Nietzsche's proliferation of metaphor is directed toward liberating human beings' metaphorical instinct for creative play, freeing humans for the play of perspectives in those domains (art, myth, illusion, dream) devalued by the nihilistic and decadent will of the scientific spirit of seriousness.

Kofman develops the emancipatory character of Nietzsche's use of metaphor, particularly in terms of the aphoristic form of his writings, as she explores his search for readers who will be able to follow his "dance with the pen" (TI "What the Germans Lack" 7). These readers will elevate reading to the level of an art (cf. GM Pr. 8): they will recognize the aphorism as the "writing itself of the will to power,"[48] and "on every metaphor will ride to every truth (Z "The Return Home"; cf. EH "Z" 3). *Nietzsche et la métaphore* concludes on this note, suggesting that the ability to dance among aphorisms is another of Nietzsche's principles of selection which distinguish those of noble instincts from the herd.

PUTTING NIETZSCHE TO WORK

Let us now move from Nietzsche's French interpreters to the second group of French Nietzscheans, those who carry his work forward. Sympathetic and critical commentators alike have noted the "Nietzscheanism" within recent French philosophy. To help understand the French link to Nietzsche, I will focus on four exemplary cases – Jacques Derrida, Michel Foucault, Gilles Deleuze, and Jean-François Lyotard – in whose work we can observe several of the Nietzschean themes that circulate within recent French thought: the emphasis on interpretation, the critique of binary thinking, the link between power and knowledge, the emphasis on becoming and process over being and ontology, and the necessity of judging in the absence of criteria.

In the early works of Jacques Derrida, Nietzsche appears as a constant reference. Derrida frequently cites him as one of his deconstructive precursors,[49] and on at least two occasions, Derrida chronicles what Nietzsche contributes to the contemporary philosophical scene. In "*Qual Quelle*: Valéry's Sources," he provides the following list of themes to look for in Nietzsche:

the systematic mistrust as concerns the entirety of metaphysics, the formal vision of philosophical discourse, the concept of the philosopher-artist, the rhetorical and philological questions put to the history of philosophy, the suspiciousness concerning the values of truth ("a well applied convention"), of meaning and of Being, of "meaning of Being," the attention to the economic phenomena of force and of difference of forces, etc.[50]

And in *Of Grammatology*, he credits Nietzsche with contributing

a great deal to the liberation of the signifier from its dependence or derivation with respect to the logos and the related concept of truth or the primary signified, in whatever sense that is understood [by his] radicalizing of the concepts of *interpretation, perspective, evaluation, difference* . . .[51]

These remarks show only some of the Nietzschean motifs which Derrida has developed in his own philosophical project. In addition, he makes numerous other remarks concerning Nietzsche as a foil to Heidegger's totalizing interpretation of the history of metaphysics,[52] Nietzsche's rhetorical strategies and multiplicity of styles,[53] the *différance* of force[54] and power,[55] the playfulness of interpretive multiplicity,[56] and what Derrida calls "the axial intention of [Nietzsche's] concept of interpretation": the emancipation of interpretation from the constraints of a truth "which always implies the *presence* of the signified (*aletheia* or *adequatio*)."[57] Rather than comment upon Derrida's particular references to Nietzsche, I would like instead to examine one specific Derridean theme which more than any other indicates Derrida's debt to Nietzsche.

The "typical prejudice" and "fundamental faith" of all metaphysicians, Nietzsche wrote, "is *the faith in opposite values*" (BGE 2). Throughout his critique of morality, philosophy, and religion, Nietzsche attempted to dismantle such oppositional hierarchies as good/evil, truth/error, being/becoming. This refusal to sanction the hierarchical relations among those privileged conceptual oppositions transmitted within the Western metaphysical tradition pervades the contemporary French philosophical scene,[58] and it is one of the primary points of contact between Nietzsche and contemporary French philosophical thought in general.

The critique of binary, oppositional thinking is, in particular, an essential component in Derrida's critical project. For Derrida, the history of philosophy unfolds as a history of certain classical philosophical oppositions: intelligible/sensible, truth/error, speech/writing, literal/figurative, presence/absence, etc. These oppositional concepts do not coexist on equal grounds, however; rather, one side of each binary opposition has been privileged while the other side has been devalued. Within these oppositions, a hierarchical "order of subordination"[59] has been established and truth has come to be valued over error, presence has come to be valued over absence, etc.

Derrida's task is to dismantle or "deconstruct" these binary oppositions. In practice, their deconstruction involves a biphasic movement that Derrida has called "double writing" or "double science." In the first phase, he overturns the hierarchy and values those poles traditionally subordinated by the history of philosophy. Although Derrida is often read as privileging, for example, writing over speech, absence over presence, or the figurative over the literal, such a reading is overly simplistic; like Heidegger before him,[60] Derrida realizes that in overturning a metaphysical hierarchy, one must avoid reappropriating the hierarchical structure. It is the hierarchical oppositional structure itself that is metaphysical, and to remain within the binary logic of metaphysical thinking reestablishes and confirms the closed field of these oppositions.

To view deconstruction as a simple inversion of these classical philosophical oppositions ignores the second phase of deconstruction's "double writing": "we must also mark the interval between inversion, which brings low what was high, and the irruptive emergence of a new 'concept,' a concept that can no longer be, and never could be, included in the previous regime."[61] These new "concepts" are the Derridean "undecidables" (e.g., "*différance*," "trace," "supplement," "*pharmakon*"): marks that in one way or another resist the formal structure imposed by the binary logic of philosophical opposition while exposing the optional character of those choices which the tradition has privileged as dominant. Throughout Derrida's early work, we find as a recurrent motif his charting the play of these undecidables: the play of the trace which is both present and absent; the play of the *pharmakon*, which is both poison and cure; the play of the supplement, which is both surplus and lack.

Returning now to Nietzsche, we can see this same critique of oppositional thinking in his assessment of traditional values, as he often proceeds by disassembling the privileged hierarchical relation that has been established among the values in question. Nietzsche's disassembling, like Derridean deconstruction, operates in two phases.[62] The first phase overturns the traditionally privileged relation between the two values while the second seeks to displace the opposition altogether by showing it to result from a prior value imposition that itself requires critique. For example, regarding the genealogy of the will to truth, we find Nietzsche inverting the traditional hierarchy of truth over falsity. Investigating the origin of the positive value placed upon truth, Nietzsche finds that it is simply a moral prejudice to affirm truth over error or appearance (see BGE 34). To this, he suggests that error might be *more* valuable than truth, that error might be a necessary condition of life.

Nietzsche's analysis does not stop here, however, as Heidegger assumed when he accused Nietzsche of "completing" the history of metaphysics through an "inversion" of Platonism. By adopting a perspectival attitude and denying the possibility of an unmediated, noninterpretive apprehension of "reality," Nietzsche displaces the truth/falsity opposition altogether. The question is no longer whether a perspective is "true" or "false"; the sole question that interests the Nietzschean genealogist is whether or not a perspective enhances life.[63]

Nietzsche discovers a certain faith in binary thinking at the center of philosophical discourse. By genealogically uncovering the will to power whose imposition of a certain value gave rise to the two poles of the opposition in question, genealogy obviates the force the opposition is believed to have. The clearest example of this strategy is his deconstruction of the good–evil opposition. Nietzsche moves *beyond* good and evil precisely by showing that both "good" and "evil" owe their meaning to a certain type of will to power – the slavish, reactive will to power of herd morality. Simply to invert the values of slave morality, making "good" what the slave judges to be "evil," is no less reactive than the original imposition of value by the slave, who judges all that differs from himself to be "evil" and defines the good in reactionary opposition to what is other than himself.

A reading of Nietzsche as an "immoralist" or "nihilist" remains at this level of mere inversion, failing to acknowledge Nietzsche's postmodern insight that by conforming to the oppositional structure, one inevitably confirms its validity and its repressive, hierarchizing power. But a reading of Nietzsche as the "transvaluer of values" locates a second movement in the Nietzschean critique of morality. This second movement flows from the *active* imposition of new values arising from a healthy will to power that has displaced the hierarchy of good/evil altogether. In rejecting the binary structure of moral evaluation, Nietzsche's transvaluation inaugurates a playful experimentation with values and a multiplication of perspectives that he labels "active interpretation."[64] The affirmation of perspectival multiplicity thus emerges as the life-enhancing alternative for those with a will to power sufficient to go beyond the reactive decadence of binary morality. This life-enhancing multiplicity continues to function within Derrida's own interpretive practice in his call for a productive style of reading that does not merely "protect" but "opens" texts to new interpretive possibilities.[65]

Nietzsche's critique of binary thinking is linked to another theme which we find operating at several places in contemporary French thought: the replacement of a dualistic account by a pluralistic, or polyvocal, monism. Nietzsche's announcement, in a remark that would become the closing entry in the non-book published as *The Will to Power*, that the solution to the riddle of his Dionysian world was that "This world is will to power – and nothing besides! And you yourselves are also will to power – and nothing besides!" (WP 1067) issued a challenge to all future dualisms: it would no longer be possible for understanding to proceed according to a model that operated in terms of a simple binary logic. We would no longer be able to divide the world neatly into dichotomous groups: good or evil, minds or bodies, truths or errors, us or them. The world is much more complicated than such dualistic thinking acknowledges. Nietzsche suggested instead that making what appear to be even simple determinations and distinctions is, in fact, radically contextual and contingent. This suggestion, in turn, made suspect any appeal to a dualistic metanarrative of binary opposition.

Like Derrida, both Michel Foucault and Gilles Deleuze are influenced by Nietzsche's antidualist rejection of philosophical binarism. They are also inspired by Nietzsche's linkage between power and knowledge. This linkage is both explicit ("Knowledge functions as an instrument of power" [WP 480]) and implicit in the fluidity of movement between "will," "will to truth," "will to knowledge," and "will to power." When Nietzsche claimed that everything was will to power, he drew our attention away from substances, subjects, and things and focused that attention instead on the relations *between* these substantives. These relations, according to Nietzsche, were relations of forces: forces of attraction and repulsion, domination and subordination, imposition and reception, and so on. If there is a metaphysics in Nietzsche, and it is not entirely clear that there is or that it is helpful to view Nietzsche in these terms (as Heidegger did), then this metaphysics will be a dynamic, "process" metaphysics and not a substance-metaphysics. It will be a metaphysics of becomings and not of beings. And these processes, these becomings, will be processes of forces: becomings-stronger or becomings-weaker, enhancement or impoverishment. There is, for Nietzsche, no escaping these becomings other than death. The goal he advocates, therefore, is not to seek Being but to strive for one's life to include more becomings-stronger than -weaker, more overcomings than goings-under.

Both Foucault and Deleuze engage in projects that reformulate traditional binary disjunctions between given alternatives in terms of a pluralistic continuum, in which choices are always local and relative rather than global and absolute. Within their respective reformulations, we see them each making double use of Nietzsche's will to power. Whether it be a continuum of power–knowledge or of "desiring production," the model they appeal to, explicitly or implicitly, seems to be that of Nietzsche's "monism" of the will to power. This monism is to be understood not in Heidegger's sense of will to power as Nietzsche's foundational answer to the metaphysical question of the Being of beings, but in Deleuze's sense of will to power as the differential of forces. This is to say, where Heidegger understood will to power in terms of a logic of Being, an onto-logic, Deleuze situates will to power within a differential logic of affirmation and negation, which facilitates the interpretation and evaluation of active and reactive forces.[66]

Will to power thus operates at the genealogical and not the ontological level, at the level of the qualitative and quantitative differences between forces and the different values bestowed upon those forces, rather than at the level of Being and beings.[67] In going beyond good and evil, beyond truth and error to the claim that all is will to power, Nietzsche attempted to think relationality without substances, relations without relata, difference without exclusion. And in so doing his thought serves as a model for both Foucault's analyses of power relations in the absence of a sovereign subject and Deleuze's account of the human "subject" as a desiring assemblage conceived in terms of a logic of events.

In addition to using Nietzsche's "formal" structure as a model, Foucault and Deleuze each seize upon what we might call the "content" of Nietzsche's will to power and together they offer expanded accounts of the two component poles: will and power. While French thought in general has been working for the past thirty years within a conceptual field framed by the three so-called masters of suspicion, Nietzsche, Freud, and Marx, we can understand Foucault and Deleuze privileging Nietzsche over Marx and Freud on precisely this point.[68] Marx operates primarily with the register of power and Freud operates primarily within the register of desire. Yet each appears blind to the overlapping of these two registers, and when they do relate them, one is clearly subordinate to the other.

Nietzsche's will to power, on the other hand, makes impossible any privileging of one over the other, and his thinking functions in terms of a complete infusion of each register within the other. That is to say, for Nietzsche, "will to power" is redundant in that will wills power and power manifests itself only through will. In privileging Nietzsche over Marx or Freud, both Foucault and Deleuze recognize the complicity between the poles of will and power. As a consequence, they can each focus on one of the poles without excluding the other pole from their analyses.

Thus Foucault engaged in a highly sophisticated analysis of power which, following Nietzsche's example, focused not on the subjects of power but on power *relations*, the relations of force that operate within social practices and social systems. And within this analysis, will and desire play an integral role in directing the relations of power. Where Nietzsche saw a continuum of will to power, Foucault saw power relations operating along a continuum of repression and production; and where Nietzsche sought to incite a becoming-stronger of will to power to rival the progressive becoming-weaker he associated with modernity, Foucault sought to draw attention to the becoming-productive of power that accompanies the increasingly repressive power of the pastoral.[69]

In a similar fashion, Deleuze, both in his own studies and especially in his collaborative works with radical psychoanalyst Félix
Guattari, has focused on the *willing* of power – desire. Like Foucault, he refrains from subjectifying desire, while recognizing the
intimate and multiple couplings of desire and power. In *Nietzsche
and Philosophy*, Deleuze first linked the notion of desire with will
to power, and the insight that desire is productive develops out of his
reflection on will to power in terms of the productivity of both
active and reactive forces. In *Anti-Oedipus*, Deleuze and Guattari
introduce the concept of "the desiring machine" as a machinic, functionalist translation of Nietzschean will to power. A desiring machine is a functional assemblage of a desiring will and the object
desired. Deleuze places desire into a functionalist vocabulary to
avoid the personification/subjectification of desire in a substantive
will, ego, unconscious, or self. In so doing, he can avoid the paradox
Nietzsche sometimes faced when speaking of a will to power without a subject doing the willing, or when implying that will to power
was both the producing "agent" and the "object" produced (see GM I
13, BGE 17, WP 484). To speak of desire as part of an assemblage, to
refuse to reify or personify desire (as psychoanalysis does), is to recognize that desire and the object desired arise together.

Deleuze rejects the account of desire as lack, an account which we
can trace back to Plato's *Symposium* and which is shared by Freud,
Lacan, Sartre, and many others.[70] Desire does not arise in response to
the perceived lack of the object desired, nor is desire a state produced
in the subject by the lack of the object. Desire is a part of the infrastruc-
ture:[71] it is constitutive of the objects desired as well as the social field
in which they appear. Desire, in other words, again like Nietzsche's
will to power, is productive; it is always already at work within the
social field, preceding and "producing" objects *as* desirable.

As Nietzsche sought to keep will to power multiple so that it
might appear in multiple forms, at once producer and product, a
monism and a pluralism, so too Deleuze wants desire to be multiple,
operating in multiple ways and capable of multiple and multiplying
productions. Nietzsche encouraged the maximization of strong,
healthy will to power while acknowledging the necessity, the inevi-
tability of weak, decadent will to power. Deleuze advocates that
desire be productive while recognizing that desire will sometimes be
destructive and will at times have to be repressed while at other

times it will seek and produce its own repression. Analyzing this phenomenon of desire seeking its own repression is one of the goals of Deleuze and Guattari's "schizoanalysis" (the analysis based on a productive and non-Oedipal account of desire that they propose in opposition to Freudian psychoanalysis). We should take note of the structural similarity between desire desiring its own repression and Nietzsche's discovery in *On the Genealogy of Morals* (III 1 and 28) of the *meaning* of the ascetic ideal: The will would rather will nothingness than not will.

Transforming Nietzsche's will to power into a desiring-machine, Deleuze and Guattari's affirmation of desiring-production appears as a post-Freudian repetition of Nietzsche's affirmation of healthy will to power. This is only one of the places where we can see the influence the author of the *Antichrist* has had on the development of the argument by the authors of the *Anti-Oedipus*. A close reading of chapter three of *Anti-Oedipus* will reveal an analysis of the relationship between capitalism and psychoanalysis that follows an analytic pattern elaborated nearly a century earlier by Nietzsche in *On the Genealogy of Morals*.

In particular, one can show that Deleuze and Guattari base much of their critique of psychoanalytic practice on grounds first articulated in Nietzsche's genealogical critique of church practice, as they claim that the psychoanalyst is the latest incarnation of the ascetic priest.[72] Nietzsche showed how much of Christianity's practice requires convincing its adherents of their guilt and sin in order to make tenable its claim of redemptive power. Deleuze and Guattari take a similar approach, developing at length the ways in which the psychological liberation promised by psychoanalysis requires first that it imprison libidinal economy within the confines of the family. To Nietzsche's "internalization [*Verinnerlichung*] of man" (GM II 16), they add man's "Oedipalization": Oedipus repeats the split movement of Nietzschean bad conscience – projecting onto the other while turning its hostility back against itself – as the unsatisfied desire to eliminate and replace the father is accompanied by guilt for having such desire.

Like Nietzsche's ascetic priests, psychoanalysts have created for themselves a mask of health that has the power to tyrannize the healthy by poisoning their conscience. Where Nietzsche notes the *irony* of the Christian God sacrificing himself for humanity *out of love*, Deleuze and Guattari ironically chronicle the various expressions of psychoanalysts' concern for their Oedipally crippled patients. The ultimate outcomes of these ironic twists also parallel one another: where Christianity's self-sacrificing God makes infinite its adherents' guilt and debt, psychoanalysis creates its own infinite debt in the form of inexhaustible transference and interminable analysis.[73] And, to draw one final parallel, just as Nietzsche's priests reduce all events to a moment within the economic logic of divine reward and punishment, Deleuze and Guattari's psychoanalysts reduce all desire to a form of familial fixation.[74]

Before closing, let me address one last Nietzschean issue and its appearance in a thinker much less frequently associated with Nietzsche than Derrida, Deleuze, or Foucault. Jean-François Lyotard has been a leading figure in the discussions of postmodernity, and he has also been a major discussant of the problem of making ethical judgments from within a postmodern perspective. Stated most simply, this problem can be put as follows: How can we make ethical judgments without appealing to absolute moral principles or a moral law? Lyotard puts the question this way: if "one is without criteria, yet one must decide," where does the ability to judge come from?

Lyotard proceeds to offer a Nietzschean answer to this Kantian question, as this ability "bears a name in a certain philosophical tradition, namely Nietzsche's: the will to power."[75] For Lyotard, Nietzsche's will to power provides an answer similar to that provided for aesthetic judgment by Kant in the third *Critique*, but Nietzsche extends this answer beyond aesthetics to all judgment: "The ability to judge does not hang upon the observance of criteria. The form that it will take in the last *Critique* is that of the imagination. An imagination that is constitutive. It is not only an ability to judge; it is a power to invent criteria."[76] Where Kant located within aesthetic judgment the ability to judge in the absence of a rule, Nietzsche's philosophical viewpoint subsumes all judgment – political, metaphysical, epistemological, ethical, and aesthetic – under these conditions. There are no universally given rules, no absolutely privileged criteria in any of these realms; it is our task to invent these criteria and make our judgments accordingly.

By making its judgments in terms of the criteria invented (masterly or slavish, life-affirming or life-negating) rather than the specific choices made, Nietzschean genealogy was able to distinguish between the worth of apparently similar actions or judgments (e.g., the differences between creating out of need or out of excess [see GS Pr. 2, 370] or between the good–evil and good–bad criteria [GM I]). In so doing, it serves as a model for Lyotard's pagan project of conceiving judgment other than as the application of a valid and validating general rule to a particular case.

Elsewhere, in *The Differend*, Lyotard develops his Nietzschean solution to the Kantian question of judgment with the help of the Wittgensteinian language game of language games.[77] There is no universal criterion to justify or legitimate the translation from the language games of description to those of prescription. Because there is no higher order rule of judgment to which these heterogeneous language games could both appeal, the criterion will always remain in dispute, incapable of proof, a *differend* [point of incommensurable and unresolvable difference].

When he suggests that postmodernity's "criterion" is "the absence of criteria"[78] and when he offers "the end of great narratives" as postmodernity's "great narrative,"[79] Lyotard appears to affirm openly the self-referentiality that plagues Nietzsche's perspectival view that there are no "truths," only "interpretations." In other words, Lyotard too follows the path traveled earlier by Nietzsche when he acknowledged that the absence of truth left open the possibility of infinite interpretations (cf. GS 374). When Lyotard writes that "one can never reach the just by a conclusion," or that "prescriptives, taken seriously, are never grounded,"[80] he makes the ultimate Nietzschean gesture: he accepts that the nonresolution of oppositions, the affirmation of differences and dissensus, and the acceptability of multiple and discordant voices are the inevitable consequences of refusing to sanction the move to a metanarrative in the ethical and political as well as aesthetic and metaphysical domains.

CONCLUSION

In bringing this discussion to a close, let me emphasize that the theme that has continued to appear in the discussion of the French appropriation and use of Nietzsche, the critique of oppositional thinking, is not simply one theme among others. Rather, this rejection of binary, oppositional thinking accompanies the suspicion towards grand, legitimating metanarratives that appears in many of the leading contemporary philosophical voices in France. Each of the thinkers we have examined recasts the forced choice or exclusive disjunction between binary opposites in terms of a continuum that is at once monistic and pluralist: for Foucault, a continuum of power–knowledge; for Deleuze, of desiring production; for Lyotard, of *differends* and phrase universes; and for Derrida, of undecidability.

These thinkers all, in diverse and multiple ways, follow the strategy suggested by Nietzsche's introduction of the will to power, which recast all substantive differences in kind in terms of differences in degree of will to power. In his attempt to think difference differently, Nietzsche's recasting was not reductive, nor should it be seen as privileging exclusively one analytic framework. Instead, the monistic framework of will to power supports Nietzsche's pluralist response to the privileging of oppositional thinking. Likewise, I would like to close with the suggestion that we view the various French descendants of Nietzsche discussed above, not as competing voices seeking an absolute analytic privilege for their respective accounts, but as complementary voices in a chorus that calls for an end to the repression that has heretofore accompanied hierarchical, oppositional thinking. They thus take their place as the philosophers of the future to whom Nietzsche addressed his writings, philosophers who, appropriating Nietzsche's description of an earlier generation of French philosophers with whom he identified, create *"real ideas . . .* ideas of the kind that produce ideas"(WS 214).[81]

NOTES

1 See, for example, Vincent Descombes, *Modern French Philosophy*, translated by L. Scott-Fox and J. M. Harding (Cambridge: Cambridge University Press, 1980), pp. 186–90; and Luc Ferry and Alain Renaut, *French Philosophy of the Sixties: An Essay on Antihumanism*, translated by Mary Schnackenberg Cattani (Amherst: University of Massachusetts Press, 1990), pp. 68–121. Disclosing French philosophy's "Nietzscheanism" is also a persistent theme in Jürgen Habermas's *The Philosophical Discourse of Modernity*, translated by Frederick Lawrence (Cambridge, MA: MIT Press, 1987).

2 See, for example, BGE 253–4; also NCW "Where Wagner Belongs." Unless otherwise noted, references to Nietzsche's works are identified by the following acronyms of their English titles:

BGE   *Beyond Good and Evil* (Kaufmann translation)
D   *Daybreak* (Hollingdale translation)
EH   *Ecce Homo* (Kaufmann translation)
GM   *On the Genealogy of Morals* (Kaufmann translation)
GS   *The Gay Science* (Kaufmann translation)
NCW   *Nietzsche Contra Wagner* (Kaufmann translation)
PTA   *Philosophy in the Tragic Age of the Greeks* (in KGW)
TI   *Twilight of the Idols* (Hollingdale translation)
WP   *The Will to Power* (Kaufmann and Hollingdale translation)
WS   *The Wanderer and His Shadow* (Hollingdale translation)
Z   *Thus Spoke Zarathustra* (Kaufmann translation)

Arabic numerals refer to paragraphs, and Roman numerals refer to parts of works. In addition, citations from the Colli–Montinari *Kritische Gesamtausgabe* are identified as KGW and translated by myself.

3 See, for example, BGE 246; see also Nietzsche's unpublished note from Fall, 1887, where he writes in a draft to a preface of one of his books: "That it is written in German is, to say the least, untimely: I wish I had written it in French, so that it might not appear to be a confirmation of the aspirations of the German Reich. [. . .] (Formerly, I wished I had not written my *Zarathustra* in German.)" (KGW VIII, 2: 9[188]).

4 Where these German philosophers are regarded as "unconscious counterfeiters" (EH "The Case of Wagner" 3), Nietzsche says of these French philosophers that their books "contain more *real ideas* than all the books of German philosophers put together: ideas of the kind that produce ideas [. . .]" (WS 214).

5 Heidegger's two-volume work *Nietzsche* was published in Germany in 1961. Its central importance for understanding Nietzsche's French reception will be discussed in what follows.

6 Let me, at this point, make several cautionary remarks about "poststructuralism." I do not want to put too much emphasis on this proper name, and I mean by it nothing more than what as a matter of historical fact came *after* structuralism. I prefer "poststructuralism" to "deconstruction," which I take as the name of a style of philosophical-critical analysis associated primarily with *one* poststructuralist philosopher – Jacques Derrida. I also prefer it to "postmodernism," which in the context of the discipline of philosophy I take to refer to the "politicization" of poststructuralism. Finally, let me explicitly acknowledge that I am aware of the dangers involved in trying to "totalize" contemporary French thought under a single "movement." One of the themes that brings together contemporary French thinkers is precisely their rejection of totalization and totalizing strategies. I recognize that many differences underlie my "unifi-

cation" of the "French," but I will continue to join them within the context of this discussion insofar as it is clear to me that one of the themes "unifying" contemporary French thought is precisely the appeal to "Nietzsche," again acknowledging that this "appeal" takes different forms in thinkers as diverse as Derrida, Deleuze, Foucault, Luce Irigaray, Lyotard, and Klossowski, to name only a few of the more prominent.

7 There are many other ways to understand the relationships between existentialism, structuralism, and poststructuralism. For example, we can distinguish these three "movements" in terms of the different ways they appeal to Hegel. (Derrida in fact does this in his essay "The Ends of Man," in *Margins of Philosophy*, translated by Alan Bass [Chicago: University of Chicago Press, 1982].) There is much to gain from comparing Sartre or Merleau-Ponty's use of Hegel with Hegel's appearance in the texts of Lacan, Jean Hyppolite, or Althusser, or with Derrida's or Deleuze's critiques of Hegelian dialectics.

8 The best known example here is provided by the works "on" Nietzsche by Jacques Derrida. Of the three works directed explicitly toward Nietzsche, *Spurs: Nietzsche's Styles* (translated by Barbara Harlow [Chicago: University of Chicago Press, 1978]) and "Interpreting Signatures (Nietzsche/Heidegger): Two Questions" (translated by Diane Michelfelder and Richard E. Palmer in Michelfelder and Palmer, eds., *Dialogue and Deconstruction: The Gadamer-Derrida Encounter* [Albany: State University of New York Press, 1989], pp. 58–71) provide a context for Derrida to challenge both the Heideggerian reading of Nietzsche and Heidegger's philosophy in general, while *Otobiographies: The Teaching of Nietzsche and the Politics of the Proper Name* (translated by Avital Ronell in *The Ear of the Other: Otobiography, Transference, Translation*, edited by Christie V. McDonald and translated by Peggy Kamuf [New York: Schocken Books, 1985]) offers Derrida the opportunity to discuss the "politics" of interpretation. For a detailed analysis of *Spurs* as one of the places in which Derrida most directly challenges Heidegger, see my *Nietzsche and the Question of Interpretation: Between Hermeneutics and Deconstruction* (New York: Routledge, 1990), Chapter Four: "Derrida: Nietzsche contra Heidegger," pp. 95–119.

9 Much of the discussion in the following section is taken, with minor changes, from Chapter Three of my *Nietzsche and the Question of Interpretation*.

10 Georges Bataille, *Sur Nietzsche* (Paris: Gallimard, 1945). English translation: *On Nietzsche*, translated by Bruce Boone (New York: Paragon House, 1992).

11 Gilles Deleuze, *Nietzsche et la philosophie* (Paris: Presses Universitaires de France, 1962). English translation: *Nietzsche and Philosophy*, trans-

lated by Hugh Tomlinson (New York: Columbia University Press, 1983).
We should note that Deleuze himself, in *Différence et répétition* (Paris:
Presses Universitaires de France, 1968), credits two essays by Pierre
Klossowski for "renovating or reviving the interpretation of Nietzsche"
(pp. 81–2). These essays are "Nietzsche, le polythéisme et la parodie,"
first presented in 1957 and published in *Un si funeste désir* (Paris: NRF,
1963), pp. 185–228, and *"Oubli et anamnèse dans l'expérience vécue de
l'éternel retour du Même,"* presented at the Royaumont Conference on
Nietzsche in 1964 and published, along with the other addresses and
discussions, in *Nietzsche: Cahiers du Royaumont,* Philosophie No. VI
(Paris: Éditions de Minuit, 1967), pp. 227–35.

12 Jean Granier, *Le problème de la vérité dans la philosophie de Nietzsche*
(Paris: Éditions du Seuil, 1966); Maurice Blanchot, *L'Entretien infini*
(Paris: Gallimard, 1969); Pierre Klossowski, *Nietzsche et le cercle
vicieux* (Paris: Mercure de France, 1969) [Klossowski also translated
Heidegger's two-volume *Nietzsche* for publication by Gallimard in
1971]; Jean-Michel Rey, *L'enjeu des signes. Lecture de Nietzsche* (Paris:
Éditions du Seuil, 1971); Bernard Pautrat, *Versions du soleil. Figures et
système de Nietzsche* (Paris: Éditions du Seuil, 1971); Pierre Boudot,
L'ontologie de Nietzsche (Paris: Presses Universitaires de France, 1971);
Sarah Kofman, *Nietzsche et la métaphore* (Paris: Payot, 1972) [English
translation: *Nietzsche and Metaphor,* translated by Duncan Large (London: Athlone Press, 1993)]; Paul Valadier, *Nietzsche et la critique du
christianisme* (Paris: Éditions du Cerf, 1974).

13 See, for example, *Bulletin de la Société française de philosophie,* No. 4
(Oct.–Dec. 1969), on "Nietzsche et ses interprètes"; *Poétique,* Vol. V
(1971) on "Rhétorique et philosophie"; *Revue Philosophique,* No. 3 (1971)
on "Nietzsche"; *Critique,* No. 313 (1973) on "Lectures de Nietzsche."

14 Over 800 pages of presentations and subsequent discussions from this
conference were published in two volumes as *Nietzsche aujourd'hui*
(Paris: Union Générale D'Éditions, 1973). In addition to many of the
authors cited in note 12 above, papers were presented at Cerisy by E.
Biser, E. Blondel, E. Clémens, G. Deleuze, J. Delhomme, J. Derrida, E.
Fink, L. Flam, E. Gaede, D. Grlic, Ph. Lacoue-Labarthe, K. Löwith, J.-F.
Lyotard, J. Maurel, J.-L. Nancy, N. Palma, R. Roos, J.-N. Vuarnet, and H.
Wismann.

15 *Nietzsche: Cahiers du Royaumont,* pp. 183–200. An English translation
by Alan D. Schrift appears in *Transforming the Hermeneutical Context:
From Nietzsche to Nancy,* edited by Gayle L. Ormiston and Alan D.
Schrift (Albany: State University of New York Press, 1990), pp. 59–67.

16 Michel Foucault, *Nietzsche: Cahiers du Royaumont,* p. 189; *Transforming the Hermeneutic Context,* p. 64.

17 Foucault, *The Order of Things* (New York: Random House, 1970), p. 305.

18 Foucault, *The Order of Things*, p. 305.

19 Foucault, *The Order of Things*, p. 342. Deleuze comments on Foucault's coupling the disappearance of man with the death of God in "On the Death of Man and Superman" in *Foucault*, translated by Séan Hand (Minneapolis: University of Minnesota Press, 1988), pp. 124–32; see also the discussion on pp. 87–93. These remarks should be compared with Deleuze and Guattari's comments on the death of God and the death of the Oedipal father in *Anti-Oedipus*, translated by Robert Hurley, Mark Seem and Helen R. Lane (Minneapolis: University of Minnesota Press, 1983), pp. 106ff.

20 See Foucault, *The Order of Things*, pp. 312–13.

21 See Kant's *Introduction to Logic*, translated by T. K. Abbott (New York: Philosophical Library, 1963), where we find the three perennial philosophical questions (What can I know? What ought I to do? What may I hope?) referred to a fourth: What is man? Of these four questions, Kant remarks: "The first question is answered by Metaphysics, the second by Morals, the third by Religion, and the fourth by Anthropology. In reality, however, all these might be reckoned under anthropology, since the first three questions refer to the last" (p. 15). Foucault here follows a move first made by Heidegger in his Kant interpretation (see Martin Heidegger, *Kant and the Problem of Metaphysics*, translated by James S. Churchill [Bloomington: Indiana University Press, 1962], pp. 213–15), when he locates within this reckoning the birth of the discipline of philosophical anthropology. For Foucault's own appraisal of the relation between Heidegger and Nietzsche in connection with the evolution of his own thought, see his "Last Interview," Michel Foucault, *Politics, Philosophy, Culture: Interviews and Other Writings 1977–1984*, edited by Lawrence D. Kritzman (New York: Routledge, 1988), pp. 242–54, esp. pp. 250–1.

22 See Kant's introduction to the *Prolegomena to any Future Metaphysics*.

23 Cf. the following: "The antithesis of the *Übermensch* is the *last man*: I created him conjointly with the former" (KGW VII, 1: 4[171]).

24 Foucault, *The Order of Things*, p. 385.

25 Not coincidentally "La question du style" was the title of Jacques Derrida's presentation at the Cerisy conference "Nietzsche aujourd'hui," which in its revised form was published as *Spurs: Nietzsche's Styles*.

26 Pautrat, *Versions du soleil*, pp. 36–9.

27 See Foucault, *The Order of Things*, p. 305.

28 Jacques Derrida, "La question du style" in *Nietzsche aujourd'hui*, Vol. I., p. 270.

29 Philippe Lacoue-Labarthe, "La Dissimulation" in *Nietzsche aujourd'hui*, Vol. II, p. 12.

30 See, for example, WP 818: "One is an artist at the cost of regarding that which all non-artists call 'form' as content, as 'the thing in itself.' " See also WP 817, 828; D 268.

31 This is particularly true in the case of Nietzsche's first American commentators, most of whom either apologize for what they see as Nietzsche's stylistic excesses or attempt to separate Nietzsche's philosophical merit from his stylistic mastery. Arthur C. Danto exemplifies the former attitude: "If one takes the trouble to eke his philosophy out, to chart the changes in signification that his words sustain in their shiftings from context to context and back, then Nietzsche emerges almost as a systematic as well as an original and analytic thinker. This task, however, is not a simple one. His thoughts are diffused through many loosely structured volumes, and his individual statements seem too clever and topical to sustain serious philosophical scrutiny" (*Nietzsche as Philosopher* [New York: Columbia University Press, 1965], p. 13). Walter Kaufmann, on the other hand, adopts the latter strategy when he claims that, in writing a book on Nietzsche, "I had been reacting against the view that Nietzsche was primarily a great stylist, and the burden of my book had been to show that he was a great thinker" (*Nietzsche: Philosopher, Psychologist, Antichrist* [Princeton: Princeton University Press, 1974], p. viii.). In the past few years, there have been several notable exceptions to this inattention to style on the part of Nietzsche's English-speaking commentators. In particular, the question of style is central to Alexander Nehamas's *Nietzsche: Life as Literature* (Cambridge, Mass.: Harvard University Press, 1985); Bernd Magnus's recent focus on what he calls the self-consuming or self-deconstructing quality of Nietzsche's major themes (especially perspectivism, eternal recurrence and *Übermensch*) in "Self-Consuming Concepts," in *International Studies in Philosophy*, Vol. XXI, No. 2 (1989), pp. 63–71; Allan Megill's *Prophets of Extremity: Nietzsche, Heidegger, Foucault, Derrida* (Berkeley: University of California Press, 1985); Gary Shapiro's *Nietzschean Narratives* (Bloomington: Indiana University Press, 1989); and Henry Staten's *Nietzsche's Voice* (Ithaca: Cornell University Press, 1990).

32 See Deleuze, *Nietzsche and Philosophy*, p. 197.

33 Deleuze, *Nietzsche and Philosophy*, p. 180

34 Deleuze, *Nietzsche and Philosophy*, p. 50.

35 Granier, *Le problème de la vérité dans la philosophie de Nietzsche*, p. 463.

36 Granier, p. 325.

37 Granier, pp. 604–9.

38 Pautrat, *Versions du soleil*, p. 9.

39 Kofman and Pautrat were students of Derrida and they both make fre-

quent use of Derridean terminology. Not coincidentally, these two texts appeared shortly after Derrida's seminar at the École Normale Supérieure, in the winter of 1969–70, devoted to a theory of philosophical discourse with a particular emphasis on the status of metaphor in philosophy. Kofman and Pautrat participated in this seminar and both presented early versions of their texts to that assembly.

40 These notes were translated into French by Kofman's fellow seminar participants Jean-Luc Nancy and Philippe Lacoue-Labarthe in 1971 as "Rhétorique et langage" in *Poétique* 5 (1971), pp. 99–142. An English translation of these notes has been published under the title *Friedrich Nietzsche on Rhetoric and Language*, edited and translated by Sander L. Gilman, Carole Blair, and David J. Parent (Oxford: Oxford University Press, 1989).

41 The editors of the *Musarionausgabe* gave the title "*Philosophenbuch*" (Vol. VI, pp. 1–119) to a collection of notes that was to be the "theoretical" section of a work which, accompanied by a "historical" section (part of which appeared as PTA), was to be on pre-Platonic philosophy. These notes are edited and translated by Daniel Breazeale in *Philosophy and Truth* (Atlantic Highlands, New Jersey: Humanities Press, 1979).

42 The full text of Nietzsche's "definition" reads: "What then is truth? A mobile army of metaphors, metonymies, and anthropomorphisms – in short, a sum of human relations which have been poetically and theatrically enhanced, transposed, and embellished, and which after long use seem fixed, canonical and binding to a people: truths are illusions which we have forgotten are illusions; metaphors which are worn out and without sensuous power, coins which have lost their picture and now matter only as metal, no longer as coin." (Walter Kaufmann, ed., *The Portable Nietzsche* [New York: Viking Press, 1954], pp. 46–7. Translation altered.)

43 Cf. Kofman, *Nietzsche et la métaphore*, pp. 29, 121; English translation, pp. 16, 82.

44 Focusing in particular on the architectural transformations that appear in "Truth and Lies."

45 For example, the eye as metaphor for perceptual knowledge (e.g., GM III 12), the ear as metaphor for understanding (e.g., EH III 1), the nose as metaphor for the capacity to discern decadence (e.g., EH I 1), taste as metaphor for the power to impose and assess value (e.g., PTA 3 in KGW III, 2, p. 310).

46 For Kofman's discussion of these metaphors, see pp. 87–117 and 149–63; English translation, pp. 59–80 and 101–12.

47 See Kofman, p. 89, p. 171; English translation, p. 60, pp. 185–6.

48 Kofman, p. 167; English translation, p. 115.

49 For example, in the essay *"Différance"* in *Margins of Philosophy*, pp. 17–18.

50 Derrida, *Margins of Philosophy*, p. 305.

51 Jacques Derrida, *Of Grammatology*, translated by Gayatri C. Spivak (Baltimore: Johns Hopkins University Press, 1976), p. 19.

52 Let me take this opportunity to expand on a point raised earlier in note 8. Many of the French appeal to Nietzsche in distancing themselves from the Heideggerian project of recuperating Being from its metaphysical oblivion. Derrida, in particular, has chosen Nietzsche's texts as a site from which to confront Heidegger's thinking. For example, in *Of Grammatology* he writes:

> Nietzsche, far from remaining *simply* (with Hegel and as Heidegger wished) *within* metaphysics, contributed a great deal to the liberation of the signifier from its dependence or derivation with respect to the logos and the related concept of truth or the primary signified, in whatever sense that is understood. . . . [R]ather than protect Nietzsche from the Heideggerian reading, we should perhaps offer him up to it completely, underwriting that interpretation without reserve; in a *certain way* and up to the point where, the content of the Nietzschean discourse being almost lost for the question of being, its form regains its absolute strangeness, where his text finally invokes a different type of reading, more faithful to his type of writing: Nietzsche has *written what* he has written. He has written that writing – and first of all his own – is not originally subordinate to the logos and to truth. And that this subordination has *come into being* during an epoch whose meaning we must deconstruct. Now in this direction (but only in this direction, for read otherwise, the Nietzschean demolition remains dogmatic and, like all reversals, a captive of that metaphysical edifice which it professes to overthrow. On that point and in that *order of reading*, the conclusions of Heidegger and Fink are irrefutable), Heideggerian thought would reinstate rather than destroy the instance of the logos and of the truth of being as *"primum signatum:"* . . . (pp. 19–20).

Compare this also with the following remark: "No doubt that Nietzsche called for an active forgetting of Being: it would not have the metaphysical form imputed to it by Heidegger" ("The Ends of Man" in *Margins of Philosophy*, p. 136). See also the remark on Nietzsche, Freud, and Heidegger in "Structure, Sign, and Play in the Discourse of the Human Sciences" in *Writing and Difference*, translated by Alan Bass (Chicago: University of Chicago Press, 1978), pp. 281–2.

53 See "The Ends of Man" in *Margins of Philosophy*, p. 135, and *Spurs*, passim.

54 See "Différance" in Margins of Philosophy, pp. 17–18. Editors' note: Différance is a Derridean coinage, which plays on the words différence [difference] and différer [defer or differ]. Derrida emphasizes with this wordplay the importance of context to meaning, the gap between a term and any definition offered, and an indication that no difference makes no difference. (Even the change of a vowel in an unstressed syllable, which makes no difference to pronunciation, makes a difference, although one might debate about precisely what this difference is.)

55 See Jacques Derrida, The Post Card from Socrates to Freud and Beyond, translated by Alan Bass (Chicago: University of Chicago Press, 1987), pp. 403–5.

56 See Derrida, Writing and Difference, p. 292.

57 Derrida, Of Grammatology, p. 287.

58 See for example, Jean-François Lyotard's remark that "oppositional thinking . . . is out of step with the most vital modes of postmodern knowledge," in The Postmodern Condition, translated by Geoff Bennington and Brian Massumi (Minneapolis: University of Minnesota Press, 1983), p. 14.

59 See Jacques Derrida, "Signature, Event, Context" in Margins of Philosophy, p. 329.

60 See, for example, Heidegger's discussion of Nietzsche's inversion of Platonism in Nietzsche. Vol. One. The Will to Power as Art, translated by David F. Krell (San Francisco: Harper and Row, Publishers, Inc., 1978), pp. 200–20.

61 Derrida, Positions, p. 42; see also Margins of Philosophy, p. 329.

62 For a more detailed discussion of Nietzschean genealogy and Derridean deconstruction, see my "Genealogy and/as Deconstruction: Nietzsche, Derrida, and Foucault on Philosophy as Critique" in Postmodernism and Continental Philosophy, edited by Hugh Silverman and Donn Welton (Albany: State University of New York Press, 1988), pp. 193–213, and "The becoming-post-modern of philosophy," in Postmodernism: Histories, Structures, Politics, edited by Gary Shapiro (Albany: State University of New York Press, 1990), pp. 99–113.

63 This same critical strategy operates in the closing stage of the famous chapter of Twilight of the Idols where Nietzsche traces the history of the belief in the "true world": "The true world we have abolished: what world then remains? The apparent one perhaps? . . . But no! with the true world we also abolished the apparent one!" (TI "How the 'True World' Finally Became a Fable"). We have abolished the apparent world because it was defined as "apparent" only in terms of its opposition to the "true" world. Without the "true world" to serve as a standard, the designation "apparent" loses its meaning and the opposition itself loses its critical force. In other words, the traditional (de)valuation of "appear-

ance" depends upon its being the negation of that which the tradition has affirmed as "truth."

64 See WP 600, 604, 605. Derrida has also used the term "active interpretation" to distinguish deconstructive reading from the textual doubling of commentary; see *Of Grammatology*, pp. 157–64.

65 See Derrida, *Of Grammatology*, pp. 158ff. As a counter to the Derridean emphasis on interpretation, but a counter equally indebted to Nietzsche, see Deleuze's call for "textual experimentalism" in Deleuze and Claire Parnet, *Dialogues*, translated by Hugh Tomlinson and Barbara Habberjam (New York: Columbia University Press, 1987), pp. 46–8, and in Deleuze and Félix Guattari, "Rhizome," translated by Paul Patton in *I&C*, No. 8 (Spring, 1981), pp. 67–8. This version of "Rhizome" was published separately prior to the appearance in 1980 of *Mille Plateaux* (*A Thousand Plateaus*, translated by Brian Massumi [Minneapolis: University of Minnesota Press, 1987]), and it differs slightly from the version that introduced *A Thousand Plateaus*.

66 See Deleuze, *Nietzsche and Philosophy*, pp. 49–55.

67 Cf. Deleuze, *Nietzsche and Philosophy*, p. 220: "Heidegger gives an interpretation of Nietzschean philosophy closer to his own thought than to Nietzsche's. [. . .] Nietzsche is opposed to every conception of affirmation which would find its foundation in Being, and its determination in the being of man." I address and criticize Heidegger's interpretation of will to power in some detail elsewhere; see my *Nietzsche and the Question of Interpretation*, pp. 53–73.

68 It must be remembered that this privileging of Nietzsche is neither absolute nor exclusive: both Marx and Freud remain major influences on virtually all French thought of the past three decades. Another way to understand the privileging of Nietzsche in contemporary French philosophical thought, and one not incompatible with the interpretation offered here, is suggested by Pierre Bourdieu in the Preface to the English translation of *Homo Academicus*, translated by Peter Collier (Stanford: Stanford University Press, 1988). In a remark about Foucault (p. xxiv), Bourdieu suggests that the philosophical appeal to Nietzsche may be a response to the general decline of influence among philosophers within French academic institutions that followed the privileging of the social sciences by the structuralists. In this regard, Nietzsche's having been overlooked by "traditional" philosophers made him "an acceptable philosophical sponsor" at a time when it was not in fashion in France to be "philosophical." Foucault made a similar point concerning Nietzsche's relation to "mainstream" academic philosophy in a 1975 interview, translated as "The Functions of Literature" by Alan Sheridan and reprinted in *Politics, Philosophy, Culture*, p. 312.

69 See Foucault's discussion of pastoral power in "*Omnes et Singulatim*: Towards a Criticism of 'Political Reason,' " two lectures delivered in 1979 and published in *The Tanner Lectures on Human Values*, edited by Sterling McMurrin (Salt Lake City: University of Utah Press, 1981), pp. 225–54.

70 See *Symposium* 200a–d, where Socrates remarks that one who desires something is necessarily in want of that thing. I discuss the Deleuzian critique of "desire as lack" in more detail elsewhere; see my "Spinoza, Nietzsche, Deleuze: An other discourse of desire" in Hugh Silverman, ed., *Philosophy and the Discourse of Desire* (New York: Routledge, forthcoming).

71 See the discussion of this point in *Anti-Oedipus*, p. 348.

72 See, for example, *Anti-Oedipus*, pp. 108–12, 269, and 332–33; see also *A Thousand Plateaus*, p. 154. I have discussed Nietzsche's influence on Deleuze and Guattari's critique of psychoanalysis elsewhere; see my "Nietzsche's becoming-Deleuze: Genealogy, Will to Power, and Other Desiring Machines," from which much of the preceding discussion of Deleuze is drawn, and forthcoming in *Nietzsche: A Critical Reader*, edited by Peter Sedgwick (Oxford: Blackwell, 1995).

73 Cf. Deleuze and Guattari, *Anti-Oedipus*, pp. 64–5.

74 We can only note here two other Nietzschean developments in Deleuze and Guattari's critique of psychoanalysis that warrant serious consideration: their claim that GM is "the great book of modern ethnology" (*Anti-Oedipus*, p. 190), and their appropriation of Nietzsche's link between the rise of Christianity and the rise of the modern state (in GM II) in their own discussion of libidinal and political economy.

75 Jean-François Lyotard and Jean-Loup Thébaud, *Just Gaming*, translated by Wlad Godzich (Minneapolis: University of Minnesota Press, 1985), p. 17.

76 Lyotard and Thébaud, p. 17.

77 Editor's Note: Ludwig Wittgenstein contended in *Philosophical Investigations* that language involves a variety of activities and that various languages may bear only a general family resemblance, much as games do.

78 Lyotard and Thébaud, p. 18; cf. 98.

79 Jean-François Lyotard, *The Differend: Phrases in Dispute*, translated by Georges Van Den Abbeele (Minneapolis: University of Minnesota Press, 1988), p. 135; cf. *Just Gaming*, p. 59.

80 Lyotard and Thébaud, p. 17.

81 Many of the points raised in my discussion of Derrida, Foucault, Deleuze, and Lyotard have been developed in much greater detail in my *Nietzsche's French Legacy: A Genealogy of Poststructuralism* (New York: Routledge, 1995).

11 Nietzsche and East Asian thought: Influences, impacts, and resonances

I imagine future thinkers in whom European-American indefati-
gability is combined with the hundredfold-inherited contempla-
tiveness of the Asians: such a combination will bring the riddle
of the world to a solution. (1876)

The conjunction signified by the "and" of the main title is to be
taken in three ways. First of all the question of what influence, if
any, ideas from Asian philosophies may have exerted on the development of Nietzsche's thinking. Conversely, there is the issue of the
enormous impact Nietzsche's ideas have had in Asia and the enthusiasm with which he continues to be studied there today – especially
in China and Japan. A subsidiary theme here concerns the ways his
thought has been appropriated by those quite alien cultures and
thereby transformed, as well as the relevance of such appropriations
to Nietzsche scholarship in the West. And finally the field of comparative research, which embraces a variety of styles of discourse. A
comparison of Nietzsche's ideas on a certain topic with those of an
appropriate Asian philosophy can enhance our appreciation of both
sides. For people familiar with Nietzsche, a comparison with an
East-Asian thinker might serve as a way into hitherto unfamiliar
modes of thought. And since Chinese and Japanese philosophies are
for the most part *un*metaphysical in outlook, insofar as Nietzsche's
ideas can be shown to resonate sympathetically with features of
those quite alien traditions of thinking, such resonances may boost
his standing in the competition, among such figures as Hegel and
Heidegger, for the distinction of being the first Western thinker to
"overcome" the metaphysical tradition.

Since the relations between Nietzsche and Indian ideas have already been the subject of some study, the primary – though not exclusive – focus of what follows will be on East Asian thought.[1]

I. THE PAUCITY OF INFLUENCE

It is hardly surprising that Nietzsche should have had some acquaintance with Asian thinking, in view of the long history of the engagement of German philosophers with ideas from India and China – even though those engagements may not, until recently, have gone very deep. Leibniz was fascinated by the Chinese classic *The Book of Changes* (*I jing*) and Neo-Confucian philosophy. Hegel treated Indian and Chinese philosophy in his comprehensive *History*, and Schelling engaged in some brief – and more positive – discussion of Buddhism and Daoism. Schopenhauer, in his research into Indian philosophy, appears to have attained the most comprehensive understanding among nineteenth-century German thinkers of a system of Asian thought.[2]

Nietzsche came into contact with ideas from the Indian tradition during his later schooldays at Schulpforta (1862–4), where he gained at least some acquaintance with the two great Indian epics, the *Mahabharata* and the *Ramayana*.[3] He appears also to have been exposed to some of the basic ideas of Hinduism and Buddhism during this period, such as the doctrines of karma and rebirth. It is easy to assume, in view of his long friendship with the Sanskrit scholar Paul Deussen and also the many allusions to Indian ideas scattered throughout Nietzsche's work, that he had a keen interest in Indian philosophy which prompted him to acquaint himself with the subject as far as the extant translations allowed. But it now appears that his interest was not as great after all: one can account for the mentions of Indian ideas in his works on the basis of his having actually read a rather small number of books on the topic.[4]

Nietzsche's discussions of Hindu and Buddhist ideas suggest that his grasp of those philosophies was less than firm. And even if he had been more inquisitive, relatively few translations were available at the time, and many of those poor quality. While Nietzsche's intuition granted him some insight into certain aspects of Indian culture, his views were conditioned to a large extent by his own projections.[5] Nevertheless, a passage in a letter to Paul Deussen in which

Nietzsche claims to possess a "trans-European eye" shows that he was by no means parochial in his understanding of philosophy, and that he was open to a broader, cross-cultural perspective.

I have, as you know, a profound sympathy with everything that you have in mind to undertake. And it belongs to the most essential fostering of my freedom from prejudice (my "trans-European eye") that your existence and work remind me again and again of the one great parallel to our European philosophy. With respect to this Indian development there still reigns here in France the same old absolute ignorance. The followers of Comte, for example, are making up totally naive *laws* for a historically necessary development and succession of the main stages of philosophy, in which the Indians are not taken into account at all – laws that are in fact *contradicted* by the development of philosophy in India.[6]

Nietzsche did possess a "trans-European eye," even if its sight was not much clearer than that of his physical eyes, and even if he chose not to cast it farther than Asia Minor and India. Even if he was not so interested in understanding Indian thought per se, and more in excursions into the realm of "the foreign" – *das Fremde* – for the hermeneutic purpose of distancing himself from his contemporary situation in order better to understand the phenomenon of European modernity.[7] And yet there does appear in the unpublished notes from 1884 the following fascinating resolution: "I must learn to think *more orientally* [orientalischer] about philosophy and knowledge. *Oriental* [Morgenländischer] *overview of Europe.*"[8]

The occasional comments Nietzsche makes about China and Japan do not suggest that he knew any more about East Asian culture than one would expect from the well-educated German of his time. The only mention of a Chinese thinker in the published works occurs in *The Antichrist* (aph. 32), where he suggests that if Jesus had appeared among the Chinese he would have employed concepts drawn from Laozi (Lao Tzu). In view of the context of this remark, Nietzsche appears to have picked up on the mystical and transcendent strain in the great classic of philosophical Daoism, the *Dao de jing*, rather than reading it as a political handbook addressed to a ruler in power.[9] The only other mention of Laozi is to be found in a late letter in which he announces his discovery of a French translation of the Hindu *Laws of Manu* and adds an utterly fanciful remark to the effect that Confucius and Laozi may have been influenced by that ancient text.[10]

There appear to be only two mentions of the Japanese in Nietzsche's published works, neither of them of much philosophical consequence, though there are several references in his letters to the "Japonisme" of his friend Reinhart von Seydlitz.[11] Indeed the brief references to the Japanese in *Beyond Good and Evil* and *Toward the Genealogy of Morals* probably stem from conversations with von Seydlitz about Japanese culture. But the most remarkable mention of Japan is in a letter to his sister in which, after the usual complaints about his health, he writes:

> If only I were in better health and had sufficient income, I would, simply in order to attain greater serenity, emigrate to *Japan*. (To my great surprise I discovered that Seydlitz too has undergone a similar inner transformation: artistically he is now the first German Japanese – read the enclosed newspaper articles about him!) I like being in Venice because things could be somewhat Japanese there – a few of the necessary conditions are in place.[12]

Since the paragraph ends with a lament over the general ruin and corruption of Europe, the fantasy of emigration is to be taken more as a reaction against the contemporary situation than as a sign of genuine attraction to Japan. (It is nonetheless fascinating to speculate on what the post-*Zarathustra* writings would have looked like had they been written in the Japan Alps rather than the Upper Engadin.)

As a philologist Nietzsche may have known that Japanese is generally counted among the Ural-Altaic languages – he in any case makes an interesting remark about that family in *Beyond Good and Evil*. On the premise that the singular "family resemblance" between "Indian, Greek, and German philosophizing" arises from "the common philosophy of grammar" that comes with affinities among languages, he surmises that "Philosophers in the domain of the Ural-Altaic languages (in which the concept of the subject is most poorly developed) will most probably look 'into the world' differently and be found on different paths from Indo-Germans or Muslims" (BGE 20). This is remarkably apropos with respect to Japanese, though Nietzsche may not have realized it. In invoking "the spell of particular grammatical functions" Nietzsche is not engaging in any kind of competitive philology by suggesting that a strong sense of the subject makes for more powerful thinking. The epithet "most poorly developed" is purely descriptive; and since the context is the culmination of a series of devastating attacks on precisely "the concept of the subject," the implication is that a weak concept of the subject may well conduce to some quite robust philosophizing.[13] Indeed the lack of a well developed concept of the subject in Japanese syntax does appear to conduce to styles of philosophy from which the metaphysical subject is absent – some of which are on this account eminently comparable to Nietzsche's own.

2. INITIAL IMPACTS IN EAST ASIA

In view of the minor influence of Asian ideas on Nietzsche's thought, the impact of his philosophy on the intellectual worlds of China and Japan has been enormous. Indeed its magnitude suggests a prior and more than superficial affinity between his ideas and the indigenous ways of thinking. Nietzsche's influence in India has probably been no more powerful than was the influence of Indian ideas on him, though this question has apparently not been the object of serious study.[14] Let us then look to the reception of Nietzsche's thought in East Asia.

Even though Nietzsche's fantasy of emigrating to Japan came to naught, his ideas arrived in that distant land within a decade, in the mid-eighteen-nineties – while he was still alive, though unaware of the world beyond his sick-room in the Villa Silberblick on a hill overlooking the city of Weimar. Just after the turn of the century the name "Nietzsche" – the figure of "the mad philosopher" who went "beyond good and evil" rather than the texts written by the author bearing that name – helped precipitate a crisis of conscience in the intellectual world of Japan. From 1901 to 1903 the "aesthetic life" debate was ignited by the proposal, supposedly drawn from Nietzsche, that the highest experience is guided by mere instinct and constrained only by aesthetic considerations. Fueled mainly by uncritical readings of secondary literature rather than Nietzsche's own texts, the debate raged throughout the land, leaving in its wake a number of ruined reputations and – in the worst cases – careers on the part of its less fortunate participants. It was a classic case of an external fuse's setting off accumulated tensions within the Japanese intellectual community, centering around problems of instinctual life, moral strictures, and individualism.[15]

A number of Chinese students were studying in Japan at this time, and when they returned home some brought with them a fascination for the figure of the recently deceased thinker who had been the occasion for such vitriolic controversy in that otherwise civilized land. Two major figures in the early Nietzsche reception in China are Wang Guowei and Lu Xun,[16] who began to publish discussions of his ideas in 1905 and 1907 respectively. Such was their stature in the Chinese intellectual world that there arose a surge of interest in Nietzsche that reached a peak around the May Fourth Movement of 1919, when many revolutionary enthusiasts espoused the German thinker as a source for ideas with which to build a "new China." Interest peaked again in the early forties at the opposite end of the political spectrum, when right-wing intellectuals associated with the Guomindang (Kuomintang) selected an alternate set of passages from Nietzsche's works to prosecute a quite different ideological agenda. Needless to say, enthusiasm for Nietzsche's ideas waned – or, rather, the people were weaned from them – with the takeover by the Communists in 1949.

In the past few decades, however, there has been a tremendous resurgence of interest in Nietzsche in the People's Republic, and a replay of many of the ideological debates of the first forty years.[17] The apparently eternal return of conflicting views of "the same" thinker serves to underscore the remarkable phenomenon – more pronounced perhaps with Nietzsche than with any other author – of the successive appropriation of his ideas by proponents of extremes at either end of the ideological spectrum. Weakened by the ever-present tendency to vulgarize Nietzsche's ideas, the resurgence faltered – understandably – in the aftermath of the Tiananmen Square massacre. Nevertheless, a visit to Beijing in 1992 left the impression that interest in Nietzsche is very much on the rise again, and is reaching – as a result of revised translations and increasing access to better secondary sources – a more sophisticated intellectual level than before.[18]

Since most of the combatants in the "aesthetic life" debate in Japan had gained what little understanding of Nietzsche's ideas they had from the secondary literature, the reception of the texts proper did not begin in Japan until 1911, when the first translations of his writings into Japanese were made. (The complete works were not available in Japanese until 1929.) Once accessible in a Japanese edition, Nietzsche's books would exert a considerable influence on the literary world of Japan, especially by way of such figures as Akutagawa Ryūnosuke and Mishima Yukio. There was initial resistance – as there always is – to the acceptance of Nietzsche as a philosopher, but considerable inroads were made by the publication in 1913 of a volume entitled *Nīchie kenkyū* (Research on Nietzsche) by a young philosopher named Watsuji Tetsurō.

Although Watsuji remarks in one of his prefaces that his version of Nietzsche is a very personal one, the book is a landmark in Nietzsche studies in Japan. Considering the level of discussion in the Nietzsche literature in Western languages up to 1913, it also has to be said that Watsuji's detailed analyses were ahead of their time. The twenty-four-year-old author enjoyed a remarkable attunement with the spirit of Nietzsche and his philosophical project which afforded him insight into several of its major themes. Watsuji's book long enjoyed a well-deserved reputation as the definitive study of Nietzsche's philosophy in Japan.

Although he was active early on as a writer of stories and plays, and also as editor of a literary magazine (he was a personal friend of two of the most famous novelists of the time, Tanizaki Jun'ichirō and Natsume Sōseki), Watsuji eventually opted to study philosophy at Tokyo Imperial University. He proposed a doctoral dissertation on Nietzsche, but the proposal was rejected and he was advised to write on a "real" philosopher, such as Schopenhauer. He submitted a thesis entitled "Schopenhauer's Pessimism and Theory of Salvation," and two years later he published his study on Nietzsche. While the study shows some influence by Schopenhauerian ideas, Watsuji is clearly aware of the important respects in which Nietzsche differed from his erstwhile spiritual mentor. The book also undertakes some apt comparisons of Nietzsche with Bergson and William James, both of whom were being much discussed in Japanese philosophical circles at that time.

The plan of Watsuji's book is based on the sketches Nietzsche made for a philosophical *Hauptwerk*, as adopted (and adapted) by Peter Gast and Elisabeth Förster-Nietzsche in their collection entitled *Der Wille zur Macht* and published in the *Grossoktavausgabe* of 1911. (Watsuji also makes use of some of the *Nachlass* published in the Kröner

Taschenausgabe of 1906.) The study is divided into two parts, of which the first bears a title corresponding to that of the third book of *Der Wille zur Macht*, "Principles for the Establishment of New Values." After an introductory chapter entitled simply "Will to Power," which discusses Nietzsche's methods and explicates the idea of will to power as "life," the remaining four chapters correspond to the subsections of the third book of *Der Wille zur Macht* – dealing with will to power as knowledge or cognition, as nature, as "character" (the original German has "Will to power as Society and Individual"), and as art. The second part of the study bears the title "The Destruction and Construction of Values," and the structure of its first half corresponds to that of the second book of *Der Wille zur Macht*, with chapters entitled "Critique of Religion," "Critique of Morality," and "Critique of Philosophy." The remaining three chapters are "Critique of Art," "The Decadence of European Civilization" (which deals with some of the topics in the first book of *Der Wille zur Macht*, "European Nihilism"), and "New Standards of Value." While Watsuji does mention Dionysus and the idea of eternal recurrence, there is little discussion of the idea of the order of rank, which is the main theme of the fourth book of *Der Wille zur Macht*, "Zucht und Züchtung" (Discipline and Cultivation/Breeding). On the publication of the second edition, the author added an appendix dealing with *Ecce Homo*.

While Watsuji places considerable emphasis on material from the *Nachlass* – in this he is an archetypal "lumper," in Bernd Magnus's felicitous coinage – he also discusses themes in Nietzsche's published works. It should be mentioned that conventions of scholarship in Japan are quite different from those prevailing in most Western circles: In explicating the thought of a philosopher, the Japanese scholar will paraphrase passages of text far more than quote them verbatim, and is thus relatively parsimonious with footnotes. (Some writers presumably wish to avoid insulting the reader's intelligence by assuming that he doesn't know where to find the passage under discussion; others may be motivated by considerations of Confucian pedagogy, according to which the reader is expected to learn better if he has to work for it. Nor are these motives mutually exclusive.) Watsuji is relatively forthcoming, insofar as he supplies at the end of the book a list of passages from Nietzsche's texts on which the discussion in each of his chapters is based.

Being himself a writer with literary sensibilities, Watsuji was especially sensitive to the artistic aspects of Nietzsche's work, and fully appreciative (as expressed in the introduction to his study) of the remarkable way in which Nietzsche's artistic talents were synthesized with his abilities as a thinker and a scholar. Watsuji is renowned for the clarity and elegance of his prose, and the engagement with Nietzsche's texts inspires him on occasion to flights of complementary lyricism.

A sense of Watsuji's philosophical orientation and approach to his subject can be gained from the beginning of his first chapter:

True philosophy is not simply the accumulation and organization of concepts but the ideational expression of the most direct inner experience. Direct pure inner experience signifies *living* as the essence of existence. . . . If we refer to direct inner experience as intuition, this intuition *lives* as "life itself." "Cosmic life" is of course ceaseless creation; accordingly, direct inner experience, too, operates creatively. Self expression is this creative activity. The arts and philosophy all derive from this.[19]

Watsuji clearly takes seriously Nietzsche's contention that the thought of a philosopher is an expression of his life and of the life that moves through him in the form of instinctual drives (BGE 3–6). He takes equally seriously the thought experiment Nietzsche proposes in which he suggests that we understand our entire instinctual life – and ultimately the world as a whole – as a play of will to power (BGE 36). Throughout his study Watsuji gives a distinctly "vitalist" reading of Nietzsche (in part, perhaps, under influence from Bergson) that takes the main aim of the Nietzschean project to be the recovery of the full flow of ascending life.

Some readers will be unhappy with Watsuji's talk of "cosmic life" and his penchant for identifying the fully realized human self with the self of the cosmos. The temptation to ascribe this orientation to a projection onto Nietzsche's text of Buddhist ideas is mitigated by the consideration that until 1917 Watsuji's works dealt exclusively with Western topics. (In 1915 he published a substantial tome on Kierkegaard, which was to remain for many years the definitive study in Japanese.) However, recent research into his unpublished notes shows that Watsuji was in fact already familiar with Buddhist ideas by the time he wrote his study of Nietzsche. In these notes Watsuji asserts a basic harmony between Nietzsche's philosophy and the Buddhist idea of self-negation in the sense of the elimination of the ego, on the grounds that the self of Nietzsche's "selfishness" refers to "a deep, supraconscious self." If one understands nirvana not negatively, as Schopenhauer did, as extinction of desire, but rather as "pure activity" or "life" in the Bergsonian sense, then the affirmation of the self as "Buddha-nature" will be consonant with Nietzsche's life-affirming stance.[20] Even though recent comparative studies on Nietzsche suggest that Watsuji was very much ahead of his time with these ideas, some readers will no doubt resist them as misinterpretations of the texts. At the very least, however, readings such as Watsuji's from the East Asian perspective highlight themes in Nietzsche's writings that have tended to be downplayed or over-looked in the West.

Watsuji's emphasis on "intuition" in Nietzsche, which is a recur-rent theme in the first part of his study, is somewhat puzzling – especially since he nowhere says which term in Nietzsche's texts the Japanese term (chokkaku) corresponds to. It is true that Nietzsche early on praises Heraclitus for his tremendous powers of "intuition [intuitiv Vorstellung]," a term he borrows from Schopenhauer (and with which Watsuji must have been familiar).[21] But Nietzsche hardly ever uses the terms intuitiv or Vorstellung in his subsequent works, nor does he exalt any faculty of "intuition." The idea of intuitive experience or understanding does, however, play an important role in a text that is regarded as the first masterpiece of modern Japanese philosophy, An Inquiry into the Good by Nishida Kitarō, which was published in 1911. Since Watsuji's study shows a number of influ-ences from this work, it is likely that the emphasis on intuition has its major source there. On the other hand, Watsuji also engages in some salutary discussion of the importance for Nietzsche of scientific method, and speaks of the "fusion of intuition and scientific method" (p. 53) in Nietzsche's works – an apt characterization, surely, if one understands "intuition" as something more like imagination.[22]

A major theme in the first part of Watsuji's study is the idea that consciousness is a superficial and paltry power in comparison with the vigorous forces of life that underlie and sustain it. He fully appre-ciates Nietzsche's discussions of the dark wisdom of the instinctual drives, and of the decisive importance of unconscious mental or psychical processes. (Again, his acquaintance with Schopenhauer will have sensitized him to this kind of theme.) Approaching Nietz-sche, as he does, from a tradition that emphasizes the unity of mind-

and-body and frequently privileges the somatic over the psychical aspects of human existence, Watsuji is naturally attentive to the corresponding themes in Nietzsche's thinking. He places similar emphasis on Nietzsche's analyses of the "I" into a multiplicity and his exposure of the ego as a conceptual synthesis or fiction.

To sum up Watsuji's reading of Nietzsche in his 1913 study: The predominant trait is a vehement anti-intellectualism that, while it may present a faithful enough picture of the author of *The Birth of Tragedy*, gives a somewhat biased view of the philosopher as a whole. While it is true that Nietzsche is concerned to point up the narrowness and superficiality of consciousness and to acknowledge the limitations of reason in fathoming the depths of existence, after *The Birth of Tragedy*, with its apotheosis of unconscious instinct, he moves to a less extreme position in which the exercise of intellect (albeit understood as a certain configuration of instinctual drives) is regarded as the sine qua non for a fully human life. (It is significant that Watsuji makes hardly any reference at all to *Human, All Too Human*.) Notwithstanding, Watsuji's reading is insightful and comprehensive – and his achievement especially remarkable coming, as it did, from the hand of an author in his early twenties.

After publishing his study of Kierkegaard in 1915, Watsuji turned his attention away from Western thinkers and toward the history of Japanese culture. Although there is hardly a mention of Nietzsche in the series of studies that flowed from his pen after the 1918 collection *Gūzō saikō* (*Restoration of the idols* – an interestingly Nietzschean title), these works still show traces of Nietzsche's influence. Just as Nietzsche had gained from the ancient Greeks a vantage point from which to criticize the decadence of contemporary German culture, so Watsuji adduced the cultural achievements of ancient Japan in order to highlight the shortcomings of a country in the throes of enthusiastic modernization. It is as if he later acknowledged Nietzsche's early rejection of Romantic individualism and came to appreciate his classicism.

3. THE CASE OF NISHITANI KEIJI

Between the wars there was something of a lull in Nietzsche studies in Japan – in part because of the prevalence of Marxist thinking in the twenties, which was followed by a repression of intellectual

life in general by the militarists and fascists in the thirties – though
one major figure in Japanese philosophy, Miki Kiyoshi, did produce
some significant Nietzsche commentary during that period. Interest in Nietzsche was rekindled after the Second World War, in the
atmosphere of general disorientation and in the context of attempts
to understand the postwar situation in Japan. Nishitani Keiji was,
like Miki, a philosopher of the "Kyoto School" who had also (following the example of Miki and another philosopher from Kyoto,
Tanabe Hajime) studied with Heidegger.[23] The year before his return from Freiburg to Japan in 1939, Nishitani wrote a long essay
comparing Meister Eckhart and Nietzsche's Zarathustra.[24] This essay marked the beginning of a lengthy engagement with Nietzsche
on Nishitani's part as well as a new turn in Nietzsche studies in
Japan.

Like Watsuji before him, Nishitani experienced as a young man an
immediate empathy with Nietzsche and his ideas. In an autobiographical essay entitled "The Days of My Youth," he writes of the
utter hopelessness that pervaded his early youth and of his despair's
being compounded by the death of his father when he was sixteen.[25]
Shortly thereafter, Nishitani was struck down by an illness similar
to the tuberculosis that had killed his father, in the course of
which – in an uncanny parallel to Nietzsche's situation some fifty
years earlier – the young student felt "the specter of death taking
hold" of him. It was the ensuing mental torment that brought him
to the enterprise of philosophy as an attempt to plumb the experience of nihilism to its depths.

My life as a young man can be described in a single phrase: it was a period
absolutely without hope. . . . My life at that time lay entirely in the grips of
nihility and despair. . . . My decision, then, to study philosophy was in fact –
melodramatic as it might sound – a matter of life and death.[26]

Like many intellectuals of his generation (he was born the year
Nietzsche died, in 1900), Nishitani was not only raised on the Chinese classics but was also exposed to a wide range of European and
American literature. He thus embarked on the study of philosophy
from a grounding in a remarkable range of reading.

Before I began my philosophical training as a disciple of Nishida, I was most
attracted by Nietzsche and Dostoevsky, Emerson and Carlyle, and also by
the Bible and St. Francis of Assisi. Among things Japanese, I liked best

Natsume Sōseki and books like the [Zen] Buddhist talks of Hakuin and Takuan.[27]

Such a grounding in two quite disparate traditions gave Nishitani a philosophical starting point of a kind possessed by no major thinker in the Western tradition. Since many Japanese philosophers of his generation were similarly well versed in the tradition of Mahāyāna Buddhist philosophy that originated in India and became sinified in China with admixtures of Confucian and Daoist thought before arriving in Japan, and since they also undertook thorough appropriations of the European and Anglo-American literary and philosophical traditions, their contributions to modern philosophy deserve to be taken very seriously indeed.

A great advantage enjoyed by Nishitani in his approach to Nietzsche derives from the perspective afforded him by his hermeneutic distance from the metaphysical tradition. Western commentators on Nietzsche themselves stand in the current of the tradition that he strove to overcome, which makes it difficult to attain sufficient perspective to evaluate the success of that striving. Nishitani's standing outside that tradition grants him a synoptic overview of Western intellectual history, so that as he works toward a comprehensive grasp of the major trends in Western philosophy he is able to retain a salutary sense of perspective on Nietzsche's position relative to those currents.[28] Another advantage for the Japanese thinker approaching Nietzsche is that his native philosophical tradition is quite unmetaphysical (indeed sometimes resolutely *anti*-metaphysical in reaction against the speculative tendencies of Indian philosophy), so that there is little danger of his interpreting ideas like will to power metaphysically.

The title of the first section of Nishitani's essay on Eckhart and Zarathustra, "The Primordiality of Life in Nietzsche," suggests that his reading will proceed along the lines projected by Watsuji's study. The essay begins with a close reading of the first two sections of "Zarathustra's Prologue," in which Nishitani talks of "fully overflowing life," "the infinite depth of great life," and "pressure pushing up from the deep bottom of life."[29] But the force of the contrast he draws between Zarathustra and the old saint in the forest concerns a difference in the kind of life that animates them, in remarking which Nishitani takes Watsuji's understanding of "life" in Nietzsche a step further.

Nishitani argues that though the saint has died away from the human world to be reborn in "the life of God in the world of great nature" in the forest, this "higher life" is still one that forms a duality with "holy life" and in which God is experienced as an object vis-à-vis the self. This life with God thus means that the saint "has lost the path that connects him to human life" (p. 7). Zarathustra is already at a stage beyond the saint, insofar as a further negation of that higher life has taken place (as evidenced by his realization that "God is dead"), a negation that issues dialectically in a creative affirmation of life – as symbolized in the "overflowing" that is propelling Zarathustra back down the mountain so that he may become human again. Nishitani alludes to Bergson's notion of *élan vital* in emphasizing that the creative life embodied by Zarathustra issues only from the second dialectical movement and is not to be found in "direct, simple [Watsuji would have said "pure"] life" (p. 12).

Thanks to his appreciation of Eckhart's intellectualism, Nishitani is able to go beyond Watsuji's anti-intellectualist emphasis on "pure, direct life" in Nietzsche: "In contrast to what is popularly believed, Nietzsche did not simply advocate direct life and will" (p. 30). His comparison of Zarathustra with Eckhart is judicious and enlightening – and prompts one to wonder how much of Nietzsche's vivid imagery concerning the soul has a source in Eckhart's lyrical effusions concerning *Gottheit* and overflowing.[30] In spite of the vast differences between their respective historical (not to mention a/theological) situations, Nishitani suggests that it might be possible to see Eckhart and Nietzsche "as having met up unexpectedly at the zenith of great life (or at its root)," and as standing together "at the point where the bottomless depth of life alone combusts in the present instant . . . at the life of life" (pp. 28–30). Nishitani's reading of Eckhart downplays the Neoplatonic strains in his thinking just as it highlights its "transcendence-in-immanence" elements, which in turns allows him to harmonize it with a religious view of Nietzsche's resolutely "this-worldly" orientation.[31]

The suggestion made above to the effect that it is to Nishitani's advantage as a reader of Nietzsche to be standing outside the Western tradition gives negative expression, as it were, to the value of his reading. The more positive contribution of his view comes from his immersion in the tradition of East Asian Buddhist thinking – and in Zen in particular. The Buddhist standpoint continues in Nishitani, as it did with Watsuji, to bring into relief a nexus of issues in Nietzsche's thought that have not generally been emphasized in Western readings. This first becomes evident in a work Nishitani first published in 1949, which has been translated into English as *The Self-Overcoming of Nihilism*, almost half of which deals with Nietzsche. Although there is relatively little explicit mention of Buddhist ideas in the text itself, it is obvious to the reader familiar with the doctrine of karma and ideas such as "dependent arising" and the "momentariness" of the elements of existence that such ideas are behind Nishitani's treatments of the complex interrelationships between *amor fati*, will to power, and the eternal recurrence.

A brief sketch of the premises of Nishitani's discussion of *amor fati* may suffice as an illustration. Nietzsche's equation of the self with fate is, for most readers, an enigma. While this idea (adumbrated in the *Untimely Meditations* and developed more fully in *Human, All Too Human*) plays an important role in *Zarathustra* and recurs as late as *Nietzsche contra Wagner*, Nishitani begins his discussion by quoting a posthumously published note from 1884 which ends with the emphasized words, "*Ego fatum.*"[32] (Nishitani is, like Watsuji, something of a "lumper.") If one approaches this idea from the perspective of the karmic doctrine that all actions proceeding from the self eventually – perhaps only after numerous cycles of reincarnation – come back on it, the equation of the self with fate immediately becomes more comprehensible. In discussing a passage from the epilogue to *Nietzsche contra Wagner* in which Nietzsche emphasizes that "only great pain is the ultimate liberator of the spirit," Nishitani writes as follows:

What Nietzsche calls "the abyss of the great suspicion" and "the ultimate depths" of the philosopher is nihilism. In this rebirth from the depths "with a higher health" and "with a second and more dangerous innocence" one's innermost nature bursts forth like a natural spring from which the covering debris has been removed. At this point the spring proclaims as its liberator the sharp pick-axe of necessity that has pierced down through the debris and brought it pain. . . . And ultimately the spring will come to affirm even the debris it burst through and which now floats in it. (SN 51)

The image of the pick-axe – a graphic analogue of Nietzsche's hammer – is very much in the spirit of Zen. When one's inner creativity is able to burst through the overlay of conventional values and conceptualizations, the resultant condition is not one of pristine purity but rather one in which the pool of the psyche is still polluted by debris from the barriers that have been breached. The point is that such debris need not be rejected, but may rather be used in the reconstruction of the new self. Though Nishitani does not himself suggest this, the self's affirmation of the debris from an earlier obstruction would point up the idea that, for Nietzsche, certain features of a tradition previously regarded as repressive may in fact be reappropriated after the appropriate transformation of the self has taken place.

In this same context, Nishitani offers an illuminating reading of the idea of the *Wende der Not* ("turn of need") which Zarathustra plays off against the idea of *Notwendigkeit* (necessity).[33]

Under the compulsion of the need or necessity [*Not*] that prevents one from becoming oneself and from becoming free, one is forced to descend into the abyss within. But once one is freed within the abyss, the need is turned into an element of this life of freedom. When Zarathustra calls his own soul "turn of need" [*Wende der Not*] and "fate" [*Schicksal*], he means that the turn of need, in which necessity is turned into an element of the life of the free soul, is the soul itself. In this case necessity becomes one with the creative. (SN 52)

Not only does this reading make more sense of the relevant passages than most commentators have been able to do, but together with the karma-tinged understanding of fate it sets the stage for a satisfying treatment of *amor fati* combined with eternal recurrence as leading to "the self-overcoming of nihilism" (SN 60–8).

It is this last idea that is the outcome of Nishitani's careful analysis of the various stages in nihilism as understood by Nietzsche.[34] Given that Nishitani attended Heidegger's lectures on Nietzsche from 1937 to 1939, the difference between his account of Nietzsche's nihilism and Heidegger's much longer treatment (in the second volume of his *Nietzsche*) is remarkable. Whereas Heidegger insists on seeing Nietzsche as a subjectivist of hyper-Cartesian proportions and on understanding will to power metaphysically, thereby concluding that Nietzsche's thought is nihilistic in a none too positive sense, Nishitani regards it as leading to the ultimate self-overcoming of nihilism – and thereby coming close to the distinctively nonmetaphysical standpoint of Mahāyāna Buddhism.[35] As in the essay on Eckhart and Zarathustra, Nishitani emphasizes the religious aspect of Nietzsche's thinking, seeing it as embodying a form of Dionysian pantheism that issues in a fully creative affirmation of life.

In Nishitani's masterwork, *Religion and Nothingness*, originally published in Japan in 1961, the focus on figures in Western philosophy has been replaced by a predominance of Mahāyāna Buddhist ideas – though his engagement with such thinkers as Eckhart, Nietzsche, and Heidegger continues. While the English translation of this work is excellent and the writing style clear, it is an extremely subtle text that demands considerable time and effort for the fathoming of its depths. (It may not be overly rash to suggest that it will eventually come to be seen as one of the most important philosophical texts of the mid-twentieth century.) Somewhat puzzling, however, is the shift in Nishitani's estimation of Nietzsche, which now seems to be conditioned by a Heideggerian bias toward taking the idea of will to power metaphysically. There is consequently a definite sense that Nietzsche "falls short" of the Mahāyāna Buddhist standpoint, to which he was said to have come so close in *The Self-Overcoming of Nihilism*. Since considerations of space prohibit an examination of this difficult issue, the reader is simply asked to entertain the possibility that the duplex genealogy of Nishitani's thinking may give it greater breadth than philosophies originating in a single tradition.[36]

4. NIETZSCHE AS A WAY IN TO EAST ASIAN THOUGHT

One of the grounds for the enthusiastic reception of Nietzsche's philosophy in China and Japan has to do with its resonance with the ideas of several major thinkers in the Asian traditions. Some work has already been done to show certain affinities between Nietzsche's ideas and early Buddhism in India, the pioneering text in the field being Freny Mistry's *Nietzsche and Buddhism*. Although this is a somewhat unpolished work written in an occasionally idiosyncratic style, and while it relies heavily on the unpublished *Nachlass*, the author undertakes a comprehensive review of all Nietzsche's remarks about or discussions of Buddhism and intelligently evaluates their validity. The study also marshals a considerable amount of evidence to show that much of Nietzsche's thinking is consonant with the basic insights of early Buddhism. To summarize briefly: the Buddhist emphasis on impermanence and its concomitant antimetaphysical and atheistic tendencies; the denial of any substantial soul, or ego, which is viewed as a merely conventional unity of a number of "energy-aggregates"; a sense that whatever "self" there may be is better understood as the lived body than as anything mental or psychical – all these are shown to have counterparts among Nietzsche's ideas.

If Mistry's comparison eventually becomes overdrawn, it is in connection with the goal of nirvana as understood by early Buddhism and the ideal human existence as exemplified by the arhant (saint). These are simply farther from Nietzsche's ideal of unconditional affirmation of life, whether or not one understands this through the condition of the *Übermensch*, than Mistry would have us believe. The detachment of the arhant who has attained nirvana issues in a condition that is insufficiently *of* the world – albeit still *in* it – to be comparable with the results of a full living out of the Nietzschean program. The author occasionally tries to close the gap by invoking the later Buddhist (Mahāyāna) denial that nirvana is different from samsara, that the world of enlightenment is different from the world of everyday life; but that denial is precisely the distinguishing feature of Mahāyāna Buddhism, which thus makes for a more fruitful comparison with Nietzsche than does the earlier tradition. Indeed, Mistry from time to time mentions the ideas of Nāgārjuna, the philosophical founder of the Mādhyamika school in the second century; and it is with his denial that nirvana is different from samsara, and the consequent reverence for *this* world, that the interesting resonances with Nietzsche's thinking begin.[37]

With respect to the Chinese tradition, it has been shown that there are some remarkable parallels between Nietzsche's thinking and Daoist philosophy – but there are some even more remarkable resonances with the ideas of the master himself, Confucius. A brief example will suffice to show the way in which a comparative approach to Nietzsche can point up hitherto neglected strains in his thinking.

The predominant image of Nietzsche in the West is of the great iconoclast, the revolutionary who proclaims the death of God and calls for a revaluation of all values. This image tends, however, to obscure an important aspect of his thought that is in fact quite conservative – and is embodied in the idea that we have a tremendous *responsibility* as participants in a heritage stretching back thousands of years. The Chinese tradition in general, and Confucius in particular, places great emphasis on the individual's indebtedness to the ancestors, an acknowledgment of which is a necessary condition of the full realization of one's humanity and of appropriate, creative activity in the present.

To fully realize one's humanity (*ren*) for Confucius, it is necessary for the individual not only to acknowledge the role of tradition in constituting the self, but also to appropriate the tradition creatively, to help "broaden the Way (*dao*)." Central to this task is somatic *practice* as exemplified in ritual activity as an outgrowth of sacred ceremony (*li*) – this emphasis on physical discipline and refinement being characteristic of the East Asian tradition in general (and of Japanese culture in particular). The idea of a responsibility stretching far back into the past is one that is developed in Nietzsche's works from the time of *The Gay Science*, but it is given an especially forceful formulation in the section entitled "Skirmishes of an Untimely One" in *Twilight of the Idols*. In this section Nietzsche (whose putative individualism caused such an uproar in China and Japan) emphasizes that the "individual" is an *error*: "he is nothing in himself, not an atom, not a 'link in the chain,' not something merely inherited from the past – he is the entire line of humanity all the way up to himself" (§ 33). His criticism of modernity stresses the shortsighted irresponsibility of its proponents, who lack "the will to tradition, to authority, to a responsibility ranging over centuries" (§ 39). But the most Confucian feature of this line of thinking is its somatic-accented conclusion, in which Nietzsche argues that beauty is, like genius, "the final result of the accumulated labor of generations" (§ 47).

Everything good is the result of inheritance; what is not inherited is incomplete, a mere beginning ... But one must not misunderstand the method: a mere disciplining of feelings and thoughts amounts to almost nothing ... one must first persuade the *body*. ... It is decisive for the fate of peoples and humanity that one begins inculcating culture in the *proper* place – *not* in the "soul" ... the proper place is the body, gestures, diet, physiology; the *rest* will follow.

Nietzsche sees that lesson as having been forgotten after the age of the Greeks; but the same teaching of Confucius continues to be followed to this day in various spheres of Chinese and Japanese culture.

One other Confucian idea deserves mention in this context, the notion of "reciprocity" (*shu*) that informs Confucius's understanding of the central virtue of "human-heartedness" (*ren*). Confucius frequently exhorts people "not to impose on others what one does not oneself desire," but the theme is best expressed by the following passage from the *Analects* (7/22): "When walking in the company of two other men, I am bound to be able to learn from them. The good points of the one I emulate; the bad points of the other I correct *in myself*" (emphasis added). This "reflective" turn to one's own case first – a theme that runs throughout the *Analects* – has its counterparts in the Christian tradition (the mote in the other person's eye), and especially in Montaigne (from whom Nietzsche learned a great deal).³⁸ But it is easily overlooked in Nietzsche's thinking. Something similar to the Confucian technique is to be found in Zarathustra's love for his fellow human beings, a "great love" that is intimately bound up with the "great contempt," and which is impossible to attain unless one has learned both to love and despise *oneself* first. Zarathustra's almost fatal nausea at the prospect of the eternal recurrence of the rabble is thus prompted as much by the rabble within his own most comprehensive soul as by the "other."³⁹

Similarly, one can obviate misunderstanding of the role of the *evil* that Zarathustra believes needs to be cultivated if human existence is to be enhanced – the theme in Nietzsche his detractors most love to hate – if one sees it in the light of Confucian reciprocity. The cruelty and violence that are said to be necessary elements in the "great economy" are to be practiced on oneself first, before one would have the right to inflict them on others: and such cruelty may be necessary for true creativity.⁴⁰ This is not to deny that one might, for Nietzsche, have earned the right to be hard on others after whipping oneself into shape – just as Confucius was well known for his sternness toward any disciple who was not exerting himself fully.

After Confucius came the two greatest philosophers of Daoism, known as Laozi and Zhuangzi (Chuang Tzu), who filled what they saw as a lacuna in Confucian thought by bringing in the world of nature for philosophical consideration. While the tone of the classic attributed to Laozi, the *Dao de jing*, harmonizes more with Heidegger's thinking, the longer and more complex text of the *Zhuangzi* resonates profoundly with Nietzsche's styles and ideas.[41] Both works are regarded as gems of classical Chinese literature as well as thought. The *Zhuangzi* was highly regarded by the Chinese Buddhist thinkers, especially those of the Chan School, and thereby became equally important for the development of Japanese Zen, and of the Rinzai School in particular. (Several of the great modern Japanese thinkers acknowledge a debt to Zhuangzi, including Nishida, Kuki Shūzō, and Nishitani.)

The *Zhuangzi* is a composite text, only the seven "Inner Chapters" of which are held to have been composed by the historical Zhuangzi, the remaining twenty-six chapters being supplements from the hands of later Daoist thinkers. The Inner Chapters themselves are a riot of styles and modes of discourse, similar in many ways to Nietzsche's multifarious stylistic experiments. In some ways Zhuangzi is the Chinese Heraclitus: though perhaps not quite as obscure as his Ephesian counterpart, and a whole lot more cheerful, Zhuangzi shares a number of structural similarities with that dark thinker and is every bit as deep. But the similarities with Nietzsche run deeper, and anyone familiar with *Thus Spoke Zarathustra* in particular will feel quite at home navigating through the complexities of the *Zhuangzi* (substituting the figure of Confucius for that of Jesus in *Zarathustra* and of Socrates in Nietzsche's other works).[42]

In the Japanese philosophical tradition, where Confucian and Daoist ideas have played an important role, there have also been several Zen Buddhist thinkers whose ideas are comparable with Nietzsche's – especially with respect to their affirmation of this very life. The thirteenth-century Zen master Dōgen, whom the Sōtō school regards as its founder, is a profound and subtle thinker who effected an iconoclastic revolution in a writing style that is comparable to Nietzsche's. Dōgen's texts are not only pervaded by highly poetic imagery but are so dense as to resist easy understanding – especially on the topic that is considered by many to be his most original: his conception of temporality. It is in this area, where the experience of the moment is crucial, that readers may find an acquaintance with Nietzsche's ideas about time to be of some help.[43]

There are resonances, too, between Nietzsche and the eponymous founder of the other major school of Zen, Rinzai, as well as with the greatest of Rinzai Zen's later representatives, the eighteenth-century master Hakuin. Practitioners of the Rinzai school tend to be the most dynamic and wild of the Zen tradition, vehemently rejecting what they deride as "dead sitting and silent illumination" in favor of "practice in the midst of activity." They are also the most concerned with retaining and cultivating the energies of the emotions and passions within what Nietzsche calls the "great economy," the common goal being transmutation of the passions rather than their annihilation. The unbridled style of the writings of Hakuin in particular, whose lifelong struggles with "Zen sickness" (illness stemming from Zen practice) are uncannily parallel with Nietzsche's bouts, matches the hyperbolic extravagance of the latter's styles.[44]

This is surely a most fertile field for Nietzsche studies, the common ground between the hermit of Sils-Maria and the life-artist-sages from the Chan and Zen traditions. The first wave of Zen to reach Western shores struck mainly *littérateurs* and religious types; now that Nietzsche is finally coming into his own is the time for a more philosophical engagement with thinkers of those Asian traditions, in which dialogue based on correspondences between both sides aims at precise elucidation of the divergences. Time, finally, for more of us to cast a trans-European eye over Nietzsche's legacy, entertain East-Asian perspectives on his person and work, and let his example be a stimulus to reconsider – as "good cosmopolitans" – our own philosophical traditions in relation to those of China and Japan.

NOTES

1 The first book to discuss Nietzsche in relation to Indian thought is Max Ladner, *Nietzsche und der Buddhismus* (Zürich, 1933). This is sadly a quirky work, written from a partisan, quasi-Buddhist standpoint and with an interpretation of Nietzsche that is unsympathetic to the point of perversity. Much more worthwhile is the thorough study by Freny Mistry, *Nietzsche and Buddhism* (Berlin and New York, 1981), the aim of which is "to investigate the proximity of spiritual outlook in Nietzsche and the Buddha, both of whom, despite marked differences in expression and perspective, showed complementary ways to self-redemption" (p. 4). The book focuses almost exclusively on early (Theravada or Hīnayāna) Buddhism, rather than the Mahāyāna tradition that was developed later in India, China, and Japan.

2 An interesting anthology of writings on China from the pens of German thinkers from Leibniz to Jaspers is Adrian Hsia, ed., *Deutsche Denker über China* (Frankfurt, 1985).

3 See Johann Figl, "Nietzsche's Early Encounters with Asian Thought," in Graham Parkes, ed., *Nietzsche and Asian Thought* (Chicago, 1991), 51–63. (Subsequent references to be abbreviated "NAT.")

4 See Mervyn Sprung, "Nietzsche's Trans-European Eye," in NAT 76–90.

5 See Michel Hulin, "Nietzsche and the Suffering of the Indian Ascetic," in NAT 64–75, as well as the essay by Sprung.

6 Letter to Paul Deussen, 3 January 1888. This passage is all the more remarkable in the light of Nietzsche's frequently callous condescension toward the Schopenhauerian Deussen after his (Nietzsche's) break with Wagner and his former intellectual mentor. For a fine analysis of the strange ambivalence that has informed the reception of Indian philosophy in modern Europe, see Roger-Pol Droit, *L'oubli de l'Inde: Une amnésie philosophique* (Paris, 1989).

7 See Eberhard Scheiffele, "Questioning One's 'Own' from the Perspective of the Foreign," in NAT 31–47.

8 KSA 11, 26[317]; 1884.

9 Nietzsche's remark is probably based on a translation of the *Laozi* that was published in Leipzig in 1870: *Lao-Tse's Tao Te King*, aus dem Chinesischen ins Deutsche übersetzt, eingeleitet und commentiert von Victor Von Strauss. This is also the translation Heidegger cites, in one of his rare references to Daoist ideas, in "Grundsätze des Denkens," *Jahrbuch für Psychologie und Psychotherapie* 6 (1958): 33–41.

10 Letter to Peter Gast, 31 May 1888.

11 In *Toward the Genealogy of Morals* Nietzsche mentions "Japanese nobility" in connection with the first occurrence of the infamous "blond beast" (I, 11); and in *Beyond Good and Evil* he mentions "the Japanese of today, flocking to tragedies" among examples of the drive for cruelty (229). It is interesting that both references to the Japanese should be in the context of the "savage cruel beast," insofar as Nietzsche's claim that "higher culture" is based on "the spiritualization and deepening of *cruelty*" would apply especially well to the case of Japanese culture.

Reinhart von Seydlitz, a German aristocrat, was a painter and writer and a keen Japanophile. In 1888 he received a letter from the Japanese Emperor thanking him for his services to the cause of disseminating understanding of Japanese culture (see Nietzsche's letter to his mother of 30 August 1888).

12 Letter to Elisabeth Förster of 20 December 1885. The letter carries an amusing postscript: "Why don't you [and Bernhard] go to Japan? The cost of living is low and life there is so much fun!" While Nietzsche would

probably have enjoyed living in Japan (given a suitable climate), the idea of the Försters' establishing their pure Aryan colony there is hard to countenance.

13 For a more detailed discussion, see Graham Parkes, "From Nationalism to Nomadism: Wondering about the Languages of Philosophy," in Eliot Deutsch, ed., *Culture and Modernity: East and West* (Honolulu, 1991), 455–67.

14 One figure in India who was deeply influenced by Nietzsche was the Islamic thinker and poet Mohammad Iqbal; see Subhash C. Kashyap, *The Unknown Nietzsche* (Delhi, 1970), and R. A. Nicholson's introduction to his translation of Iqbal's most Nietzschean work, *Secrets of the Self* (Lahore, 1944). For a brief overview of the global reach of Nietzsche's influence, see "The Orientation of the Nietzschean Text," in NAT 3–19.

15 For a more detailed account, see Graham Parkes, "The Early Reception of Nietzsche's Philosophy in Japan," in NAT 177–99.

16 Chinese and Japanese names are given in the East Asian order, with the family name first, followed by the given name(s).

17 See David Kelly, "The Highest Chinadom: Nietzsche and the Chinese Mind, 1907–1989," in NAT 151–74. For a recent account from a conservative Chinese perspective, see Yue Daiyun, "Nietzsche in China," *Journal of the Oriental Society of Australia* 20 and 21 (1990).

18 When asked about the restrictions on teaching such figures as Nietzsche and Heidegger in university courses after 1949, one of mainland China's foremost experts in German philosophy recounted how, after what he referred to (with a leaven of irony) as "the liberation of the country," it was permissible to discuss their works in his courses – but only *"mit Kritik,"* of course. Nowadays, he said, he was free to teach such thinkers without bothering with the *Kritik* at all.

19 Watsuji Tetsurō, *Nīchie kenkyū*, in *Watsuji Tetsurō zenshū* (Tokyo, 1961), vol. 1, 41. The translation is by David Gordon, to whom I am grateful for making available his translation of the first two chapters of Watsuji's study.

20 Watsuji, *Kōdō* [Memoranda] (Tokyo, 1965), 281–2. I am grateful to David Gordon for bringing these notes to my attention, and have again borrowed his translations.

21 *Philosophy in the Tragic Age of the Greeks*, § 5, and Schopenhauer, *The World as Will and Representation* I, § 3.

22 For an account of the important – and generally neglected – role played by imagination, or phantasy, in Nietzsche's philosophy, see Graham Parkes, *Composing the Soul: Reaches of Nietzsche's Psychology* (Chicago, 1994), chapter eight.

23 It is highly probable that Heidegger's personal association with such thinkers as Tanabe and Nishitani had a significant influence on the development of his thought; see Graham Parkes, "Heidegger and Japanese Philosophy: How Much Did He Know, and When Did He Know It?" in Christopher Macann, ed., *Heidegger: Critical Assessments* (London, 1992), vol. 4, pp. 377–406.

24 Nishitani Keiji, "Nīchie no Tsuaratsusutora to Maisutā Ekkuharuto," in *Shūkyō to bunka* (Religion and culture) (Tokyo, 1940).

25 Nishitani Keiji, "Watakushi no seishun jidai," in *Kaze no kokoro* (Heart in/of the wind) (Tokyo, 1980).

26 Nishitani, "The Days of my Youth," cited in the translator's introduction to Nishitani Keiji, *Religion and Nothingness*, trans. Jan Van Bragt (Berkeley, 1982), xxxv (hereafter abbreviated as "RN"). See also Nishitani's account of his early development in his *Nishida Kitarō*, trans. Yamamoto Seisaku and James W. Heisig (Berkeley, 1991), 3–9. He speaks there of being stimulated by Watsuji's study of Nietzsche to learn German – so as to be able to read *Thus Spoke Zarathustra*, which he read "over and over."

27 Nishitani, "Watakushi no tetsugakuteki hossokuten" (My philosophical starting point), as translated by Van Bragt in RN, xxxiv–xxxv. Later in this essay he writes of his enthusiastic reading of Plotinus, Eckhart, Boehme, and the later Schelling. In "The Days of My Youth," Nishitani mentions his avid readings of Tolstoy, Ibsen, and Strindberg, as well as of Nietzsche's *Thus Spoke Zarathustra*. In a conversation in Kyoto in 1988, Nishitani said that as a young man he used to carry *Zarathustra* around with him wherever he went: "It was like my Bible."

28 The breadth and depth of Nishitani's understanding of the history of Western philosophy is evidenced by his treatment (in the third section of his essay on Eckhart and Nietzsche's Zarathustra) of the various intellectual currents that fed into Meister Eckhart's thinking. The benefits of hermeneutic distance are manifested especially by Nishitani's discussion of the history of European nihilism in *The Self-Overcoming of Nihilism*, trans. Graham Parkes with Setsuko Aihara (Albany, 1990) – hereafter "SN" – which will be discussed shortly.

29 "Nīchie no Tsuaratsusutora to Maisutā Ekkuharuto," 4–6; draft translation by David Gordon. Nishitani acknowledges Watsuji's study of Nietzsche as a major influence.

30 For example (aside from images mentioned by Nishitani): in attempting to characterize the abyss of Godhead (*Gottheit*), Eckhart speaks of it as "the ground, the soil, the stream, the source of Godhead" (Josef Quint, ed., *Deutsche Predigten und Traktate*, Predigt 26). He speaks also of God's great "joy in giving, insofar as he wants the soul to widen itself, so

that it can receive *much* and He can give *much* to the soul" (Predigt 36). In *Zarathustra*, abysmally deep life as will to power would correspond to Godhead in Eckhart – as suggested by Eckhart's own remark that "life lives from out of its own ground and wells up out of its Own [*aus seinem Eigenen*]" (Predigt 6).

31 Nishitani went on to write a great deal more on Eckhart, and his work has been a major basis of the widespread view among Japanese philosophers that, of all the thinkers the West has produced, it is Eckhart who is closest to the spirit of Zen.

32 KSA 11, 25[158]; literally translated: "I fate," or "I, something fated." Nietzsche's ideas about fate were deeply influenced by his reading of Emerson's essay "Fate" at the age of seventeen. Emerson's general influence on Nietzsche's thinking is considerable; see the many references to Emerson in *Composing the Soul*.

33 *Thus Spoke Zarathustra*, III.14; also I.22, §1 and III.12, §30. Kaufmann's translation of *Wende der Not* as "cessation of need" misses the point of the *turn* – though it is preferable to Hollingdale's rendering, "Dispeller of Care."

34 It should be mentioned that "The Self-Overcoming of Nihilism" was only a section heading in the original text, the title of which was simply *Nihilism*. However, Nishitani approved the choice of the longer English title as conveying the main idea of the book. The phrase apparently occurs only in a rather obscure note in the *Nachlass* (XVI, 422 of the *Grossoktavausgabe*).

35 See *The Self-Overcoming of Nihilism*, chapter nine, section 4.

36 Nishitani did concede in private conversation, after reading my essay "Nietzsche and Nishitani on the Self through Time" (*The Eastern Buddhist* 17/2 [1984]), that the parallels between Nietzsche's thinking and his own run farther than he was prepared to allow in *Religion and Nothingness*. Some related themes are discussed in Graham Parkes, "Nietzsche and Nishitani on the Self-Overcoming of Nihilism," *International Studies in Philosophy* 25/2 (1993): 585–90.

37 For a sketch of how such a comparison would proceed, see Glen T. Martin, "Deconstruction and Breakthrough in Nietzsche and Nāgārjuna," in NAT 91–111.

38 See, especially, Montaigne, *Essays* III: 8 ("On the Art of Discussion"), and the discussion of this technique in *Composing the Soul*, "Interlude 2 – The Psychical Feminine."

39 At the culmination of a magnificent passage in one of the unpublished notes, Nietzsche writes of how, owing to continual retroflection of the drives upon the self, even such things as "the stock exchange and the newspaper" (!) have become a part of us (KSA 9, 6[80]; 1880).

40 See, for example, *Beyond Good and Evil* 229–30 and *Toward the Genealogy of Morals* II, 18.

41 On the relation of Heidegger's thinking to Daoism, see Otto Pöggeler, "West–East Dialogue: Heidegger and Lao-tzu," in Graham Parkes, ed., *Heidegger and Asian Thought* (Honolulu, 1987), 47–78, and Graham Parkes, "Thoughts on the Way: *Being and Time* via Lao-Chuang," in *Heidegger and Asian Thought*, 105–44.

42 On the relations between Daoism and Nietzsche, see: Graham Parkes, "The Wandering Dance: Chuang-Tzu and Zarathustra," *Philosophy East and West* 29/3 (1983): 235–50, and "Human/Nature in Nietzsche and Taoism," in J. Baird Callicott and Roger T. Ames, eds., *Nature in Asian Traditions of Thought: Essays in Environmental Philosophy* (Albany, 1989), 79–98; also Roger T. Ames, "Nietzsche's 'Will to Power' and Chinese 'Virtuality' (*De*): A Comparative Study," and Chen Guying, "Zhuangzi and Nietzsche: Plays of Perspectives," in NAT 130–50 and 115–29 respectively. A recent book on the topic of Nietzsche in China – Cheng Fang, *Nicai zai zhong guo* (Nanjing, 1992) – discusses the "Wandering Dance" essay, which appeared in Chinese translation in an anthology on Daoism and culture. After quoting the essay's final paragraph, the author writes: "It is surely not easy for a foreigner to make such progress along this path [of comparing Nietzsche and Zhuangzi], and the comparison he carries out is most impressive in its details" (pp. 385–6). I mention this less out of a desire for self-aggrandizement than as evidence of the effectiveness of Nietzsche as a way into classical Daoist thinking, insofar as the essay was my first philosophical foray into the world of Zhuangzi, aided by a minimal acquaintance with the Chinese language and the kind assistance of a colleague familiar with the original text. To the extent that the comparison worked, it was on the basis of a fairly sound grasp of Nietzsche. (Indeed, if this entire essay reads like an exercize in self-aggrandizement, with its frequent references to my own writings, this is owing to a general paucity of work in this field.)

43 The interpretation offered by Joan Stambaugh in her *Nietzsche's Thought of Eternal Return* (Baltimore, 1972) is in many respects reminiscent of Dōgen. Her recent book *Impermanence is Buddha-Nature: Dōgen's Understanding of Temporality* (Honolulu, 1990) proceeds from the eminently sensible premise that to adduce some ideas from appropriate Western thinkers may help one "use what is more familiar and better understood as a bridge to what at first would appear to most Western readers . . . as simply unintelligible" (p. 3). However, the subsequent brief discussion of Nietzsche's ideas fails to pursue the parallels, in my opinion, as far as they might helpfully go. Her reason for not taking them further – that Nietzsche "still retains remnants of substantializing and objectifying

tendencies in his thought" (p. 41) – fails to do justice to the extent to which the thought of recurrence not only subverts the idea of duration but also shatters the substantiality of any self or thing that might be said to recur.

44 For a sketch of a comparison, see Graham Parkes, "Nietzsche and Zen Master Hakuin on the Roles of Emotion and Passion," in Joel Marks and Roger T. Ames, eds., *Emotions in Asian Thought: A Dialogue in Comparative Philosophy* (Albany, 1994), 213–233.

SELECTED BIBLIOGRAPHY

NIETZSCHE'S WORKS: GERMAN EDITIONS

Kritische Gesamtausgabe: Briefwechsel. Edited by Giorgio Colli and Mazzino Montinari. Berlin: De Gruyter, 1975 onward.
Kritische Gesamtausgabe: Werke. Edited by Giorgio Colli and Mazzino Montinari. Berlin: De Gruyter, 1967 onward.
Werke in Drei Bänden. 3 vols. Edited by Karl Schlechta. 3rd edition. Munich: Carl Hansers, 1965.

ENGLISH TRANSLATIONS

Multiple works

Basic Writings of Nietzsche. Translated and edited with commentaries by Walter Kaufmann. New York: The Modern Library, 1968.
A Nietzsche Reader. Edited and translated by R. J. Hollingdale. Harmondsworth: Penguin, 1977.
Nietzsche: Selections. Ed. Richard Schacht. New York: Macmillan, 1993.
The Poetry of Friedrich Nietzsche. Edited by Grundlehner, Philip. Oxford: Oxford University Press, 1986.
The Portable Nietzsche. Translated and edited by Walter Kaufmann. New York: Viking, 1954.

Individual works

Beyond Good and Evil. Translated by R. J. Hollingdale. Harmondsworth: Penguin, 1961.
Beyond Good and Evil. Translated by Walter Kaufmann. New York: Vintage, 1966.
The Birth of Tragedy (with *The Case of Wagner*). Translated by Walter Kaufmann. New York: Vintage, 1966.

385

The Case of Wagner (with *The Birth of Tragedy*). Translated by Walter Kaufmann. New York: Vintage, 1966.

Daybreak: Thoughts on the Prejudices of Morality. Translated by R. J. Hollingdale. Cambridge: Cambridge University Press, 1982.

Ecce Homo. Translated by Walter Kaufmann. (With *On the Genealogy of Morals*, translated by Walter Kaufmann and R. J. Hollingdale). New York: Vintage, 1967.

The Gay Science. Translated by Walter Kaufmann. New York: Vintage, 1974.

Human, All Too Human. Translated by R. J. Hollingdale. Cambridge: Cambridge University Press, 1986.

Human, All Too Human. Volume I. Translated by Marion Faber, with Stephen Lehmann. Lincoln: University of Nebraska Press, 1984.

Nietzsche contra Wagner. Translated by Walter Kaufmann. In *The Portable Nietzsche*, edited by Walter Kaufmann. New York: Viking, 1954.

On the Advantage and Disadvantage of History for Life. Translated by Peter Preuss. Indianapolis, Ind.: Hackett, 1980.

On the Genealogy of Morals. Translated by Walter Kaufmann and R. J. Hollingdale. (Together with *Ecce Homo*, translated by Walter Kaufmann). New York: Vintage, 1967.

Philosophy in the Tragic Age of the Greeks. Translated by Marianne Cowan. South Bend, Indiana: Gateway, 1962.

Thus Spoke Zarathustra. Translated by R. J. Hollingdale. Harmondsworth: Penguin, 1973.

Thus Spoke Zarathustra. Translated by Walter Kaufmann. In *The Portable Nietzsche*, edited by Walter Kaufmann. New York: Viking, 1954.

Twilight of the Idols. Translated by Walter Kaufmann. In *The Portable Nietzsche*, edited by Walter Kaufmann. New York: Viking, 1954.

Unmodern Observations. Edited by William Arrowsmith. New Haven: Yale University Press, 1990.

Untimely Meditations. Translated by R. J. Hollingdale. Cambridge: Cambridge University Press, 1983.

Unfashionable Observations. Translated by Richard Gray. Stanford: Stanford University Press, 1995.

Letters and unpublished works

Nietzsche: A Self-Portrait from His Letters. Eds. Peter Fuss and Henry Sharpio. Cambridge: Harvard University Press, 1971.

Nietzsche on Rhetoric and Language. Ed. and trans. Sander L. Gilman, Carole Blair, and David J. Parent. New York: Oxford University Press, 1989.

Nietzsche: Unpublished Letters. Edited and translated by Kurt F. Leidecker. New York: Philosophical Library, 1959.

Philosophy and Truth: Selections from Nietzsche's Notebooks of the Early 1870's. Edited and translated by Daniel Breazeale. Atlantic Highlands, New Jersey: Humanities Press, 1979.

Selected Letters of Friedrich Nietzsche. Edited and translated by Christopher Middleton. Chicago: University of Chicago Press, 1969.

The Will to Power. Translated by Walter Kaufmann and R. J. Hollingdale. New York: Vintage, 1967.

BIOGRAPHIES AND GENERAL SURVEYS

Ansell-Pearson, Keith. *Nietzsche and Modern German Thought*. New York: Routledge, 1991.

Behler, Ernst. *Confrontations*. Trans. Steven Taubeneck. Stanford: Stanford University Press, 1991.

Breazeale, Daniel. "Ecce Psycho: Remarks on the Case of Nietzsche." *International Studies in Philosophy* 23, 2 (1991): 19–34.

Clark, Maudemarie. *Nietzsche on Truth and Philosophy*. Cambridge: Cambridge University Press, 1990.

Cooper, David E. *Authenticity and Learning: Nietzsche's Educational Philosophy*. Brookfield, Vermont: Avebury, 1991.

Copelston, Frederick, S. J. *Friedrich Nietzsche: Philosopher of Culture*. New York: Barnes and Noble, 1975.

Danto, Arthur. *Nietzsche As Philosopher*. New York: Macmillan, 1965.

Fink, Eugen. *Nietzsches Philosophie*. 3rd rev. ed. Stuttgart: W. Kohlhammer, 1973.

Gilman, Sander L., ed. *Conversations with Nietzsche*. Trans. David Parent. New York: Oxford University Press, 1987.

Hayman, Ronald. *Nietzsche: A Critical Life*. New York: Oxford University Press, 1980.

Heidegger, Martin. *Nietzsche*. 2 vols. Pfullingen: Neske, 1961. Trans. David Farrell Krell. 4 vols. New York: Harper and Row, 1979–86.

The Question Concerning Technology, trans. William Lovitt. New York: Harper Colophon Books, 1977.

Hollingdale, R. J. *Nietzsche*. London and New York: Routledge and Kegan Paul, 1973.

Nietzsche, the Man and His Philosophy. Baton Rouge: Louisiana State University Press, 1965.

Hollinrake, Roger. *Nietzsche, Wagner and the Philosophy of Pessimism*. London: George Allen and Unwin, 1982.

Janz, Curt Paul. *Friedrich Nietzsche Biographie.* 3 vols. Munich: Carl Hanser, 1979.

Jaspers Karl. *Nietzche, An Introduction to the Understanding of His Philosophical Activity,* trans. Charles F. Wallraff and Frederick J. Schmitz. Tucson: University of Arizona Press, 1965.

Kaufmann, Walter. *Nietzsche: Philosopher, Psychologist, Antichrist.* 4th ed., rev. and enlarged. New York: Vintage, 1974.

Lavrin, Janko. *Nietzsche: A Biographical Introduction.* New York: Charles Scribner's Sons, 1972.

Nietzsche and Modern Consciousness. New York: Haskell House Publishers, 1973.

Lea, F. A. *The Tragic Philosopher: A Study of Friedrich Nietzsche.* London: Methuen, 1957; New York: Barnes and Noble, 1973.

Magnus, Bernd. With Jean-Pierre Mileur, Stanley Stewart. *Nietzsche's Case: Philosophy as/and Literature.* New York: Routledge, 1993.

Morgan, George. *What Nietzsche Means.* New York: Harper Torchbooks, 1965 (1941).

Nehamas, Alexander. *Nietzsche: Life as Literature.* Cambridge, Massachusetts: Harvard University Press, 1985.

Ogilvy, James. *Many Dimensional Man: Decentralizing Self, Society, and the Sacred.* New York: Oxford University Press, 1977.

Parkes, Graham. *Composing the Soul: Reaches of Nietzsche's Psychology.* Chicago and London: University of Chicago Press, 1994.

Pfeffer, Rose. *Nietzsche: Disciple of Dionysus.* Lewisburg: Bucknell University Press, 1972.

Pletsch, Carl. *Young Nietzsche: Becoming a Genius.* New York: Free Press, 1991.

Salomé, Lou Andreas. *Friedrich Nietzsche in seinen Werken.* Vienna: Konegen, 1911.

Salomé, Lou. *Nietzsche.* Edited and translated by Siegfried Mandel. Redding Ridge, Connecticut: Black Swan Books, 1988.

Schacht, Richard. *Nietzsche.* London: Routledge and Kegan Paul, 1983.

Simmel, Georg. *Schopenhauer and Nietzsche.* Trans. Helmut Loiskandle, Deena Weinstein, and Michael Weinstein. Urbana and Chicago: University of Illinois Press, 1991.

Stack, George J. *Nietzsche and Emerson: An Elective Affinity.* Athens: Ohio University Press, 1992.

Stern, J. P. *Nietzsche.* Glasgow: William Collins Sons, 1978.

A Study of Nietzsche. Cambridge: Cambridge University Press, 1979.

Solomon, Robert C., editor. *Nietzsche: A Collection of Critical Essays.* New York: Doubleday, 1973.

Stack, George J. *Nietzsche: Man, Knowledge, and Will to Power.* Wolfeboro, New Hampshire: Longwood Press, 1991.

CLASSICS AND ANTIQUITY

Ackermann, Robert John. *Nietzsche: A Frenzied Look*. Amherst: University of Massachusetts Press, 1990.

Calder, William Musgrave III. "The Wilamowitz-Nietzsche Struggle: New Documents and a Reappraisal," *Nietzsche-Studien* 12 (1983): 214–54.

Dannhauser, Werner J. *Nietzsche's View of Socrates*. Ithaca: Cornell University Press, 1974.

Grant, George. "Nietzsche and the Ancients: Philosophy and Scholarship," *Dionysius* 3 (1979): 5–16.

O'Flaherty, James, Timothy F. Sellner and Robert M. Helm. *Studies in Nietzsche and the Classical Tradition*. Chapel Hill: University of North Carolina Press, 1976. Second ed., Chapel Hill, 1979.

Silk, M. S. and J. P. Stern. *Nietzsche on Tragedy*. London: Cambridge University Press, 1981.

Small, Robin. "Nietzsche and the Platonist Tradition of the Cosmos: Center Everywhere and Circumference Nowhere." *Journal of the History of Ideas* 44 (January–March 1983): 89–104.

Tejera, N. *Nietzsche and Greek Thought*. The Hague: Nijhoff, 1987.

EPISTEMOLOGY, METAPHYSICS, AND PHILOSOPHY
OF SCIENCE

Breazeale, Daniel. "Lange, Nietzsche, and Stack: The Question of 'Influence.' " *International Studies in Philosophy* 21, 2 (1989): 91–103.

Clark, Maudemarie. *Nietzsche on Truth and Philosophy*. Cambridge: Cambridge University Press, 1990.

Gallo, Beverly E. "On the Question of Nietzsche's 'Scientism.' " *International Studies in Philosophy* 22, 2 (1990): 111–19.

Grimm, Ruediger Hermann. *Nietzsche's Theory of Knowledge*. Berlin: Walter de Gruyter, 1977.

Moles, Alistair. *Nietzsche's Philosophy of Nature and Cosmology*. New York: Peter Lang, 1990.

Wilcox, John. "The Birth of Nietzsche Out of the Spirit of Lange." *International Studies in Philosophy* 21, 2 (1989): 81–9.

Truth and Value in Nietzsche: A Study of His Metaethics and Epistemology. Ann Arbor: University of Michigan, 1974.

ETERNAL RECURRENCE, GENEALOGY, THE ÜBERMENSCH,
AND WILL TO POWER

Bergoffen, Debra B. "The Eternal Recurrence Again." *International Studies in Philosophy* 15, 2 (1983): 35–46.

Foucault, Michel. "Nietzsche, Genealogy, History." In *Language, Counter-Memory, Practice.* Trans. Donald F. Bouchard and Sherry Simon. Ithaca, New York: Cornell University Press, 1977.

Golomb, Jacob. *Nietzsche's Enticing Philosophy of Power.* Ames: Iowa State University Press, 1989.

Hatab, Lawrence J. *Nietzsche and Eternal Recurrence: The Redemption of Time and Becoming.* Washington, D.C.: University Press of America, 1978.

Löwith, Karl. *Nietzsches Philosophie der Ewigen Wiederkehr des Gleichen.* 3rd rev. ed. Hamburg: Felix Meiner, 1978.

Magnus, Bernd. "Author, Writer, Text: *The Will to Power.*" *International Studies in Philosophy* 22, 2 (1990): 49–57.

"Eternal Recurrence." *Nietzsche-Studien* 8 (1979): 362-377.

Nietzsche's Existential Imperative. Bloomington: Indiana University Press, 1978.

"Nietzsche's Philosophy in 1888: *The Will to Power* and the *Übermensch.*" Journal of the History of Philosophy 24/1 (January, 1986): 79–98.

"Perfectability and Attitude in Nietzsche's *Übermensch.*" *Review of Metaphysics* 36 (March 1983): 633–60.

Small, Robin. "Three Interpretations of Eternal Recurrence." *Dialogue, Canadian Philosophical Review* 22 (1983): 21–112.

Stambaugh, Joan. *Nietzsche's Thought of Eternal Return.* Baltimore: Johns Hopkins University Press, 1972.

The Problem of Time in Nietzsche. Philadelphia: Bucknell University Press, 1987.

Zimmerman, Michael E. "Heidegger and Nietzsche on Authentic Time." *Cultural Hermeneutics* 4 (July 1977): 239–64.

FEMINIST PERSPECTIVES ON NIETZSCHE

Bertram, Maryanne J. "God's Second Blunder – Serpent Woman and the Gestalt in Nietzsche's Thought." *Southern Journal of Philosophy* 19 (Fall 1981): 252–78.

Diethe, Carol. "Nietzsche and the Woman Question." *History of European Ideas* (1989): 865–76.

Frisby, Sandy. "Woman and the Will to Power." *Gnosis* 1 (Spring 1975): 1–10.

Graybeal, Jean. *Language and "The Feminine" in Nietzsche and Heidegger.* Bloomington: Indiana University Press, 1990.

Hatab, Lawrence J. "Nietzsche on Woman." *Southern Journal of Philosophy* 19 (Fall, 1981): 333–46.

Irigaray, Luce. *Marine Lover of Friedrich Nietzsche.* Trans. Gilliam C. Gill. New York: Columbia University Press, 1991.

Kennedy, Ellen, and Susan Mendus, eds. *Women in Western Philosophy: Kant to Nietzsche*. New York: St. Martin's Press, 1987.

Krell, David Farrell. *Postponements: Woman, Sensuality, and Death in Nietzsche*. Bloomington: Indiana University Press, 1986.

Oliver, Kelly A. "Nietzsche's 'Women': Poststructuralist Attempt to Do Away with Women." *Radical Philosophy* 48 (Spring 1988): 25–9.

"Woman as Truth in Nietzsche's Writing." *Social Theory and Practice* 10 (Summer 1984): 185–99.

Parsons, Katherine Pyne. "Nietzsche and Moral Change." In Robert C. Solomon, ed. *Nietzsche: A Collection of Critical Essays*. Garden City: Doubleday, 1973; reissued, Notre Dame: University of Notre Dame Press, 1980, pp. 169–93.

Platt, Michael. "Woman, Nietzsche, and Nature." *Maieutics* 2 (Winter 1981): 27–42.

Tomas, R. Hinton. "Nietzsche, Women and the Whip." *German Life and Letters: Special Number for L. W. Forester* 34 (1980): 117–25.

INDIVIDUAL WORKS

Bennholdt-Thomsen, Anke. *Nietzsches Also Sprach Zarathustra als Literarisches Phänomen*. Rev. ed. Frankfurt am Main: Athenäum, 1974.

Clark, Maudemarie. "Deconstructing *The Birth of Tragedy*." *International Studies in Philosophy* 19, 2 (1987): 67–75.

Gadamer, Hans-Georg. "Das Drama Zarathustras." *Nietzsche Studien* 15 (1986): 1–15.

Goicoechea, David. *The Great Year of Zarathustra (1881–1981)*. Lanham: University Press of America, 1983.

Gooding-Williams, Robert. "The Drama of Nietzsche's *Zarathustra*: Intention, Repetition, Prelude." *International Studies in Philosophy* 20, 2 (1988): 105–16.

Heidegger, Martin. "Who is Nietzsche's Zarathustra?" trans. Bernd Magnus. In *The New Nietzsche: Contemporary Styles of Interpretation*, ed. David B. Allison. New York: Delta, 1977, pp. 64–79.

Higgins, Kathleen Marie. *Nietzsche's "Zarathustra."* Philadelphia: Temple University Press, 1987.

"Zarathustra is a Comic Book." *Philosophy and Literature* 16 (April 1992): 1–14.

Jung, Carl G. *Nietzsche's "Zarathustra."* Ed. James L. Jarrett. Princeton: Princeton University Press, 1988.

Kofman, Sarah. *Explosion I: de l'Ecce Homo de Nietzsche*. Trans. Jessica George, David Blacker, and Judith Rowan. Paris: Galilée, 1991.

Lambert, Laurence. *Nietzsche's Teaching: An Interpretation of "Thus Spoke Zarathustra."* New Haven: Yale University Press, 1987.

Rethy, Robert A. "The Tragic Affirmation of *The Birth of Tragedy.*" *Nietzsche-Studien* 17 (1988): 1–44.

Sallis, John C. *Crossings: Nietzsche and the Space of Tragedy.* Chicago: University of Chicago Press, 1991.

Schacht, Richard. "Nietzsche on Art in *The Birth of Tragedy.*" In *Aesthetics: A Critical Anthology*, edited by Dickie and Sclafani. New York: Saint Martin's Press, 1977, 268–312.

Nietzsche, Genealogy, Morality: Essays on Nietzsche's "On the Genealogy of Morals." Berkeley/Los Angeles/London: University of California Press, 1994.

Solomon, Robert C., and Higgins, Kathleen M., editors. *Reading Nietzsche.* New York: Oxford University Press, 1988.

INFLUENCE AND RECEPTION

Aschheim, Steven E. *The Nietzsche Legacy in Germany, 1890–1990.* Berkeley and Los Angeles: University of California Press, 1993.

Bauschinger, Sigrid, Susan L. Cocalis, and Sara Lennox, eds. *Nietzsche Heute: Die Rezeption seines Werkes nach 1968.* Berlin: Francke Verlag, 1988.

Harrison, Thomas, ed. *Nietzsche in Italy.* Saratoga, California: ANMA Libri, 1988.

Mistry, Freny. *Nietzsche and Buddhism.* New York and Berlin: Walter de Gruyter, 1981.

Nishitani, Keiji. *The Self-Overcoming of Nihilism.* Trans. Graham Parkes with Setsuko Aihara. Albany: State University of New York Press, 1990.

O'Hara, Daniel, ed. *Why Nietzsche Now?* Bloomington: Indiana University Press, 1985.

Parkes, Graham, ed. *Nietzsche and Asian Thought.* Chicago: University of Chicago Press, 1991.

Rickels, Laurence A., ed. *Looking After Nietzsche.* Albany: State University of New York Press, 1990.

Rosenthal, Bernice Glatzer, ed. *Nietzsche in Russia.* Princeton: Princeton University Press, 1986.

Talmor, Ezra and Sascha, eds. *Nietzsche's Influence on Contemporary Thought.* Part Three of *History of European Ideas*, Vol. II (1989). Special Issue. *Turning Points in History* (Oxford: Pergamon Press, 1990): 675–1035.

Thatcher, David S. *Nietzsche in England 1900–1914: The Growth of a Reputation.* Toronto: University of Toronto Press, 1970.

LITERARY INTERPRETATION AND STYLE

Alderman, Harold. *Nietzche's Gift.* Athens: Ohio University Press, 1977.

Allison, David B., ed. *The New Nietzsche: Contemporary Styles of Interpretation.* New York: Dell, 1977.

Ansell-Pearson, Keith, ed. *The Fate of the New Nietzsche.* Brookfield, Vermont: Avebury, 1993.

Babich, Babette E. "On Nietzsche's Concinnity: An Analysis of Style." *Nietzsche-Studien* 19 (1990): 59–80.

"Self-Deconstruction: Nietzsche's Philosophy as Style." *Soundings* 73, 1 (Spring 1990): 107–16.

Bataille, Georges. *On Nietzsche.* London: Athlone, and New York: Paragon House, 1992.

Behler, Ernst. *Confrontations: Derrida, Heidegger, Nietzsche.* Trans. Steven Taubeneck. Stanford: Stanford University Press, 1991.

Irony and the Discourse of Modernity. Seattle: University of Washington Press, 1990.

Blondel, Eric. *Nietzsche, the Body and Culture: Philosophy as a Philological Genealogy.* Trans. Sean Hand. Stanford: Stanford University Press, 1991.

Bloom, Harold, ed. *Friedrich Nietzsche.* New York: Chelsea House, 1987.

Conway, D. W. "Nietzsche's Art of This-Worldly Comfort: Self-Reference and Strategic Self-Parody." *History of Philosophy Quarterly* 9 (July 1992): pp. 343–357.

Conway, D. W., and J. E. Seery, eds. *The Politics of Irony: Essays in Self-Betrayal.* New York: St. Martin's Press, 1992.

Crawford, Claudia. *The Beginnings of Nietzsche's Theory of Language.* Berlin: Walter de Gruyter, 1988.

Del Caro, A. *Nietzsche contra Nietzsche: Creativity and the Anti-Romantic.* Baton Rouge: Louisiana University Press, 1989.

Deleuze, Gilles. *Nietzsche and Philosophy.* Trans. Hugh Tomlinson. New York: Columbia University Press, 1983.

de Man, Paul. *Allegories of Reading: Figural Language in Rousseau, Nietzsche, Rilke, and Proust.* New Haven: Yale University Press, 1979.

Derrida, Jacques. *The Ear of the Other: Otobiography, Transference, Translation.* Ed. Christie V. McDonald. Schocken Books, 1985.

Spurs: Nietzsche's Styles, trans. Barbara Harlow. Chicago: University of Chicago Press, 1979.

Foucault, Michel. "Ecce Homo, or the Written Body." Trans. Judith Still. *Oxford Literary Review* 7, 1–2 (1985): 3–24.

"Nietzsche, Freud, Marx." Trans. John Anderson and Gary Hentzi. *Critical Texts* 3, 2 (1986): 1–5.

Gilman, Sander L. *Nietzschean Parody.* Bonn: Bouvier Verlag, 1976.

Harries, Karsten. "Boundary Disputes." *The Journal of Philosophy* 83 (November, 1986): 676–7.

Heller, Erich. *The Artist's Journey into the Interior and Other Essays.* New York: Vintage, 1968.

The Disinherited Mind. 3rd edition. New York: Barnes and Noble, 1971.

The Importance of Nietzsche. Chicago: University of Chicago Press, 1988.

Heller, Peter. *Dialectics and Nihilism: Essays on Lessing, Nietzsche, Mann, and Kafka.* Amherst, Massachusetts: University of Massachusetts Press, 1966.

Studies in Nietzsche. Bonn: Bouvier, 1980.

Klossowski, Pierre. *Nietzsche and the Vicious Circle.* London: Athlone, 1993.

Koelb, Clayton, ed. *Nietzsche as Postmodernist: Essays Pro and Contra.* Albany, New York: State University of New York Press, 1990.

Kofman, Sarah. *Nietzsche and Metaphor.* London: Athlone; and Stanford: Stanford University Press, 1993.

Krell, David Farrell, and David Wood, eds. *Exceedingly Nietzsche: Aspects of Contemporary Nietzsche Interpretation.* London: Routledge, 1988.

Magnus, Bernd. "The End of 'The End of Philosophy'." In *Hermeneutics and Deconstruction.* Ed. Hugh Silverman. Albany: State University of New York Press, 1985. 2–10.

"Nietzsche and Postmodern Criticism." *Nietzsche-Studien* 18 (1989): 301–16.

Jean-Pierre Mileur, Stanley Stewart. *Nietzsche's Case: Philosophy as/and Literature.* New York: Routledge, 1993.

Miller, J. Hillis. "Ariadne's Thread: Repetition and the Narrative Line." *Critical Inquiry* 3 (Autumn 1976): 57–77.

"The Disarticulation of the Self in Nietzsche." *Monist* 64 (April 1981): 247–61.

Pasley, Malcolm, editor. *Nietzsche: Imagery and Thought.* Berkeley: University of California Press, 1978.

Reichert, Herbert W. *Friedrich Nietzsche's Impact on Modern German Literature.* Chapel Hill: University of North Carolina Press, 1975.

Ronell, Avital. "Queens of the Night: Nietzsche's Antibodies." *Genre* 16 (1983): 404–22.

Rosen, Stanley. "Nietzsche's Image of Chaos." *International Philosophical Quarterly* 20 (1980): 3–23.

Schrift, Alan D. *Nietzsche and the Question of Interpretation: Between Hermeneutics and Deconstruction.* New York: Routledge, 1990.

Shapiro, Gary. *Alcyone: Nietzsche on Gifts, Noise and Women*. Albany: State University of New York Press, 1991.
Nietzschean Narratives. Bloomington: Indiana University Press, 1989.
Staten, Henry. *Nietzsche's Voice*. Ithaca: Cornell University Press, 1990.
Taylor, Mark C. *Deconstruction in Context: Literature and Philosophy*. Chicago: University of Chicago Press, 1986.
Williams, Robert J. "Literary Fiction as Philosophy: The Case of Nietzsche's *Zarathustra*." *The Journal of Philosophy* 83 (November 1986): 667–75.

MORAL THEORY

Ansell-Pearson, Keith. *Nietzsche contra Rousseau: A Study of Nietzsche's Moral and Political Thought*. Cambridge: Cambridge University Press, 1991.
Conway, Daniel. "A Moral Ideal for Everyone and No One." *International Studies in Philosophy* 22, 2 (1990): 17–29.
Cosineau, Robert Henri. *Zarathustra and the Ethical Ideal*. Amsterdam: J. Benjamins, 1991.
Hunt, Lester H. *Nietzsche and the Origin of Virtue*. London: Routledge, 1991.
MacIntyre, Alasdair. *After Virtue: A Study of Moral Theory*. Notre Dame: Notre Dame University Press, 1981.
Scott, Charles E. *The Question of Ethics: Nietzsche, Foucault, Heidegger*. Bloomington: Indiana University Press, 1990.
Seigfried, Hans. "Nietzsche's Natural Morality." *Journal of Value Inquiry* 26 (1992): 423–31.
White, Alan. *Within Nietzsche's Labyrinth*. New York: Routledge, 1990.
Yovel, Yirmiyahu, ed. *Nietzsche as Affirmative Thinker: Papers Presented at the Fifth Jerusalem Philosophical Encounter, April 1983*. Dordrecht: Martinus Nijhoff, 1986.

PHILOSOPHY OF ART/AESTHETICS

Barker, Stephen, *Autoaesthetics: Strategies of the Self after Nietzsche*. Atlantic Highlands, New Jersey: Humanities Press, 1993.
Del Caro, Adrian. *Nietzsche contra Nietzsche: Creativity and the Anti-Romantic*. Baton Rouge: Louisiana State University Press, 1989.
Eagleton, Terry. *The Ideology of the Aesthetic*. Oxford: Basil Blackwell, 1990.
Gillespie, Michael Allen and Tracy B. Strong, eds. *Nietzsche's New Seas: Explorations in Philosophy, Aesthetics, and Politics*. Chicago: University of Chicago Press, 1988.

Schacht, Richard. "Nietzsche's Second Thoughts about Art." *Monist* 64 (April 1981): 241–6.
Stambaugh, Joan. *The Other Nietzsche*. Albany: State University of New York Press, 1993.
Young, Julian. *Nietzsche's Philosophy of Art*. Cambridge: Cambridge University Press, 1992.

PHILOSOPHY OF RELIGION

Geffre, Claude and Jean-Pierre Jossua, eds. *Nietzsche and Christianity*. Edinburgh and New York, 1981.
Jaspers, Karl. *Nietzsche and Christianity*, trans. E. B. Ashton. Chicago: Regnery, 1961.
O'Flaherty, James C., Timothy F. Sellner, and Robert M. Helm, eds. *Studies in Nietzsche and the Judaeo-Christian Tradition*. Chapel Hill: University of North Carolina Press, 1985.

POLITICAL PHILOSOPHY

Bergmann, Peter. *Nietzsche: The Last Antipolitical German*. Bloomington, Indiana: Indiana University Press, 1987.
Bergoffen, Debra B. "Posthumous Popularity: Reading, Privileging, Politicizing Nietzsche." *Soundings* 73, 1 (Spring 1990): 37–60.
Darby, Tom, Béla Egyed and Ben Jones, eds. *Nietzsche and the Rhetoric of Nihilism: Essays on Interpretation, Language, and Politics*. Ottawa: Carleton University Press, 1989.
Detwiler, Bruce. *Nietzsche and the Politics of Aristocratic Radicalism*. Chicago: University of Chicago Press, 1990.
Kuenzli, Rudolf E. "The Nazi Appropriation of Nietzsche," *Nietzsche-Studien* 12 (1983): 428–35.
Lukács, György. *The Destruction of Reason*. Trans. Peter Palmer. Atlantic Highlands, N.J.: Humanities Press, 1981.
Schutte, Ofelia. *Beyond Nihilism: Nietzsche without Masks*. Chicago: University of Chicago Press, 1984.
Stauth, Georg, and Bryan S. Turner. *Nietzsche's Dance: Resentment, Reciprocity, and Resistance in Social Life*. Oxford: Basil Blackwell, 1988.
Strong, Tracy. *Friedrich Nietzsche and the Politics of Transfiguration*. Berkeley: University of California Press, 1975.
Thiele, Leslie Paul. *Friedrich Nietzsche and the Politics of the Soul: A Study of Heroic Individualism*. Princeton: Princeton University Press, 1990.

Thomas, R. Hinton. *Nietzsche in German Politics and Society 1890–1918.* Manchester: Manchester University Press, 1983.

Warren, Mark. *Nietzsche and Political Thought.* Cambridge, Massachusetts: MIT Press, 1988.

Yack, Bernard. *The Longing for Total Revolution: Philosophic Sources of Social Discontent from Rousseau to Marx and Nietzsche.* Princeton: Princeton University Press, 1986.

REFERENCE WORKS

International Nietzsche Bibliography. Compiled and edited by Herbert W. Reichert and Karl Schlechta. Chapel Hill: The University of North Carolina Press, 1968.

Nietzsche-Studien: Internationales Jahrbuch für die Nietzsche-Forschung. New York and Berlin: Walter de Gruyter, 1972ff.

Reichert, Herbert and Karl Schlechta, compiled and eds. *International Nietzsche Bibliography.* Second Edition, continued. *Nietzsche-Studien* 2 (1973): 320–39.

INDEX

Lightning Source UK Ltd.
Milton Keynes UK
UKOW01f1647160616

276414UK00001B/72/P